I0321941

THE EMBASSY, THE AMBUSH, AND THE OGRE

The Embassy, the Ambush, and the Ogre

Greco-Roman Influence in Sanskrit Theater

Roberto Morales-Harley

OpenBook Publishers

https://www.openbookpublishers.com

Any digital material and resources associated with this volume will be available at https://doi.org/10.11647/OBP.417#resources

ISBN Paperback: 978-1-80511-361-4

ISBN Hardback: 978-1-80511-362-1

ISBN Digital (PDF): 978-1-80511-363-8

ISBN Digital eBook (EPUB): 978-1-80511-364-5

ISBN HTML: 978-1-80511-365-2

DOI: 10.11647/OBP.0417

Cover image: Head of a woman, Hadda, Eastern Afghanistan, Greco-Buddhist period, 4th-5th century AD, stucco. Wadsworth Atheneum - Hartford, Connecticut, USA, https://commons.wikimedia.org/wiki/File:Head_of_a_woman,_Hadda,_Eastern_Afghanistan,_Greco-Buddhist_period,_4th-5th_century_AD,_stucco_-_Wadsworth_Atheneum_-_Hartford,_CT_-_DSC05145.jpg
Cover design: Jeevanjot Kaur Nagpal.

Contents

List of Abbreviations vii

1. Can Literary Parallelisms Prove Cultural Contact?: Theater Following in Epic's Footsteps 1

    Let's Go to the Greek Theater (in India) 7

    The Case of Classicists v. Sanskrit Playwrights 17

    The Building Blocks of Tradition and Adaptation 26

    If It Looks like a Duck... 33

2. The Embassy: A "Potifar's Wife" Story 41

    Don't Shoot the Messenger! 48

    Ekphrasis and It-fiction 66

3. The Ambush: The Tale of the Tricked Trickster 79

    Give Me Five! – Villages or Nights? 96

    Tokens of Recognition and Other Telling Details 118

4. The Ogre: "Nobody Seeks to Kill Me!" 133

    "Hey! Middle One, Come Quick!" 156

    (Plautine) Mistaken Identities 184

    Emily B. West's Ogres 196

5. Sanskrit Authors Adapting Greco-Roman Texts: Influences in the Adaptation Techniques 207

    Folk, Indo-European, or Greco-Roman Literary Motifs? 217

    Borrowings in the Adapted Elements 228

    Greco-Indian Historical Contexts? 236

Proposed Influences 245

Proposed Borrowings 246

Followed Chronologies 247

References 249

List of Tables 267

Index 269

List of Abbreviations

ad Aen.	Servius' commentary on the *Aeneid*
Ael.	Aelian
Aen.	*Aeneid* by Virgil
Ag.	*Agamemnon* by Aeschylus
AitBr.	*Aitareyabrāhmaṇa*
Alex.	*Alexander* by Plutarch
AM	Ambush Motif
An.	*Andria* by Terence
Andr.	*Andromache* by Euripides
Anth. Pal.	*The Greek Anthology* (*Anthologia Palatina*)
Arthaś.	*Arthaśāstra* by Kauṭilya
Asin.	*Asinaria* by Plautus
b.	birth
c.	century
Bacch.	*Bacchides* by Plautus
BC	*Bālacaritam* by (Ps.-)Bhāsa
BhP.	*Bhāgavatapurāṇa*
Bibl.	*Bibliotheca* by Apollodorus mythographus
ca.	*circa*
Capt.	*Captivi* by Plautus

Cas.	*Casina* by Plautus
Cist.	*Cistellaria* by Plautus
Crass.	*Crassus* by Plutarch
Curc.	*Curculio* by Plautus
Cyc.	*Cyclops* by Euripides
d.	death
Dio Chrys.	Dio Chrysostom
DV	*The Embassy* (*Dūtavākyam*) by (Ps.-)Bhāsa
e.g.	*exempli gratia*
EM	Embassy Motif
Ep.	*Epistulae* by Seneca de Younger
Epid.	*Epidicus* by Plautus
Epigr.	*Epigrammata* by Martial
Eun.	*The Eunuch* (*Eunuchus*) by Terence
Fast.	*Fasti* by Ovid
GA	Greek Ambush
GE	Greek Embassy
GO	Greek Ogre
Gr.	Greek
Hariv. App.	Appendix to *Harivaṃśa*
Haut.	*H(e)autontimorumenos* by Terence
Hec.	*Hecuba* by Euripides
Hel.	*Helen* by Euripides
Hipp.	*Hippolytus* by Euripides
IA	*Iphigenia at Aulis* by Euripides
Ib.	*Ibis* by Ovid

i.e.	*id est*
Il.	*Iliad* by Homer
Karp.	*Karpūramañjarī* by Rājaśekhara
KBh.	*Karṇabhāram* by (Ps.-)Bhāsa
Lach.	*Laches* by Plato
Lat.	Latin
Lucr.	Lucretius
Mālatīm.	*Mālatīmādhava* by Bhavabhūti
Mālav.	*Mālavikāgnimitra* by Kālidāsa
MBh.	*Mahābhārata* by Vyāsa
Men.	*The Two Menaechmuses* (*Menaechmi*) by Plautus
Merc.	*Mercator* by Plautus
Met.	*Metamorphoses* by Ovid
Mil.	*Miles gloriosus* by Plautus
Mor.	*Moralia* by Plutarch
Mṛcch.	*Mṛcchakaṭikā* by Śūdraka
MV	*The Middle One* (*Madhyamavyāyoga*) by (Ps.-)Bhāsa
NA	*Noctes Atticae* by Gelius
Nāg.	*Nāgānanda* by Harṣa
Nāṭyaś.	*Nāṭyaśāstra* by Bharata
Nic.	*Nicias* by Plutarch
Od.	*Odyssey* by Homer
OM	Ogre Motif
Or.	*Orationes* by Dio Chrysostom
OT	*Oedipus Tyrannus* by Sophocles
PCG	*Poetae Comici Graeci*

Phd.	*Phaedo* by Plato
Phdr.	*Phaedrus* by Plato
Philostr.	Philostratus
Plut.	Plutarch
PMGF	*Poetarum Melicorum Graecorum Fragmenta*
Poen.	*The Little Carthaginian* (*Poenulus*) by Plautus
Poet.	*Poetics* by Aristotle
Posth.	posthumous
POxy.	*Papyrus Oxyrhynchus*
PR	*The Five Nights* (*Pañcarātram*) by (Ps.-)Bhāsa
Ps.-	Pseudo-
Pun.	*Punica* by Silus Italicus
R.	*Rāmāyaṇa* by Vālmīki
r.	*regnavit*
Raghuv.	*Raghuvaṃśa* by Kālidāsa
Ratn.	*Ratnāvalī* by Harṣa
Rhes.	*Rhesus* by Ps.-Euripides
Rud.	*The Rope* (*Rudens*) by Plautus
RV.	*Ṛgveda*
SA	Sanskrit Ambush
Śak.	*Śakuntalā* by Kālidāsa
Sat.	*Satirae* by Horace
Satur.	*Saturnalia* by Macrobius
sc.	*scilicet*
Schol. ad Il.	Scholium to the *Iliad*
SE	Sanskrit Embassy

Skr.	Sanskrit
SO	Sanskrit Ogre
Stich.	*Stichus* by Plautus
Suas.	*Suasoriae* by Seneca de Elder
Supp.	*The Suppliants* by Aeschylus
Suppl.	*Suppliant Women* by Euripides
SV	*Svapnavāsavadattam* by (Ps.-)Bhāsa
s.v.	*sub voce*
Theb.	*Thebaid* by Statius
Tht.	*Theaetetus* by Plato
TrGF	*Tragicorum Graecorum Fragmenta*
Tro.	*Trojan Women* by Euripides
ŪBh.	*Ūrubhaṅgam* by (Ps.-)Bhāsa
Uttar.	*Uttararāmacarita* by Bhavabhūti
V A	*Life of Apollonius of Tyana* (*Vita Apollonii*) by Philostratus
VH	*Historical Miscellany* (*Varia Historia*) by Aelian
Viddh.	*Viddhaśālabhañjikā* by Rājaśekhara
Vikr.	*Vikramorvaśī* by Kālidāsa
V.P.	*Viṣṇupurāṇa*

1. Can Literary Parallelisms Prove Cultural Contact?

Theater Following in Epic's Footsteps

Epic (Gr. ἔπος, Skr. *itihāsa*) and theater (Gr. δρᾶμα, Skr. *nāṭya*) exist as literary genres both in the Greco-Roman world and in India. In both contexts, epic is an older literary genre and theater a newer one, so epic can function as a model for later literary production. Indeed, Greek theater and Sanskrit theater take their inspiration from their respective epics. For Ancient Greece, the *Iliad* and the *Odyssey* represent the main benchmarks, whereas for Ancient India, the *Mahābhārata* and the *Rāmāyaṇa* fill in that position.

The adaptation of epic materials is part of a process of tradition (Lat. *trāditiō*, Skr. *smṛti*), through which works from the past are assessed in terms of aesthetics and ethics, and accordingly reinterpreted in the present as an acknowledgment of their authority. Not only the Greco-Roman world, but also India reaches a classical period for their literature and language. In Greece, it is the Age of Pericles (fifth century BCE); in Rome, the Age of Augustus (first century BCE to first century CE); and in India, the Gupta Empire (fourth century CE to sixth century CE). Both in Greece and in India, theater constitutes the most conspicuous form of the *Belles Lettres*.

This book deals, first, with the adaptation of Greek epic into Greek theater; second, with the adaptation of Sanskrit epic into Sanskrit theater; and third, with the parallelisms between both

 https://doi.org/10.11647/OBP.0417.01

sets of adaptation products/processes. Furthermore, it argues that, not only do the adapted elements and adaptation techniques coincide, but also that it is possible that such coincidence is due to a hypothetical setting of influences and borrowings from the Greco-Roman world into India.

For this study, Greek epic will be represented by the Homeric Epics, that is, the *Iliad* (*Il.*) and the *Odyssey* (*Od.*).[1] These are narrative texts: the first one, about anger, fighting, withdrawal and return, power struggles, and the destruction of a generation of heroes; the second one, about homecoming, wandering, and reunion. They were probably dictated by Homer in the Aegean Islands between 800 BCE and 750 BCE.[2] The *Iliad* is structured in three sections: books 1-8, from the loss of Briseis and Zeus' promise to its fulfillment; books 9-16, from the embassy to Achilles and Agamemnon's promise to the loss of Patroclus; and books 17-24, from the war around Patroclus' corpse, to the peace-offering release of Hector's corpse.

The *Odyssey*, in turn, is structured in six sections: books 1-4, with Telemachus' adventures; books 5-8, with Odysseus' post-Calypso adventures; books 9-12, with Odysseus' pre-Calypso adventures; books 13-16, with the father/son encounter; books 17-20, with the much-awaited return; and books 21-24, with the trail, the punishment, the reunion, and Laertes' adventures. The ingenious author of these epics seems to have borrowed materials both from Greek myth and Near Eastern sources to put together a work concurrently producing aesthetic pleasure and serving didactic, religious, and moral purposes.[3]

In the Homeric Epics, the focus will be on the *Presbeia* (*Il.* 9), the *Doloneia* (*Il.* 10), and the *Cyclopeia* (*Od.* 9), which correspond, respectively, to the literary motifs of the embassy, the ambush, and the ogre. These three books have been viewed from various

1 I follow the Greek text by Murray & Wyatt (Homer, 1999a and 1999b) for the *Iliad*, and by Murray & Dimock (Homer, 1995a and 1995b) for the *Odyssey*. The translations are my own. See Finkelberg (2011), Bierl (2015), and Pache (2020) for an overview of the Homeric Epics.

2 See Powell (2004, pp. 30-34).

3 See Edmunds (1997) and Graf (2011) for the "Greek myth" influence; and M. L. West (1971, 1997), Burkert (1992, 2004a, 2004b), Morris (1997), and Powell (2011) for the "Near East" influence.

perspectives within the tendencies of the so-called analysts, unitarians, oral theory researchers, and neoanalysts.[4] Within the *Presbeia*, analysists have seen Phoenix's intervention as an interpolation for its oddity in terms of both cultural values and dual forms, while unitarians have found common ground for integration in the folktale-nature of Meleager's story.[5]

As for the *Doloneia*, analysts, unitarians, oral theory researchers, and neoanalysts alike have almost unanimously regarded it as being a latter insertion. However, recent studies, from a conciliatory perspective combining neoanalysis and oral theory research, have contributed to a better understanding of the book within both the narrative and its tradition, by emphasizing the poetics involved in its composition.[6] Finally, regarding the *Cyclopeia*, both analysts and unitarians have profited from the tools of folklore studies, the consensus being the proposal of one or several previous folktales functioning as its sources.[7]

4 Within Homeric scholarship, analysts view the plurality of the text as the result of either one originally shorter poem by a previous author that served as a kernel and was expanded through later insertions, or a series of originally shorter poems that functioned as lays and were given shape by a later author. On the contrary, unitarians understand the coherence of the plots as a mark of either their themes being developed during a first phase of creative activity but the poems themselves being ultimately composed during a second one, or them being the works of two different poets, one of them original and the other an imitator. Over time, the unitarian perspective split into those of oral theory research and neoanalysis: the former sees the Homeric Epics as traditional texts which result from a combination of an individual poet's performance and a style inherited from oral, pre-Homeric literature; the latter considers the *Iliad* (and to a lesser degree the *Odyssey*) a traditional text which results from a mixture of an individual author's intentions and materials drawn from written, pre-Homeric literature.

5 From an analytical perspective, see Page (1959, pp. 297-315) and Kirk (1962, p. 217). From a unitarian perspective, see Scodel (1982, p. 128) for an oral-theory view; and Kakridis (1944/1949, p. 14), Swain (1988, p. 271), and Burgess (2017, p. 51) for a neoanalytical view.

6 From an analytical perspective, see von Wilamowitz-Moellendorf (1916, pp. 60-67). From a unitarian perspective, see Hainsworth (1993, pp. 151-155) for an oral-theory critique; and Schadewaldt (1938, p. 142), Reinhardt (1961, pp. 243-250), and Danek (1988) for a neoanalytical critique. See Dué & Ebbott (2010) and Dué (2012) on the poetics of "ambush", and Bierl (2012) on the poetics of "night/light" and "death/life".

7 From an analytical perspective, see Page (1955, p. 17). From a unitarian perspective, see Schein (1970, p. 74) and Glenn (1971, pp. 141-142) for an oral-theory view; and Burgess (2001, p. 111) for a neoanalytical view.

If the Homeric Epics will provide the corpus for Greek epic, (Ps.-)Euripides will do so for Greek theater.[8] The playwright Euripides lived in Athens and Macedon from 485/480 BCE to 407/406 BCE. There are nineteen plays attributed to him, which tend to be separated into three groups: nine early plays, from 438-416 BCE (*Alcestis, Medea, Children of Heracles, Hippolytus, Andromache, Hecuba, Suppliant Women, Electra*, and *Heracles*); eight later plays, from after 416 BCE (*Trojan Women, Iphigenia in Tauris, Ion, Helen, Phoenician Women, Orestes, Iphigenia at Aulis*, and *Bacchae*); and the miscellanea (*Cyclops, Rhesus*, and fragments).

Even more so than those authored by Aeschylus and Sophocles, the plays associated with (Ps.-)Euripides rework epic subjects.[9] The fragmentary *Phoenix* borrows from *Il.* 9; the *Rhesus* (*Rhes.*), from *Il.* 10, as well as from Greek myth and literature; and the *Cyclops* (*Cyc.*), from the *Od.* 9, as well as from Greek myth and literature.[10] These three plays are, respectively, examples of the literary motifs of the embassy, the ambush, and the ogre.

Regarding the other side of the comparison, Sanskrit epic will be represented by the *Mahābhārata* (*MBh.*).[11] This is a narrative text

---

8 I follow the Greek text by Kovacs (Euripides, 1994, 2003) and Collard & Cropp (Euripides, 2008). The translations are my own. The (Ps.-) is for acknowledging that the *Rhesus* is only attributed.

9 Aeschylus wrote a trilogy from the *Iliad* and another one from the *Odyssey*: the trilogy from *Il.* 16-24 included *The Myrmidons, The Nereids*, and *The Phrygians*; the trilogy from *Od.* 11-24, *The Ghost-Raisers, Penelope*, and *The Bone-Gatherers* (followed by the satyr play *Circe*). Sophocles composed three plays based on the *Odyssey*: *Nausicaa or The Washerwomen* from *Od.* 6, *The Phaeacians* from *Od.* 7-12, and *The Foot-Washing* from *Od.* 19. See Murnaghan (2011), Zimmermann (2014), and Sommerstein (2015) for an overview of the adaptation of Greek epic into Greek theater.

10 *Phoenix* is a tragedy, written by Euripides ca. 425 BCE (Collard & Cropp, in Euripides, 2008, p. xv). See Papamichael (1982) and Collard & Cropp (Euripides, 2008) for an overview of *Phoenix*'s sources. *Rhesus* is a tragedy, written by an imitator of Euripides ca. 336 BCE (Liapis, 2017, p. 342; Fantuzzi, 2020, p. 41). See Liapis (2012, Chapter 1), Fries (2014, Chapter 2), and Fantuzzi (2020) for an overview of *Rhesus*' sources. Lastly, *Cyclops* is a satyr drama, written by Euripides ca. 408 BCE (Seaford, 1982). See O'Sullivan & Collard (2013, pp. 28-39), Shaw (2018), and Hunter & Laemmle (2020) for an overview of the *Cyclops*' sources.

11 I follow the Sanskrit text by Sukthankar, Belvalkar, Vaidya, et al. (1933/1971). The translations are my own. See Sullivan (2016), Fitzgerald (2018), and Adluri & Bagchee (2018) for an overview of the *Mahābhārata*.

about *dharma* (duty), *bhakti* (devotion), *pravṛtti* (active life) and *nivṛtti* (ceasing from worldly acts), education, genealogies, power struggles, and the destruction of a generation of heroes. It was probably written by Vyāsa in Northern India between 1 CE and 100 CE.[12] The text is structured through two successive narrative frames.

In the outer frame, the *sūta* (bard) Ugraśravas tells the story to the *kulapati* (family chieftain) Śaunaka at the Naimiṣa Forest during a twelve-year sacrifice; in the inner frame, the Brahman Vaiśampāyana tells the story to the *rāja* (king) Janamejaya at the city of Takṣaśilā during a snake-sacrifice. The ingenious author of this epic seems to have borrowed materials both from Vedic myth and Greco-Roman sources to put together a work concurrently producing aesthetic pleasure and serving didactic, religious, moral, and political purposes.[13]

In the *Mahābhārata*, the focus will be on the *Udyogaparvan* (*MBh.* 5), the *Virāṭaparvan* (*MBh.* 4), and the *Ādiparvan* (*MBh.* 1), which include, respectively, the literary motifs of the embassy, the ambush, and the ogre. These three books have been viewed from various perspectives within the tendencies of the so-called analysts and synthetists.[14] From an analytic perspective, the *Hiḍimbavadhaparvan* (*MBh.* 1.139-144) and the *Bakavadhaparvan* (*MBh.* 1.145-152) have been read in terms of postcolonialism, and the *Bhagavadyānaparvan* (*MBh.* 5.70-135) in terms of ethics; from

12 See Wulff Alonso (2018a, p. 92; 2018b, p. 459).

13 See Minkowski (1989, 1991, 2001) and Feller (2004) for the "Vedic myth" influence; and Arora (1981, 2011) and Wulff Alonso (2008a, 2008b, 2013, 2014, 2015, 2018a, 2018b, 2019a, 2019b, 2020) for the "Greco-Roman" influence.

14 Within *Mahābhārata* studies, analysts assume an original kernel to which later layers would have been added, during a long process of oral composition ending in some form of redaction of the text. For them, the additions, mostly of didactic materials, would account for the epic's all-encompassing nature, which, in turn, would result in an aesthetically inferior quality. On the contrary, synthetists assume the text as having some form of cohesion and intention, be it in terms of law, philosophy, or literature. For them, the critical edition has provided a reliable point of departure for a unified view of the text.

a synthetic point of view, the *Virāṭaparvan* (*MBh.* 4) has been interpreted based on its supposed sources.[15]

If the *Mahābhārata* will provide the corpus for Sanskrit epic, (Ps.-)Bhāsa will do so for Sanskrit theater.[16] The playwright Bhāsa probably lived in Northern India between 100 CE and 200 CE.[17] There are thirteen plays attributed to him, which tend to be separated into three groups: seven *Mahābhārata*-and-Kṛṣṇa-inspired plays (*The Middle One, The Five Nights, The Embassy, Ghaṭotkaca as an Envoy, Karṇa's Task, The Broken Thighs*, and *The Adventures of the Boy Kṛṣṇa*); two *Rāmāyaṇa*-inspired plays (*The Consecration* and *The Statue Play*); and the miscellanea (two legendary plays, i.e., *Avimāraka* and *Cārudatta in Poverty*; and two historical plays, i.e., *The Minister's Vows* and *The Vision of Vāsavadatta*).

Even more so than Kālidāsa, Bhaṭṭa Nārāyaṇa, Vatsarāja, Kulaśekhara Varman, Rājaśekhara, Kṣemendra, and Vijayapāla after him, (Ps.-)Bhāsa reworked epic subjects.[18] Focusing only on the literary motifs of the embassy, the ambush, and the ogre, one

15 See S. K. Menon (2016) for the *Hiḍimbavadhaparvan* (*MBh.* 1.139-144) and the *Bakavadhaparvan* (*MBh.* 1.145-152), and Greer (2005) for the *Bhagavadyānaparvan* (*MBh.* 5.70-135). See Wulff Alonso (2018a, 2019a, 2019b, 2020) for the *Virāṭaparvan* (*MBh.* 4).

16 I follow the Sanskrit text by the Bhasa-Projekt Universität Würzburg (2007). The translations are my own. The (Ps.-) is for acknowledging that, to some, all the plays would be only attributed. See Pusalker (1940) for the "pro-Bhāsa" view; and Tieken (1993) and Brückner (1999/2000) for the "against-Bhāsa" view.

17 This dating, a little earlier than the traditional 200 CE–300 CE (Keith, 1924, p. 95; Bansat-Boudon, 1992, p. 38; Ganser, 2022, p. 30), responds to the presumed Greco-Roman influence.

18 Considering only the *Mahābhārata*-inspired plays, (Ps.-)Bhāsa wrote *The Middle One* from *MBh.* 1, *The Five Nights* from *MBh.* 4, *The Embassy* from *MBh.* 5, *Ghaṭotkaca as an Envoy* from *MBh.* 7, *Karṇa's Task* from *MBh.* 8, and *The Broken Thighs* from *MBh.* 9. On the other hand, Kālidāsa composed *The Recognition of Śakuntalā* from *MBh.* 1.62-69 and *On Purūravas and Urvaśī* from *Harivaṃśa* 10.26; Bhaṭṭa Nārāyaṇa, *The Binding Up of the Braided Hair* from the entire *MBh.*; Vatsarāja, *On the Mountaineer and Arjuna* from *MBh.* 3.13-42 and *The Burning of Tripura* from *MBh.* 8.24; Kulaśekhara Varman, *On Tapatī and Saṃvāraṇa* from *MBh.* 1.160-163 and *Subhadrā and Arjuna* from *MBh.* 1.211-213; Rājaśekhara, *The Little Mahābhārata* from the entire *MBh.*; Kṣemendra, *The Blossom-Cluster of the Rāmāyaṇa* from *MBh.* 3.257-276; and Vijayapāla, *The Self-choice of Draupadī* from *MBh.* 1.174-185. See Ghosh (1963) and Thapar (1984) for an overview of the adaptation of Sanskrit epic into Sanskrit theater.

respectively notices that *The Embassy* (*DV*) borrows from *MBh.* 5; *The Five Nights* (*PR*), from *MBh.* 4; and *The Middle One* (*MV*), from *MBh.* 1.[19] The selection, from among several available options, of these three plays for the book was motivated precisely because they deal with the same three motifs that are present in the only three remaining plays by (Ps.-)Euripides that adapt Homer.

In sum, the aim of this book is to compare, by means of a philological and literary analysis, the adaptation of the embassy, ambush, and ogre motifs, on one hand, in (Ps.-)Euripides' Homeric-inspired *Phoenix*, *Rhesus*, and *Cyclops*, and on the other, in (Ps.-) Bhāsa's *Mahābhārata*-inspired *The Embassy*, *The Five Nights*, and *The Middle One*, towards the goal of supporting the hypothesis of influences and borrowings from the Greco-Roman world into India. Based on this comparison, I will argue that the techniques for adapting epic into theater could have been Greco-Roman influences in India; and some of the elements adapted within the literary motifs of the embassy, the ambush, and the ogre, could have been Greco-Roman borrowings by Sanskrit authors.

Let's Go to the Greek Theater (in India)

The earliest attestation of Greek epic influencing Sanskrit epic would coincide with the dating that I follow for the *MBh.* It comes from Dio Chrysostom's (40-115 CE) *Orationes* (*Or.*),[20] specifically from his discourse *On Homer*. The relevant passage offers three pieces of information that are noteworthy. First, the Homeric Epics would have been "sung" and "translated" in India. If the singing part already presupposes an influence in the form of an exposure

19 *The Embassy* is a *vyāyoga* or one-act, epic-inspired play (Keith, 1924, pp. 95-105). See Esposito (1999/2000, 2010) for an overview of *The Embassy*'s sources. *The Five Nights* is a *samavakāra* or three-act, heroic play (Keith, 1924, pp. 95-105). See Tieken (1997), Steiner (2010), and Hawley (2021) for an overview of *The Five Nights*' sources. Lastly, *The Middle One*, as its Sanskrit title suggests, is also a *vyāyoga* (Keith, 1924, pp. 95-105). See Salomon (2010) and Sutherland Goldman (2017) for an overview of *The Middle One*'s sources.

20 I follow the Greek text by Crosby (Dio Chrysostom, 1946). The translations are my own.

to Greek language and literature, the translating part also opens the door for linguistic and literary borrowings.

Second, Indian people, and presumably Sanskrit authors as well, would have been "acquainted" with epic Greek themes and characters.[21] And third, there are two modes of interacting with epic Greek sources: one, with which other non-Greek speakers would have engaged, that would not have gone past mere enchantment; and another, which the Indians would have followed, that would have included a knowledge of the epic Greek "tongue" and "deeds".

> Ἔτι δὲ καὶ αὐτὸς τῆς χάριτος ἐπαινῶν τὴν ποίησιν σφόδρα ἄγαται τὸν ἄνδρα. ἀτεχνῶς γὰρ οὐκ ἄνευ θείας τύχης οὐδ' ἄνευ Μουσῶν τε καὶ Ἀπόλλωνος ἐπιπνοίας δυνατὸν οὕτως ὑψηλὴν καὶ μεγαλοπρεπῆ καὶ προσέτι ἡδεῖαν γενέσθαι ποίησιν, ὥστε μὴ μόνον τοὺς ὁμογλώττους καὶ ὁμοφώνους τοσοῦτον ἤδη κατέχειν χρόνον, ἀλλὰ καὶ τῶν βαρβάρων πολλούς· καὶ τοὺς μὲν διγλώττους καὶ μιγάδας σφόδρα ἐμπείρους εἶναι τῶν ἐπῶν αὐτοῦ, πολλὰ τῶν ἄλλων ἀγνοοῦντας τῶν Ἑλληνικῶν, ἐνίους δὲ καὶ τῶν σφόδρα μακρὰν διῳκισμένων· ὁπότε καὶ παρ' Ἰνδοῖς φασιν **ᾄδεσθαι** τὴν Ὁμήρου ποίησιν, **μεταλαβόντων** αὐτὴν εἰς τὴν σφετέραν διάλεκτόν τε καὶ φωνήν.
>
> ὥστε καὶ Ἰνδοὶ τῶν μὲν ἄστρων τῶν παρ' ἡμῖν πολλῶν εἰσιν ἀθέατοι· τὰς γὰρ ἄρκτους οὔ φασι φαίνεσθαι παρ' αὐτοῖς· τῶν δὲ Πριάμου παθημάτων καὶ τῶν Ἀνδρομάχης καὶ Ἑκάβης θρήνων καὶ ὀδυρμῶν καὶ τῆς Ἀχιλλέως τε καὶ Ἕκτορος ἀνδρείας **οὐκ ἀπείρως** ἔχουσιν. τοσοῦτον ἴσχυσεν ἑνὸς ἀνδρός μουσική· καὶ δοκεῖ ἔμοιγε τῇ δυνάμει ταύτῃ τάς τε Σειρῆνας ὑπερβαλέσθαι καὶ τὸν Ὀρφέα.
>
> τὸ γὰρ λίθους τε καὶ φυτὰ καὶ θηρία κηλεῖν καὶ ἄγειν τί ἔστιν ἕτερον ἢ τὸ βαρβάρους ἀνθρώπους ἀσυνέτους τῆς Ἑλληνικῆς φωνῆς οὕτως ἄγαν χειρώσασθαι, μήτε τῆς **γλώττης** μήτε τῶν **πραγμάτων** ἐμπείρους ὄντας ὑπὲρ ὧν ὁ λόγος, ἀλλὰ ἀτεχνῶς καθάπερ, οἶμαι, πρὸς κιθάραν κηλουμένους; ἡγοῦμαι δὲ ἔγωγε πολλοὺς καὶ τῶν ἀμαθεστέρων ἔτι βαρβάρων τό γε ὄνομα ἀκηκοέναι τὸ Ὁμήρου, ὅ τι δὲ δηλοῖ, τοῦτο μὴ εἰδέναι σαφῶς, εἴτε ζῷον εἴτε φυτὸν εἴτε πρᾶγμα ἕτερον.
>
> Furthermore, he [sc. Plato] himself praising the poetry for its charm, greatly admires the man [sc. Homer]. Indeed, without

21 See J. Allen (1946) on the Gandharan "*tabula iliaca*", an Indian depiction of the Trojan Horse. Also, see Derrett (1992, pp. 48-51).

> a divine cause or without the Muses' and Apollo's intervention, it is simply not possible for an elevated, magnificent, and sweet poetry to appear and to enthrall for quite some time, not only those of the same tongue and of the same language, but also many of the barbarians. The bilingual ones and the mixed ones, not knowing much else about the Greeks, are versed in his poetry, and so are some living very far away. Among the Indians, so they say, Homer's poetry **is sung**, after they **translated** it into their own dialect and language.
>
> In this way, even if the Indians are not looking at many of the stars that are near us –they say, indeed, that the Great Bear does not appear near them; still, in terms of Priam's sufferings, of Andromache's and Hecuba's laments and wailings, and of Achilles' and Hector's courage, they conduct themselves **not in an unacquainted manner**. So influential was the poetry of a single man! It seems to me that, in puissance alone, he surpasses the Sirens and Orpheus.
>
> Indeed, how is enchanting and steering rocks, plants, and beasts any different than utterly subduing barbarian men who do not understand the Greek language, and who are unacquainted with the **tongue** and the **deeds** about which the text is, but are, I believe, simply enchanted by the lyre? Moreover, I think that many of the barbarians that are even more ignorant have certainly heard Homer's name, it is clear, not knowing well if it was an animal, a plant, or other thing.
>
> (Dio Chrys. *Or.* 53.6-8)[22]

As a speculative interpretation of all this information I suggest the following: if Sanskrit authors would have had a mastery of the epic Greek language and an appreciation for the epic Greek literature, they could have profited from them, to re-create Greek epic, however freely, when coming up with the Sanskrit epic.

Contemporaneous to Dio Chrysostom is Plutarch (46-119 CE). From him, there is reason to include as many as four passages. In the first one, from *Moralia* (*Mor.*),[23] specifically from *On the Fortune of Alexander*, alongside Homer, he mentions Sophocles and Euripides. Although he is not speaking of India, but of its vicinities

22 Throughout the book, I have added the boldfaced emphasis in the quotations/translations.

23 I follow the Greek text by Babbit (Plutarch, 1962). The translations are my own.

(Persia, Susa, and Gedrosia), he notes that these works of Greek literature, both epic and dramatic, would have been "read" and "sung". In the second one, from *Parallel Lives*, specifically from *Alexander* (*Alex.*),[24] he reveals that Alexander the Great traveled to Asia with Aristotle's "edition" of Homer's *Iliad*, and that once he was stationed there, he ordered for more "books", among others, by Aeschylus, Sophocles, and Euripides.

> θαυμάζομεν τὴν Καρνεάδου δύναμιν, εἰ Κλειτόμαχον, Ἀσδρούβαν καλούμενον πρότερον καὶ Καρχηδόνιον τὸ γένος, ἑλληνίζειν ἐποίησε · θαυμάζομεν τὴν διάθεσιν Ζήνωνος, εἰ Διογένη τὸν Βαβυλώνιον ἔπεισε φιλοσοφεῖν. ἀλλ᾽Ἀλεξάνδρου τὴν Ἀσίαν ἐξημεροῦντος Ὅμηρος ἦν **ἀνάγνωσμα**, καὶ Περσῶν καὶ Σουσιανῶν καὶ Γεδρωσίων παῖδες τὰς Εὐριπίδου καὶ Σοφοκλέους τραγῳδίας **ᾖδον**. καὶ Σωκράτης ὡς μὲν ξένα παρεισάγων δαιμόνια δίκην τοῖς Ἀθήνησιν ὠφλίσκανε συκοφάνταις· διὰ δ᾽Ἀλέξανδρον τοὺς Ἑλλήνων θεοὺς Βάκτρα καὶ Καύκασος προσεκύνησε.
>
> We admire Carneades' power, if it did Hellenize Cleitomachus, formerly known as Hasdrubal and Carthaginian by birth. We admire Zeno's character, if it persuaded Diogenes the Babylonian to philosophize. But while Alexander was civilizing Asia, Homer was habitual **reading**, and the children of the Persians, the Susianians, and the Gedrosians, **sang** Euripides' and Sophocles' tragedies. When even Socrates was condemned by Athenian slanderers for the charge of introducing foreign deities, through Alexander, Bactria and the Caucasus still worshiped the gods of the Greeks.
>
> (Plut. *Mor*. 328d)

> καὶ τὴν μὲν Ἰλιάδα τῆς πολεμικῆς ἀρετῆς ἐφόδιον καὶ νομίζων καὶ ὀνομάζων, ἔλαβε μὲν Ἀριστοτέλους **διορθώσαντος** ἣν ἐκ τοῦ νάρθηκος καλοῦσιν, εἶχε δὲ ἀεὶ μετὰ τοῦ ἐγχειριδίου κειμένην ὑπὸ τὸ προσκεφάλαιον, ὡς Ὀνησίκριτος ἱστόρηκε, τῶν δὲ ἄλλων βιβλίων οὐκ εὐπορῶν ἐν τοῖς ἄνω τόποις Ἅρπαλον ἐκέλευσε πέμψαι.
>
> κἀκεῖνος ἔπεμψεν αὐτῷ τάς τε Φιλίστου **βίβλους** καὶ τῶν Εὐριπίδου καὶ Σοφοκλέους καὶ Αἰσχύλου τραγῳδιῶν συχνάς,

24 I follow the Greek text by Perrin (Plutarch, 1967). The translations are my own.

> καὶ Τελέστου καὶ Φιλοξένου διθυράμβους. Ἀριστοτέλην δὲ θαυμάζων ἐν ἀρχῇ καὶ ἀγαπῶν οὐχ ἧττον, ὡς αὐτὸς ἔλεγε, τοῦ πατρός, ὡς δι᾽ἐκεῖνον μὲν ζῶν, διὰ τοῦτον δὲ καλῶς ζῶν, ὕστερον ὑποπτότερον ἔσχεν, οὐχ ὥστε ποιῆσαί τι κακόν, ἀλλ᾽ αἱ φιλοφροσύναι τὸ σφοδρὸν ἐκεῖνο καὶ στερκτικὸν οὐκ ἔχουσαι πρὸς αὐτόν ἀλλοτριότητος ἐγένοντο τεκμήριον.
>
> Considering the *Iliad* "provisions" for warlike excellencies, and calling it so, he [sc. Alexander] took – after Aristotle **revised** it – the one called "of the casket", and he always kept it near his dagger, placed under his pillow, as Onesicritus has reported; and other books not being available at the inland regions, he ordered Harpalus to send some.
>
> And he [sc. Harpalus] sent him [sc. Alexander] Philistus' **books** and lots of Euripides', Sophocles', and Aeschylus' tragedies, as well as Telestus' and Philoxenus' dithyrambs. Admiring Aristotle at first and loving him no less than he did his father, as he said – for thanks to one he lived, but thanks to the other he lived well – later, he [sc. Alexander] held him more under suspicion, not up to doing him harm, but his kindnesses no longer having such profusion and affection towards the other: thus, surfaced the proof of their estrangement.
>
> (Plut. *Alex.* 8.2-3)

If the orality of chanting suffices for positing a general influence, writing would be much more likely to account for specific borrowings, which naturally need not be copies. Following up the speculative interpretation, I postulate that if authors of Sanskrit theater would have had a mastery of Greek language (both epic and classical), an appreciation for Greek literature (both epic and dramatic), and written versions of Greek texts (both Homer and Euripides), they could have profited from them, to re-create Greek theater, however freely, when coming up with Sanskrit theater.

In the third and fourth passages, Plutarch is also in the context of speaking about India's vicinities. *Parallel Lives*, still in *Alexander* (*Alex.*), stretches the reach of Greek theater up to Media. In Ecbatana, there would have been Greek "theaters" and "artists". Similarly, *Parallel Lives*, specifically *Crassus* (*Crass.*),[25] extends

25 I follow the Greek text by Perrin (Plutarch, 1932). The translations are my own.

Euripides' influence up to Parthia and Armenia. There, king Orodes II (r. 57-37 BCE) is said to have become acquainted with Greek "language" and "literature", and king Artavasdes II (r. 55-34 BCE), to have composed, among other things, "tragedies". Moreover, the passage notably suggests a Parthian adaptation of "Euripides' *Bacchae*", during the staging of which, the head of Crassus would have taken the place of the head of Pentheus.

> Ὡς δὲ ἧκεν εἰς Ἐκβάτανα τῆς Μηδίας καὶ διῴκησε τὰ κατεπείγοντα, πάλιν ἦν ἐν θεάτροις καὶ πανηγύρεσιν, ἅτε δὴ τρισχιλίων αὐτῷ **τεχνιτῶν** ἀπὸ τῆς Ἑλλάδος ἀφιγμένων. ἔτυχε δὲ περὶ τὰς ἡμέρας ἐκείνας Ἡφαιστίων πυρέσσων· οἷα δὲ νέος καὶ στρατιωτικὸς οὐ φέρων ἀκριβῆ δίαιταν, ἅμα τῷ τὸν ἰατρὸν Γλαῦκον ἀπελθεῖν εἰς τὸ **θέατρον** περὶ ἄριστον γενόμενος καὶ καταφαγὼν ἀλεκτρυόνα ἑφθὸν καὶ ψυκτῆρα μέγαν ἐκπιὼν οἴνου κακῶς ἔσχε καὶ μικρὸν διαλιπὼν ἀπέθανε.
>
> When he [sc. Alexander] came to Ecbatana of Media and attended pressing matters, once again, he partook in theaters and festivals, after three thousand **artists** from Greece appeared before him. But around that time, Hephaestion happened to have a fever. Since he was young and a soldier, he was not following a strict regimen: as soon as his physician Glaucus took off to the **theater**, he turned up for breakfast, ate a cooked chicken, and having drunk a huge decanter of wine, fell ill and died shortly thereafter.
>
> (Plut. *Alex*. 72.1)
>
> ἦν γὰρ οὔτε **φωνῆς** οὔτε **γραμμάτων** Ὑρώδης Ἑλληνικῶν ἄπειρος, ὁ δ᾽Ἀρταοθάσδης καὶ **τραγῳδίας** ἐποίει καὶ λόγους ἔγραφε καὶ ἱστορίας, ὧν ἔνιαι διασῴζονται. τῆς δὲ κεφαλῆς τοῦ Κράσσου κομισθείσης ἐπὶ θύρας ἀπηρμέναι μὲν ἦσαν αἱ τράπεζαι, τραγῳδιῶν δὲ ὑποκριτὴς Ἰάσων ὄνομα Τραλλιανὸς ᾖδεν **Εὐριπίδου Βακχῶν** τὰ περὶ τὴν Ἀγαύην. εὐδοκιμοῦντος δ᾽ αὐτοῦ Σιλλάκης ἐπιστὰς τῷ ἀνδρῶνι καὶ προσκυνήσας προὔβαλεν εἰς μέσον τοῦ Κράσσου τὴν κεφαλήν.
>
> Indeed, neither with the **language** of the Greeks nor with their **literature** was Orodes unacquainted, and Artavasdes even composed **tragedies**, and wrote discourses and histories, some of which are preserved. And when the head of Crassus was taken to the door, the tables had been removed and an

> actor of tragedies from Tralles, named Jason, was singing the scene about Agave from **Euripides' *Bacchae***. When he was being cheered, Sillaces stood before the hall, and having kneeled, he cast Crassus' head in the middle.
>
> (Plut. *Crass*. 33.2)

What this would mean is that Greek theater would have been susceptible not only to repetition, but also to re-creation. Still in the same speculative manner, with the mastery of Greek language, the appreciation for Greek literature, and the availability of Greek texts in their favor, authors of Sanskrit theater could have re-created Greek theater *while* re-creating Sanskrit epic into Sanskrit theater. This is a key point: Greek theater alone does not account for Sanskrit theater. The similarities between Sanskrit theater and Sanskrit epic are too numerous to admit such a simplistic explanation. However, as an alternative setting I propose the following: authors of Sanskrit theater could have borrowed, *simultaneously*, themes coming from Sanskrit epic, themes coming from Greek theater, and techniques for the epic-to-theater adaptations, also coming from Greek theater.

The last two ancient sources are about a century later than Dio Chrysostom and Plutarch. They are Aelian and Philostratus. Aelian (175-235 CE), in *Historical Miscellany* (*VH*),[26] retransmits Dio Chrysostom's ideas about "translating" and "chanting" the Greek epic in India.

> ...ὅτι Ἰνδοὶ τῇ παρά σφισιν ἐπιχωρίῳ φωνῇ τὰ Ὁμήρου **μεταγράψαντες ᾄδουσιν** οὐ μόνοι ἀλλὰ καὶ οἱ Περσῶν βασιλεῖς, εἴ τι χρὴ πιστεύειν τοῖς ὑπὲρ τούτων ἱστοροῦσιν.
>
> ...that Indians, **having translated** Homer's poetry into their native language, **sing** it, and so too do the kings of the Persians, if one must trust those who report these things.
>
> (Ael. *VH* 12.48)

Philostratus (170-250 CE) provides the last attestations of Greek epic and theater bearing an influence on Sanskrit literature. With him, the number of passages goes up to five, all of which come from

26 I follow the Greek text by Wilson (Aelian, 1997). The translations are my own.

the *Life of Apollonius of Tyana* (*V A*),[27] a source that, on account of its tendency to fiction, must be considered with the utmost care. The first two passages refer to the mastery of Greek language in India itself, a practice that would have been so run-of-the-mill as to be qualified as "not remarkable", and as to be exemplified by pointing out the omission of a "single character".

> ...προσδραμόντα δὲ τῷ Ἀπολλωνίῳ φωνῇ Ἑλλάδι προσειπεῖν αὐτόν, καὶ τοῦτο μὲν **οὔπω θαυμαστὸν** δόξαι διὰ τὸ καὶ τοὺς ἐν τῇ κώμῃ πάντας ἀπὸ Ἑλλήνων φθέγγεσθαι...
>
> ...that after having run up to Apollonius, he [sc. the Indian] addressed him in the Greek language, and with this, he did not appear **remarkable at all**, since following the Greeks, everyone at the village spoke it...
>
> (Philostr. *V A* 3.12)
>
> ...τὸν δὲ Ἀπολλώνιον ἰδὼν φωνῇ τε ἠσπάσατο Ἑλλάδι καὶ τὰ τοῦ Ἰνδοῦ γράμματα ἀπῄτει. θαυμάσαντος δὲ τοῦ Ἀπολλωνίου τὴν πρόγνωσιν καὶ **γράμμα γε ἓν** ἔφη λείπειν τῇ ἐπιστολῇ, δέλτα εἰπών, παρῆλθε γὰρ αὐτὸν γράφοντα·
>
> ...after seeing Apollonius, he [sc. Iarchas] greeted him in the Greek language and asked for the Indian's letter. When Apollonius became puzzled by his foreknowledge, he told him that a **single character** was missing from the letter, adding that a "delta" had escaped the writer.
>
> (Philostr. *V A* 3.16)

The last three passages deal with the appreciation for Greek literature in India itself. They also serve to reinforce the assertion that Greek epic and theater would have been susceptible not only to repetition, but also to re-creation. According to the Indian character, respectively, the literary situation of the *Iliad*'s "Achaeans" could have applied to the historical situation of the Greeks, the Greek

27 I follow the Greek text by Conybeare (Philostratus, 1912). The translations are my own. Regarding this source, it is worth mentioning that it is the literary work of a third-century author (Philostratus) about a much-mythologized first-century holy man (Apollonius). Therefore, the data gathered from it is not necessarily as credible as was the case with the previous sources.

"Palamedes" could just as easily have reincarnated as an Indian "young man", and the plot of Euripides' *"Children of Heracles"* could very well have been about an Indian king's "sovereignty".[28]

> ...ὁ δὲ Ἰνδὸς "Τροία μὲν ἀπώλετο," εἶπεν, "ὑπὸ τῶν πλευσάντων **Ἀχαιῶν** τότε, ὑμᾶς δὲ ἀπολωλέκασιν οἱ ἐπ' αὐτῇ λόγοι· μόνους γὰρ ἄνδρας ἡγούμενοι τοὺς ἐς Τροίαν στρατεύσαντας, ἀμελεῖτε πλειόνων τε καὶ θειοτέρων ἀνδρῶν, οὓς ἥ τε ὑμετέρα γῆ καὶ ἡ Αἰγυπτίων καὶ ἡ Ἰνδῶν ἤνεγκεν."
>
> ...and the Indian replied: "Troy was destroyed by the **Achaean** sailors and your own words have destroyed you all. Indeed, while considering as heroes only those who fought against Troy, you are neglecting more numerous and more divine heroes, whom your land produced, as well as that of the Egyptians and the Indians."
>
> (Philostr. *VA* 3.19)

> γέγονε μὲν οὖν τὸ **μειράκιον** τοῦτο **Παλαμήδης** ὁ ἐν Τροίᾳ, κέχρηται δὲ ἐναντιωτάτοις Ὀδυσσεῖ καὶ Ὁμήρῳ, τῷ μὲν ξυνθέντι ἐπ' αὐτὸν τέχνας, ὑφ' ὧν κατελιθώθη, τῷ δὲ οὐδὲ ἔπους αὐτὸν ἀξιώσαντι. καὶ ἐπειδὴ μήθ' ἡ σοφία αὐτόν τι, ἣν εἶχεν, ὤνησε, μήτε Ὁμήρου ἐπαινέτου ἔτυχεν, ὑφ' οὗ πολλοὶ καὶ τῶν μὴ πάνυ σπουδαίων ἐς ὄνομα ἤχθησαν, Ὀδυσσέως τε ἥττητο ἀδικῶν οὐδέν, διαβέβληται πρὸς φιλοσοφίαν καὶ ὀλοφύρεται τὸ ἑαυτοῦ πάθος. ἔστι δὲ οὗτος Παλαμήδης, ὃς καὶ γράφει μὴ μαθὼν γράμματα.
>
> Indeed, this **young man** was once born as **Palamedes** of Troy and has had Odysseus and Homer as his worst enemies: the former, plotting tricks by which he ended up being stoned to death; and the latter, not even having deemed him worthy of a word. And since neither the wisdom that he possessed was of any use to him, nor did he find praise in Homer, by whom many of the not so earnest made a name for themselves, and since he was defeated by Odysseus while not doing anything wrong, he is at variance with philosophy and bewails his sufferings. So, this is Palamedes, who writes while not knowing the alphabet.
>
> (Philostr. *VA* 3.22)

28 See Mills (2015, p. 262) for a reference to the play *Charition* (second century CE), a similar, India-inspired adaptation of Euripides' *Iphigenia in Tauris*.

> καί μοι ἀναγιγνώσκοντι τοὺς **Ἡρακλείδας** τὸ δρᾶμα, ἐπέστη τις ἐντεῦθεν ἐπιστολὴν φέρων παρὰ ἀνδρὸς ἐπιτηδείου τῷ πατρί, ὅς με ἐκέλευσε διαβάντα τὸν Ὑδραώτην ποταμὸν ξυγγίγνεσθαί οἱ περὶ τῆς **ἀρχῆς** τῆς ἐνταῦθα, πολλὰς γὰρ ἐλπίδας εἶναί μοι ἀνακτήσασθαι αὐτὴν μὴ ἐλινύοντι.
>
> And when I [sc. Phraotes] was reading the play ***Children of Heracles***, someone from that place stood near me, bringing a letter from a man favorable to my father, who ordered me to cross the river Hydraotes to meet with him about my **sovereignty** there, for there was a lot of hope for me to recover it, if I were not to stand idly by.
>
> (Philostr. *VA* 2.32)

If Greek testimonies of their influence in India are abundant, Indian testimonies of a Greek influence therein are altogether nonexistent.[29] Oddly enough, this Indian lack of acknowledgement agrees with the *sui generis* form of acculturation, evidenced for instance, in the Muslim philosophical influence in India. According to Nair (2020, p. 18),

> If one should ask why, for instance, despite centuries of sharing the same soil, Sanskrit philosophical writings never discussed – and, overwhelmingly, never even acknowledged the existence of – Muslim thought, the controls set up by the philosophical "discursive tradition" are a significant part of the explanation: if the tradition has no precedent for such an endeavor, and if no foundational texts within the tradition provide any particular encouragement or even pretext to

29 However, although a lack of documentation is not tantamount to a lack of influences and borrowings, there is certainly documentation of diplomatic contacts (Jairazbhoy, 1963, p. 63) since Aśoka (third century BCE), of bilingual coins (Jairazbhoy, 1963, p. 64) since Demetrius I (second century BCE), of Greek scripts in India (Jairazbhoy, 1963, p. 89) since Patañjali (second century BCE), and at least, of one instance of literary borrowing: Yavaneśvara (second century CE) would have translated the astronomical treatise entitled *Yavanajātaka* from Greek into Sanskrit, and Sphujidhvaja (third century CE) would have adapted it from prose into verse (Pingree, in Sphujidhvaja, 1978, p. 3). Moreover, there is a tendency to accept influences and borrowing from the Greco-Roman world to India in astronomy and mathematics (Pingree, 1971, 1976, 1993; Falk, 2002; Plofker, 2011), as well as in architecture, painting, and sculpture (Acharya, 1927; Nehru, 1989; Boardman, 2015).

> do so, then, in such an environment, any dramatically new intellectual initiative would find scarcely any space to take root.

Anyhow, since someone asserting that something happens in a certain way is not quite the same as it having happened in that way, testimonies will never suffice. Therefore, in mid-nineteenth-century Germany, where the Greek influence hypothesis resurfaces, and in late-nineteenth-century France, where it finds its fiercest adversary, the attention is redirected towards the primary sources. As I will show, the straightforward rejection from most Indologists, paired with the inconsequential acceptance from the few classicists who have even dealt with the question, has resulted in relatively little progress having been made.

The Case of Classicists v. Sanskrit Playwrights

The idea that Greek theater had somehow influenced Sanskrit theater was first suggested by Weber in 1852:

> From the foregoing exposition it appears that the drama meets us in an already finished form, and with its best productions. In almost all the prologues, too, the several works are represented as new, in contradistinction to the pieces of former poets; but of these pieces, that is, of the early beginnings of dramatic poetry, not the smallest remnant has been preserved. Consequently the conjecture that it may possibly have been the representation of Greek dramas at the courts of the Grecian kings in Bactria, in the Panjáb, and in Gujarát (for so far did Greek supremacy for a time extend), which awakened the Hindú faculty of imitation, and so gave birth to the Indian drama, does not in the meantime admit for direct verification. But its historical possibility, at any rate, is undeniable, especially as the older dramas nearly all belong to the west of India. No internal connection, however, with the Greek drama exists. (Weber, 1852/1878, p. 207)

This first exposition argues for *influence*, but not necessarily for *borrowing*. The influence, expressed through the wording of a "birth", would explain "the idea of theater itself" (Walker, 2004, p. 6), and would only represent the "general thesis" (Bronkhorst,

2016, p. 392) that there was a Greek influence in Sanskrit theater, somewhere along the lines of what Diamond (1997) calls "idea diffusion" (p. 224). This is as far as Weber got.

The borrowing, on the other hand, thought of in terms of an "internal connection", would need "a certain type of theater" (Walker, 2004, p. 6), and would refer to a "specific thesis" (Bronkhorst, 2016, p. 392) about how that Greek or Roman theater relates to Sanskrit theater, in the sense of what Diamond (1997) refers to as "blueprint copying" (p. 224). Following Weber, came two explanations, both concerned with borrowing: Windisch sought answers in Greek New Comedy,[30] and Reich in Greek Pantomime.[31] Contrary to what might be expected, I will follow neither of these paths.

A turning point in the development of the hypothesis was due to Lévi, whose chapter on the subject was conceived as a challenge to Windisch. Lévi rules out the parallelisms one by one, whether by taking them as being broad enough not to be necessarily correlated, or by focusing on their differences more than their similarities. However, apart from striking details like the *yavanikā* (curtain), which is still regarded as a non-Greek term,[32] there are deeper similitudes that might have been overlooked. A case in point is the epic-to-theater procedure, which Lévi saw as an argument in favor of an Indian origin, and therefore, as one against Greek influence.

> La fable des drames classiques est tirée directement des épopées ou des contes, mis en œuvre et transformés à l'aide de procédés et de ressources empruntés au fonds commun de l'esprit indien, et qui portent tous une garantie incontestable d'origine.
>
> The fable of classic dramas is taken directly from epics or tales, it is implemented and transformed with the aid of processes and resources borrowed from the common stock of the Indian spirit, all of which bear an indisputable guarantee of originality.
>
> (Lévi, 1890/1963, p. 365)

30 See Windisch (1882, pp. 14-15).
31 See Reich (1903, p. 694).
32 See Mayrhofer (1976), s.v. *yavanáḥ*. Cf. Bharata, *Nāṭyaś.* 5.11-12; Amarasiṃha, 2.6.3.22; and Halāyudha, 2.154.

There are three major assumptions behind this statement: borrowing is the same as being influenced, borrowing/being influenced is at odds with being original, and borrowing from/being influenced by Indian texts is at odds with borrowing from/being influenced by Greek texts. Additionally, a fourth assumption is also at work elsewhere, in Lévi's one-dimensional concept of influence/borrowing: borrowing/being influenced is always an explicit procedure.[33] According to him, if Europe borrowed from/was influenced by the Greco-Roman Classics in an announced manner, then India too would have had to proceed thusly. Against Lévi's claim that borrowing from Sanskrit epic disproves borrowing from Greek theater, I contend that the textual evidence on this matter could be interpreted as signaling that the idea itself of theater borrowing from epic is part of the Greek influence in India.

Even though Lévi himself partly modified his position later on in his career,[34] after him scholars gravitated either towards admitting

33 See Lévi (1890/1963): "Les littératures savantes de l'Europe, créées ou remaniées sur le modèle des classiques anciens, nous ont familiarisés avec les caractères ordinaires de l'emprunt: il ne se devine pas, il éclate; il ne se cache pas, il s'avoue orgueilleusement. L'admiration de l'œuvre originale, qui provoque l'imitation, porte l'imitateur à la copier avec une fidélité presque servile; il peut essayer d'adapter son modèle au goût du temps et du pays, de le naturaliser par une transposition habile; il ne réussit pas, il ne cherche pas même à en effacer les traits principaux. Les sujets, les sentiments essentiels, l'allure générale de l'action ne se modifient pas [The learned literatures of Europe, created or reworked on the model of the ancient classics, have familiarized us with the ordinary characteristics of borrowing: it is not to be guessed, it explodes; it does not hide, it proudly announces itself. The admiration of the original work, which provokes imitation, leads the imitator to copy it with almost servile fidelity: he can try to adapt his model to the taste of the time and the country, to naturalize it by a skillful transposition; he fails, he does not even try to erase its main features. The subjects, the main feelings, the general pace of the action do not change]" (p. 365).

34 See Lévi (1902): "Si le théâtre sanscrit est né à la cour des Kṣatrapas, la théorie de l'influence grecque semble gagner en vraisemblance. Le pays des Kṣatrapas était sans doute le plus hellénisé de l'Inde, puisqu'il était le marché le plus important du commerce hellénistique [If Sanskrit theater was born at the court of the Kṣatrapas, the theory of Greek influence seems to be gaining in credibility. The land of the Kṣatrapas was arguably the most Hellenized in India, as it was the most important market for Hellenistic commerce]" (p. 124).

defeat when faced with lack of evidence, or simply towards accepting the question as settled. For instance, Keith (1924), who in principle is open to the idea, ends up rejecting it: "But we do find in the epic indications that it was not necessary for Greece to give to India the ideas presented in the drama" (Keith, 1924, p. 63). Keith seems to be working under the same assumptions that Lévi did. In agreement with Keith's view, I argue that Sanskrit theater certainly borrowed from Sanskrit epic, but after further consideration, I also posit that the *why* (the idea itself of theater borrowing from epic) and the *how* (the techniques for adapting epic into theater) of such borrowing could have been Greco-Roman influences.

If, after Lévi, Indologists seemed ready to turn the page, classicists remained curious. This is the case with Tarn (1938), who with unprecedented clarity, is willing to delimit what to look for, i.e., general influences instead of specific borrowings, as well as where to look for it, i.e., Homer and Euripides instead of Menander: "And Egypt has at least taught us that whatever other works Greeks might take with them to foreign lands they would certainly take Homer and Euripides" (Tarn, 1938, p. 382). Indeed, literary motifs appearing in both Homer and (Ps.-)Euripides seem like a great starting point to investigate *what* (the elements adapted from epic to theater) could have been borrowed. But would the results of such research suffice? After all, as Thieme (1966) puts it, "Nach Lage der Dinge muss die Last des Beweises bei denen ruhen, die griechischen Einfluss behaupten [As things stand, the burden of proof must rest with those who affirm a Greek influence]" (p. 51).

Since themes and characters of the Attic New Comedy and the Greek Pantomime had already been presented as "evidence", but deemed inadequate, the question must be raised as to what would be considered "evidence", how would it be expected to "prove" a Greek influence, or even what would be regarded as an "influence". Trying to answer these questions, which have not been openly posed but seem to be awaiting a response anyway, I infer that only some sort of "borrowing" would amount to influence, that only something close to "imitation" would serve as proof, and that only a systematic exposition of "several such instances" within Sanskrit theater would once and for all settle the question. Such evidence exists nowhere, which is why some scholars have made up their minds, while others expect indefinitely, as if some "new" evidence could appear at any moment.

The truth is that the expectations are too high for such a meagre reality: when it comes to the literary sources of the Ancient World, new discoveries occur once in a blue moon. For the philologist, even a few blurred lines on a torn manuscript could be the finding of a lifetime. For the archaeologist, on the other hand, the sight of new evidence is certainly a more usual experience. Nonetheless, even archaeological evidence has been deemed inadequate by a very demanding circle. In the 1970s, Bernard (1976) reported a piece of information that could have been the milestone that stirred the debate back to at least the possibility of Greek influence: there was, by the third to second century BCE, a Greek building serving as a theater in India.[35] According to him, this replaced the question of whether there had been an influence with that of what type of influence would it have been.

Bernard, like Tarn, distinguishes between general influence and specific borrowing. He also adds, as a third option, the most modest of contributions to a process that would have happened with or without it. This additional attenuation of the claim has much to do with the modern notion of originality, only now not from the point of view of the European colonizer, but from that of the colonized Indian. For the former, acknowledging the extra help would be a sign of merit that stresses their achievement in the light of their legacy, whereas for the latter it would signify demerit. A natural response to the discourse of colonialism is nationalism. Where the modern is foreign, the ancient is native. It is an independent accomplishment. Or at least, it should be.

Closing in on the research problem, in colonial India, where Elizabethan theater would have been seen as foreign, Sanskrit theater would have been thought of as native. Its invention would positively articulate Indian identity; contrarywise, the mere suggestion of its imitation would negatively affect it. Hence, Indian nationalism could have been one of the reasons for an *a*

35 See Walker (2004, p. 9) and Bronkhorst (2016, p. 398).

priori rejection of the Greek influence hypothesis. The fact that two cultures, coinciding in space and time, and having contacts in other branches of the sciences (e.g., astronomy) and the arts (e.g., sculpture), would have both independently developed and mastered theater, without any borrowing, influence, or even contribution, seems, to say the least, unlikely.

Within other fields, the Greek influence hypothesis endured, as it did with the classicist Tarn and the archaeologist Bernard. A case in point is Free (1981), whose background is in theatre arts. Free does not differentiate between borrowing and influence, but she does distinguish between coincidence and intentionality. Coincidence could account for some parallelisms, but not all of them. According to her, to explain every similarity, one must accept influence/borrowing in both directions, that is, from the Greco-Roman world to India, and the other way around. The last option is certainly possible but seems less likely, based on the dating of the playwrights. In addition, Free's (1981) article offers one of only two statements that I have been able to identify,[36] suggesting a possible Greek influence in terms of the epic-to-theater procedure, as I postulate here: "The epic sweep of Sanskrit drama and the indebtedness of the subjects of the earliest plays to the Indian epic offer a further parallel with Greek tragedy" (p. 84). Regrettably, the idea is subject to no further consideration.

Sinha & Choudhury (2000) and Lindtner (2002) are probably the first Indologists since Windisch to openly accept the hypothesis as possible. For the former, not only could (Ps.-)Bhāsa have been influenced by Greek theater, but he could have even borrowed the device of the Greek chorus for his triads of characters (e.g., *The Middle One, The Five Nights, The Broken Thighs*, and *The Consecration*).[37] For the latter, a long study on the matter is still pending.[38] Following them, there are two studies with a lot in common: they are recent, they provide historiographical and bibliographical contributions, and they openly defend the Greek hypothesis. As differences, one can point out that one is by an expert

36 The other is Wells (1968, p. iii).
37 See Sinha & Choudhury (2000, p. 32).
38 See Lindtner (2002, p. 199).

in comparative literature, while the other is by an Indologist; and that one favors borrowing, while the other prefers influence.

The first of these studies is by Walker (2004), who revisits the comparison with Greek New Comedy. The old theory is refurbished with new "circumstantial evidence".[39] This encompasses a text that had not been considered before, as well as a text that was not even available before. These are, respectively, the parallel example of religious borrowing in the adapted Latin theater of Hrostvitha (ca. 935-973),[40] and the lucky discovery of the plays attributed to Bhāsa. Walker's take on the hypothesis is quite ingenious. On one hand, (Ps.-)Bhāsa's *The Broken Thighs* has much in common with Greek Tragedy;[41] on the other, so do the *prakaraṇa* and the Greek New Comedy. This could mean that, at an early stage, Sanskrit theater could have begun with borrowings from both Greek tragedy and Greek comedy, only to abandon them later, to develop other dramatic genres that were more relatable to their audiences. As advanced when discussing Windisch, I will not follow this line of inquiry.

In fact, I advance two major criticisms against Walker's proposal. First, the *nāṭaka*, with its epic-to-theater procedures, is closer to Greek theater than the *prakaraṇa*; second, Sanskrit theater and Roman theater, although influenced by the same Greek models, yielded such contrasting results, not because of a language barrier that Walker presupposes, but by reason of conscious choice. If the authors of Sanskrit theater knew Greek and Latin, and if they were aware that there is more than one way to adapt a text,[42] they could have consciously designed their adaptations in a new way, that

39 See Walker (2004, pp. 4-5) and Bronkhorst (2016, p. 397).

40 See Walker (2004): "As regards Greco-Roman New Comedy as a subtext for didactic religious plays, parallels between Hrotswitha and the Buddhist playwright Asvaghosa might prove especially striking, if more of the text of Asvaghosa's *prakaranas* had survived" (p. 6, n. 6). Walker's example could be strengthened by mention of the adapted Greek theater of Gregorius of Nazianzus (ca. 329-390), who borrowed from none other than Euripides.

41 Walkerś example could be strengthened by mention of (Ps.-)Bhāsa's *Karṇa's Task*.

42 For instance, Euripides adapts Homer's *Embassy* by emphasizing *Phoenix*, but Seneca adapts Euripides' *Trojan Women* by merging its plot with that of *Hecuba*.

could be called "Greco-Indian *anukaraṇa*",[43] mirroring the concept of Greco-Roman *imitatio*.

The texts and genres having much in common is not tantamount to them being the same. If Walker's similarities are noticeable, so too are the differences that have been adduced time and again by those who reject the influence hypothesis. Just like arguing in favor of what is similar does not entail proving the hypothesis, so too, counterarguing with what is different does not mean disproving it. The Greek influence hypothesis is not a scientific one, precisely because it is not falsifiable. In Classics, Indology, and other disciplines of the Humanities, analysis and interpretation, rather than data and hard evidence, tend to guide the process from hypotheses to conclusions. Unlike Science's empirical methods, their critical ones hardly ever lead to definitive answers, yet the field of knowledge profits from the debate. Hence, any reframing of the hypothesis of a Greek influence in the Sanskrit theater should be intended to reignite this debate.

To put in an analogy, up until now, Sanskrit borrowing has been approached as if it were a case of copyright infringement: classicists, the plaintiffs, have been seen as alleging that Sanskrit playwrights, the defendants, would have been making unauthorized use of Greco-Roman plays, and since academia, the jury, is not yet convinced by a preponderance of the evidence, therefore, it should have already been determined that there has been no harm done. This picture is troubling in various ways: copyright infringement is a felony, but imitation used to be the norm, e.g., in Rome; neither ancient authors nor modern critics have any exclusive rights over the Greco-Roman Classics; and far from any harm, the supporters of the influence hypothesis have repeatedly emphasized the benefits of acknowledging such interactions for achieving a better understanding of the Ancient World as a whole. Innocent until

43 This term would presuppose the Indian imitation of both Greek *and* Roman models. Moreover, if said imitation did occur in India, its very motivation might lie in Rome. After all, classical Rome was chronologically closer to classical India than classical Greece was, and by the first century CE, Roman authors had already under their belt several centuries of productively imitating another literary canon.

proven guilty is not a model that works here, and in consequence, a higher standard of proof should not be required. All that the academic jury needs to accept is the possibility of an influence: it is a hypothesis, after all.

The most recent study is Bronkhorst (2016), who openly acknowledges that the mainstream view is still that there is no need for further research into the Greek influence hypothesis. The author is aware of the flawed assumptions that have guided this line of reasoning that started with Lévi. Following Bernard, he distinguishes between borrowing, influence, and contribution; even if he opposes borrowing, he does support influence and contribution. And finally, in overt opposition with the generally accepted view, he even encourages new research to be done in pursuit of influences and contributions: "...in the form which Weber had given to it, the thesis of Greek influence on the Sanskrit theater still awaits its first serious criticism" (Bronkhorst, 2016, p. 403). Still having in mind borrowings, although not of the kind that have been looked for, this book was conceived, in part, in the hopes of filling in this void.

A final word on implications: the fact that two entities resemble each other is, certainly, no proof for one being derived from the other, and even when such resemblances are quantitatively and qualitatively relevant, there is still not just one single explanation; but it might at least amount to a matter worth considering. As objections to a book like this one, one could foresee the claim that it still has not provided any definitive "proof" of an "influence" of the Greco-Roman world in India. "Proof", indeed, there will not be; "influences" and "borrowings", on the contrary, there might have been, and it is about time to start discussing them.

The Building Blocks of Tradition and Adaptation

A text modeled upon another text works on two basic levels: it keeps some of the components of the original text and it makes some changes of its own. This mixture of something old and something new can be further analyzed in terms of two counterbalancing theories: the theory of tradition and the theory of adaptation. Both concepts have their roots in Roman Antiquity.

In English, *tradition* is attested since the sixteenth century and refers, among other things, to "a literary, artistic, or musical method or style established by a particular person or group, and subsequently followed by others" ("Tradition", n.d., para. 1). This definition, encompassing two crucial moments, i.e., the establishment and the follow-up, retains, to some degree, the idea of handing over that comes from the word's etymon. In Latin, *trāditiō* becomes frequent after the Age of Augustus and means "a saying handed down from former times" (Lewis & Short, 1879, s.v. *trādĭtĭo*).

Likewise, in English, *adaptation* is documented from the thirteenth century onwards and designates "an altered or amended version of a text, musical composition, etc., (now *esp.*) one adapted for filming, broadcasting, or production on the stage from a novel or similar literary source" ("Adaptation", n.d., para. 4). This meaning also comprises two pivotal moments, i.e., the production and the alteration. The word derives from the Latin *adaptō*, which gives form to an abstract noun during the Middle Ages, and signifies "to fit, adjust, or adapt to a thing" (Lewis & Short, 1879, s.v. *ăd-apto*).

Tradition has been studied from a theoretical standpoint by several authors. Alexander (2016) distinguishes between three forms of tradition: a) anthropological, b) literary, and c) religious. Each of them is characterized by the presence of specific elements of tradition, which also add up to three: a) continuity, b) canon, and c) core. In his model, the three forms of tradition are organized in terms of the increasing number of elements that constitute them. Hence, an anthropological tradition is one whose sole element is continuity; a literary tradition, one that contains continuity plus the additional element of canon; and a religious tradition, one that is composed of all three elements, that is, continuity, canon, and core.

Anthropological traditions are merely continuous. This continuity exists because the cultural phenomena present in these traditions are characterized by these three features: "(i) they are instances of social interaction; (ii) they are repeated; (iii) they are psychologically salient" (Boyer, 1990, p. 1). The features serve as criteria of recognition, meaning that by their presence or absence an anthropological tradition is recognizable as such. As instances of social interaction, traditional phenomena are to be understood only as actual events and never as hypothetical explanations for such events; as repeated instances, these phenomena refer to previous, similar occurrences; and as psychologically salient instances, traditional phenomena are "attention-demanding".[44] Two additional features are worth noticing, for they complement this basic formulation: on one hand, anthropological traditions cannot be written; and on the other, their members tend not to be self-aware. To put it another way, in such traditions, events are always oral, and the participants are usually unaware of the theoretical implications of such practices.

Conversely, literary traditions[45] are both continuous and canonical. The element of canon is key, since it allows for the repetitiveness, the orality, and the unawareness of anthropological traditions to turn, respectively, into creativity, literacy, and criticality. Creativity, unlike repetitiveness, is an active endeavor. In this sense, an adaptation of a text would never be solely the repetition of its form or content, but an independent text altogether. In the Greco-Roman world, this is what is meant by the term Gr. μίμησις / Lat. *imitatio*,[46] defined as "the study and conspicuous deployment of features recognizably characteristic of a canonical author's style or content, so as to define one's own generic affiliation" (Conte & Most, 2015, para. 1).

This way of interacting with authoritative texts differs from three other parallel modes of interaction: plagiarism, parody, and intertextuality. In plagiarism (Gr. κλοπή / Lat. *furtum*), there is derivative copying, whereas in imitation this turns into creative re-use, which is why even though plagiarism was condemned, imitation was encouraged, not only as a pedagogic means towards literary proficiency, but also as a form of artistic mastery by

44 See Lewis (1980).

45 See Grafton, Most, & Settis (2010), for a study on Greco-Roman literary tradition; and Patton (1994), for a study on Indian literary tradition.

46 In its rhetorical use, which differs from the poetical one, see Seneca the Elder, *Suas.* 3.7, and Seneca the Younger, *Ep.* 114.

itself. In parody (Gr. παρῳδία / Lat. *ridicula imitatio*), the re-use is intended as mockery, and not as a manifestation of admiration towards a revered author, as is the case with imitation. Even satyr plays, such as Euripides' *Cyclops*, are not to be interpreted as a parodies;[47] instead, they are meant as "mythological burlesques" (Shaw, 2014, p. 109). Finally, in intertextuality, the entire body of literature works as a system; in contrast, imitation is limited to individual authors like Homer, or at the most, to specific genres like epic.

Even more so than orality, literacy is suited for tradition. In fact, the emergence of writing is "the most significant event in the history of tradition" (Alexander, 2016, p. 12), because it broadens the temporal frame of tradition. Whereas anthropological traditions tend to focus on mortality and its temporal correlate, the present, literary traditions pay attention to immortality and its temporal correlate, the past. The link between literature, immortality, and the past is a relatively obvious one, especially within the epic genre. This is the reason why the element of canon is the most valuable one for a study encompassing literary traditions, as represented by Greek and Sanskrit ancient cultures and their respective written texts. A canon results from the dialectics of the old and the new, as Eliot (1919, p. 55) clearly puts it:

> The existing order is completed before the new work arrives; for order to persist after the supervention of novelty, the *whole* existing order must be, if ever so slightly, altered; and so the relations, proportions, values of each work of art toward the whole are readjusted; and this is conformity between the old and the new.

If a canon were a qualitative system of measurement, then the classic would be its qualitative unit of measurement, in which, similarly, the dialectics of ancient and modern tend towards a synthesis or "organic unity"[48] of form and content. However, such dialectics,

47 If one were to accept, for the sake of argument, that Euripides' *Cyclops* is indeed a parody, it would then be a parody of tragedy (Arnott, 1972), but never a parody of Homer's *Odyssey*.

48 See Matarrita Matarrita (1989).

since they allow for differences of opinions, also imply criticality, whether in the form of positive criticism or in that of its negative counterpart. In any case, there is to be expected some degree of underlying tension, as Kermode (1975, pp. 15-16) explains it:

> The doctrine of the classic as model or criterion entails, in some form, the assumption that the ancient can be more or less immediately relevant and available, in a sense contemporaneous with the modern – or anyway that its nature is such that it can, by strategies of accommodation, be made so. When this assumption is rejected the whole authority of the classic as model is being challenged, and then we have – whether in Alexandria or in twelfth- or seventeenth- or nineteenth or twentieth-century Europe – the recurrent *querelle* between ancient and modern.

Lastly, religious traditions are, at once, continuous, canonical, and core oriented. The extra element of core accounts for these types of traditions being hierarchical, immutable, and indisputable. The shared events and the shared texts, belonging, respectively, to anthropological and literary traditions, are shared through horizontal interaction; contrarywise, the shared truths of religious traditions are conveyed from a position of knowledge towards one of ignorance, in an expository fashion. Such exposition, as one of immutable truths, comes closer to the repetitiveness of traditions having only continuity than it does to the cumulative creativity of those adding canon. Immutable truths, as a matter of faith, are never subject to dispute, not because of unawareness, like in anthropological traditions, but because of lack of criticality, unlike in literary traditions. For these reasons, religious traditions transcend both mortality and immortality through the notion of eternity and they go beyond present, past, and even future, in a timeless manner.

Adaptation, in turn, has also been the subject of various theoretical projects. Hutcheon & O'Flynn (2012) identify three perspectives for looking at an adaptation: a) as a product; b) as a process of creation; and c) as a process of reception. Each perspective focuses on one of the key participants in an adaptation, respectively, text, author, and audience. Moreover, each perspective results in a specific definition, adding up to three parallel definitions of adaptation: a) adaptation, as a product, is a transposition or a transcoding; b) adaptation, as a process of creation, is a reinterpretation and a re-creation; and c) adaptation, as a process of reception, can be a subtype of intertextuality.

When taken as a product, an adaptation is a transposition that must be extended, deliberate, specific, and announced; it could also be intermedial. The criteria of extension and deliberateness rule out shorter or unintentional interactions, such as echoes or allusions; the criterion of specificity leaves out more general forms of intertextuality; and the criterion of announcement excludes instances of plagiarism. Most importantly, the fact that these transpositions need not change media (e.g., literary adaptations of literary works) but may vary in genre (e.g., theater adaptations of epic works) allows for the type of study that I am undertaking: "This 'transcoding' can involve a shift of medium (a poem to a film) or genre (an epic to a novel), or a change of frame and therefore context" (Hutcheon & O'Flynn, 2012, pp. 7-8). The textual elements being transposed in the product of an adaptation are "themes" (p. 10), "characters" (p. 11), "time and space" (p. 13), among others.

When seen as a process of creation, an adaptation is both a reinterpretation and a re-creation. In two inverted juxtapositions, intended more as a reflection than as a mere play on words, the former is to be thought of as a creative interpretation, and the latter as an interpretative creation. To put it another way, the creative process consists of two intertwined facets: the interpretation of the traditional text, which must be undertaken with creativity, that is, with one of the distinctive qualities of literary traditions; and the creation of the adapted text, which ought to be assumed with criticality, that is, with the other distinctive quality of literary traditions. Some of the authorial techniques at stake in the process of creation are "contraction" and "expansion" (Hutcheon & O'Flynn, 2012, p. 19), as well as "omissions and additions" (Corrigan, 2017, p. 1).

A relevant example of adaptation as a process of creation within the Indian tradition is that of "adaptive reuse", a concept borrowed from the fields of architecture and city planning, and itself reused in those of philosophy and literature by Freschi & Maas (2017, p. 13):

> The concept of reuse comprises four main aspects, viz. (1.) the involvement of at least one consciously acting agent, who, (2.) in order to achieve a certain purpose, (3.) resumes the usage (4.) of a clearly identifiable object after an interruption in its being used. The attribute "adaptive" presupposes that the reusing person pursues a specific purpose by adapting something already existent to his or her specific needs.

Like adaptation as a product, adaptive reuse is characterized by deliberateness (the agency from aspect 1) and specificity (the attribute *adaptive*); also, like adaptation as a process of creation, adaptive reuse is defined by creativity (the purpose from aspect 2). In this sense, adaptative reuses appear as instances of adaptation whose key features are the interruption and the resuming of the use (aspects 3 and 4). However, just as not all adaptations are adaptive reuses, so too, not all reuses are adaptive ones: the interruption and the resuming of the use, by themselves, account only for simple reuses, whereas the deliberateness and the creativity, not to mention the more obvious aspect of specificity, procure the necessary components for adaptive reuses.

If adaptation and reuse come together in the concept of adaptive reuse, adaptation can be further linked to tradition through the notion of textual reuse, as explained by Freschi & Maas (2017, p. 17):[49]

> In the case of textual reuse, adaptive reuse highlights the fact that the textual material has been reused. Its reuse emphasizes the text and its connotations. For example, it possibly adds prestige to the newly created text or situates that text within a continuous and illustrious tradition.

Textual reuse, the manifestation of adaptive reuse in literary traditions, should be both intended and identified as such: without intention, instead of a textual reuse all that is left is simple reuse; and without identification, mere recycling. Even though textual

49 Cf. Hutcheon & O'Flynn (2012, p. 32): "Adaptation, like evolution, is a transgenerational phenomenon".

reuse operates more directly at the level of the text (i.e., of adaptation as a product), it also, through the standard of intention, lays part of the responsibility on the author (i.e., on adaptation as a process of creation), and, through the standard of identification, lays the rest of it on the audience (i.e., on adaptation as a process of reception).

Going back to Hutcheon & O'Flynn (2012), when understood as a process of reception, adaptation can be a subtype of intertextuality, if, and only if, two conditions are met: "if the receiver is acquainted with the adapted text", and if "they are also acknowledged as adaptations of specific texts" (p. 21). For adaptation to be intertextuality, in the reception end of the spectrum, acquaintance (like identification in textual reuses) is a *sine qua non*; and in the creation end of the spectrum, acknowledgment (like intention in textual reuses) is. Nonetheless, for adaptation to be adaptation, acknowledgement and acquaintance are optional.[50] This nuance fits better in the Greco-Roman and Indian contexts: even though in most cases a play based on the Homeric Epics or on the *Mahābhārata* would certainly be intended as such (given the canonical status of the texts) and identified as such (given the cultural background of the audience), this could not be asserted of every single case.[51]

In sum, adaptation is a "double-faceted" (Elliott, 2020, p. 198) concept: it *is* product and process, production and consumption, old and new, creativity and criticality; and it *can be* deliberate or unintentional (or even unconscious).

A combination of the views from the theory of tradition, with its dialectics of the old and the new and its ways of understanding written literature and a canon of classical texts, on one side, and the theory of adaptation, with its integrations of products

50 This clearly contradicts Hutcheon & O'Flynn's (2012) theory, and is more in line with Elliott's (2020, pp. 198-199) theory.

51 What if the author is not adapting the canonical text but previous adaptations of it, as might be the case with Euripides' *Cyclops*? What if the audience does not identify all the conflated canonical sources, as might be the case with (Ps.-)Bhāsa's *The Middle One*? What if the references can only be retrieved by means of scholarly commentaries and digital humanities? Can one even address the matter of ancient reception when the dating of authors and texts (and, therefore, audiences as well) is still subject to large scholarly debate?

and processes and its ways of conceiving reinterpretations and re-creations, on the other, can benefit my proposal by way of delimiting the conceptual building blocks upon which an appropriate methodology can be supported.

If It Looks like a Duck...

Concepts provide an appropriate methodological basis for research in the Humanities in general and in Philology specifically. While in a narrow sense philology refers to the collecting, editing, and commentating activities associated with textual criticism, in a broader sense this discipline deals with making sense of texts. This second view is to be thought of, not in terms of higher criticism, but as a form of close reading. Notoriously present in the Greco-Roman world, where the term was coined,[52] philology is also well represented in India, the phenomenon at least, if not an equivalent concept. For this book, I intend for the philological and literary analysis to bridge theory and practice, concepts and methods, tradition and adaptation, epic and theater, the Greco-Roman world and India. The key concepts for the following analyses are "motifs", "adapted elements", and "adaptation techniques".

A motif is "a situation, incident, idea, image, or character-type that is found in many different literary works, folktales, or myths" (Baldick, 2001, p. 162). Moreover, a literary motif is a "unidad temática mínima con valor de contenido y situación dentro del texto [minimum thematic unit with content and situation value within the text]" (Orea Rojas, 2018, p. 181). This unit, smaller than the text itself but larger than one of its themes, can be identified by answering the following questions (Bremond, 1980): When? Where? Who? What? To whom? How? With what result? With what consequences?

Much like concepts themselves, motifs travel within traditions, as adaptations from epic to theater, and sometimes even across cultures, if they come into contact. Rather than presenting all the Greco-Roman epic-to-theater transitions, followed by all the Indian

52 See Plato, *Phdr.* 236e, *Tht.* 146a, *Lach.* 188c-e, *Phd.* 89d-e and *Phd.* 90b-91a.

ones, in this book I structure the contents according to motifs. Also, for all relevant passages, I successively present textual contexts,[53] emphasized summaries, parallel quotations, and commentaries.

The first literary motif is that of the embassy (Gr. πρεσβεία, Lat. *legatio*, Skr. *dūtya*). It relates how, *during the war/before the war, at a bivouac/at a city, three ambassadors/one ambassador deliver(s) a message to the opposing side, with the aid of applicable substories, and the speakers fail to convince the estranged party to fight/not to fight, thus almost producing total annihilation.* It is found in *Il.* 9, from where Euripides reworks the substory of the eponymous character in the fragmentary *Phoenix*, as well as in *MBh.* 5, out of which (Ps.-)Bhāsa fashions *The Embassy*. The second chapter of this book is dedicated to analyzing this motif.

To that end, I first give a side-by-side translation[54] of relevant epic and dramatic passages, whose similarities have for the most part been noticed by the critics. This serves to determine the main adapted elements. Second, I provide a comparative analysis of such passages with the aim of identifying the chief adaptation techniques. I present all this separately for each literary tradition. Then, as a third and final step, I bring together the two sets of information, and I postulate a list of possible influences and borrowings from the Greco-Roman world into India.

The third chapter deals with the ambush motif (Gr. λόχος, Lat. *insidiae*, Skr. *sauptika*), present, on one hand, in *Il.* 10 and Ps.-Euripides' *Rhesus*; and on the other, in *MBh.* 4 and (Ps.-)Bhāsa's *The Five Nights*. This motif depicts how, *during the night/during the day-to-night transition, at a bivouac/at a city, two soldiers/two armies attack the opposing side, without them expecting it, and the attackers massacre enemies/seize cattle, thus obtaining valuable intelligence.*

53 See Baldick (2001): "**context,** those parts of a *TEXT preceding and following any particular passage, giving it a meaning fuller or more identifiable than if it were read in isolation" (p. 50).

54 The sole exception is the *Phoenix*, whose fragmentary nature makes a side-by-side presentation much more difficult. In that case, the entirety of the epic version is provided from the start, and then, all the relevant dramatic passages are organized and analyzed.

Likewise, the fourth chapter focuses on the ogre motif (Gr. κύκλωψ, Lat. *sēmifer*, Skr. *rākṣasa*), which stages how, *after the war/ before the war, while traveling through the sea/through the forest, a hero faces a man-eating ogre, with the aid of wine/food coming from a priest and his family, and the hero defeats/kills the ogre, thus freeing his companions/the townsfolk*. This motif appears, on the Greco-Roman side, in *Od.* 9 and Euripides' *Cyclops*; and on the Indian side, in *MBh.* 1 and (Ps.-)Bhāsa's *The Middle One*. In both cases, I follow the same three-stage process of reviewing adapted elements, adaptation techniques, and Greco-Roman influences and borrowings.

The fifth and concluding chapter builds on all the parallelisms that previous scholars have identified between the Greco-Roman and Sanskrit theatrical traditions, both in theory and in practice, and it does so by bringing together not only the postulated influences and borrowings from the three motifs, but also their distinctive literary features and their hypothetical historical context, with the intention of proposing a preliminary model for Greco-Indian *anukaraṇa*, mirroring that of Greco-Roman *imitatio*.

Elements and techniques are useful for analyzing adaptations within the same tradition, like that of Greek epic into Greek theater or that of Sanskrit epic into Sanskrit theater; but they can also contribute to the examination of cross-cultural adaptations, be they well-accepted, such as that from the Greek literary tradition into the Roman literary tradition, or hypothetical, such as that from the Greco-Roman literary tradition into the Sanskrit literary tradition. In this sense, additional methodological criteria, such as those brought forward by Wulff Alonso (2019a, pp. 2-3; 2019b; 2020, pp. 18-23) for the also hypothetical adaptation of the Greco-Roman literary tradition into the Sanskrit epic, may also be useful when considering such cross-cultural adaptation into the Sanskrit theater. Especially, the "argument of improbability" and the "argument of oddity" appear relevant and are worthy of my reformulation here.

In my opinion, the argument of improbability would mean that a higher quantity and quality of shared elements between two versions of a literary motif coming from historically connected cultures is proportional to a lower probability of explanations other than adaptation.[55] It is possible for two literary motifs to belong to the realm of folklore, and so, to be completely unrelated to each other.[56] It is also possible for them to exist exclusively – or to share more elements – within Indo-European traditions, thus suggesting a relation via common heritage.[57] And cultural contact is no less of a possibility, as the Greco-Roman *imitatio* itself demonstrates.[58] Just as coots, grebes, and loons resemble ducks without actually being ducks, so too, folk motifs and Indo-European motifs might resemble Greco-Roman motifs. Therefore, a review of the shared elements between two versions of the same literary motif, paired with an examination of the opinions of those who have classified it one way or the other, will reveal a higher or lower probability of such motif pertaining to one of these three categories.

If a *culture hero being susceptible to wounds* is generally regarded as pertaining to folklore, if an *otherwise invulnerable hero having a weak spot* (Achilles in the *Iliad*, Kṛṣṇa in the *Mahābhārata*, Esfandiyar in the *Shāh-nāma*, or Siegfried in the *Nibelungenlied*) tends to be narrowed down to the Indo-European realm, and if a *group of heroes carrying out an unexpected night attack* (Dolon, but also Diomedes and Odysseus in the *Iliad*; Nisus and Euryalus in the *Aeneid*) is usually accepted as a Greco-Roman feature; then, why could the latter not be regarded as a Greco-Indian feature as well? After all, Suśarman and Duryodhana, but also Aśvatthāman, Kṛpa, and Kṛtavarman in the *Mahābhārata*, can just as easily exemplify those elements too.

In my view, the argument of oddity would entail, first, that odd elements which are shared between two versions of a literary motif coming from historically connected cultures increase the probability of an adaptation more than ordinary elements do; and second, that when they are coherent within one culture

55 Cf. Wulff Alonso's (2020) view that this principle "denies the possibility of explaining repetition by chance or other explanations" (p. 18).
56 On "folk motifs", see Thompson (1955/1958).
57 On "Indo-European motifs", see Mallory & Adams (1997), and M. L. West (2007), and N. J. Allen (2020).
58 On "Greco-Roman motifs", see West & Woodman (1979).

but incoherent within the other, such odd elements suggest the directionality of the adaptation, from the former towards the latter. For instance, remuneration for a job done is ordinary, but asking for it when not offered is odd; and remuneration for a soldier or for a teacher is ordinary, but depending on the cultural context, them demanding it would be odd.

If motifs are thematic units for the analysis, which are delimited by a series of questions, adapted elements respond to one specific question: the “what?” or the “forms” in Hutcheon & O’Flynn’s (2012) categories. My proposed typology of adapted elements includes themes, characters, times, and spaces.

A theme is “a salient abstract idea that emerges from a literary work’s treatment of its subject-matter” (Baldick, 2001, p. 258). Among the elements of the story, themes are the most easily recognizable as “adaptable” (Hutcheon & O’Flynn, 2012, p. 10). In turn, a character might refer either to “(the representation of) a human(-like) individual in a literary text” (de Temmerman & van Emde Boas, 2018, p. xii) or to “the sum of relatively stable moral, mental and social traits and dispositions pertaining to an individual” (de Temmerman & van Emde Boas, 2018, p. xii). In adaptations, characters additionally relate to the “how?” or the “audiences”, since they convey “rhetorical and aesthetic effects” (Hutcheon & O’Flynn, 2012, p. 11).

Time and space are correlated. Even though obviously linked to the categories of “when?” and “where?”, that is, of “contexts” in Hutcheon & O’Flynn’s (2012) nomenclature, they can also be part of the things being adapted, and as such, they can serve some specific functions. Time is determined by the “story” (the events when ordered according to the text), rather than the “fabula” (the events when ordered according to time itself), because storytelling profits from variation: “the events in the story may differ in frequency (they may be told more than once), rhythm (they may be told at great length or quickly), and order (the chronological order may be changed)” (de Jong & Nünlist, 2007, p. xiii). Similarly, space fulfills “thematic”, “mirror”, “symbolic”, “characterizing”, “psychologizing”, and “personification” functions (de Jong, 2012, pp. 13-17).

Now, if adapted elements respond to the "what?" or the "forms" of adaptations, then adaptation techniques are determined by the "who?" and "why?", that is, by the "adapters" themselves, according to Hutcheon & O'Flynn's (2012) paradigm, and by their intentions. Just as I advanced a typology of adapted elements, so too am I putting forward one for the adaptation techniques, which comprise the contrasting pairs of maintaining/changing, adding/subtracting, emphasizing/ignoring, and merging/splitting.

The maintaining/changing pair resonates with the dialectics of tradition/adaptation. Theatrical versions of epic motifs maintain some features, not only to be recognizable as their reworkings, but also out of respect for their canonical status. The changes, in turn, even when intended to provoke laughter, are tokens of said deferential attitude. The adding/subtracting pair recalls Corrigan's (2017) observation about "omissions and additions" (p. 1). Two basic sub procedures of changing are, precisely, to add new elements or to subtract some of the previously existing ones. Although subtraction, given the performative nature of theater, is a far more common technique in the epic-to-theater transitions, additions are not at all atypical, whether it be for resolving problems caused by previous subtractions, or as the result of other authorial choices.

Similarly, the emphasizing/ignoring pair suggests Hutcheon & O'Flynn's (2012) "contraction" (p. 19) and "expansion" (p. 19). This is a technique usually related to the element of time, whose features of frequency, rhythm, and order, make it ideal for various kinds of emphases. On the opposite end of the spectrum, the intentional ignoring of something might be very telling, since sometimes silence speaks louder than words. And the last pair, formulated as merging/splitting, arises from the Greco-Roman term of *contaminatio*, "a word used by modern scholars to express the procedure of *Terence (and perhaps *Plautus) in incorporating material from another Greek play into the primary play which he was adapting" (Brown, 2015, para. 1).[59] This is very similar to what (Ps.-)Bhāsa does in *The Middle One*, borrowing materials from two

59 See Terence's *An.* 9 and *Haut.* 17.

separate *Mahābhārata* episodes and combining them into a single play. For that reason, this is one of my main arguments in support of the influence hypothesis.

Having explained the gist of the book in terms of contents and procedures, it is now time to proceed to the analysis itself.

2. The Embassy

A “Potifar’s Wife” Story

Book 9 of the *Iliad* encompasses an assembly, a council of chiefs, and an embassy. At the assembly, king Agamemnon proposes to flee but young Diomedes insists on fighting. During the council of chiefs, old Nestor suggests the conciliation of the hero Achilles, and Agamemnon offers him compensation. Then, the orator Odysseus, the preceptor Phoenix, and the companion Ajax are chosen as ambassadors, and each delivers a speech for the benefit of the enraged hero, who, in turn, gradually and slightly yields his grudge. Phoenix’s speech includes three substories: the story of Phoenix, the story of the Prayers, and the story of Meleager.

The story of Phoenix (*Il.* 9.447-477) narrates a father-son νείκεα (strife). It involves not only the son Phoenix and the father Amyntor, but also the latter’s unnamed ἄκοιτις (wife) and παλλακίς (concubine). As a tale of two men disputing over a concubine, it resembles the plot of the *Iliad* itself. Nonetheless, when compared with other embedded narratives such as the story of Meleager, it appears “almost parodical” (Scodel, 1982, p. 133, n. 13): the anger is aimed not at the offender but at the offended, the supplication seeks to take the hero not to the battlefield but to bed, and the curse threatens not his life but his fertility.

The epic version is as follows: Amyntor favors his concubine over his wife. The wife, determined to divide Amyntor and the concubine, begs Phoenix to interfere by sleeping with the concubine. Her reasoning is that having slept with the young man, the concubine would prefer him to the old one. Phoenix reluctantly

 https://doi.org/10.11647/OBP.0417.02

obeys his mother's pleading and, in turn, faces his father's wrath. He gets cursed not to bear any children. Then, he thinks about killing his father, but a god makes him desist.[60] He wants to leave his father's palace, but friends and relatives prevent him from doing so, by guarding him day and night by turns. On the tenth night, he bursts open the door of his chamber, leaps over the fence of the court, and escapes without being noticed by the watchmen or the slave women.

> οἷον ὅτε πρῶτον λίπον Ἑλλάδα καλλιγύναικα,
> φεύγων νείκεα πατρὸς Ἀμύντορος Ὀρμενίδαο,
> ὅς μοι **παλλακίδος** περιχώσατο καλλικόμοιο,
> τὴν αὐτὸς φιλέεσκεν, ἀτιμάζεσκε δ'ἄκοιτιν,
> **μητέρ** ἐμήν. ἣ δ'αἰὲν ἐμὲ **λισσέσκετο** γούνων
> παλλακίδι προμιγῆναι, ἵν'ἐχθήρειε γέροντα.
> τῇ πιθόμην καὶ ἔρεξα· πατὴρ δ'ἐμὸς αὐτίκ'ὀισθεὶς
> πολλὰ κατηρᾶτο, **στυγερὰς** δ'ἐπεκέκλετ'Ἐρινῦς,
> μή ποτε γούνασιν οἷσιν ἐφέσσεσθαι φίλον υἱὸν
> ἐξ ἐμέθεν γεγαῶτα· θεοὶ δ'ἐτέλειον ἐπαρὰς,
> Ζεύς τε καταχθόνιος καὶ ἐπαινὴ Περσεφόνεια.
> τὸν μὲν ἐγὼ βούλευσα κατακτάμεν ὀξέι χαλκῷ·
> ἀλλά τις ἀθανάτων παῦσεν χόλον, ὅς ῥ' ἐνὶ θυμῷ
> δήμου θῆκε φάτιν καὶ ὀνείδεα πόλλ' ἀνθρώπων,
> ὡς μὴ πατροφόνος μετ' Ἀχαιοῖσιν καλεοίμην.
> ἔνθ'ἐμοὶ οὐκέτι πάμπαν ἐρητύετ'ἐν φρεσὶ θυμὸς
> **πατρὸς χωομένοιο** κατὰ μέγαρα στρωφᾶσθαι.
> ἦ μὲν πολλὰ ἔται καὶ ἀνεψιοὶ ἀμφὶς ἐόντες
> αὐτοῦ λισσόμενοι κατερήτυον ἐν μεγάροισι,
> πολλὰ δὲ ἴφια μῆλα καὶ εἰλίποδας ἕλικας βοῦς
> ἔσφαζον, πολλοὶ δὲ σύες θαλέθοντες ἀλοιφῇ
> εὑόμενοι τανύοντο διὰ φλογὸς Ἡφαίστοιο,
> πολλὸν δ'ἐκ κεράμων μέθυ πίνετο τοῖο γέροντος.
> εἰνάνυχες δέ μοι ἀμφ'αὐτῷ παρὰ νύκτας ἴαυον·
> οἳ μὲν ἀμειβόμενοι φυλακὰς ἔχον, οὐδέ ποτ'ἔσβη
> πῦρ, ἕτερον μὲν ὑπ'αἰθούσῃ εὐερκέος αὐλῆς,
> ἄλλο δ'ἐνὶ προδόμῳ, πρόσθεν θαλάμοιο θυράων.
> ἀλλ'ὅτε δὴ δεκάτη μοι ἐπήλυθε νὺξ ἐρεβεννή,
> καὶ τότ'ἐγὼ θαλάμοιο θύρας πυκινῶς ἀραρυίας
> ῥήξας ἐξῆλθον, καὶ ὑπέρθορον ἑρκίον αὐλῆς
> ῥεῖα, λαθὼν φύλακάς τ'ἄνδρας δμῳάς τε γυναῖκας.

60 The verses containing this intention (*Il.* 9.458-461) were transmitted only by Plutarch, *Mor.* 26 ff.

> ...like when, at first, I left Greece, of beautiful women, fleeing from a strife with my father Amyntor, the son of Ormenus, who was exceedingly angry at me about a **concubine** of beautiful hair. He loved her and dishonored his wife, my **mother**, who repeatedly **begged** me at my knees to sleep with the concubine, so that she would hate the old man. I obeyed her and acted on it. My father, immediately having suspected it, called down many **curses** and invoked the loathed Erinyes, so that he would never set on his knees a dear son, born from me. And the gods fulfilled his curses, both Zeus, the belowground, and the dreaded Persephone. I decided to kill him with the sharp sword, but one of the immortals held my wrath: into my mind he put the people's gossip and various recriminations, so that among the Achaeans I would not be called a parricide. Then the heart in my breast could not at all keep me living any longer in the palaces of my **wrathful father**. Truly, my fellows and my relatives, surrounding me and begging me, held me back there in the palaces. Many fat sheep, and cattle of curved horns and rolling gait did they slaughter; many swine, swelling with fat, did they lay to singe over the flame of Hephaistos; and much wine was drunk from the jars of that old man. For nine nights, they passed the night around me. Alternating, they kept guards, and the fire never went out: one beneath the portico of the well-fenced court, and the other in the porch in front of the doors of my chamber. But when the tenth dark night fell upon me, then, having broken the closely fitted doors of my chamber, I came out and easily leapt over the fence of the court, having escaped the notice of the male guards and the female servants.
>
> (*Il.* 9.447-477)

In Euripides' fragmentary *Phoenix*, the father-son strife turns into a "Potiphar's Wife" story. From the two main sources available, i.e., Apollodorus the mythographer (ca. 1-100 CE) and Hieronymus of Rhodes (ca. 300-200 BCE),[61] the plot can be roughly put together like this: the concubine makes sexual advances towards Phoenix, but he rejects her. Then, the concubine takes the matter to Amyntor, and falsely accuses Phoenix of rape. Amyntor blinds Phoenix and imprisons him. The outcome is tragic for Amyntor, who sees his son

61 I follow the Greek text by Collard & Cropp (Euripides, 2008). The translations are my own.

leave, as well as for the concubine, who dies with regret; but it is favorable for Phoenix, who recovers his sight and gets enthroned elsewhere.

The evidence from Apollodorus the mythographer is direct; however, in terms of dramatic action, it only mentions the blinding, the accusation, the treatment, and the enthronement. Regarding the characters, it offers further help, since it refers to the name of the concubine as Phthia,[62] as well as to the role of the centaur Chiron within the story.[63]

> ...Φοῖνοξ ὁ Ἀμύντορος... ὑπὸ τοῦ πατρὸς **ἐτυφλώθη καταψευσαμένης** φθορὰν Φθίας τῆς τοῦ πατρὸς παλλακῆς. Πηλεὺς δὲ αὐτὸν πρὸς Χείρωνα κομίσας, ὑπ' ἐκείνου **θεραπευθέντα** τὰς ὄψεις **βασιλέα κατέστησε** Δολόπων.
>
> ...Phoenix, the son of Amyntor... **was blinded** by his father, **having been falsely accused** of rape by Phthia, his father's concubine. And having taken him to Chiron, by whom he **was treated** for his eyes, Peleus **made him king** of the Dolopians.
>
> (Apollodorus mythographus, *Bibl.* 3.13.8)

The testimony of Hieronymus of Rhodes is indirect since it speaks of the story of the Anagyrasian deity in comparison with the story of Phoenix. When it comes to dramatic action, it recounts the accusation, the blinding, and the imprisonment, and even though it remains silent about Phoenix's treatment and enthronement, it suggests Amyntor's and the concubine's tragic endings.

> 'Ἀναγυράσιος δαίμων'· ἐπεὶ τὸν παροικοῦντα πρεσβύτην καὶ ἐκτέμνοντα τὸ ἄλσος ἐτιμωρήσατο Ἀνάγυρος ἥρως. Ἀναγυράσιοι δὲ δῆμος τῆς Ἀττικῆς. τούτου δέ τις ἐξέκοψε τὸ ἄλσος. ὁ δὲ τῷ υἱῷ αὐτοῦ ἐπέμηνε τὴν παλλακήν, ἥτις μὴ δυναμένη συμπεῖσαι τὸν παῖδα **διέβαλεν** ὡς ἀσελγῆ τῷ πατρί. ὁ δὲ **ἐπήρωσεν** αὐτὸν καὶ **ἐγκατῳκοδόμησεν**. ἐπὶ τούτοις καὶ ὁ πατὴρ ἑαυτὸν ἀνήρτησεν, ἡ δὲ παλλακὴ εἰς φρέαρ ἑαυτὴν

62 On Clytia as the name for the concubine, assuming either an involuntary confusion with the toponym or a motivated change in the name, see Papamichael (1982, p. 217, n. 2).

63 On Chiron as a mediator between Amyntor and Phoenix after the blinding, see Collard & Cropp (Euripides, 2008, p. 406).

> ἔρριψεν. ἱστορεῖ δὲ Ἱερώνυμος... ἀπεικάζων τούτοις τὸν Εὐριπίδου Φοίνικα.
>
> 'The Anagyrasian deity' is such because the hero Anagyrus revenged himself upon an old neighbor who cut down his grove. The Anagyrasians were a deme of Attica. One of them cut down his grove, and he [sc. Anagyrus] drove his concubine mad about his son. Not being able to persuade the son, she **denounced** him to his father for lewd behavior. He [sc. the father] **blinded** him and **confined** him. After that, the father hanged himself, and the concubine threw herself into a well. Hieronymus reports this... comparing Euripides' *Phoenix* with it.
>
> (Hieronymus of Rhodes, *On Tragedians* fr. 32 Wehrli, in Photius α 1432 Theodoridis and other lexica)

This product/process of adaptation deals mainly with characterization. Its author exploits the following six procedures: [GE1][64] he subtracts the mother's pleading, [GE2] he adds the concubine's advances, [GE3] he merges the mother and the concubine into a single character, [GE4] he ignores the dilemma of whether to obey the mother or to respect the father, [GE5] he emphasizes the father's wrath, and [GE6] he changes the outcome of the story.

[GE1] The subtraction of the mother's pleading is the result of the broader authorial decision of dispensing with the character of the mother.[65] In the epic version, the pleading of the mother, much like that of Thetis towards Zeus in favor of Achilles (*Il.* 1.503 ff.), is presented as the external force impelling Phoenix to act. [GE2] In the dramatic version, the subtraction of this component entails the addition of the concubine's advances.[66] In this case,

64 GE stands for "Greek Embassy". Hence, numbers GE1-GE6 refer to the adaptation of *Il.* 9 into *Phoenix*.

65 On the subtraction of the mother's pleading, see Papamichael (1982): "The role of his mother was almost certainly discarded and her figure as such is of very minor importance" (p. 220); and Collard & Cropp (Euripides, 2008): "...Amyntor's wife, of whose anger nothing is attested in the fragments, only in Homer" (p. 406).

66 On the addition of the concubine's advances, see Papamichael (1982): "In their [sc. the mother's pleas] place come the open, seductive advances on the part of the young mistress, who is clearly not the innocent girl we see in

the external force appears more negative in essence, considering Ancient Greece's ideological take on gender roles and male/female infidelities. Unlike the worried mother from the *Iliad*, the concubine from the *Phoenix* is worrisome. The topic of the false accusation by the father's wife/concubine is also presented, through Phaedra's character, in Euripides' *Hippolytus* (856 ff.).

[GE3] According to the economy of the play, the subtraction of one cause for action and the subsequent addition of a different one is possible because the characters that partake of such actions experience something of a merging.[67] In the absence of the mother, the concubine fills in both as Amyntor's paramour and as Phoenix's stepmother. In this sense, the two characters that come between father and son, and that end up provoking their antagonism, can be viewed as merged into one. Moreover, if the character inciting the sexual encounter and the character such an encounter must be held with are the same, the tragedy of the situation becomes much more manifest.

[GE4] In the epic, Phoenix, even though pushed by an external force, faces an internal dilemma: is it better to obey a mother's pleading or to respect a father's position? Choosing either party would result in mistreating the other. After some consideration, he sides with his mother, and his father becomes so enraged that he curses the young man, who becomes sterile. In the drama, there is no dilemma or inner conflict.[68] The whole ambiguity of the situation is derived from the setup. If the epic Phoenix was guilty of executing the mother's plan, the dramatic Phoenix is innocent,

---

the previous [sc. Homer's] account" (p. 220); and Collard & Cropp (Euripides, 2008): "In his [sc. Euripides'] version, moreover, Phoenix refused his mother's pleading, only to be falsely accused of rape by the concubine" (p. 406).

67 On the merging of the mother and the concubine into a single character, see Papamichael (1982): "The tightening of the bond between Amyntor and concubine and to some extent between the concubine and Phoenix, who in a way becomes her stepson in consequence of the removal of the mother, is the core of the tragic plot" (p. 220).

68 On the ignoring of the dilemma of whether to obey the mother or to respect the father, see Papamichael (1982): "He [sc. Phoenix] is under no great psychological compulsion to do or not to do anything imposed upon him from outside" (p. 220).

but framed by the concubine's trickery. As a matter of fact, the *Schol. ad Il.* 9.453 states: "But Euripides stages a guiltless hero in the *Phoenix* [Εὐριπίδης δὲ ἀναμάρτητον εἰσάγει τὸν ἥρωα ἐν τῷ Φοίνικι]".

[GE5] The emphasis on the father's wrath relates to the dramatic perspective.[69] The *Iliad*'s Amyntor gets angry when he finds out about a consensual relationship between Phoenix and the concubine, but the *Phoenix*'s Amyntor gets angrier when he hears about the alleged assault from the concubine herself. Therefore, the guiltless behavior receives a much harsher punishment than the guilty one. The anger, a very Homeric topic (e.g., *Il.* 1.1), is also dramatically explored in very Homeric ways (e.g., *Il.* 9.443): Homer, through the words of Phoenix, only grants access to Amyntor's deeds; Euripides, on the contrary, makes room for Amyntor's words.[70]

In fragments 803a, 803b, 804, 805, and 807, Amyntor complains about life, children, wives, and old age. His complaint in 803a, "before, falling over his eyes, darkness has already reached him [πρὶν ἂν κατ' ὄσσων κιγχάνῃ σφ' ἤδη σκότος]" recalls Euripides' *Hippolytus* 1444: "Oh! Oh! Falling over my eyes, darkness is already reaching me [αἰαῖ, κατ' ὄσσων κιγχάνει μ' ἤδη σκότος]". After that, introspection gives way to interaction, and father and son argue, in an ἀγὼν λόγων (verbal contest) about the concubine's allegations.

Fragments 809, 810, and 811 refer to proofs, evidence, and the well-known "nature versus nurture" debate. The statement in 810, "Then, the most important thing is nature, since no one, by being nurtured, would ever adequately turn evil into good [μέγιστον ἄρ' ἦν ἡ φύσις· τὸ γὰρ κακὸν οὐδείς τρέφων εὖ χρηστὸν ἂν θείη ποτέ]",

69 On the emphasis on the father's wrath, see Papamichael (1982): "In other words Euripides could never have effectively permitted Amyntor to blind his son in fury, if he had kept the Homeric setting with a wife still rather close to her husband and a very young girl whom the old Amyntor had not yet touched" (p. 221); and Collard & Cropp (Euripides, 2008): "Euripides' purpose is plain, to maximize the pathos of Phoenix's tragedy and, so the fragments suggest, to create room for much introspection and agony in the disillusioned Amyntor... together with tense argument between father and son over the concubine's allegations" (p. 406).

70 On words/deeds in Euripides, see *Hipp.* 486 ff.

brings to mind Euripides' *Hippolytus* 921-922:[71] "A wonderful Sophist – you say – is whoever will be able to force those thinking wrongly to think rightly [δεινὸν σοφιστὴν εἶπας, ὅστις εὖ φρονεῖν τοὺς μὴ φρονοῦντας δυνατός ἐστ'ἀναγκάσαι]".

[GE6] Lastly, the change in the outcome of the story is also motivated by dramatic choices.[72] Instead of being cursed with sterility, Phoenix is blinded by Amyntor. The blinding and the accusation, if originally introduced by Euripides, would be the playwright's two main innovations to the Homeric model. After the corrupt fragment 815, which may have contained the actual reference to the blinding, in fragments 816 and 817 Phoenix himself speaks of his ill fate, and bids farewell to his fatherland. It is not unreasonable to suppose a *deus ex machina*, in a manner like that in which they appear in other Euripidean plays.[73]

Don't Shoot the Messenger!

Book 5 of the *Mahābhārata* is composed of twelve minor books. Minor book 49 includes, like *Iliad* 9, a council of chiefs and an embassy of king Drupada's priest to the Kauravas, as well as the siding of the divine Kṛṣṇa with the Pāṇḍavas, and the substory of the victory of Indra; minor book 50, a second embassy, of king Dhṛtarāṣṭra's bard to the Pāṇḍavas; minor books 51 and 52, respectively, steward Vidura's and sage Sanatsujāta's instructions; minor book 53, Dhṛtarāṣṭra's failed attempt at swaying his son Duryodhana from the war; minor book 54, a third embassy, of Kṛṣṇa to the Kauravas, as well as the substory of Dambhodbhava, the deeds of Mātali and Gālava, and the colloquy of Vidurā and her son.

Minor book 55 details Kṛṣṇa's and Kuntī's revelations about the warrior Karṇa's true origin; minor book 56, the yoking of the armies

71 Cf. Euripides' *Hec.* 592-602 and *Suppl.* 911-917.

72 On the change of the outcome of the story, see Papamichael (1982): "What happened after the blinding of Phoenix can only be surmised from parallel tragedies" (p. 226); and Collard & Cropp (Euripides, 2008): "Euripides may have introduced the blinding to the story" (p. 406).

73 See Euripides' *Hipp.* 1283 ff.

for battle, which gives name to the entire book 5;[74] minor book 57, the consecration of Dhṛṣṭadyumna and Bhīṣma as marshals, respectively, of the Pāṇḍavas and the Kauravas; minor book 57, a fourth embassy, of Duryodhana's cousin to the Pāṇḍavas; minor book 59, a review of the warriors from both sides; and minor book 60, the substory of Ambā. Out of the four embassies,[75] that of Kṛṣṇa is the most prominent, both quantitively and qualitatively.

The embassy of Kṛṣṇa (*MBh.* 5.83-129) narrates Kṛṣṇa's *yāna* (coming). The *dūta* (messenger) addresses, among several others, the father Dhṛtarāṣṭra and the son Duryodhana. The epic version is as follows: Dhṛtarāṣṭra knows that Kṛṣṇa is coming, and like Agamemnon in *Iliad* 9, Dhṛtarāṣṭra is willing to offer him various gifts. However, Vidura reminds him that Kṛṣṇa, similarly to Achilles in *Iliad* 9, will only settle for the one offering he expects, i.e., peace. Duryodhana agrees with recognizing Kṛṣṇa's dignity, but he disagrees with the gifts, which he thinks could be seen as a sign of fear. Instead, he expresses his intention to capture Kṛṣṇa.

One day later, Kṛṣṇa arrives at Dhṛtarāṣṭra's house, where all the noblemen rise from their seats to honor him. After visiting Vidura and his aunt Kuntī, Kṛṣṇa arrives at Duryodhana's house, where the noblemen also rise from their seats. Kṛṣṇa rejects a meal offering and eats at Vidura's place. Another day later, he enters the assembly hall, where for a third time he is welcomed by a standing crowd. Kṛṣṇa addresses his first speech to Dhṛtarāṣṭra, who as king has the power to restrain Duryodhana from combat. His speech contains quotes from the Pāṇḍavas' speech. Then, as in Phoenix's speech in *Iliad* 9, follow three stories: the story of Dambhodbhava, the story of Mātali, and the story of Gālava.

The sage Rāma Jāmadagnya tells the story of king Dambhodbhava's challenging of Nara and Nārāyaṇa, intended to reveal the true nature of Arjuna and Kṛṣṇa. The sage Kaṇva

74 Cf. *MBh.* 5.149.47.
75 The topic of embassies/messengers offers several examples within the Sanskrit literary tradition. As a Vedic precedent, there is the hymn about the dog messenger Saramā (*RV.* 10.108); and as classical reinterpretations, pertaining to the genre of *Saṃdeśakāvya* (Messenger Poems), there is Kālidāsa's *Meghadūta* (Cloud Messenger) and Dhoyin's *Pavanadūta* (Wind Messenger).

narrates the story of Indra's charioteer Mātali, who while procuring the snake Sumukha as a husband for his daughter, causes the eagle Garuḍa to inappropriately challenge a more powerful enemy. The goal of this story is for Duryodhana to learn his place. The sage Nārada recounts the story of the student Gālava, who to pay his *gurudakṣiṇā* (graduation fee), prostitutes princess Mādhavī to three kings and to his own teacher. From such unions, four sons are born, with the power to restore king Yayāti, Mādhavī's father and their own grandfather, to heaven, from where he had fallen because of pride. The aim of this story is for Duryodhana to give up his own pride. Unsurprisingly, all three stories fall on deaf ears.

After the stories, Dhṛtarāṣṭra admits his powerlessness and requests Kṛṣṇa to redirect his efforts towards Duryodhana. Accordingly, Kṛṣṇa addresses his second speech to Duryodhana. As he himself later comments,[76] he tries *sāman* (conciliation), *bheda* (alienation), and *dāna* (gifts), leaving no other option than *daṇḍa* (punishment).[77] The grandfather Bhīṣma, the preceptor Droṇa, and the father Dhṛtarāṣṭra comment upon Kṛṣṇa's speech. Duryodhana rejects the accusations, for he thinks not even in the game of dice was there any wrongdoing. At his brother Duḥśāsana's instigation, Duryodhana leaves the assembly hall, only to be promptly brought back. Then, because of his mother Gāndhārī's intervention, he once again leaves.

Duryodhana plots Kṛṣṇa's capture with his uncle Śakuni, his brother Duḥśāsana, and his ally Karṇa. Dhṛtarāṣṭra is warned about the plot by Kṛṣṇa's companion Sātyaki but is instructed by Kṛṣṇa himself not to impede it. Duryodhana is brought back for a second time by Dhṛtarāṣṭra and listens to Vidura's account of Kṛṣṇa's deeds. Kṛṣṇa shows his *viśvarūpa* (universal form), including his weapons: discus, bow, mace, conch, and sword, as well as spear and plough. The grandfather Bhīṣma, the preceptor Droṇa, the steward Vidura, and the bard Saṃjaya are given divine eyesight. The visit ends with Dhṛtarāṣṭra reminding Kṛṣṇa that he is in favor of peace but unable to control the bloodthirsty Duryodhana.

76 See *MBh.* 5.148.7 ff.
77 On the four *upāyas* (means of success against an enemy), see Kauṭilya's *Arthaś.* 2.10.47.

In (Ps.-)Bhāsa's *The Embassy*, the plot goes like this: after the standard invocation of the god Viṣṇu, the prologue has the stage manager draw the attention of the audience towards the council chamber, around which the events are about to unfold. Then, the one and only act moves through all the facets of wickedness that make up the character of king Duryodhana: the fine for standing up, the painting of Draupadī's humiliation, the dialogue with the ambassador, the attempted capture of the deity, and the intervention of the weapons.

The fine serves to introduce Duryodhana. After a lengthy monologue that has the appearance of a dialogue, Duryodhana consecrates the grandfather Bhīṣma as commander in chief of the Kaurava army. Then, through a brief exchange with a chamberlain, he starts insulting the ambassador Kṛṣṇa before even letting him into his chamber. And it is this self-centered and rude character who the audience eventually hears giving the order to fine anybody who stands up upon the arrival of Kṛṣṇa. All this display of prospective impertinence is nothing but a taste of what he is truly capable of. In retrospect, he comes out much worse.

The painting of Draupadī's humiliation is the darkest possible trip down memory lane. Duryodhana not only failed to impede the crimes against Draupadī in the assembly hall, but he is also gloating over them right now. It is all there: prince Duḥśāsana pulling her hair, her husband Bhīma struggling not to burn the entire assembly hall to the ground, her husband Yudhiṣṭhira being the voice of reason, her husband Arjuna daydreaming about revenge, her husbands Nakula and Sahadeva being just as enraged, not to mention the utter schadenfreude of the gambler Śakuni, or the impotence of the preceptor Droṇa and the grandfather Bhīṣma. The painting suffices to relive the whole experience. It is obvious that Duryodhana's crimes, both past and future, are just framing the present ones, those that this repulsive character commits during the embassy itself.

The dialogue represents the axis in this circle of evil. After all the noblemen cave in and after even Duryodhana sits down for the tricky newcomer, Kṛṣṇa transmits, word for word, the message that the Pāṇḍavas have sent to Duryodhana: they have kept their side of the deal, and so should Duryodhana. But soon, the straightforward claim turns into a heated debate about the legitimacy of the Bhārata lineage and the appraisal of Kṛṣṇa's deeds. Then, Kṛṣṇa changes the carrot for the stick. Has Arjuna not been one step ahead of Duryodhana at every turn? Why should this time be any different?

Angry at Kṛṣṇa, Duryodhana expects his underlings to capture the messenger, whom he considers to be an inferior man, when, in fact, he is a supreme god, about to captivate the deities themselves. As if by magic, Kṛṣṇa keeps getting away with it, but he is growing more and more impatient. Kṛṣṇa summons his discus Sudarśana, who ends up having to calm him down. After all, Kṛṣṇa has descended into this earthly existence to help alleviate the Earth from her burden. Then comes a parade of divine weapons, including the bow Śārṅga, the mace Kaumodakī, the conch Pāñcajanya, and the sword Nandaka, and leading up to the arrival of the mount Garuḍa. Just before wrapping things up, king Dhṛtarāṣṭra is granted a cameo, in which he recognizes the divine nature of Kṛṣṇa.

This product/process of adaptation focuses on characters and events. Its author exploits these six procedures: [SE1][78] he subtracts talking characters, [SE2] he adds the painting of the humiliation, [SE3] he merges the father and the son into a single character, [SE4] he adds the questioning of the genealogy, [SE5] he adds the fine for anyone who stands up, and [SE6] he adds the personified weapons.

[SE1] The subtraction of characters responds to the economy of the play.[79] According to the epic source, those present during

---

78 SE stands for "Sanskrit Embassy". Hence, numbers SE1-SE6 refer to the adaptation of *MBh.* 5 into *The Embassy*. These are just the adaptation techniques that will allow me to argue for parallelisms with the Greco-Roman world. Other techniques at play include changing the embassy's site and timing, emphasizing the grudge between cousins, maintaining the messenger's divinity but changing his characterization, merging several humiliations of the son into one and emphasizing his failure, changing the *viśvarūpa* (universal form), and splitting the final bewilderment between kings and gods.

79 On the subtraction of characters, see Esposito (2010): "Die Anzahl der Personen wird auf Kṛṣṇa, Duryodhana, den Kämmerer, Sudarśana und Dhṛtarāṣṭra reduziert, alle ubrigen Charaktere werden durch die Technik

Kṛṣṇa's message to Dhṛtarāṣṭra were Vidura (*MBh.* 5.92.32a), Sātyaki (*MBh.* 5.92.32b), Duryodhana and Karṇa (*MBh.* 5.92.33b), Kṛtavarman (*MBh.* 5.92.33c), Dhṛtarāṣṭra (*MBh.* 5.92.34a), Bhīṣma and Droṇa (*MBh.* 5.92.34c), Duḥśāsana (*MBh.* 5.92.47a), Viviṃśati (*MBh.* 5.92.47c), and Śakuni (*MBh.* 5.92.49a), alongside the innumerable hosts of Kauravas and Vṛṣṇis. However, in the dramatic adaptation, from the eleven characters mentioned by name, only four are alluded to: Droṇa ("preceptor [*ācārya*]", *DV* 4.14), Bhīṣma ("grandfather [*pitāmaha*]", *DV* 4.16), Śakuni ("maternal uncle [*mātula*]", *DV* 4.18), and Karṇa (*DV* 4.22). Two more partake in the dialogue: Duryodhana and Dhṛtarāṣṭra. And five are altogether subtracted: Vidura, Sātyaki, Kṛtavarman, Duḥśāsana, and Viviṃśati.

As sons of Dhṛtarāṣṭra, Duḥśāsana and Viviṃśati, have no place in the play,[80] provided that even their father has had to make room for the sole focus on Duryodhana as representative of the Kaurava cause; and as Vṛṣṇis, neither do Sātyaki and Kṛtavarman, because this same highlight on the Kaurava side is to explain Kṛṣṇa as having come alone. Vidura's absence can be accounted for in a similar manner, since he always remains partial towards the Pāṇḍavas and Kṛṣṇa.[81] The remaining characters are enough to situate the audience among the Kauravas.[82]

[SE2] The addition of a painting of the humiliation is an authorial decision.[83] The author of the play could have opted

des *ākāśabhāṣita* dargestellt [The number of people is reduced to Kṛṣṇa, Duryodhana, the chamberlain, Sudarśana, and Dhṛtarāṣṭra, all other characters are represented through the technique of *ākāśabhāṣita*]" (p. 18).

80 Although Vaikarṇa, one of the two invented silent characters, resounds with Vikarṇa, another one of Dhṛtarāṣṭra's sons.

81 In fact, during Kṛṣṇa's visit in the *MBh.*, Vidura's house serves as his hub: he goes to Dhṛtarāṣṭra's house and then to Vidura's (*MBh.* 5.87); and after meeting with Kuntī (*MBh.* 5.88), he goes to Duryodhana's house and then again to Vidura's (*MBh.* 5.89), where the two of them can openly discuss the matters at hand (*MBh.* 5.90-91).

82 Bhīṣma and Droṇa defend the Pāṇḍavas, while Karṇa and Śakuni oppose them. Cf. (Ps.-)Bhāsa's *The Five Nights*.

83 On the addition of the painting of the humiliation, see Esposito (2010): "Durch das neu eingeführte Motiv des Gemäldes wird ein Rückblick auf die Ursachen des Konflikts ermöglicht, der im Epos durch Anspielungen während der Diskussionen in der *sabhā* geleistet wird [The newly introduced motif of the painting enables a review of the causes of the

to include the causes of the conflict as part of the interactions between the ambassador and his addressee, as did the author of the epic. In the *MBh.*'s dialogue, Kṛṣṇa berates Duryodhana for humiliating Draupadī, among other things, by the way in which she was brought to the assembly hall against her will.

> kaś cānyo jñātibhāryāṃ vai viprakartuṃ tathārhati |
> **ānīya** ca sabhāṃ vaktuṃ yathoktā draupadī tvayā ||
> kulīnā śīlasaṃpannā prāṇebhyo 'pi garīyasī |
> mahiṣī pāṇḍuputrāṇāṃ tathā vinikṛtā tvayā ||
>
> Who else would be capable of dishonoring the wife of a relative and, **having brought** her to the assembly hall, of speaking to her like you spoke to Draupadī? The wellborn, the well-behaved, the queen of Pāṇḍu's sons, even dearer to them than their lives, was thus dishonored by you!
>
> (*MBh.* 5.126.8-9)

Instead, the adaptation turns words into images, and opts for an ekphrasis, i.e., a verbal description of a work of art. The procedure is of Greco-Roman origin. Its most conspicuous representative in this context is the depiction of Achilles' shield (*Il.* 18.478-608), and it is already adapted by Virgil for describing the pictures at Juno's temple (*Aen.* 1.418-493). In fact, the idea of referencing paintings in plays is already common within Roman theater (Plautus, *Asin.* 174 ff. and 762, *Capt.* 998 ff., *Epid.* 620 ff., *Men.* 141 ff., *Merc.* 313 ff., *Poen.* 1271 ff., and *Stich.* 270 ff.; and Terence, *Eun.* 584 ff.).[84] And it could have been borrowed by Sanskrit theater ((Ps.-)Bhāsa, *DV* 6 and *SV* 6; Śūdraka, *Mṛcch.* 2; Kālidāsa, *Mālav.* 1, *Vikr.* 2, and *Śāk.* 6; Harṣa, *Ratn.* 2 and *Nāg.* 2; Bhavabhūti, *Mālatīm.* 2 and *Uttar.* 1; and Rājaśekhara, *Karp.* 2 and *Viddh.* 1).[85]

The painting in *The Embassy* depicts two separate moments of Draupadī's humiliation in the *Sabhāparvan*. One concerns Duḥśāsana grabbing her by the hair to bring her to the assembly hall against her will. The other one occurs a few moments later,

---

conflict, which is made in the epic through allusions during the discussions in the *sabhā*]" (p. 19).

84 See Knapp (1917, p. 156).

85 See Saunders (1919) and S. S. Dange (1994b).

and it relates to Duḥśāsana pulling her dress, whilst in the middle of the assembly hall, and unsuccessfully trying to undress her.

> tato javenābhisasāra roṣād; duḥśāsanas tām abhigarjamānaḥ |
> dīrgheṣu nīleṣv atha cormimatsu; **jagrāha keśeṣu** narendrapatnīm | |
>
> Out of anger, Duḥśāsana quickly rushed towards her roaring, and then, he **grabbed** the king's wife by her long, dark, and flowing **hair**.
>
> (*MBh.* 2.60.22)
>
> tato duḥśāsano rājan draupadyā **vasanaṃ** balāt |
> sabhāmadhye **samākṣipya** vyapakraṣṭuṃ pracakrame | |
>
> Then, O king, **having** forcibly **pulled** Draupadī's **dress** in the middle of the assembly hall, Duḥśāsana began to undress her.
>
> (*MBh.* 2.61.40)

The author of *The Embassy* merges the two offenses into one. He also pushes them from their past timing, during the events of the *Sabhāparvan*, and into a present timing, set during the events of the *Udyogaparvan*; all this, whilst incorporating the ekphrasis device. The merging is not at all unexpected, since pictorial representations tend to operate within a single time frame, whereas verbal representations can more easily afford to develop multiple time frames. The solution provided to this challenge by (Ps.-)Bhāsa, that is, to depict both the hair-grabbing and the dress-pulling scenes as a single "pregnant moment", is not dissimilar to what a painter would do. A case in point is the painting *Draupadi Vastraharan*, by Raja Ravi Varma (1848-1906), in which Duḥśāsana appears grabbing Draupadī's hair with his right hand and pulling her dress with his left hand.

> bādarāyaṇānīyatāṃ sa citrapaṭo nanu yatra draupadī**keśāmbarāvakarṣaṇam** ālikhitam
>
> O Bādarāyaṇa, please fetch me that painting, where Draupadī's **hair-and-dress dragging** is depicted.
>
> (*DV* 6.5)

[SE3] Merging father and son results in Duryodhana being presented as king.[86] In the *MBh.*, Dhṛtarāṣṭra is addressed as "king [*rājan*]", for instance, by Vidura (*MBh.* 5.85.1a), and even by Duryodhana (*MBh.* 5.86.12a). For Duryodhana, in turn, the text is ambiguous: sometimes he is a king and other times he is a prince. In the *DV*, there is no ambiguity: Duryodhana is presented as "great king [*mahārājo*]" by the chamberlain (*DV* 2.7).[87] This title is befitting to his self-portrait, which mentions both the umbrella as a symbol of royalty and the water as a sign of the royal consecration.

> aham avadhṛtapāṇḍar**ātapatro** dvijavarahastadhṛt**ambu**si ktamūrdhā |
> avanatanṛpamaṇḍalānuyātraiḥ saha kathayāmi bhavadvidhair na bhāṣe ||
>
> I, of the known white **umbrella**, of head sprinkled with **water** prepared by the hand of the best of Brahmans, I, and the attendant company of kings who have bowed, say: I do not speak with people like yourselves.
>
> (*DV* 37)

Since father and son have been merged into one antagonist, the speeches towards them also need to be merged. One adversary, one attempted dissuasion. The simplification provides immediacy. Vyāsa, first, presents Kṛṣṇa's speech towards Dhṛtarāṣṭra (*MBh.* 5.93.3-61). A summary of its contents would go as follows: the speech is pronounced expressly in pursuit of "peace [*śamaḥ*]" (*MBh.* 5.93.3). Despite the merits of the Bhārata lineage (*MBh.* 5.93.4-8), the Kauravas' ill conduct could lead to the destruction of the earth (*MBh.* 5.93.9-11), unless Dhṛtarāṣṭra steadies them (*MBh.* 5.93.12-15). If united, the Kauravas and Pāṇḍavas would be

---

86 On merging father and son, see Esposito (2010): "Im Gegensatz zum Epos aber tritt er [sc. Duryodhana] als Herrscher auf und fuhrt den Vorsitz der *sabhā* [But in contrast to the epic, he appears as ruler and presides over the *sabhā*]" (p. 18). In any case, it is a matter of functions, since Dhṛtarāṣṭra does briefly appear as a talking character in the play. Cf. S. A. Dange's (1994a) view that Duryodhana remains "childish": "Bhāsa wants us to know that Duryodhana is still boyish (*bāliśa*) in this first drama on the life of Duryodhana" (p. 36).

87 Cf. Vāsudeva's address to Dhṛtarāṣṭra as "Your Majesty [*atrabhavān*]" (*DV* 55.3).

invincible (*MBh.* 5.93.16-27); at war, they would annihilate each other (*MBh.* 5.93.28-32). Only king Dhṛtarāṣṭra, their father figure, can protect them (*MBh.* 5.93.33-39).

The Pāṇḍavas send Dhṛtarāṣṭra their message, quoted in full by Kṛṣṇa (*MBh.* 5.93.40-46). They also send one to the assembly (*MBh.* 5.93.47-49). Then, Kṛṣṇa asks Dhṛtarāṣṭra not to fall victim to anger, and instead, to give the Pāṇḍavas their share of the kingdom (*MBh.* 5.93.50-53). Despite numerous offenses against him, Yudhiṣṭhira would still abide by what is right (*MBh.* 5.93.54-58). In sum, the Kauravas are in the wrong, the Pāṇḍavas are ready either way, and the ball is in Dhṛtarāṣṭra's court (*MBh.* 5.93.59-61).

After the substories comes Kṛṣṇa's speech to Duryodhana (*MBh.* 5.122.5-61). Similarly, an outline comes in handy: despite the merits of his lineage (*MBh.* 5.122.5-8), Duryodhana's conduct goes against what is right and profitable (*MBh.* 5.122.9-12). Uniting with the Pāṇḍavas would prove fruitful for everyone (*MBh.* 5.122.13-17), as has already been admitted by Dhṛtarāṣṭra; and there is nothing better than a father's advice (*MBh.* 5.122.18-26). As he did with his father, Kṛṣṇa asks Duryodhana not to fall victim to anger (*MBh.* 5.122.27-31), because emotion is not as good as profit, which, in turn, is no match for duty (*MBh.* 5.122.32-41). Likewise, the Kauravas are inferior to the Pāṇḍavas (*MBh.* 5.122.42-50). Despite their best efforts, Arjuna will remain invincible (*MBh.* 5.122.51-56). In conclusion, by restoring their "half [*ardhaṃ*]" to the Pāṇḍavas, Dhṛtarāṣṭra could be rightfully enthroned as "senior king [*mahārājye*]", and Duryodhana as "young king [*yauvarājye*]", all while achieving the much-desired "peace [*saṃśamaṃ*]" (*MBh.* 5.122.57-61). Certainly, a win-win deal.

The Bhāratas' merits, Duryodhana's ill conduct, the cousins' allegiance, Dhṛtarāṣṭra's fatherly advice, the dangers of anger, the safety of duty, and the overarching goal of peace; all these topics bridge together two speeches that are related both in length and in depth. Peace was at the beginning of the speech to Dhṛtarāṣṭra, and it is also at the end of the speech to Duryodhana. Half a kingdom does not seem such a high price to pay for full-fledged peace. But the master plan of relieving the Earth from her burden must proceed, and Duryodhana will help.

The advice from Bhīṣma (*MBh.* 5.123.2-8), Droṇa (*MBh.* 5.123.10-17), Vidura (*MBh.* 5.123.19-21), Dhṛtarāṣṭra (*MBh.* 5.123.23-27), and again Bhīṣma and Droṇa together (*MBh.* 5.124.2-18) does not suffice to dissuade Duryodhana. In his response to Kṛṣṇa (*MBh.* 5.125.2-26), Duryodhana sees no wrongdoing in the dicing match, or in any of his actions for that matter (*MBh.* 5.125.2-9). Working under the "warrior duty [*kṣatradharmam*]", Duryodhana believes that he is right, and that it is his army which is unlikely to be vanquished; and even in that scenario, heaven would still await them (*MBh.* 5.125.10-21). The response ends with Duryodhana putting his foot down (*MBh.* 5.125.22-26): that "share of the kingdom [*rājyāṃśaś*]" is going nowhere, not even "as much as could be pierced with the tip of a sharp needle [*yāvad dhi sūcyās tīkṣṇāyā vidhyed agreṇa*]".

For the comparison between epic and drama, I focus on the section of Kṛṣṇa's speech to Dhṛtarāṣṭra where Kṛṣṇa quotes the Pāṇḍavas' message (*MBh.* 5.93.40-46). Here, the whole aftermath of the dicing match is summarized as a suffering encompassing the twelve-year exile and the extra year incognito. However, this suffering was always supposed to be temporary, and the thirteenth year was expected to bring an end to it. Such was the "agreement [*samaya-*]" (*MBh.* 5.93.42a, *MBh.* 5.93.42c, *MBh.* 5.93.43a), which, by an instance of an emphatic triple-mention, is accentuated as the main basis for the demand, involving both the part of the kingdom and the accompanying peace.

The standing by required by such agreement is stressed by a repetition of "*sthā*". Originally, the Pāṇḍavas thought that Dhṛtarāṣṭra would stand by the agreement, but now he appears to not have done so; therefore, they ask him to stand by it, given that they themselves are doing just that. Moreover, even if they ever stood on the wrong path, it would be up to him to set them straight; so, they ask for him to help them and help himself in the process. Those are seven examples (*sthatā, tiṣṭha, sthitānāṃ, sthāpayitavyā, āsthitāḥ, saṃsthāpaya,* and *tiṣṭha*), coming from the exact same number of verses. The importance of the "*sthā*" theme is clear. Evident too is its connection to the theme of the agreement. Other themes seem to reverberate around those two, like Dhṛtarāṣṭra being a father figure: "our father [*pitā*]" (*MBh.* 5.93.42c), "O father [*tata*]" (*MBh.* 5.93.42c), "like a father and a mother [*mātṛpitṛvad*]" (*MBh.* 5.93.45a), "by our father [*pitrā*]" (*MBh.* 5.93.46a); or like duty being the key to it all: "duty [*dharmam*]" (*MBh.* 5.93.44a).

> āhus tvāṃ pāṇḍavā rājann abhivādya prasādya ca |
> bhavataḥ śāsanād **duḥkham anubhūtaṃ** sahānugaiḥ | |
> dvādaśemāni varṣāṇi vane nirvyuṣitāni naḥ |
> trayodaśaṃ tathājñātaiḥ sajane parivatsaram | |
> **sthātā** naḥ **samaye** tasmin piteti kṛtaniścayāḥ |
> nāhāsma **samayaṃ** tāta tac ca no brāhmaṇā viduḥ | |
> tasmin naḥ **samaye tiṣṭha sthitānāṃ** bharatarṣabha |
> nityaṃ saṃkleśitā rājan **svarājyāṃśaṃ** labhemahi | |
> tvaṃ **dharmam** arthaṃ yuñjānaḥ samyaṅ nas **trātum arhasi** |
> gurutvaṃ bhavati prekṣya bahūn kleśāṃs titikṣmahe | |
> sa bhavān mātṛpitṛvad asmāsu pratipadyatām |
> guror garīyasī vṛttir yā ca śiṣyasya bhārata | |
> pitrā **sthāpayitavyā** hi vayam utpatham **āsthitāḥ** |
> **saṃsthāpaya** pathiṣv asmāṃs **tiṣṭha** rājan svavartmani | |
>
> O king, having greeted and propitiated you, the Pāṇḍavas said: "At your command, we **experienced suffering**, together with our companions, during these twelve years of us living in exile in the forest, and a thirteenth year incognito among people. We were certain that our father **would stand by the agreement**. O father, we have not backed out on **the agreement**, and our Brahmans know this. O bull of the Bharatas, **stand by** this **agreement** with us **who are standing by it**. O king, after always being harassed, we should attain **our share of the kingdom**. Adequately bringing together **duty** and profit, **you can protect** us. Having observed the mastery in you, we are enduring many hardships. Behave towards us like a father and a mother. O Bhārata, the conduct of a teacher is very important, and so is that of a pupil. Having **stood** on the wrong path, we **should be made to stand straight** by our father. **Make us stand straight** on our paths, O king, and **stand** on your own road."
>
> (*MBh.* 5.93.40-46)

The Pāṇḍavas' quoted message within Kṛṣṇa's speech towards Dhṛtarāṣṭra is a major influence on the message brought by the *DV*'s Kṛṣṇa. An easier path would have probably been to borrow only from the speech to Duryodhana, since after all, he is the only one with which the *DV*'s Kṛṣṇa is debating. But easier is not always better, and (Ps.-)Bhāsa recreates the quoted message in at least two of the *DV*'s verses. The first one states that the Paṇḍavas "experienced a great suffering [*anubhūtaṃ mahad duḥkhaṃ*]", which seems to reinterpret the epic's "experienced suffering [*duḥkham anubhūtaṃ*]" (*MBh.* 5.93.40c-d). It also mentions their inheritance being "dutiful [*dharmyaṃ*]", which echoes the epic's "duty [*dharmam*]" (*MBh.* 5.93.44a).

> **anubhūtaṃ mahad duḥkhaṃ** saṃpūrṇaḥ samayaḥ sa ca |
> asmākam api **dharmyaṃ** yad dāyādyaṃ tad vibhajyatām ||
>
> We **experienced a great suffering**, and our time span is completed. Let the inheritance that is **dutiful** towards us be distributed.
>
> (*DV* 20)

The other verse conveys the demand that "half of the kingdom [*rājyārdhaṃ*]" must be given, which appears to recreate the epic's "our share of the kingdom [*svarājyāṃśaṃ*]" (*MBh.* 5.93.43d). A share suddenly becomes a half, a partition previously attempted in the epic source by Dhṛtarāṣṭra, when he sent the Pāṇḍavas to the Khāṇḍava tract, and offered them to take it as "half of the kingdom [*ardhaṃ rājyasya*]" (*MBh.* 1.199.25e). But the verse also evinces another example of adaptation, through the by-now-known technique of repetition with variation. Thus, the epic's "you can protect [*trātum arhasi*]" (*MBh.* 5.93.44b) becomes the drama's "you can give [*dātum arhasi*]". With this, the general possibility of 'being able to protect' turns into the specific compulsion of 'being obliged to give'. In a much shorter version, the message needs to be much more straightforward.

> **dātum arhasi** madvākyād **rājyārdhaṃ** dhṛtarāṣṭraja |
> anyathā sāgarāntāṃ gāṃ hariṣyanti hi pāṇḍavāḥ ||
>
> O son of Dhṛtarāṣṭra, based on my speech, **you can give** them **half of the kingdom**; otherwise, the Pāṇḍavas will seize the earth up to the ocean.
>
> (*DV* 34)

One last feature that might be worth mentioning is the phrasing "based on my speech [*madvākyād*]" (*DV* 34), within what is presented as the speech itself. This does not happen in the epic Kṛṣṇa's speech towards Dhṛtarāṣṭra, which is referred to as a "speech [*vākyam*]" only before and after it is spoken (*MBh.* 5.93.1c, *MBh.* 5.93.62a). Nonetheless, in the epic Kṛṣṇa's speech towards Duryodhana it occurs twice. The first time is as part of a *tatpuruṣa*-compound "my speech [*madvākyaṃ*]" (*MBh.* 5.122.6b), which is the same one that appears in *DV* 34, thus indicating the source of the adaptation. The second time is at about one third of the way through the speech, as part of the expression "word of advice [*niḥśreyasaṃ vākyāṃ*]" (*MBh.* 5.122.21a). This word is relevant, since it also functions, as part of another *tatpuruṣa*-compound, to give a name to the entire play: *Dūtavākyam* literally means "The messenger's speech".

[SE4] After the speeches, the epic source includes a debate centered on the Kauravas' wrongdoings (*MBh.* 5.126); but the dramatic adaptation adds the questioning of the genealogy.[88] Where Vyāsa focuses on the characters' actions, such as the humiliation of Draupadī, (Ps.-)Bhāsa reinterprets this by looking into the characters' relationships: is Pāṇḍu the legitimate father of the Pāṇḍavas, or is Vicitravīrya the legitimate father of Dhṛtarāṣṭra? The fact that Pāṇḍu's curse led to Kuntī's summonses, and then to Dharma, Vāyu, Indra, and the Aśvins fathering, respectively, Yudhiṣṭhira, Bhīma, Arjuna, and the twins, as well as the fact that Vicitravīrya's death led to Vyāsa begetting Dhṛtarāṣṭra on Ambikā and Pāṇḍu himself on Ambālikā are obviously known to the author of the *MBh.* In fact, they are narrated as early as the very first book. The novelty in treatment by the author of the *DV* is that one is used by Duryodhana to question the Pāṇḍavas' claim to the kingdom, while the other is adduced by Kṛṣṇa as a counterargument against that exact claim by the Kauravas.

88 On the addition of the questioning of the genealogy, see Esposito (2010): "Weitere Rückblicke finden, wie im Epos, während der Diskussion statt [Further retrospectives take place, like in the epic, during the discussion]" (p. 19).

tvayāhaṃ hiṃsito yasmāt tasmāt tvām apy asaṃśayam |
dvayor nṛśaṃsakartāram avaśaṃ kāmamohitam |
jīvitāntakaro bhāva **evam evāgamiṣyati** | |

Since you injured me, then I will certainly make you, who caused the harm of this couple, unwillingly deluded by love. You will be the cause of your own death; **just so, it will happen**.

(*MBh*. 1.109.25)

vane pitṛvyo mṛgayāprasaṅgataḥ kṛtāparādho **muniśāpam** āptavān |
tadāprabhṛty eva sa dāranisspṛhaḥ **parātmajānāṃ pitṛtāṃ kathaṃ vrajet** | |

In the forest, my paternal uncle went hunting, made a mistake, and received **a sage's curse**; ever since then, he was deprived of desire for his wives. **How could one reach a conclusion about the paternity of those born from others?**

(*DV* 21)

tayor **utpādayāpatyaṃ** samartho hy asi putraka |
anurūpaṃ kulasyāsya saṃtatyāḥ prasavasya ca | |

O son, since you are the right person, on those two [sc. Ambikā and Ambālikā] **beget children**, who are worthy of this family and of increasing the lineage.

(*MBh*. 1.99.35)

vicitravīryo viṣayī vipattiṃ
kṣayeṇa yātaḥ punar ambikāyām |
vyāsena jāto dhṛtarāṣṭra eṣa
labheta rājyaṃ janakaḥ kathaṃ te | |

The voluptuous Vicitravīrya met his death through sickness, and yet, Dhṛtarāṣṭra was born to Vyāsa from Ambikā. **How could your father have obtained the kingdom?**

(*DV* 22)

[SE5] The addition of the fine for standing up evinces a superb mastery of the *Udyogaparvan*. For Vyāsa, the action of standing up is telling in terms of courtesy towards the ambassador.[89] He emphasizes this procedure by mentioning it on three separate occasions during the embassy: first, during Kṛṣṇa's arrival at Dhṛtarāṣṭra's palace; second, during Kṛṣṇa's first arrival at Duryodhana's palace, which gets interrupted because the ambassador will not eat until he has spoken his mind; and third, during Kṛṣṇa's second arrival at Duryodhana's palace, where the audience listens to the speech towards the father, and then, to the speech towards the son, a doubling down on the former, and a last-ditch attempt to avert disaster.

After being introduced by an absolute construction about Kṛṣṇa's arrival, the first scene about standing up offers two expressions that will turn out to be key in terms of the text's self-referencing: *udatiṣṭhan* (stood up) and *āsanebhyo 'calan* (rose from their seats). The enumeration of those who stand is structured in descending order, from Dhṛtarāṣṭra, passing through Droṇa and Bhīṣma, and down to the rest.

> **abhyāgacchati dāśārhe** prajñācakṣur nareśvaraḥ |
> sahaiva droṇabhīṣmābhyām **udatiṣṭhan mahāyaśāḥ** ||
> kṛpaś ca somadattaś ca mahārājaś ca bāhlikaḥ |
> **āsanebhyo 'calan** sarve **pūjayanto** janārdanam ||
>
> **When the Dāśārha arrived**, the **renowned** king whose sight was knowledge, as well as Droṇa and Bhīṣma, **stood up**. Kṛpa, Somadatta, and the great king Bāhlika all **rose from their seats**, **honoring** Janārdana.
>
> (*MBh.* 5.87.13-14)

The second scene repeats the absolute construction about Kṛṣṇa's arrival, and it offers a variation on one of the expressions from the previous scene: *udatiṣṭhat* (stood up). The plural is substituted by the singular since now the subject is just Duryodhana. As in the previous case, the enumeration begins with the most prominent character. That the passages are to be taken in tandem is further signaled by Duryodhana's renown, mirroring that of Dhṛtarāṣṭra, as well as by Kṛṣṇa's being honored.

---

89 Cf. the courtesy involved in presenting the first gift to the guest of honor, as exemplified by Kṛṣṇa during Yudhiṣṭhira's royal consecration (*MBh.* 2.33).

abhyāgacchati dāśārhe dhārtarāṣṭro **mahāyaśāḥ** |
udatiṣṭhat sahāmātyaḥ **pūjayan** madhusūdanam | |

When the Dāśārha arrived, the **renowned** son of Dhṛtarāṣṭra **stood up**, together with his advisors, **honoring** Madhusūdana.

(*MBh*. 5.89.6)

The third scene provides greater variation. It opens with Dhṛtarāṣṭra, whom, in similar order, the others follow: Bhīṣma, Droṇa, and the rest. Then comes the expression *āsanebhyo 'calan* (rose from their seats), which occupies the same metrical position as before. In fact, *MBh*. 5.92.34c-d = *MBh*. 5.87.14c-d. After this, there is the absolute construction about Kṛṣṇa's arrival, immediately followed by two of Dhṛtarāṣṭra's recurring features: his renown and his special kind of sight. By realizing that *MBh*. 5.92.35 ~ *MBh*. 5.87.13, it becomes clearer that the passages are to be taken conjointly. By now, the expression *udatiṣṭhan* (stood up) reverberates with the one from *MBh*. 5.89.6c and the one from *MBh*. 5.87.13d. If all these repetitions were not enough of a token, *MBh*. 5.92.36 presents two additional variations on the "*ud-* + *sthā*" theme: *uttiṣṭhati* (stood up), as part of a new absolute construction; and *samuttasthuḥ* (stood up), with an additional prefix. As in *MBh*. 5.89.6, the last verse mentions one prominent character and fills in with several unnamed ones.

dhṛtarāṣṭraṃ puraskṛtya bhīṣmadroṇādayas tataḥ |
āsanebhyo 'calan sarve **pūjayanto** janārdanam | |
abhyāgacchati dāśārhe prajñācakṣur mahāmanāḥ |
sahaiva bhīṣmadroṇābhyām **udatiṣṭhan mahāyaśāḥ** | |
uttiṣṭhati mahārāje dhṛtarāṣṭre janeśvare |
tāni rājasahasrāṇi **samuttasthuḥ** samantataḥ | |

Following Dhṛtarāṣṭra, Bhīṣma, Droṇa, and the rest all **rose from their seats, honoring** Janārdana. **When the Dāśārha arrived**, the **renowned** and magnanimous one, **whose sight was knowledge**, as well as Bhīṣma and Droṇa, **stood up**. When the great king Dhṛtarāṣṭra, the lord of the people **stood up**, those thousands of kings **stood up** around him.

(*MBh*. 5.92.34-36)

(Ps.-)Bhāsa subtracts these threefold repetition, and in its place, adds the fine for standing up. Three epic variations on the same theme become one new dramatic theme. Could it have been that the playwright deemed this treatment excessive or inadequate for the new genre? This is unlikely since he himself turns the triple acknowledgement of Karṇa's curses (*MBh.* 8.29, *MBh.* 8.66, and *MBh.* 12.2-3) into Karṇa's three calls for action in *Karṇa's Task* (*KBh.* 5, *KBh.* 14, and *KBh.* 24). An authorial decision seems more suitable, because the addition of the fine maintains the emphasis on the action of standing up that the traditional text already reveals, but it does so in a creative way. Such adaptation is suggested by the phrasing *pratyutthāsyati* (stands up), a new variation on the "*ud-* + *sthā*" theme. On a separate note, when presented with the detail of a twelve-coin penalty, a reader of the *MBh.* cannot help but remember the twelve-year exile.

> api ca yo 'tra keśavasya **pratyutthāsyati** sa mayā dvādaśasuvarṇabhāreṇa daṇḍyaḥ
>
> Moreover, he who **stands up** here for Keśava, will be penalized by me with a fine of twelve gold coins.
>
> (*DV* 6.1)

[SE6] As stated, another major addition is that of the personified weapons.[90] The weapons in the play are the same ones, minus the spear and the plough, as in the narrative. What is new is that one of them speaks. The personification of the discus Sudarśana allows for the introduction of themes that are already present in the *MBh.*, such as the relieving of the Earth. The themes are so close that there can be little doubt about the source of the adaptation: "to relieve Earth's burden [*bhūmer nirasituṃ bhāraṃ*]" and "the relief of Earth's burden [*mahībhārāpanayanaṃ*]". However, the technique is much more innovative. Since "it-fiction", i.e., speaking

90 On the addition of the personified weapons, see Esposito (1999/2000): "In my opinion these verses were not modelled on the *Bālacarita*, where each weapon of Viṣṇu is introducing itself in a separate verse, because of the very simple style of the *Bālacarita*'s verses" (p. 557). Cf. *Hariv.* App. 31, vv. 908ff and 1029ff; *V.P.* 5.37.47; (Ps.-)Bhāsa's *BC* 1.21-28; and Kālidāsa's *Raghuv.* 10.60.

objects, is common in Roman lyric (Catullus, 4, 66, and 67; Horace, *Sat.* 1.8; and Martial, *Epigr.* 13.50, 14.39, 14.41, 14.44, and 14.64),[91] and since examples involving weapons are already a feature of Hellenistic lyric (Hegesippus, *Anth. Pal.* 6.124; Mnasalces, *Anth. Pal.* 6.125; Nicias, *Anth. Pal.* 6.127; and Meleager, *Anth. Pal.* 6.163),[92] this could have been another borrowing by Sanskrit theater.

> asyā **bhūmer nirasituṃ bhāraṃ** bhāgaiḥ pṛthak pṛthak |
> asyām eva prasūyadhvaṃ virodhāyeti cābravīt ||
>
> And he said, "**To relieve Earth's burden**, one by one you must be partly born on her for the sake of strife."
>
> (*MBh.* 1.58.46)
>
> **mahībhārāpanayanaṃ** kartuṃ jātasya bhūtale |
> asminn eva gate deva nanu syād viphalaḥ śramaḥ ||
>
> After you were born on earth to achieve **the relief of Earth's burden**, O god, if he passes away, your effort, indeed, would be fruitless.
>
> (*DV* 46)

Ekphrasis and It-fiction

After analyzing the motif of the embassy in *Il.* 9 and *Phoenix*, as well as in *MBh.* 5 and *The Embassy*, I put forward two cases of possible Greek influence in the adaptation techniques: [EM1][93] *epic characters that are not essential are subtracted in the plays, provided that their functions are merged into other characters*, and [EM2] *dramatic themes which have no precedent in the source texts are added with the intention of providing an emphasis.*

[EM1] Epic characters that are not essential are subtracted in the plays, provided that their functions are merged into other characters. It is a truism that any theatrical work must compress

91 See Cuvardic García & Cerdas Fallas (2020).
92 See Gutzwiller (2017).
93 EM stands for "Embassy Motif". Hence, numbers EM1-EM2 refer to the proposed influences from *Phoenix*'s adaptation of *Il.* 9 into *The Embassy*'s adaptation of *MBh.* 5.

when adapting from a narrative text. However, the combined technique of subtracting one or more characters, and then merging their functions into other characters, is something that can be identified even in a fragmentary play such as Phoenix, where the subtraction of the mother (GE1) is correlated with the merging of the mother and the concubine (GE3). Then, a single character comes between Phoenix and his father.

If the author of *The Embassy* knew these sources, the procedure could have influenced his parallel subtraction of characters (SE1), which is also linked to the instances of merging involving the father and the son, as well as the speeches directed towards them (SE3). The merging of father and son is, certainly, the more relevant one, for it results in a single character opposing Kṛṣṇa. Moreover, the father/son conflict between Amyntor and Phoenix would have offered an epic model, which already had been proven to be adaptable to the theater in Greece, and therefore, its adaptation into the father/son conflict between Dhṛtarāṣṭra and Duryodhana, would have had an influence in India.

If this were an instance of Greco-Indian *anukaraṇa*, its trademark would be reversal: the Greek texts (*Il.* 9 and *Phoenix*) about an embassy's addresser (*Phoenix*) who opposes his father (Amyntor), would have become the Indian texts (*MBh.* 5 and *The Embassy*) about an embassy's addressee (Duryodhana) who opposes his father (Dhṛtarāṣṭra).

[EM2] Dramatic themes which have no precedent in the source texts are added with the intention of providing an emphasis. In *Phoenix*, apart from ignoring the dilemma (GE4) and changing the outcome (GE6), the two main innovations would be the accusation and the blinding: the concubine falsely accuses Phoenix of rape, and in turn, his father blinds him. In this sense, the addition of the concubine's advances (GE2) entails the emphasis on the father's wrath (GE5). And, in *The Embassy*, the two chief contrivances are the painting and the personified weapons: at the beginning of the play, the keepsake of the humiliation attests Duryodhana's ethos; and at the end of the play, the speech by the discus reveals Kṛṣṇa's ethos. Minor additions, such as the fine for anyone who stands up (SE5) and the questioning of the genealogy (SE4), highlight certain details too: respectively, the honoring of the messenger figure and the legitimacy of the father figures. However, it is the major additions, like the painting (SE2) and the personified weapons (SE6), that better exemplify the technique of emphasizing.

One of *The Embassy*'s chief contrivances, i.e., the painting, is introduced by an ingenious combination of flashback and ekphrasis, both common procedures in the Homeric epics (e.g., *Od.* 9-12 and *Il.* 18.478-608, respectively). Nonetheless, the specific choice of a painting could have been borrowed from Roman theater.

Among Romans playwrights, Plautus (254-184 BCE)[94] employs, mostly for the purpose of comparisons, eight references to paintings: in *Asin.* 174, a well-wishing bawd is something that has never been "painted [*pictum*]"; in *Asin.* 762, an exclusive courtesan should be made to get rid of every undesirable "painting [*pictura*]" so that she is deprived of any writing surfaces; in *Capt.* 998, several "paintings [*picta*]" of the Acheron's tortures are no match to certain quarries; in *Epid.* 624, a scene depicting a maiden and a usurer is compared to a "beautifully painted picture [*signum pictum pulchre*]"; in *Men.* 143, a youth is likened to the mythical Ganymede and Adonis that one can see in any "picture painted on a wall [*tabulam pictam in pariete*]"; in *Merc.* 315, a decrepit old man is said to be worth as much as a "picture painted on a wall [*signum pictum in pariete*]"; in *Poen.* 1272, a scene depicting a youth and a courtesan is something that only a famous painter "would have painted [*pingeretis*]"; and in *Stich.* 271, a slave's pose is equated to that "from a painting [*ex pictura*]".

Terence (185-159 BCE)[95] only has one reference to a painting, but it is by far the most relevant one. If Plautus falls short of expectations in not describing the paintings and in not exploiting them enough as artistic devices, the situation with Terence is very different. Not only does *The Eunuch*'s painting entail ekphrasis, with the description of how Zeus sends a shower of gold, turns

94 I follow the Latin text by Nixon (Plautus, 1916, 1917, 1924, 1930, and 1952). The translations are my own.

95 I follow the Latin text by Sargeaunt (Terence, 1918). The translations are my own.

himself into a man, enters a house, and tricks a woman; but also, it is central to the plot:[96] in the painting, a god (Jupiter) turns into someone else (a man) and rapes a woman (Danae); in the play, a youth (Chaerea) dresses up as someone else (a eunuch) and rapes a woman (Pamphila).

It is striking that *The Eunuch*'s painting has not yet been linked to *The Embassy*'s painting. The commonalities are numerous. They are both presented as nearby paintings: "this painting [*pictura haec*]", "this painting [*ayaṃ citrapaṭaḥ*]". In both cases, there is an explicit reference to the painting process: "a painted picture [*tabulam quandam pictam*]", "this picture was carefully painted [*suvyaktam ālikhito 'yam citrapaṭaḥ*]". They function as ekphrases: "in which [*quo pacto*]", "this one right here [*eṣa*]". A sexual assault is the main event: "as they say, sent a shower of gold to her lap [*misisse aiunt quondam in gremium imbrem aureum*]", "grabbed her by the lock of her hair [*keśahaste gṛhītavān*]". The offender and the victim are the first ones to be mentioned: "Jupiter [*Iovem*]" and "Danae [*Danaae*]", "Duḥśāsana [*duḥśāsano*]" and "Draupadī [*draupadīṃ*]".

Then, both descriptions are further elaborated: "a god that turned himself into a man and secretly came under another man's tiles, through the impluvium, all as a hoax aimed at a woman [*deum sese in hominem convortisse atque in alienas tegulas / venisse clanculum: per inpluvium fucum factum mulieri*]", "manhandled by Duḥśāsana, her eyes wide open out of perplexity, she shines like the digit of the moon that has already gone inside of Rahu's mouth [*duḥśāsanaparāmṛṣṭā sambhramotphullalocanā | rāhuvaktrāntaragatā candralekheva śobhate*]". Down to the smallest details, Jupiter's shower of gold, i.e., rainwater, would turn into Rahu's mouth devouring the moon, i.e., an eclipse.

Lastly, both pictures condone a previous offense and serve to rationalize an impending one. Through *The Eunuch*'s painting, Jupiter raping Danae sets an example for Chaerea raping Pamphila: "And I, a puny man, would not do it? I certainly did it, and gladly!

96 On the centrality of the painting to the plot of *The Eunuch*, see Germany (2016, Chapter 1).

[*ego homuncio hoc non facerem? ego illud vero ita feci ac lubens*]". Through The Embassy's painting, Duḥśāsana grabbing Draupadī sets an example for Duryodhana attempting to take Kṛṣṇa captive: "Then, how am I the vile one of perverted mind? O experts in conduct and misconduct, let go of your anger today! Unforgiving of the dishonor related to the dicing match, may they have their heroism censured among the truly courageous ones [*nīco 'ham eva viparītamatiḥ kathaṃ vā roṣaṃ parityajatam adya nayānayajñau | dyūtādhikāram avamānam amṛṣyamāṇāḥ sattvādhikeṣu vacanīyaparākramāḥ syuḥ*]". The use of the first person, the rhetorical questions, and in general, the blunt statements, all come together to support the claim of a borrowing from Rome into India.

> ...dum adparatur, virgo in conclavi sedet
> **suspectans tabulam quandam** pictam: ibi inerat **pictura haec, Iovem**
> **quo pacto Danaae misisse aiunt quondam in gremium imbrem aureum.**
> egomet quoque id spectare coepi, et quia consimilem luserat
> iam olim ille ludum, inpendio magis animus gaudebat mihi,
> **deum sese in hominem convortisse atque in alienas tegulas**
> **venisse clanculum: per inpluvium fucum factum mulieri.**
> at quem deum! qui templa caeli summa sonitu concutit.
> **ego homuncio hoc non facerem? ego illud vero ita feci ac lubens.**
>
> While this [sc. a bath] is prepared, the maiden sits in her room, looking at **a painted picture**. On it, was **this painting in which Jupiter, as they say, sent a shower of gold to Danae's lap**. I started to look at it too, and since he had already played such a trick, my heart rejoiced even more: **a god that turned himself into a man and secretly came under another man's tiles, through the impluvium, all as a hoax aimed at a woman**; and what a god! – 'He who shakes the highest regions of heaven with his thunder'. **And I, a puny man, would not do it? I certainly did it, and gladly!**
>
> (Ter. *Eun.* 583-591)

aho darśanīyo **'yaṃ citrapaṭaḥ** | **eṣa duḥśāsano draupadīṃ keśahaste gṛhītavān** | **eṣā khalu draupadī** | |

7. **duḥśāsanaparāmṛṣṭā sambhramotphullalocanā** |
rāhuvaktrāntaragatā candralekheva śobhate | |

eṣa durātmā bhīmaḥ sarvarājasamakṣam avamānitāṃ draupadīṃ dṛṣṭvā pravṛddhāmarṣaḥ sabhāstambhaṃ tulayati | **eṣa yudhiṣṭhiraḥ** | |

8. satyadharmaghṛṇāyukto dyūtavibhraṣṭacetanaḥ |
karoty apāṅgavikṣepaiḥ śāntāmarṣaṃ vṛkodaram | |

eṣa idānīm arjunaḥ | |

9. roṣākulākṣaḥ sphuritādharoṣṭhas
tṛṇāya matvā ripumaṇḍalaṃ tat |
utsādayiṣyann iva sarvarājñaḥ
śanaiḥ samākarṣati gāṇḍivajyām | |

eṣa yudiṣṭhiro 'rjunaṃ nivārayati | **etau nakulasahadevau** | |

10. kṛtaparikarabandhau carmanistriṃśahastau
paruṣitamukharāgau spaṣṭadaṣṭādharoṣṭhau |
vigatamaraṇaśaṅkau satvaraṃ bhrātaraṃ me
harim iva mṛgapotau tejasābhiprayātau | |

eṣa yudhiṣṭhiraḥ kumārāv upetya nivārayati | |

11. **nīco 'ham eva viparītamatiḥ kathaṃ vā**
roṣaṃ parityajatam adya nayānayajñau |
dyūtādhikāram avamānam amṛṣyamāṇāḥ
sattvādhikeṣu vacanīyaparākramāḥ syuḥ | |

iti | **eṣa gāndhārarājaḥ** | |

12. akṣān kṣipan sakitavaṃ prahasan sagarvaṃ
saṅkocayann iva mudaṃ dviṣatāṃ svakīrttyā |
svairāsano **drupadarājasutāṃ rudantīṃ**
kākṣeṇa paśyati likhaty abhikhāṃ nayajñaḥ | |

etāv ācāryapitāmahau tāṃ dṛṣṭvā lajjāyamānau paṭāntāntarhitamukhau sthitau | aho asya varṇāḍhyatā | aho bhāvopapannatā | aho yuktalekhatā | **suvyaktam ālikhito 'yam citrapaṭaḥ** | prīto 'smi | |

Ah, **this painting** is beautiful! **This Duḥśāsana right here, grabbed Draupadī by the lock of her hair. Indeed, this one here is Draupadī.**

7. **Manhandled by Duḥśāsana, her eyes wide open out of perplexity, she shines like the digit of the moon that has already gone inside of Rahu's mouth.**

Having seen Draupadī despised before the eyes of all the kings, **this evil-minded Bhīma right here**, of pent-up anger, is examining the columns of the assembly hall. **This one here is Yudhiṣṭhira.**

8. Endowed with truth, duty, and compassion, his mind lost to gambling, just by casting a look at Vṛkodara, he transforms his anger into peace.

Now, this one here is Arjuna.

9. His eyes twitching from anger, his lower lip quivering, having regarded that entire circle of foes as just a straw, as if intending to annihilate all the kings, he gently draws Gāṇḍiva's string.

This Yudhiṣṭhira right here is holding Arjuna back. **These two here are Nakula and Sahadeva.**

10. The binding of their girdles done, shield and sword in their hands, the reddening of their faces harshly prompted, their lower lips discernibly bitten, deprived of the fear of death, they hastily and fiercely set out against my brother, like two fawns against a lion.

This Yudhiṣṭhira right here, having come near the youths, is refraining them.

11. **Then, how am I the vile one of perverted mind? O experts in conduct and misconduct, let go of your anger today! Unforgiving of the dishonor related to the dicing match, may they have their heroism censured among the truly courageous ones.**

There, I have said it. **This one here is the king of Gāndhāra.**

12. Casting the dice like a gambler, laughing with arrogance, as if blithely degrading the condition of his opponent with his own glory, sitting where he wants, with a frown he looks at **the weeping daughter of king Drupada**, and being skilled in the game, he scrapes the ground.

The preceptor and the grandfather right here, ashamed after having seen her, stood with their faces covered by the edges of their robes. Ah, the richness of its colors! Ah, the lifelikeness! Ah, the skillful nature of the strokes! **This picture was carefully painted**. I am delighted.

(*DV* 6.15-12.6)

If this were another instance of Greco-Indian *anukaraṇa,* its trademark would be merging: a Greek text (*Phoenix*) about an alleged sexual assault (Phthia's pretend rape) that results in an unforgiving father (Amyntor) blinding his son (Phoenix), would have been combined with a Roman text (*The Eunuch*) about a sexual assault (Pamphila's actual rape) depicted in painting, to produce an Indian text (*The Embassy*) about a sexual assault (Draupadī's humiliation) depicted in painting, that results in a blind father (Dhṛtarāṣṭra) asking for forgiveness in the name of his son (Duryodhana).

The other one of *The Embassy*'s chief contrivances, i.e., the personified weapons, as a device intended to restrain the choleric god from harming the king, and thus impeding the divine plan, exhibits the signs of a *deus ex machina*, a frequent technique in the works of Euripides (e.g., *Hipp*. 1283 ff.). This notwithstanding, the concrete decision of utilizing personification could have been borrowed from Hellenistic/Roman lyric.

Among Roman lyric poets, it-fiction can be exemplified by Catullus (84-54 BCE),[97] Horace (65-8 BCE),[98] and Martial (40-104 CE):[99] in Catull. 4, a boat telling its life story, "says that he was [*ait fuisse*]" once a forest; in Catull. 66, a curl/constellation tells the story of the woman from whose hair it was cut, and it can even add, "I swear it [*adiuro*]"; in Catull. 67, a door reveals everyone's secrets, and it further explains, "I have heard it [*audivi*]"; in Hor. *Sat*. 1.8, a statue of the god Priapus proclaims, "once I was the trunk of a fig tree [*olim truncus eram ficulnus*]"; in Mart. *Epigr*. 13.50, some truffles say, "as fruiting bodies we are second only to mushrooms [*boletis poma secunda sumus*]"; in Mart. *Epigr*. 14.39, a lamp, ironically enough, proclaims, "I shall remain silent [*tacebo*]"; in Mart *Epigr*. 14.41, another lamp asserts, "I am called a single lamp [*una lucerna vocor*]"; in Mart. *Epigr*. 14.44, a candelabrum states, "you know me to be wood [*esse vides lignum*]"; and in Mart. *Epigr*. 14.64, a flute complains about its flutist, "she is breaking us [*nos... rumpit*]". There are many other examples of this topic.

---

97 I follow the Latin text by Cornish (Catullus; Tibullus; Pervigilium Veneris, 1962). The translations are my own.

98 I follow the Latin text by Fairclough (Horace, 1942). The translations are my own.

99 I follow the Latin text by Ker (Martial, 1920). The translations are my own.

Among Hellenistic lyric poets, examples of speaking objects are also quite common. The following poems[100] by Hegesippus the epigrammatist (ca. 300-200 BCE), Mnasalces of Sicyon (ca. 300-200 BCE), Nicias of Miletus (ca. 300-200 BCE), and Meleager of Gadara (ca. 100-1 BCE) are relevant for this study. The first three texts represent instances of a shield speaking, and therefore, appear close to the next quoted passage from *The Embassy*, in which a discus speaks. In *Anth. Pal.* 6.124, the "shield [Ἀσπὶς]" even identifies himself as such.

In all three Greek epigrams, there are verbal forms evincing that the speaker is the object itself: "I have been fastened [ἇμμαι]", "I stay [μένω]", and "I was destined [Μέλλον]". This also happens in the Sanskrit quotation: "I have sprung [*nirdhāvito 'smi*]" and "should I openly appear [*mayā pravijṛmbhitavyam*]". Furthermore, there are a couple of forms that even signal the locutionary act: "I proclaim [φαμὶ κατὰ]" and "having heard [*śrutvā*]". All the Greek poems also feature a warlike god: "Pallas [Παλλάδος]" and "Enyalius [Ἐνυαλίου]", which is the same as "Ares [Ἄρηος]". Epithets stand out as being predominant, since Pallas, probably meaning "the maiden", and Enyalius, meaning 'the warlike one', are respectively used for Athena and Ares, the two gods traditionally associated with war in Greek myth. The Sanskrit verse also opts for epithets: "the fortunate one [*bhagavato*]" and "the one of the large, lotus-like eyes [*kamalāyatākṣaḥ*]". However, a warlike demeanor is not as distinctive a feature in Kṛṣṇa's case. After all, Sudarśana says, Viṣṇu has descended, not to bring about the annihilation, but to see that it is done.

In addition, in two of the Greek texts, the shield talks about saving its owner: "always saving my bearer [τόν με φέροντ' αἰεὶ ῥυομένα]" and "having often saved my master's handsome chest [καλὸν ἄνακτος/στέρνον... πολλάκι ῥυσαμένα]". This is not explicitly stated in the quoted passage from *The Embassy*. Nonetheless, by remembering Kṛṣṇa's plan, Sudarśana kills two birds with one stone: he saves Duryodhana (from being killed by Kṣṛṇa) and he

100 I follow the Greek texts by Paton (The Greek Anthology, 1916). The translations are my own.

saves the plan (of relieving the Earth from her burden). He truly saves the day, as any *deus ex machina* would when it comes to wrapping up the plot.

Ἀσπὶς ἀπὸ βροτέων ὤμων Τιμάνορος **ἄμμαι**
ναῷ ὑπορροφία **Παλλάδος** ἀλκιμάχας,
πολλὰ σιδαρείου κεκονιμένα ἐκ πολέμοιο,
τόν με φέροντ' αἰεὶ ῥυομένα θανάτου.

As **the shield** from the mortal shoulders of Timanor, **I have been fastened** to the attic on the temple of the bravely fighting **Pallas**, considerably covered with the dust of the iron war, after **always saving my bearer** from death.

(Hegesippus, *Anth. Pal.* 6.124)

Ἤδη τῇδε **μένω** πολέμου δίχα, **καλὸν ἄνακτος**
στέρνον ἐμῷ νώτῳ **πολλάκι ῥυσαμένα**.
καίπερ τηλεβόλους ἰοὺς καὶ χερμάδι' αἰνὰ
μυρία καὶ δολιχὰς δεξαμένα κάμακας,
οὐδέποτε Κλείτοιο λιπεῖν περιμάκεα πᾶχυν
φαμὶ κατὰ, βλοσυρὸν φλοῖσβον **Ἐνυαλίου**.

Now **I stay** here, away from the war, **having often saved my master's handsome chest** with my back. Although having received far-reaching arrows, thousands of dreadful stones, and large spears, **I proclaim** that I never left Cleitus' huge forearm, at the hair-raising sound **of Enyalius**.

(Mnasalces, *Anth. Pal.* 6.125)

Μέλλον ἄρα στυγερὰν κἀγώ ποτε δῆριν **Ἄρηος**
ἐκπρολιποῦσα χορῶν παρθενίων ἀΐειν
Ἀρτέμιδος περὶ ναόν, Ἐπίξενος ἔνθα μ' ἔθηκεν,
λευκὸν ἐπεὶ κείνου γῆρας ἔτειρε μέλη.

So, at that time **I was destined** to give up the loathsome contest **of Ares**, for looking at the dances of the maidens around the temple of Artemis. Epixenus placed me there when old white age had weakened his limbs.

(Nicias, *Anth. Pal.* 6.127)

śrutvā giraṃ **bhagavato** vipulaprasādān
nirdhāvito 'smi parivāritatoyadaughaḥ |
kasmin khalu prakupitaḥ **kamalāyatākṣaḥ**
kasyādya mūrdhani **mayā pravijṛmbhitavyam** | |

Having heard the voice **of the fortunate one, I have sprung** from his great kindness, surrounded by a stream of clouds. With whom is he angry, **the one of the large, lotus-like eyes**? On whose head **should I openly appear** now?

(*DV* 42)

The last Greek epigram is not spoken by a weapon, but by the god of war himself, who was presented with weapons as a means of honoring him. It mentions "spears [αἰγανέαι]", a "helmet [πήληξ]", and on two occasions, a "shield [σάκος]" / "shields [ὅπλα]". The topic has broadened but the emphasis is still there. It also remains in the next Sanskrit quotation, in which the "discus [*cakraṃ*]" features twice. In the Greek poem, the god is identified by name (Ares) and epithet (Enyalius), as well as by a pronoun: "for me [μοι]". The Sanskrit verse opts for the god's pronoun too: "mine [*mama*]". The gruesome expression, "with human blood [λύθρῳ... βροτέῳ]", makes room for a more attenuated one: "the discus of your death [*kālacakraṃ tava*]". Finally, both gods (Ares and Kṛṣṇa) are talking to someone (the mortals and Duryodhana) while intending for their message to be heard by someone else (the weapons and Sudarśana).

Τίς τάδε **μοι** θνητῶν τὰ περὶ θριγκοῖσιν ἀνῆψε
σκῦλα, παναισχίστην τέρψιν **Ἐνυαλίου**;
οὔτε γὰρ **αἰγανέαι** περιαγέες, οὔτε τι **πήληξ**
ἄλλοφος, οὔτε φόνῳ χρανθὲν ἄρηρε **σάκος**·
ἀλλ' αὔτως γανόωντα καὶ ἀστυφέλικτα σιδάρῳ,
οἷά περ οὐκ ἐνοπᾶς, ἀλλὰ χορῶν ἔναρα·
οἷς θάλαμον κοσμεῖτε γαμήλιον· **ὅπλα** δὲ **λύθρῳ**
λειβόμενα **βροτέῳ** σηκὸς **Ἄρηος** ἔχοι.

Which of the mortals hung up **for me** these spoils here, the ones around the walls, the poorest form of enjoyment **for Enyalius**? For no broken **spears**, not a single crestless **helmet**, nor a **shield** stained with blood have been presented; only these that are gleaming like before, unbeaten by the

> iron, as if they were spoils, not of battle, but of dances. With them, embellish a bridal bed, but let the precinct **of Ares** have **shields** that are dripping **with human blood**.
>
> (Meleager, *Anth. Pal.* 6.163)

> yadi lavaṇajalaṃ vā kandaraṃ vā girīṇāṃ
> grahagaṇacaritaṃ vā vāyumārgaṃ prayāsi |
> **mama** bhujabalayogaprāptasaṃjātavegaṃ
> bhavatu capala **cakraṃ kālacakraṃ tavā**dya ||

> Even if you go to the ocean, to a cave of the mountains, or to the path of the wind, traversed by the planets, O ill-mannered one, may **my discus**, whose resulting speed is obtained by means of the strength of my arm, now be **the discus of your death**.
>
> (*DV* 45)

If this were a third instance of Greco-Indian *anukaraṇa*, its trademark would also be merging: a Greek text (*Phoenix*) probably ending with a *deus ex machina* (Phoenix's eye treatment by Chiron?), would have been combined with a selection of Hellenistic texts (*The Greek Anthology*) featuring it-fiction with weapons (speaking shields), to produce an Indian text (*The Embassy*) featuring it-fiction with weapons (a speaking discus) as a form of *deus ex machina* (Duryodhana's life being spared by Sudarśana).

In sum, I postulate a Greek influence from *Il.* 9 and *Phoenix* into *MBh.* 5 and *The Embassy*. Such influence would encompass two adaptation techniques: character subtraction-cum-merging (EM1), and theme addition-cum-emphasis (EM2). As an instance of Greco-Indian *anukaraṇa*, the key component of this Greek influence would be reversal. Furthermore, from the embassy motif, I claim two Greco-Roman borrowings: on one hand, the painting about a sexual assault, from Terence's *The Eunuch*; on the other, it-fiction with weapons, from *The Greek Anthology*. As instances of Greco-Indian *anukaraṇa*, they would both be characterized by merging.

3. The Ambush

The Tale of the Tricked Trickster

For the purposes of this book, an ambush broadly refers to "… spying missions, raids on enemy camps, cattle rustling, and other types of epic warfare that happen at night" (Dué & Ebbott, 2010, p. 32). In the Homeric Epics, ambushes seem to be valuable in terms of the overall goal of perfecting heroism. For instance, at *Il.* 13.277-278, one reads, "for an ambush, where the excellence of men better manifests itself, and where the cowardly man is brought to light, as well as the brave one [ἐς λόχον, ἔνθα μάλιστ' ἀρετὴ διαείδεται ἀνδρῶν, / ἔνθ' ὅ τε δειλὸς ἀνὴρ ὅς τ' ἄλκιμος ἐξεφαάνθη]". Even the sack of Troy could be seen as a night ambush.

The ambush motif makes for a good transition between those of the embassy and the ogre, given the fact that both of those episodes include instances of ambush. If the entire Cyclops episode (*Od.* 9.105-566) follows the poetics of ambush, at least a section of the Phoenix episode does so (*Il.* 9.474-477). However, *Iliad* 10 is the best example of the ambush motif in extant Greek epic. For this reason, as well as for the fact that the ambush from *Il.* 10 is the one adapted in Ps.-Euripides' *Rhesus*, this is the book that I will examine. Its distinctive feature is the doubling of the ambush: with two spying missions followed by two ambushes, all of which takes place during the night, this is a wonderfully detailed use of the motif, and a great starting point for the analysis.

The epic version is as follows: the book opens at nighttime and at the Greek bivouac, where everyone but king Agamemnon seems to be sleeping. Upon seeing the Trojan fires burning, he gets ready

 https://doi.org/10.11647/OBP.0417.03

by dressing himself in the skin of a lion. At that point, he is visited by his brother Menelaus, who comes wearing a leopard's skin and asking if Agamemnon is planning on a spying mission. Afraid of Hector's deeds during the previous day, Agamemnon intends to hold a night council: he sends Menelaus to wake up everyone, while he himself goes looking for old Nestor. On their way, Agamemnon and Nestor wake up Odysseus and Diomedes, who will be the key figures of the Greek ambush.

For the council, the scene moves away from the huts, through the trench, and into the open field. Nestor proposes a night attack, during which they could gather intelligence about the Trojans' plans. Whoever volunteers will obtain fame and gifts. Diomedes steps up, but he also asks for a companion. The sneaky Odysseus seems like the perfect choice. By now, two out of the three watches of the night have passed, and dawn draws near. As with the king and his brother, their animal attire is highlighted: Diomedes' helmet is made from a bull's hide; Odysseus', from the teeth of a boar. With Athena's blessing, they march through the plain, still filled with the corpses from the daytime slaughter.

With a little repetition with variation, the author then turns to the Trojan bivouac. Like Agamemnon, Hector is awake and calls for a night council; like Nestor, he sets forth the idea of a night attack, which would reveal the Greeks' intentions. As gifts, he offers a chariot and two horses. Like Diomedes, Dolon volunteers, looking forward to obtaining Achilles' horses. He puts on a wolf's hide, as well as a helmet made from the skin of a ferret. Astutely, Odysseus lets him pass them, so that when they come after him from behind, he confuses foes with friends. Diomedes chases him, and Odysseus not only asks if Dolon is spying, but also manages to gather some intelligence of his own: the Trojans keep watch but their allies do not, the Thracians are newcomers and their king Rhesus has the best horses. Afterwards, Diomedes cuts off Rhesus' head.

Having outsmarted Dolon, Diomedes and Odysseus proceed to seek out Rhesus. Diomedes' casualties add up to twelve plus one, for Rhesus is killed after twelve of his companions. Meanwhile, Odysseus removes the bodies, and he leads Rhesus' horses back to the Greek camp, not without stopping midway to gather Dolon's spoils. In favor of the Greeks, Athena oversees the ambush and intervenes when necessary; as for the Trojans, Apollo awakes the Thracian Hippocoon, who pointlessly calls for Rhesus. Diomedes and Odysseus come back as heroes, and the latter tells Nestor the deeds performed by the former: Diomedes is responsible for twelve-plus-one victims, this time, combining Rhesus' comrades and the spy Dolon. The book ends with the triumphant raiders bathing and eating.

Regarding Ps.-Euripides' *Rhesus*, its numerous sources include the Homeric Epics, the Epic Cycle, and even Aristophanes. Focusing on the tragedians, the play evinces the influence of Aeschylus and Sophocles, as well as a clear Euripides-*imitatio*. This notwithstanding, the main source for the adaptation is the ambush motif coming from *Il.* 10. The play is divided into four episodes, respectively dealing with the mission by the spy Dolon, the arrival of the hero Rhesus, his boastfulness, and his killing. Since the parodos,[101] the Chorus of Trojans makes it clear that the action starts by the tent of Hector, during the fourth watch of the night.

In the first episode, king Hector fears a night escape of the Greek army, which would leave him bloodthirsty. When he is about to wake everyone up, the warrior Aeneas offers him some advice: a spying mission might be better. Dolon volunteers and demands, as a reward, the horses of Achilles. Having dressed himself with a wolf hide, the boastful Dolon believes that he will kill the warriors Odysseus and Diomedes. After a first stasimon,[102] in which the Trojans fail to keep the champagne on ice and prematurely celebrate the mission of Dolon, the second episode turns the focus towards Rhesus. A messenger informs Hector about the arrival of Rhesus, which the shepherds mistake for a cattle raid. Uninterested at first, Hector progressively caves in. He goes from wanting nothing to do with Rhesus to accepting him, first as a guest and then as an ally.

After a second stasimon, during which the Trojans praise Rhesus in quasi-hubristic terms, the third episode begins with an

101 A parodos is the first choral part of a Greek play and it signals the entrance of the Chorus.

102 A stasimon is any choral part of a Greek play other than the first one and the last one, and it serves to separate the episodes.

explanation for the tardy arrival. Before coming to fight the Greeks at Troy, Rhesus had to fight the Scythians at Thrace. Boastful like Dolon, Rhesus believes that he can kill the Greeks within a single day. He asks to be stationed facing the tents of the hero Achilles, and Hector brings him up to speed about the well-known quarrel. Hector also warns him about Diomedes and Odysseus, shows him a place for him to spend the night, and shares with him the watchword, just in case.

Following a third stasimon that stresses both the tardiness of Dolon and the proximity of dawn, the fourth and last episode opens with Odysseus and Diomedes. Having already killed Dolon and learned the watchword from him, they are trying, without any success, to find Hector and kill him. They are not sure about their next step, and at this point the goddess Athena enters the stage to intervene in their favor. She points them towards Rhesus and orders them to kill him instead. Moreover, Athena diverts prince Paris, by posing as the goddess Aphrodite. Having already killed Rhesus, Odysseus and Diomedes are now struggling to get back to the ships. What follows is an epiparodos,[103] during which the Trojans fail to capture the Greeks, mostly because of the cunning of Odysseus.

Lastly, the exodos[104] includes some moving scenes: the dream of the charioteer, with two wolves mounted on horses; the accusation of Hector, who has left a lot to be desired as a general; and the *dea ex machina* of the Muse. The Muse curses Diomedes, Odysseus and even the infamous Helen. She laments the death of her son Rhesus, and she blames Athena for her meddling. All this helps Hector to confirm his suspicions of Greek wrongdoing. But there is more. The Muse also prophesizes the hero cult of Rhesus and the death of Achilles, and Hector never ceases to believe that he can turn his luck around. The play ends when daylight is just starting to break.

---

103 An epiparodos is a sort of second parodos or choral part of a Greek play.

104 An exodos is the last choral part of a Greek play, and it signals the departure of the Chorus.

In the dramatic version, the author profits, among others, from these nine procedures: [GA1][105] he merges two camps into one, [GA2] he merges two dialogues into one, [GA3] he adds a tricky bargaining, [GA4] he emphasizes the braggart, [GA5] he emphasizes the adaptation's sources, [GA6] he adds the anagnorisis, [GA7] he changes the perspective of the attack, [GA8] he maintains the nighttime, and [GA9] he ignores the on-stage death.

[GA1] In terms of spatial location, the narrative source begins at the Greek camp (*Il.* 10.1), transitions into the Trojan camp halfway through the book (*Il.* 10.299), and then returns to its starting point near the end (*Il.* 10.532). This twofold scenery is merged into one in the dramatic adaptation, where the two camps, together with their comings and goings, become one.[106] Agamemnon's and Hector's huts become just those pertaining to the Trojan. In this way, instead of contrasting Greeks and Trojans, the playwright

---

105 GA stands for "Greek Ambush". Hence, numbers GA1-GA9 refer to the adaptation of *Il.* 10 into *Rhesus*. Once again, these are just the adaptation techniques that will allow me to argue for parallelisms with the Greco-Roman world. Other techniques at play include maintaining the timing of Hector's speech, merging two of Nestor's opinions into one of Hector's, adding Hector's blaming of Fortune, changing the meaning of Hector's lion metaphor, merging Menealus' and Polydamas' characters into Aeneas' character, changing Dolon's character from ignoble to noble, emphasizing the wolf hide, changing Rhesus' character from noble to hero, emphasizing Odysseus' role, adding the watchword, changing the intended victim from Rhesus to Hector, changing the leaving of Dolon's spoils into a carrying of Dolon's spoils, emphasizing Athena's role, subtracting Dolon's treason, adding Athena's deception of Paris, changing Dolon's actual capture into Odysseus' and Diomedes' near capture, changing Rhesus' bad dream into the Charioteer's nightmare, changing the lion/Diomedes into the wolves/Achaeans, maintaining Diomedes' taking of Rhesus' chariot, ignoring Odysseus' and Diomedes' heroism, and changing Thetis' lament into the Muse's lament.

106 On merging two camps into one, see Liapis (2012): "In many ways, Hector is the play's central character, and his sleeping-place the visual centre of the action" (p. xlvii); Fries (2014): "Likewise, the position Hector assigns to Rhesus and his men in 518-20 (cf. 613-15) matches that of *Il.* 10.434, a telling detail after different precedents (including the τειχοσκοπία in *Iliad* 3) had to be invoked for the encounter between Hector and the Thracian king (388-526, 388-453, 467-526nn.)" (p. 9); and Fantuzzi (2020): "*Rhesus*, a play that focuses on the problem of power in the military sphere, begins appropriately enough at the bivouac of the leader of the Trojan army, Hector, and this remains the setting until the end" (p. 1).

contrasts two Trojan factions, headed by Hector and Rhesus. The topic of sleeping serves to weave together the two locations.

> ἄλλοι μὲν παρὰ νηυσὶν ἀριστῆες Παναχαιῶν
> **εὗδον παννύχιοι, μαλακῷ δεδμημένοι ὕπνῳ·**
>
> Next to their ships, the other chiefs of the Achaeans **were sleeping through the night, overcome by soft sleep**.
>
> (*Il.* 10.1-2)
>
> Οὐδὲ μὲν οὐδὲ Τρῶας ἀγήνορας εἴασεν Ἕκτωρ
> εὕδειν, ἀλλ' ἅμυδις κικλήσκετο πάντας ἀρίστους,
>
> And Hector also **did not allow the heroic Trojans to sleep**; instead, he called together all their chiefs.
>
> (*Il.* 10.299-300)
>
> Βῆθι **πρὸς εὐνὰς τὰς Ἑκτορέους·**
> τίς ὑπασπιστῶν **ἄγρυπνος** βασιλέως
> ἢ τευχοφόρων;
>
> Go **to Hector's beds**! Who is **wakeful** among the king's squires or armor bearers?
>
> (*Rhes.* 1-3)

[GA2] Ps.-Euripides changes Agamemnon's and Menelaus' dialogue into Hector's and Aeneas' dialogue.[107] Building on the awakening scene, which served as an introductory announcement to the adaptation, the conclusions reached in these dialogues mirror each other, as an instance of repetition with variation: where Agamemnon orders that Menelaus raise his voice and wake up the Greeks, Hector instructs Aeneas to lower his and to allow the Trojans to continue sleeping. At the level of the characters, Agamemnon's farsightedness seems to be replaced by a sheer lack of it on Hector's part. However, when focusing on the author's intentions, the

107 On merging two dialogues into one, see Dué & Ebbott (2010): "The dialogue between Hektor and Aeneas about how to respond (*Rhesos* 87-148) is similar in structure, although not in content, to that between Agamemnon and Menealos (*Iliad* 10.36-72). We see that, after some disagreement, their conclusion is to let the allies continue to sleep, while Agamemnon and Menelaos, cooperative throughout, resolve to wake the Achaean leaders" (p. 123).

Trojans need to be asleep for the ambush to happen. With a clear precedent in the source text, and with a deliberate reversal in the new version, this dialogue serves as a clear-cut example of what an adaptation is, both as a product and as a process of creation.

> **φθέγγεο** δ' ᾗ κεν ἴῃσθα, καὶ **ἐγρήγορθαι** ἄνωχθι,
>
> **Speak up** wherever you may go, and command them **to be awake**...
>
> (*Il.* 10.67)

> στείχων δὲ **κοίμα** συμμάχους· τάχ' ἂν στρατὸς
> κινοῖτ' **ἀκούσας** νυκτέρους ἐκκλησίας.
>
> Going there, **calm** our allies: perhaps the army might be stirred up, **having heard** about our nightly assemblies.
>
> (*Rhes.* 138-139)

[GA3] Dolon's bargaining is an addition. And the bargaining chips reveal the influence of Agamemnon's and Achilles' negotiations, as per the enumeration at *Il.* 9.122-156, on Hector's and Dolon's negotiations.[108] In the epic, Hector voluntarily offers a pair of horses together with a chariot; then, Dolon has him swear that the horses will be those of Achilles. In the drama, Hector proposes the spying mission without mentioning any reward for such effort, and Dolon calls him on it.

> ἀλλ' ἄγε μοι τὸ σκῆπτρον ἀνάσχεο, καί μοι ὄμοσσον
> ἦ μὲν **τοὺς ἵππους τε καὶ ἅρματα ποικίλα χαλκῷ**
> δωσέμεν, **οἳ φορέουσιν ἀμύμονα Πηλεΐωνα,**
>
> But come on, raise your scepter before me and swear to me that you will give me **the horses and the chariot ornamented with bronze, which carry the noble son of Peleus.**
>
> (*Il.* 10.321-323)

108 On the addition of a tricky bargaining, see Fries (2014): "The 'guessing-game' by which Dolon elicits the promise of Achilles' horses as a reward for his expedition is informed by the proxy negotiations between Agamemnon and Achilles in *Iliad* 9, and the animals themselves are described after *Il.* 16.149-51 + 23.276-8 (cf. 149-94, 185-8nn.)" (p. 9); and Fantuzzi (2020): "The debate between Dolon and Hector is a major addition to the plot of *Il.* 10" (p. 64).

> οὐκοῦν πονεῖν μὲν χρή, **πονοῦντα δ' ἄξιον μισθὸν φέρεσθαι.** παντὶ γὰρ προσκείμενον κέρδος πρὸς ἔργῳ τὴν χάριν τίκτει διπλῆν.
>
> Well, it is necessary to work for it, **and therefore, to give the worker a fair wage.** Remuneration being attached to a job brings forth twice the pleasure.
>
> (*Rhes.* 161-163)

[GA4] Rhesus goes from silent character in the Homeric epic to title character in the play attributed to Euripides.[109] Rhesus' characterization is correlated to Hector's. In the play, when warned about Rhesus' unexpected arrival, Hector is the one who determines his standing: for Hector, Rhesus is, first, an opportunist who comes "for the feast [ἐς δαῖτ']" (*Rhes.* 325) without having contributed for securing "the prey [λείαν]" (*Rhes.* 326); Rhesus is, then, "a guest at the table [χένος δὲ πρὸς τράπεζαν]" (*Rhes.* 337) but not "an ally [σύμμαχος]" (*Rhes.* 336); and Rhesus is, eventually, considered "an ally [σύμμαχος]" (*Rhes.* 341). In turn, given that Priam does not figure among the characters of the play, Rhesus addresses Hector as a king: "O king of this land [τύραννε τῆσδε γῆς]" (*Rhes.* 388).

The emphasis on Rhesus' character continues with him being given an origin story: "But when I was about to undertake my long

109 On the emphasis on the braggart, see Dué & Ebbott (2010): "In the *Iliad* we do not have any opportunity to see what Rhesos is like as a character – he is asleep and then dead the only time he appears. In the *Rhesos*, his character is presented as overconfident in his abilities to win the war in a single day of fighting, but his tragic mistake is related to ambush in particular" (p. 126); Fries (2014): "The epic Thracian [sc. Rhesus] is a nonentity, a sleeping source of booty for Odysseus and Diomedes, but the memorable description of his god-like appearance and snow-white horses (*Il.* 10.435-41) has been incorporated into the Shepherd's report of his approach (301-8) and is further elaborated in the chorus' 'cletic hymn' and entry announcement (342-79, 380-7nn.)" (p. 9); and Fantuzzi (2020): "In the play Rhesus does not have time to fight, and dies 'ingloriously' (758-61), as in the *Il.*, but at least he speaks extensively, in a long debate with Hector (388-517). This debate has two structural aims. First of all, together with Athena's claim that Rhesus could annihilate the Greeks on the battlefield in a single day (598-606), it constructs what we might call the virtual and boastful heroism of Rhesus. This in part replaces his non-existent martial glory with extreme ambition… The second aim of the debate between Hector and Rhesus is to consider in depth the risks and benefits of military alliances" (pp. 15-16).

journey to Ilium, my neighboring land, the people of Scythia, went to war with me [ἀλλ' ἀγχιτέρμων ψαῖα μοι, Σκύθης λεώς, / μέλλοντι νόστον τὸν πρὸς Ἴλιον περᾶν / ξυνῆψε πόλεμον]" (*Rhes.* 426-428). Nevertheless, probably the greatest novelty is the assertion that he could get rid of the Greeks within a single day. Coming from him, this only contributes to turning the emphasis into a sort of caricature, much along the lines of what the Roman theater (Plautus, *Mil.*) calls a *miles gloriosus* (braggart warrior).[110] Hector, Dolon, and Rhesus all have moments of boastfulness. As seen in the next three passages, respectively, Hector asserts that he could have destroyed the Greek army, Dolon proclaims that he will behead Odysseus, and Rhesus claims that he will end the war in a single day. Ironically enough, Rhesus does not make it past the night, Dolon himself is beheaded by Odysseus' coconspirator, and Hector makes it to the end of the play still believing that he can win.

> ὦ δαῖμον, ὅστις μ' εὐτυχοῦντ' ἐνόσφισας
> θοίνης λέοντα, **πρὶν τὸν Ἀργείων στρατὸν**
> **σύρδην ἅπαντα τῷδ' ἀναλῶσαι δορί.**
>
> O Fortune, in whichever form turned me, the lucky lion, away from my feast, **before I could kill the entire army of the Argives, as if dragged along, with this spear!**
>
> (*Rhes.* 56-58)

> σωθήσομαί τοι **καὶ κτανὼν Ὀδυσσέως**
> **οἴσω κάρα σοι...**
>
> I will return safely, **and having killed Odysseus, I will bring you his head...**
>
> (*Rhes.* 219-220)

> σὺ μὲν γὰρ ἤδη δέκατον αἰχμάζεις ἔτος
> κοὐδὲν περαίνεις, ἡμέραν δ' ἐξ ἡμέρας
> ῥίπτεις κυβεύων τὸν πρὸς Ἀργείους Ἄρη·
> **ἐμοὶ δὲ φῶς ἓν ἡλίου καταρκέσει**
> **πέρσαντι πύργους ναυστάθμοις ἐπεσπεσεῖν**
> **κτεῖναί τ' Ἀχαιούς...**

110 On Rhesus as a *miles gloriosus*, see Fantuzzi (2020): "Rhesus is from time to time almost a *miles gloriosus*, but he seems to have the potential to be a good fighter" (p. 46). Cf. Liapis' (2012, p. xlv ff.) critique.

> Indeed, you are now throwing your spear for the tenth year, and you are accomplishing nothing, and day after day, while playing at dice, you are casting Ares against the Argives. **But for me, a single daylight of the sun will suffice, when ravaging the towers, to burst into the roadstead and kill the Achaeans.**
>
> (*Rhes.* 444-449)

Rhesus behaves like a braggart warrior even more than Hector and Dolon. Two more examples serve to support this claim. In the first one, he wishes to take his own army to Greece, in an overt reversal of the known story. Then, so he asserts, he would singlehandedly destroy all Greece. In the second example, he once again focuses on Odysseus, whom he intends to impale with an aggressiveness like that he exhibited while threatening his beheading.

> ξὺν σοὶ στρατεύειν γῆν ἐπ' Ἀργείων θέλω
> καὶ **πᾶσαν** ἐλθὼν **Ἑλλάδ' ἐκπέρσαι δορί**,
> ὡς ἂν μάθωσιν ἐν μέρει πάσχειν κακῶς.
>
> ...together with you, I wish to advance with my army towards the land of the Achaeans, and having arrived, **to ravage all Greece with my spear**, so that they would learn, in turn, to suffer badly.
>
> (*Rhes.* 471-473)
>
> ...ζῶντα συλλαβὼν ἐγὼ
> **πυλῶν ἐπ' ἐξόδοισιν ἀμπείρας ῥάχιν**
> στήσω πετεινοῖς γυψὶ θοινατήριον.
>
> ...having taken him alive and **having impaled him through his spine by the side of the doors**, I will set him up as food for the winged vultures.
>
> (*Rhes.* 513-515)

[GA5] If the epic source mentions in passing a clamor and an uproar among the Trojans, the dramatic adaptation further elaborates such commotion.[111] The epic Trojans are too sluggish to capture

111 On the emphasis on the adaptation's sources, see Fries (2014): "The epiparodos (675-91 + 692-727) dramatises a single sentence in the epic source. The commotion caused by the searching chorus parallels that of

Diomedes and Odysseus; the dramatic Trojans, grouped together as the Chorus, are too naive to hold on to them. Furthermore, the fact that this re-created commotion is certainly an adaptation is signaled by a pun. When an unaware Trojan asks, "What is your troop? [τίς ὁ λόχος;]", any discerning audience member hears, "What sort of ambush is this? [τίς ὁ λόχος;]". The word used here for "troop [λόχος]" is the same one that is employed through the drama for the main motif: the "ambush [λόχος]".

> Τρώων δὲ **κλαγγή τε καὶ ἄσπετος ὦρτο κυδοιμὸς**
> θυνόντων ἄμυδις· θηεῦντο δὲ μέρμερα ἔργα,
> ὅσσ' ἄνδρες ῥέξαντες ἔβαν κοίλας ἐπὶ νῆας.
>
> **A clamor and an unspeakable uproar rose** among the Trojans, who were rushing all together: they gazed upon the mournful deeds that the warriors had done before they left for the hollow ships.
>
> (*Il.* 10.523-525)

675	ἔα ἔα· βάλε βάλε βάλε· θένε θένε <θένε>. τίς ἀνήρ;
677	λεῦσσε· τοῦτον αὐδῶ.
680	δεῦρο δεῦρο πᾶς.
681	τούσδ' ἔχω, τούσδ' ἔμαρψα
678-9	κλῶπας οἵτινες κατ' ὄρφνην τόνδε κινοῦσι στρατόν.
682	**τίς ὁ λόχος;** πόθεν ἔβας; ποδαπὸς εἶ;
675	Hey, hey! Throw it, throw it, throw it! Kill him, kill him, <kill him>! Who is that man?
677	Look: I am speaking about that one!

the Trojans when, alerted by Hippocoon, they discover the massacre in the Thracian camp (*Il.* 10.523-4)" (p. 10).

680	Here, here, everyone!
681	I have them, I caught them,
678-9	the thieves who are disturbing the army during the night.
682	**What is your troop?** Where did you come from? From what country are you?
	(*Rhes.* 675-682)

[GA6] Another procedure followed by the author of the *Rhesus* is the addition of the anagnorisis. According to Aristotle,[112] "Anagnorisis, as its name signals, is a change from ignorance to knowledge, either towards friendship or towards enmity, of what defines prosperity and adversity [ἀναγνώρισις δέ, ὥσπερ καὶ τοὔνομα σημαίνει, ἐξ ἀγνοίας εἰς γνῶσιν μεταβολή, ἢ εἰς φιλίαν ἢ εἰς ἔχθραν, τῶν πρὸς εὐτυχίαν ἢ δυστυχίαν ὡρισμένων]" (*Poet.* 1452a28-31). Also, anagnorises can result from various procedures: "the one by signs [ἡ διὰ τῶν σημείων]", "the ones effected by the poet [αἱ πεποιημέναι ὑπὸ τοῦ ποιητοῦ]", "the one by memory [ἡ διὰ μνήμης]", "the one from reasoning [ἡ ἐκ συλλογισμοῦ]", and "the one from events themselves [ἡ ἐξ αὐτῶν τῶν πραγμάτων]".

In *Il.* 10, Hector does not even acknowledge Rhesus' death, but in *Rhes.*, following the Muse's appearance, Hector confirms what he has suspected all along: Odysseus is responsible. Before the *dea ex machina*, the Charioteer blames Hector for Rhesus' death, and Hector, in turn, accuses Odysseus of the killing of both Rhesus and Dolon. After the anagnorisis, the true enmity is revealed, not between Trojan factions, but between the Trojans and the Greeks. The next two passages indicate, respectively, Hector's first words in the narrative after Rhesus' killing, and Hector's first words in the play after the anagnorisis.

112 I follow the Greek text by Halliwell (Aristotle; Longinus; Demetrius, 1995). The translations are my own.

Τρῶες καὶ Λύκιοι καὶ Δάρδανοι ἀγχιμαχηταί,
ἀνέρες ἔστε, φίλοι, **μνήσασθε** δὲ θούριδος ἀλκῆς.
οἴχετ' ἀνὴρ ὤριστος, ἐμοὶ δὲ μέγ' εὖχος ἔδωκε
Ζεὺς Κρονίδης· ἀλλ' ἰθὺς ἐλαύνετε μώνυχας ἵππους
ἰφθίμων Δαναῶν, ἵν' ὑπέρτερον εὖχος ἄρησθε.

O Trojans, Lycians, and Dardanians, all fighting hand by hand! O friends! Be men and **remember** your impetuous courage. Their best warrior is gone and Zeus, the son of Cronos, granted me great glory. Ride your single-hoofed horses straight towards the powerful Danaans, so that you may win greater glory.

(*Il.* 11.286-290)

ᾔδη τάδ'· οὐδὲν μάντεων ἔδει φράσαι
Ὀδυσσέως τέχναισι τόνδ' ὀλωλότα.

I knew it: there was no need for a seer to tell us that this one was killed by the tricks of Odysseus.

(*Rhes.* 952-953)

Even when aware of the deceit, Hector refuses to admit defeat. His final words in the play are tragic, for he is willing to go down defending a lost cause.

...ὡς ὑπερβαλὼν στρατὸν
τείχη τ' Ἀχαιῶν ναυσὶν αἶθον ἐμβαλεῖν
πέποιθα Τρωσί θ' ἡμέραν ἐλευθέραν
ἀκτῖνα τὴν στείχουσαν ἡλίου φέρειν.

Thus, having traversed the army and the walls of the Achaeans to set fire to their ships, I **believe** that the upcoming brightness of the sun will bring a day of freedom for the Trojans.

(*Rhes.* 989-992)

[GA7] The broader authorial decision is that of changing the perspective from the Greeks to the Trojans.[113] The beginning of

113 On the change of perspective of the attack, see Dué & Ebbott (2010): "The *Rhesos* presents the story of this night raid and ambush from the Trojan point of view, and it seems to set itself up as a parallel or alternative to the *Iliad* 10 account in its opening details" (p. 123); Fries (2014): "For lack of an

the *Rhesus* makes this quite clear by contrasting several scenes. For instance, Nestor's question, "**who is this**, coming alone by the ships, through the army, during the dark night, when the other mortals sleep? [**τίς δ' οὗτος** κατὰ νῆας ἀνὰ στρατὸν ἔρχεαι οἶος / νύκτα δι' ὀρφναίην, ὅτε θ' εὕδουσι βροτοὶ ἄλλοι;]" (*Il.* 10.82-83), is transformed into that of Hector: "**who are those**, approaching our bedsteads during the night? [**τίνες** ἐκ νυκτῶν τὰς ἡμετέρας / κοίτας πλάθουσ';]" (*Rhes.* 13-14). The patronymic in "calling each man **by their father's name** and their descent [**πατρόθεν** ἐκ γενεῆς ὀνομάζων ἄνδρα ἕκαστον]" (*Il.* 10.68-69) is reworked into a patronymic and a pretend matronymic: "who will go to **Panthus' son** or to **that of Europa**, leader of the Lycian men? [τίς εἶσ' ἐπὶ **Πανθοΐδαν**, / ἢ **τὸν Εὐρώπας**, Λυκίων ἀγὸν ἀνδρῶν;]" (*Rhes.* 28-29). In addition, the Trojan "many fires [πυρὰ πολλά]" (*Il.* 10.12) become Greek "fires [πύρ']" (*Rhes.* 41); and the Trojan "sound of flutes and pipes, and clamor of men [αὐλῶν συρίγγων τ' ἐνοπὴν ὅμαδόν τ' ἀνθρώπων]" (*Il.* 10.13) turns into a Greek "tumult [θορύβῳ]" (*Rhes.* 45).

The idea of retelling a known story from the point of view of the losing party is a common one in Greek theater (Aeschylus' *Persians*; Euripides' *Andromache*, *Hecuba*, *Helen*, and *Trojan*

adequate precedent among the Trojans in 'Homer', the sequence of 1-148 has been devised as a mirror-image of *Il.* 10.1-179, which describes the anxious commotion in the Greek naval camp" (p. 8); and Fantuzzi (2020): "From the very beginning of *Il.* 10, Greeks and Trojans behave and think in similar ways and their actions mirror each other. The same duplication can be observed in *Rhesus*. The leaders of both camps are awake and call a council; in each camp, a leader has the idea of a spy mission and asks for a volunteer; in both cases, the volunteers arm themselves in an unusual way, wearing animal pelts or unusual headgear... and the spies are promised the enemy's best horses (in the case of the Trojans) or in fact receive them (in the case of the Greeks)" (p. 58). On the borrowings from *Il.* 10, see also Liapis' (2012) list: *Rhes.* 49-51, *Rhes.*72-73, *Rhes.* 178, *Rhes.* 193-194, *Rhes.* 458-460a, *Rhes.* 477-478, *Rhes.* 480, *Rhes.* 494-495, *Rhes.* 523-525a, *Rhes.* 609b-610, *Rhes.* 611-612, *Rhes.* 627-299, *Rhes.* 702, *Rhes.* 752-753, *Rhes.* 784-786, *Rhes.* 792, and *Rhes.* 829-831 (p. lx); and Fries' (2014) cross-references: *Rhes.* 1-148 ~ *Il.* 10.1-179, *Rhes.* 149-223 ~ *Il.* 10.299-337, *Rhes.* 264-387 ~ *Il.* 10.436-441, *Rhes.* 388-526 ~ *Il.* 10.434, *Rhes.* 527-564 ~ *Il.* 10.251-253, 428-431, 561-563, *Rhes.* 565-94 ~ *Il.* 10.339-468, *Rhes.* 595-641 ~ *Il.* 10.433-441, 463-464, 474-475, 479-481, *Rhes.* 642-674 ~ *Il.* 10.509-511, *Rhes.* 675-727 ~ *Il.* 10.523-524, *Rhes.* 728-881 ~ *Il.* 10.515-521, and *Rhes.* 756-803 ~ *Il.* 10.471-497 (p. 10, n. 4).

Women). Moreover, the procedure of introducing such retelling by a specific scene, like the awakening, works in tandem with the announced nature of most adaptations.

[GA8] As for the occurrence in time, night remains the trademark of the ambush motif.[114] However, the precise moment in time is phrased differently: in Homer, two out of the three watches of the night have passed; in Ps.-Euripides, four out of five. The contingents in charge of the watches in *Rhesus* are, successively, the Paeonians, the Cilicians, the Mysians, the Trojans, and the Lycians. For the adaptation, the number five signals the deadline.

> ἄστρα δὲ δὴ προβέβηκε, **παροίχωκεν δὲ πλέων νὺξ**
> **τῶν δύο μοιράων, τριτάτη** δ' ἔτι **μοῖρα λέλειπται.**
>
> The stars are far gone, and **two full watches of the night having passed**, now **only a third watch is left.**
>
> (*Il.* 10.252-253)

> δέξαιτο νέων κληδόνα μύθων,
> οἳ **τετράμοιρον νυκτὸς φυλακὴν**
> πάσης στρατιᾶς προκάθηνται·
>
> Let him hear the news of the recent reports of those who, **during the fourth watch of the night**, are guarding the entire army.
>
> (*Rhes.* 4-6)

> – τίς ἐκηρύχθη πρώτην φυλακήν;
> – Μυγδόνος υἱόν φασι Κόροιβον.
> – τίς γὰρ ἐπ' αὐτῷ; – Κίλικας Παίων
> στρατὸς ἤγειρεν, Μυσοὶ δ' ἡμᾶς.
> – οὔκουν Λυκίους **πέμπτην φυλακὴν**
> βάντας ἐγείρειν
> καιρὸς κλήρου κατὰ μοῖραν;
>
> – Who was announced for the first watch?
> – They say that Coroebus, the son of Mygdon.
> – Who, then, after him?
> – The Paeonian army woke the Cilicians; and the Mysians, us.

114 On maintaining the nighttime, see Fantuzzi (2020): "No other tragedy is set entirely at night… although some fragmentary ones were probably set at night…" (p. 55, n. 183).

> – Then is it not time, as per the drawing of the lots, to wake the Lycians, having gone to them, **for the fifth watch**?
>
> (*Rhes.* 538-545)

[GA9] Dolon's death is gruesomely described in the epic, but it is only alluded to in the drama.[115] According to Aristotle,[116] "Suffering is a destructive and painful action, such as **deaths in public**, excessive pains, wounds, and others such as these [πάθος δέ ἐστι πρᾶξις φθαρτικὴ ἢ ὀδυνηρά, οἷον **οἵ τε ἐν τῷ φανερῷ θάνατοι** καὶ αἱ περιωδυνίαι καὶ τρώσεις καὶ ὅσα τοιαῦτα]" (*Poet.* 1452b11-13). Public deaths are not necessarily the same as deaths on stage. In Greek tragedy, the latter are *rarae aves*. Nonetheless, avoiding deaths on stage is not a rule but a convention, and it entails "the act that causes death" (Sommerstein, 2010, p. 33), rather than the actual death. In fact, death on stage occurs twice in the extant corpus of Greek tragedy (Euripides' *Alcestis* and *Hippolytus*). In this sense, ps.-Euripides' treatment agrees with the convention within Greek theater: he does not stage the beheading, i.e., the action that caused Dolon's death.

> Ἦ, καὶ ὃ μέν μιν ἔμελλε γενείου χειρὶ παχείῃ
> ἁψάμενος λίσσεσθαι, ὃ δ' **αὐχένα μέσσον ἔλασσε**
> **φασγάνῳ ἀΐξας, ἀπὸ δ' ἄμφω κέρσε τένοντε·**
> φθεγγομένου δ' ἄρα τοῦ γε κάρη κονίῃσιν ἐμίχθη.
>
> And he [sc. Dolon] was about to beg him by touching his chin with his stout hand, but having thrust at him, he [sc. Diomedes] **struck him in the middle of the neck with his sword, and severed both of his arteries,** and immediately, the head of the one still speaking mingled with the dust.
>
> (*Il.* 10.454-457)

---

115 On ignoring Dolon's death, Liapis (2012): "More importantly perhaps, the *Rh.* author takes care to refer to Dolon's eventual murder only in the vaguest terms (525-6, 557-8, 863-5 nn.) – whereas in the *Doloneia* the slaughter is described with gruesome detail (*Il.* 10.454-9)" (p. xlix); and Fries (2014): "Their entry dialogue (565-94) contains several allusions to the spy's interception and death (*Il.* 10.339-468), which allow the audience to reconstruct his fate" (p. 9).

116 I follow the Greek text by Halliwell (Aristotle; Longinus; Demetrius, 1995). The translations are my own.

πῶς δ’ οὐ δέδρακας; οὐ **κτανόντε** ναυστάθμων
κατάσκοπον **Δόλωνα** σῴζομεν τάδε
σκυλεύματ’; ἢ πᾶν στρατόπεδον πέρσειν δοκεῖς;

How have you done nothing? **Having killed Dolon**, the spy of the roadstead, are we not keeping these spoils? Are you expecting to ravage the whole camp?

(*Rhes*. 591-593)

Likewise, the number of Thracian deaths is not specified by the playwright. Even though book 10 specifies twice that the thirteen dead men are a combination of twelve plus one (*Il*. 10.487-496 and *Il*. 10.560-561), the *Rhes*. ignores the number of casualties.[117] The total of thirteen is obtained, first, by adding up the twelve Thracian warriors and Rhesus himself; and then, by considering the twelve Thracian warriors alongside Dolon. In the play, besides that of Dolon, only the death of Rhesus is mentioned. Once again, the convention within Greek theater is followed: the dramatist does not stage the action that caused Rhesus’ death.

ὣς μὲν Θρήικας ἄνδρας ἐπῴχετο Τυδέος υἱὸς,
ὄφρα δυώδεκ’ ἔπεφνεν…

…so, the son of Tydeus attacked the Thracian warriors, **until he killed twelve**.

(*Il*. 10.487-488)

ἀλλ’ ὅτε δὴ βασιλῆα κιχήσατο Τυδέος υἱός,
τὸν τρισκαιδέκατον μελιηδέα θυμὸν ἀπηύρα
ἀσθμαίνοντα…

But when the son of Tydeus approached the king, **he took the honey-sweet life of the thirteenth one** [sc. Rhesus], who was left gasping for breath…

(*Il*. 10.494-496)

…πὰρ δ’ ἑτάρους δυοκαίδεκα πάντας ἀρίστους.
τὸν τρισκαιδέκατον σκοπὸν εἵλομεν ἐγγύθι νηῶν,

117 On ignoring the number of casualties, see Fantuzzi (2020): “At *Il*. 10.495 Homer speaks of twelve Thracians plus Rhesus killed by Diomedes; *Rh*. does not give figures” (p. 49, n. 155).

> ...in addition to all twelve of his best companions. **We killed, as a thirteenth one, the spy** [sc. Dolon] **by the ships.**
>
> (*Il.* 10.560-561)

> **κεῖται** γὰρ ἡμῖν Θρῄκιος στρατηλάτης,
>
> The Thracian general [sc. Rhesus] **lies dead** before us...
>
> (*Rhes.* 670)

Give Me Five! – Villages or Nights?

Book 4 of the *Mahābhārata* is composed of four minor books, and in its compactness, it manages to encompass most of the main themes of the entire text. Minor book 45 begins with the return of the fire-drilling woods that were stollen at the end of the forest adventures. During their year incognito, Yudhiṣṭhira disguises himself as the gamester Kaṅka; Bhīma, as the cook Ballava, who also plays the part of a gladiator; Arjuna, as the eunuch Bṛhannaḍā, who works as a teacher of music and dance; Nakula, as the horse groom Granthika; Sahadeva, as the cattle tender Tantipāla; and Draupadī, as the maid Sairandhrī.

Minor book 46 depicts a new humiliation of Draupadī, which recalls the one from the assembly hall at Hāstinapura: Kīcaka, king Virāṭa's general, upon Draupadī's rejection of him, grabs her by the hair, throws her on the floor, and even kicks her. In revenge, Bhīma tricks Kīcaka in the dance pavilion, and then kills him, along with one hundred and five of his kinsmen. Minor book 47 presents a two-fold ambush: the Trigarta king Suśarman marches against the Matsya king Virāṭa; the Kaurava prince Duryodhana, against the Matsya prince Uttara. After a battle foreshadowing the one that will take place in Kurukṣetra, minor book 48 closes with the wedding of Arjuna's son, Abhimanyu, and Virāṭa's daughter, Uttarā. Their grandson Janamejaya will be the one listening to the *Mahābhārata.*

The ambushes upon Virāṭa and Uttara (*MBh.* 4.24-62) narrate Suśarman's and Duryodhana's *gograhaṇa* (cattle raid). The epic version is as follows: at Hāstinapura, Duryodhana hears from his spies the bad news that the Pāṇḍavas are nowhere to be found, and the good news that Kīcaka and his kinsmen have been slain by *gandharvas* (celestial musicians). Aware of the little time left before the concealment will be over, Duryodhana only focuses on the downside. He receives counsel, not only from Karṇa, Duḥśāsana, and Kṛpa, but also from Droṇa and Bhīṣma, who encourage Duryodhana to keep on looking for his cousins. It is up to king Suśarman to turn Duryodhana's attention towards the slain general, and to suggest the opportunity of an ambush against the country of king Virāṭa. Duryodhana adds a twist: undercover, Suśarman and the Trigartas should march there first, and on the next day, he and the Kauravas should join them to finish the job.

By now, the time of the covenant has nearly expired. In the Matsya kingdom, a herdsman travels from the country to the city to warn Virāṭa that the Trigartas are raiding his cattle. Virāṭa prepares to fight and asks Yudhiṣṭhira, Bhīma, Nakula, and Sahadeva to ride with him. The journey back from the city to the country explains their late arrival, after sunset. Then, the Matsyas and the Trigartas fight at night, and darkness makes it harder to distinguish their enemies. The casualties are countless. When the moon finally offers a glimmer, Suśarman and his brother, having dismounted their chariot, kill Virāṭa's horses and guards, and then proceed to lift Virāṭa himself, as if he were a bride. Seeing this, Yudhiṣṭhira instructs Bhīma to intervene, but without blowing their cover. At this point, the tables turn: Bhīma, having killed Suśarman's horses and guards, dismounts his own chariot, and then goes on to catch the fleeing Suśarman. The role reversal is clear. The cattle are safe.

While Virāṭa goes to the country to resist Suśarman's ambush, Duryodhana comes to the city commanding a second ambush. As with Virāṭa, a herdsman warns Uttara that the Kauravas are raiding his father's cattle. However, unlike Virāṭa, Uttara is not ready to fight since he is missing a charioteer. Unhappy about Uttara having compared himself to Arjuna, Draupadī suggests precisely the one Pāṇḍava who remains at the city. Uttara's sister, Uttarā, fetches him. Arjuna pretends to be unfit, but eventually he departs, promising the young girls to bring back, as spoils, clothes for their dolls. Uttara goes from boastful to panicked in the blink of an eye. The scene is yet another role reversal of Virāṭa's manhandling: Arjuna, having dismounted the chariot, must lift Uttara while he flees. Moreover, the image of Arjuna comforting Uttara foreshadows that of Arjuna himself being reassured by Kṛṣṇa later, during the *Gītā*.[118]

The main result of the ambushes is the recognition of the Pāṇḍavas. Having gone for their weapons that were hidden in a tree, Arjuna reveals his and his brothers' identities to Uttara, and, as proof, he proceeds to explain his ten names. Droṇa recognizes Arjuna by the sound of his conch, and Duryodhana celebrates the finding, taking it to mean a new exile for the Pāṇḍavas. Karṇa is ready to fight, and so is Kṛpa, although the latter wonders if the ambush might have been a mistake. Even Aśvatthāman, the protagonist of the text's better known *sauptika* (ambush), questions whether there should be any pride in raiding. In response to Duryodhana's question, Bhīṣma carries out the official counting, and he concludes that the due time has passed. Arjuna leads Uttara through the battlefield by pointing out to him the chief warriors on the Kaurava side. To the delight of the gods and the great seers, Arjuna vanquishes Kṛpa, Droṇa, Aśvatthāman, Karṇa, Bhīṣma, and Duryodhana. Once again, this prefigures the battle of Kurukṣetra. With his conch, Arjuna stuns everyone but Bhīṣma. Then, he instructs Uttara to gather the fallen warriors' clothes, and the herdsmen to collect the cattle and rest the horses.

After the ambushes comes the Pāṇḍavas' and Draupadī's reinstatement (*MBh.* 4.63-67), signaled by Abhimanyu's and Uttarā's wedding (*vaivāhika*). By the time Virāṭa returns to the city, Uttara is now gone. Upon finding out about the successful repelling of the second ambush, Virāṭa becomes proud: he commands a pompous reception for his son, and he orders Yudhiṣṭhira to play a celebratory dicing-match with him, which recalls the one at Hāstinapura. During the game, Virāṭa boasts that Uttara alone is responsible for the victory, while Yudhiṣṭhira insists that it would not have been possible without Arjuna. Virāṭa becomes angry and throws a die at Yudhiṣṭhira's face. To prevent Arjuna from killing Virāṭa, Yudhiṣṭhira catches the spilling blood with his hand before

118 On the parallelisms between the *Virāṭaparvan* and the *Bhagavadgītā*, see Hejib & Young (1980).

it reaches the floor, and he instructs the steward to let Uttara enter the assembly hall alone.

The revelation of the identities continues gradually. On the day of the second ambush, Uttara credits the triumph to the son of a god, so that Arjuna is still in disguise when he presents Uttarā with the plundered clothes. On the third day thereafter, the Pāṇḍavas enter Virāṭa's assembly hall and sit on his thrones. When Virāṭa asks about this behavior, Arjuna first reveals Yudhiṣṭhira's identity, and then those of Draupadī and the remaining Pāṇḍavas, including his own. Only then does Uttara admit that it was Arjuna who vanquished the Kauravas. Having become aware that it was Bhīma who rescued him, and that it was Yudhiṣṭhira whom he offended, Virāṭa offers Uttarā in marriage to Arjuna, who, in turn, accepts her for Abhimanyu. Arjuna sees her more like a daughter, and this is what ensures her chastity. For the ceremony, the Pāṇḍavas move to Upaplavya, where they will conduct the embassies; Arjuna brings Abhimanyu, who had been staying with Kṛṣṇa at Ānarta; and noblemen attend from all over the world.

In (Ps.-)Bhāsa's *The Five Nights*, the plot is divided into three acts, which move the action from Hāstinapura, where king Duryodhana is performing a sacrifice, to the Matsya kingdom, towards where he is leading a cattle raid, and again back to Hāstinapura, where Abhimanyu brings the news about the wedding. Before the first act come two sections: one is a prologue, which, by means of paronomasia, serves both to invoke the god Viṣṇu and to introduce the main characters of the plot; the other is a prelude, in which a conversation between three Brahmans sets the stage at the time of the sacrifice.

At the beginning of the first act, the preceptor Droṇa and the grandfather Bhīṣma speak about a law-abiding Duryodhana, thus setting the expectations of the audience. Then, the words coming from others make room for the deeds being performed by Duryodhana himself, when he discusses the subtleties of duty with his friend Karṇa and his maternal uncle Śakuni. Following the sacrifice, Śakuni proposes that Duryodhana carry out a royal consecration. After all, the kings are already there. Duryodhana greets all who have gathered for him, and he notices the absence of king Virāṭa. Śakuni sends a messenger to make inquiries. Then, Duryodhana brings up the matter of the graduation fee that is due to Droṇa, and, out of the blue, Droṇa expresses his intention to make a request.

In a tricky way, Droṇa pretends to cry, so that Duryodhana sees to him being brought some water. It is only after the promise has been made binding by the water that Droṇa finally reveals what he wants: Duryodhana must share the kingdom with the Pāṇḍavas. Undecided, Duryodhana turns to Śakuni and Karṇa for advice. The former pushes for a negative response, and the latter leaves the choice up to Duryodhana, not without reminding him that he is always to be counted on in times of war. Against their advice, Duryodhana intends to be true to his word by giving them a second-rate part of the realm. However, Śakuni also has a trick up his sleeve. For the agreement to take effect, news of the Pāṇḍavas must be brought to them within the next "five nights".

At this point, the messenger that Śakuni had sent to inquire about Virāṭa comes back and tells the Kauravas about the death of general Kīcaka and his kinsmen. When listening to the details of their deaths, Bhīṣma recognizes the work of the hero Bhīma, and he reveals this relevant information to Droṇa. With this unexpected turn of events, Droṇa no longer has a problem agreeing with the condition set by Śakuni. Joining in with the trickery, Bhīṣma pretends to have a feud with Virāṭa, which, on one hand, would account for Virāṭa being absent during the sacrifice, and on the other, would merit Duryodhana leading a cattle raid to remind him who is in charge. Once again, Bhīṣma reveals his true intentions to Droṇa. As soon as the Pāṇḍavas become aware of the ambush, they will take part in the defense, thus rendering themselves easily recognizable.

The second act focuses on the attack. In an interlude, an old cowherd lets slip the fact that, on that very day, Virāṭa is celebrating his birthday, which is the reason why there are currently so many cattle in the city. After that, as if playing the game of telephone, the old cowherd tells a soldier about the seizing, then, the soldier tells a chamberlain, and, although reluctant to importune the man of the hour, the chamberlain eventually tells Virāṭa. Piece by piece, Virāṭa begins to put together the picture of what is happening. First, he learns from the soldier that Duryodhana is the one responsible. Then, after he has turned to Yudhiṣṭhira in the guise of the Brahman Bhagavān for backup, Virāṭa learns from an attendant that other kings are marching alongside Duryodhana. Lastly, he learns from his own charioteer that his vehicle is no longer available, since his son, prince Uttara, has taken it to battle, with the aid of Arjuna in the guise of the eunuch Bṛhannalā.

For the remainder, it is the soldier who travels back and forth to continue with the narration. First, he informs that the chariot on which Uttara and Arjuna were riding has been smashed by a burial ground, which makes Yudhiṣṭhira rejoice, and in turn, Virāṭa gets angry at him. Then, the soldier communicates that most of the raiders have been defeated, but the young Abhimanyu is still standing, which makes Yudhiṣṭhira worry. After that, he reports that the menace is over, which immediately leads Virāṭa to credit Uttara. At this point, Arjuna enters the stage, evincing some difficulty in handling the weapons. Arjuna being present, the soldier further conveys that Abhimanyu has been taken captive by Bhīma, who is in the guise of a cook. And then, Bhīma also enters the stage and justifies the capture as the lesser of two evils.

Both Bhīma and Arjuna take pleasure in taunting Abhimanyu, who still manages to adhere to rightfulness on every occasion. After a while, Uttara also returns, and this accelerates the anagnorises. Uttara points to the scar on the arm of Arjuna, and thus, Arjuna is recognized; then, Arjuna himself reveals the identities of Bhīma and Yudhiṣṭhira. Father and son come together in an embrace. However, there is still something that troubles Virāṭa: Arjuna has been living under the same roof as his unmarried daughter Uttarā. Faced with such a conundrum, Virāṭa offers Uttarā in marriage to Arjuna, who accepts her as a suitable wife for his own son Abhimanyu. Having a three for one on rites, the marriage is to take place on the same day that begun with a sacrifice and witnessed a birthday celebration.

At the beginning of the third and last act, a charioteer explains to the stunned Kauravas how Abhimanyu was taken from his chariot by a foot soldier, who was just using his bare hands. Once again, Bhīṣma recognizes the work of Bhīma, and this time, Droṇa reaches the same conclusion all by himself. Nonetheless, Śakuni is far from convinced, even when the charioteer introduces, as an exhibit, an arrow signed by Arjuna. It is only when Uttara arrives as a messenger, not of Virāṭa but of Yudhiṣṭhira, that Duryodhana agrees to honor his deal. What happens next? Was there no war of Kurukṣetra or did the Kauravas, as they tend to do, manage to foul things up anyway? The playwright is smart enough to leave the story open-ended.

In the dramatic version, the author profits, among others, from these nine procedures: [SA1][119] he merges two ambushes into one, [SA2] he merges two addressees into one, [SA3] he adds a tricky request, [SA4] he emphasizes the braggart, [SA5] he emphasizes the adaptation's sources, [SA6] he adds the anagnorisis, [SA7] he changes the timing of the sacrifice, [SA8] he changes the five villages into the five nights, and [SA9] he ignores the on-stage anger.

[SA1] Just like his treatment of the speeches towards father and son in *The Embassy*, his re-creation of Suśarman's and Duryodhana's ambushes as Duryodhana's ambush in *The Five Nights* evinces merging as one of (Ps.-)Bhāsa's trademark adaptation techniques.[120]

119 SA stands for "Sanskrit Ambush". Hence, numbers SA1-SA9 refer to the adaptation of *MBh.* 4 into *The Five Nights*. Besides those that will allow me to argue for parallelisms with the Greco-Roman world, other adaptation techniques include merging Yudhiṣṭhira's and Duryodhana's character into Duryodhana's character, splitting Duryodhana's character into Duryodhana's, Karṇa's, and Śakuni's characters, changing the genealogy, ignoring the news about the Pāṇḍavas, adding Virāṭa's birthday celebration, merging four of the five brothers into one, changing Bhīṣma's assertion into Yudhiṣṭhira's conjecture, changing Uttara's cry for help into Uttara's resoluteness, changing Uttara's visual scrutiny into Virāṭa's multisensory scrutiny, adding Arjuna's forgetfulness, changing the pretend failure in arming into an actual failure in arming, emphasizing the name *Vijaya*, ignoring the name *Kaṅka*, changing Abhimanyu to the Kaurava side, changing Arjuna's lifting of Uttara into Bhīma's lifting of Abhimanyu, emphasizing Abhimanyu's role, changing the timing of the Pāṇḍavas' recognition, emphasizing Arjuna's link to Śiva, and subtracting the taking of the spoils after the battle.

120 On merging two ambushes into one, see Steiner (2010): "Im Virāṭaparvan (Adhyāya 30-62) ist der Kampf um die Kühe ausführlicher gestaltet mit mehreren Angriffen und Gegenagriffen. Im Stück wird dies zu nur einem indirekt beschriebenen Angriff unter Bhīṣmas Führung zusammengefasst – und dessen letzlich erfolgreicher Abwehr durch den als Bṛhannalā verkleideten Arjuna [In the *Virāṭaparvan* (*Adhyāya* 30-62) the fight for the cows is more detailed with several attacks and counterattacks. In the play, this is summarized in only one indirectly described attack under Bhīṣma's leadership – and its ultimately successful defense by Arjuna disguised as Bṛhannalā]" (p. 157).

Vyāsa presents two different herdsmen, carrying two separate messages: one to Virāṭa, about Suśarman's ambush; the other to Uttara, about Duryodhana's ambush. But at the same time, he intends for them to be taken in tandem. The assertion about the hundreds of thousands of cattle being raided by the Trigartas is clearly mirrored by the one about the sixty thousand cattle being raided by the Kauravas. Perceptive as always, the playwright reinterprets the parallelism as a merging: as in the epic's first ambush, the message's addressee is Virāṭa; as in the epic's second ambush, the message's subject is the Kauravas.

> asmān yudhi vinirjitya paribhūya sabāndhavān |
> **gavāṃ śatasahasrāṇi trigartāḥ kālayanti te** |
> tān parīpsa manuṣyendra mā neśuḥ paśavas tava ||
>
> Having defeated us in a fight and subdued our relatives, **the Trigartas are taking hundreds of thousands of cattle from you**. O best of men, try and protect them – may your cattle not be lost!
>
> (*MBh.* 4.30.7)

> **ṣaṣṭiṃ gavāṃ sahasrāṇi kuravaḥ kālayanti te** |
> tad vijetuṃ samuttiṣṭha godhanaṃ rāṣṭravardhanam ||
> rājaputra hitaprepsuḥ kṣipraṃ niryāhi vai svayam |
> tvāṃ hi matsyo mahīpālaḥ śūnyapālam ihākarot ||
>
> **The Kurus are taking sixty-thousand cattle from you**. Stand up to recover the cattle herd, the prosperity of the kingdom. O prince, desirous of your own benefit, go out quickly, for the Matsya king made you keeper of his empty kingdom.
>
> (*MBh.* 4.33.10-11)

> bho bho nivedyatāṃ nivedyatāṃ mahārājāya virāṭeśvarāya **etā** hi dasyukarmapracchannavikramair **dhārtarāṣṭrair hriyante gāva** iti
>
> Hey, hey! Let it be made known, let it be made known to the great king, to lord Virāṭa, that **the sons of Dhṛtarāṣṭra**, their prowess hidden by the deeds of robbers, **are seizing these cattle**.
>
> (*PR* 2.0.42)

[SA2] (Ps.-)Bhāsa also merges the father and the son into a single character. If *The Embassy* evinces a partial merging of Dhṛtarāṣṭra and Duryodhana, where the old king is still allowed a few words of his own, *The Five Nights* accomplishes a total merging. In *MBh.* 4, even though Dhṛtarāṣṭra plays no role during the ambushes, Duryodhana is still introduced, since the beginning and throughout the *Gograhaṇaparvan*, as "Dhṛtarāṣṭra's son" (*dhṛtarāṣṭraja-*, *MBh.* 4.27.7b; *dhṛtarāṣṭrātmaja-*, *MBh.* 4.50.12c; *dhṛtarāṣṭraputra-*, *MBh.* 4.60.1b; and *dhṛtarāṣṭrasya putraḥ*, *MBh.* 4.61.1b). In *PR*, Dhṛtarāṣṭra has been reduced to a patronymic, used not specifically for Duryodhana, but for the collective of the Kauravas (*dhārtarāṣṭra-*, *PR* 2.0.42, *PR* 2.1.2, *PR* 2.8.3, *PR* 2.15c, *PR* 2.20c, and *PR* 2.27.9).

Moreover, the dramatic Duryodhana sometimes speaks as if he were the epic Dhṛtarāṣṭra. A case in point is the offering of half of the kingdom. Vyāsa has Dhṛtarāṣṭra as the first one to suggest, as a sort of preamble to their thirteen-year exile, that the Pāṇḍavas take the Khāṇḍava tract, which constitutes half of the kingdom. On the contrary, (Ps.-)Bhāsa has Duryodhana suggest half of the kingdom, and then, propose it to be a bad, unendurable, and unfriendly country, that is, something like the Khāṇḍava tract. At *MBh.* 5, where Duryodhana is presented by Kṛṣṇa with a similar offer (*MBh.* 5.122.57-61), he responds with the categorical rejection of even what could be pierced with a needle (*MBh.* 5.125.26a-b). Here, Duryodhana is the one bringing it up, and Śakuni is the one turning it down, also in similar terms: "I will say 'nothing!' [*śūnyam ity abhidhāsyāmi*]" (*PR* 1.44a). Having Śakuni as his dramatic understudy, allows Duryodhana to fill in for the epic Dhṛtarāṣṭra.

> **ardhaṃ rājyasya** saṃprāpya khāṇḍavaprastham āviśa | |
>
> Partaking of **half the kingdom**, take possession of the Khāṇḍava tract.
>
> (*MBh.* 1.199.25e-f)
>
> mātula pāṇḍavānāṃ **rājyārdhaṃ** prati ko niścayaḥ
>
> O uncle, what is your opinion about the Pāṇḍavas having **half the kingdom**?
>
> (*PR* 1.42.4)

mātula **balavat** praty **amitro 'nupajīvyaś** ca kaścit **kudeśaś** cintyatām
tatra vaseyuḥ pāṇḍavāḥ

O uncle, think of some **bad country, unendurable** and **extremely unfriendly**. Let the Pāṇḍavas live there!

(*PR* 1.43.1-2)

[SA3] Droṇa's graduation fee is an addition. In this sense, the *Saṃbhavaparvan* (*MBh.* 1.59-123) is mined for adapted elements. There, one finds the story of Ekalavya (*MBh.* 1.123.10-39), which seems to have been adapted into *The Five Nights* in the form of Droṇa's graduation fee. Ekalavya wants to be Droṇa's pupil, but Droṇa rejects him for being the son of a Niṣāda. After touching the master's feet, Ekalavya retires to the forest and fashions a clay statue of Droṇa, under whom he studies. Thanks to a dog, the Pāṇḍavas come across the outstanding archer, who introduces himself as Droṇa's pupil, and filled with jealousy, Arjuna reminds Droṇa of his promise of a privileged position among his students. Without further clarification, Droṇa asks Ekalavya for a fee, to which Ekalavya agrees, only to later find out that what Droṇa wants for a *dakṣiṇā-* "graduation fee" is his *dakṣiṇa-* "right one", in reference to his thumb. At the cost of renouncing archery, Ekalavya pays the fee and cuts off his thumb.

In the play, in lieu of Droṇa asking, it is Duryodhana who offers him a "graduation fee [*dakṣiṇā*]" (*PR* 1.27.14), without saying what it will be. Then, Droṇa pretends to cry, and Duryodhana fetches him some "water [*āpas*]" (*PR* 1.29.8), which serves to seal the deal before even agreeing to the terms. The dramatic Droṇa's request is for the Pāṇḍavas to recover their share of the kingdom. In support of the claim that it is the epic Droṇa's petition to Ekalavya which is adapted here, it is worth remembering that, in the outer "circle of promises" around Ekalavya's thumb, there is Drupada's promise of sharing his kingdom with Droṇa himself, which is fulfilled by Droṇa receiving half of Drupada's land.[121]

121 On the "circle of promises" and the *Ringkomposition* in the story of Ekalavya, see Brodbeck (2006, especially p. 4, diagram 1).

> tato droṇo 'bravīd rājann ekalavyam idaṃ vacaḥ |
> yadi śiṣyo 'si me tūrṇaṃ **vetanaṃ** saṃpradīyatām | |
> ekalavyas tu tac chrutvā prīyamāṇo 'bravīd idam |
> kiṃ prayacchāmi bhagavann ājñāpayatu māṃ guruḥ | |
> na hi kiṃ cid adeyaṃ me gurave brahmavittama |
> tam abravīt tvayāṅguṣṭho **dakṣiṇo** dīyatāṃ mama | |
>
> O king, then Droṇa gave this order to Ekalavya, "If you are my student, quickly give me my **fee**!" Having heard that, Ekalavya said this, propitiating him, "O fortunate one, what can I give you? Let my teacher command me. O expert on the absolute, there is nothing that I shall not give to my teacher." He told him, "Give me your **right** thumb!"
>
> (*MBh.* 1.123.33-35)
>
> yeṣāṃ gatiḥ kvāpi nirāśrayāṇāṃ
> saṃvatsarair dvādaśabhir na dṛṣṭā |
> tvaṃ pāṇḍavānāṃ kuru saṃvibhāgam
> eṣā ca bhikṣā mama **dakṣiṇā** ca | |
>
> Execute the distribution with the Pāṇḍavas, the destitute ones who have had no visible means for twelve years. This boon will be my **fee**.
>
> (*PR* 1.31)

[SA4] (Ps.-)Bhāsa turns Uttara's braggartry into Virāṭa's braggartry. *MBh.* 4's Uttara is a *miles gloriosus* (braggart warrior).[122] *PR*'s Virāṭa, in turn, is a bragging father. Vyāsa paints the braggartry from the point of view of both Arjuna and Uttara himself. Like a true *katthano bhaṭaḥ* "braggart warrior", Uttara boasts about the greatness of his flag, the number of enemies that he could face, his ability to conquer the entire Kaurava troop, his capacity for terrifying their best warriors, and his resemblance to Indra and to Arjuna himself. Near the end of this nonsensical crescendo, he even trumpets his own prowess. However, his behavior at the battlefront is quite different. Arjuna, who has witnessed Uttara's boastful assertion of his supposed manliness, eventually questions

122 On Uttara as a *miles gloriosus*, see Wulff Alonso (2020): "Prince Uttara is an invention, a foil character of Arjuna. He is, at the same time, a quite typical Greco-Latin *miles gloriosus*, a braggart warrior, who ends up becoming the eunuch Arjuna's charioteer, squire and the herald of his glories" (p. 178).

it when Uttara trembles at the mere thought of fighting. The oxymoronic contrast between the epic Uttara's words and his deeds, evinces this character's comicality: he is the one who ends up belittled and terrified, looking less like a god or a hero, and more like an abducted bride. So much for his prowess.

The dramatic braggartry, on the contrary, is considered from the point of view of both Uttara himself and his father Virāṭa. According to the bragging father, one man is enough for defeating an entire army and one day suffices for Uttara to wrap up the whole ambush. But unlike Arjuna, Virāṭa is biased in favor of his son Uttara, and more importantly, unlike Arjuna, Virāṭa did not witness Uttara's deeds, but only learned about them from the Soldier's speech. If the epic source was consistent in presenting Uttara's boastfulness in terms of both his own deeds and other people's opinions about them, the dramatic adaptation separates a boastful Uttara, as borrowed from the canonic text, and as characterized by Virāṭa, on one side, and a moderate Uttara, recast by the new text, and described by himself, on the other. The dramatic Uttara, when reflecting about his situation, is aware that the report about him is specious, and he even feels ashamed about it. Uttara is just paying lip service to Arjuna, as is (Ps.-)Bhāsa to Vyāsa.

> sa labheyaṃ yadi tv anyaṃ hayayānavidaṃ naram |
> tvarāvān adya yātvāhaṃ samucchrita**mahā**dhvajam ||
> vigāhya tatparānīkaṃ gajavājiratha**ākulam** |
> śastrapratāpanirvīryān kurūñ **jitvā**naye paśūn ||
> duryodhanaṃ śāṃtanavaṃ karṇaṃ vaikartanaṃ kṛpam |
> droṇaṃ ca saha putreṇa maheṣvāsān samāgatān ||
> **vitrāsayitvā** saṃgrāme dānavān **iva vajrabhṛt** |
> anenaiva muhūrtena punaḥ pratyānaye paśūn ||
> śūnyam āsādya kuravaḥ prayānty ādāya godhanam |
> kiṃ nu śakyaṃ mayā kartuṃ yad ahaṃ tatra nābhavam ||
> paśyeyur adya **me vīryaṃ** kuravas te samāgatāḥ |
> kiṃ nu **pārtho 'rjunaḥ sākṣād** ayam asmān prabādhate ||

> If I found another man who knows how to drive my horses, after marching swiftly with my **great** flag raised, plunging into the enemy army which would be **crowded** with elephants, horses, and chariots, and **conquering** the Kurus who would become unmanly against the power of my sword,

I would bring back the cattle. After **terrifying** Duryodhana, Śāṃtanava [sc. Bhīṣma], Karṇa Vaikartana, Kṛpa, Droṇa with his son, and the great warriors that have assembled in battle, **just as he who wields the thunderbolt** did against the Dānavas, I would bring back the cattle in an instant. Having found an empty place, the Kurus march after taking our cattle herd, but what can I do if I am not there? Today the assembled Kurus shall see **my prowess** and think that it is **the Pārtha Arjuna in the flesh** who torments them.

(*MBh.* 4.34.4-9)

tathā strīṣu pratiśrutya **pauruṣaṃ** puruṣeṣu ca |
katthamāno 'bhiniryāya kimarthaṃ na yuyutsase ||

Having thus asserted your **manliness** among men and women, and having marched out **while boasting**, why do you not want to fight?

(*MBh.* 4.36.20)

nṛpā bhīṣmādayo **bhagnāḥ** saubhadro grahaṇaṃ gataḥ |
uttareṇ**ādya** saṃkṣepād arthataḥ pṛthivī jitā ||

Kings such as Bhīṣma **have been defeated**, Subhadrā's son [sc. Abhimanyu] has walked right into his capture. In short, **today** Uttara has surely conquered the earth.

(*PR* 2.41)

mithyāpraśaṃsā khalu nāma kaṣṭā yeṣāṃ tu **mithyā**vacaneṣu bhaktiḥ |
ahaṃ hi yuddhāśrayam ucyamāno vācānuvartī hṛdayena **lajje** ||

Though there is devotion in their **false** words, their **false** praise is still wrong. I might be compliant with their words while being praised in relation to the battle, but in my heart I **am ashamed**.

(*PR* 2.60)

[SA5] The dramatist also includes Bhīṣma's feud with Virāṭa. In the narrative source, while Duryodhana is dwelling on the bad news about the Pāṇḍavas not having been found, Suśarman concentrates on the bigger picture and sells it as the glass being half full. His is the idea of an ambush and his is also the justification for undertaking it to get back at Virāṭa for a very real feud between them, which antedates the events of the *Virāṭaparvan*. (Ps.-)Bhāsa subtracts Suśarman. This means, on one hand, assigning the role of proponent of the ambush to someone else; and on the other, providing them with a plausible explanation for wanting to carry it out. Bhīṣma is cast in the role, and a fictional feud between him and Virāṭa is added to the mix.

A close reading reveals four occurrences of the compound *gograha(ṇa)-*, meaning "cattle raid", near the end of the first act (*PR* 1.52.3, *PR* 1.53d, *PR* 1.54b, and *PR* 1.55.3). This can be interpreted as the play announcing itself as an adaptation of the *Gograhaṇaparvan* from *MBh.* 4.

> **asakṛn** matsyarājñā **me rāṣṭraṃ bādhitam** ojasā |
> praṇetā kīcakaś cāsya balavān abhavat purā ||
> krūro 'marṣī sa duṣṭātmā bhuvi prakhyātavikramaḥ |
> nihatas tatra gandharvaiḥ pāpakarmā nṛśaṃsavān ||
> tasmiṃś ca nihate rājan hīnadarpo nirāśrayaḥ |
> bhaviṣyati nirutsāho virāṭa iti me matiḥ ||
> tatra **yātrā** mama matā yadi te rocate 'nagha |
> kauravāṇāṃ ca sarveṣāṃ karṇasya ca mahātmanaḥ ||
>
> The Matsya king **has repeatedly oppressed my kingdom** with his might. Before, his general was the powerful Kīcaka, cruel, intransigent, and evil-minded, but of known prowess throughout the earth. Then, the violent wrongdoer was killed by some gandharvas. O king, him being dead, it is my opinion that Virāṭa will be deprived of his pride, destitute, and dispirited. O faultless one, if it pleases you, I favor **an ambush** of all the Kauravas and the eminent Karṇa.
>
> (*MBh.* 4.29.4-7)

> pautra duryodhanāsti mama virāṭen**āprakāśaṃ vairam**
> atha bhavato yajñam anubhavitum anāgata iti
> tasmāt kriyatāṃ tasya **gograhaṇam**
>
> O grandson Duryodhana, I have **a secret feud** with Virāṭa, which is why he did not come to assist at your sacrifice. So, let there be **a cattle raid** against him!
>
> (*PR* 1.52.2-3)

[SA6] Regarding the emphasis on the anagnorisis, (Ps.-)Bhāsa splits the explanation for the scar.[123] In *MBh.* 4, Arjuna's scar is due to the bowstring slapping the interior of his forearm. In *PR*, there are two contrasting explanations. First, and in agreement with what the epic Arjuna says, the dramatic Uttara interprets the scar as coming from string slap, and he tries to present it as proof for convincing Virāṭa that Bṛhannalā is, in truth, Arjuna. Then, and as if arguing with his epic counterpart, the dramatic Arjuna clarifies that it has an altogether different origin. Just as archers get slapped by their bowstring, so too can eunuchs bear the marks of their trade: since they must wear bracelets, their forearms can become pale through lack of exposure to sunlight. To the untrained eye, a scarred forearm and one that is just pale would look very much alike, even though they are not so. Of course, the character is just being crafty, as is the playwright.

> pratijñāṃ ṣaṇḍhako 'smīti kariṣyāmi mahīpate |
> **jyāghātau** hi mahāntau me saṃvartuṃ nṛpa duṣkarau ||
> karṇayoḥ pratimucyāhaṃ kuṇḍale jvalanopame |
> veṇīkṛtaśirā rājan nāmnā caiva bṛhannaḍā ||
>
> O lord of the earth, I will vow that I am a eunuch. O lord of men, my great arms, **scarred by the bowstring**, are difficult to hide. O king, after putting fire-like earrings on my ears and having a braid done on my head, I will go by the name of Bṛhannaḍā.
>
> (*MBh.* 4.2.21-22)

> prakoṣṭhāntarasaṅgūḍhaṃ **gāṇḍīvajyāhataṃ kiṇam** |
> yat tad dvādaśavarṣānte naiva yāti savarṇatām ||
>
> The **scar**, which was **inflicted by the string of Gāṇḍīva** and remains hidden in the interior of his forearm, does not vanish, having the same appearance even at the end of the twelve years.
>
> (*PR* 2.63)

123 On splitting the explanation for the scar, see Hawley (2021): "He [sc. Arjuna] speaks of how he'll wear ornaments – which we later discover to be bangles, an image that the *Pañcarātra* will go on to spotlight – that cover the bowstring scars of his forearms" (p. 96), and "Arjuna's account of the scar – that it was created by his bracelets – recalls the reasoning that the *Virāṭaparvan*'s Arjuna uses to support his choice of custom" (p. 114).

etan me **pārihāryāṇāṃ vyāvartana**kṛtaṃ kiṇam |
sannirodhavivarṇatvād godhāsthānam ihāgatam | |

This scar of mine was produced **by me removing my bracelets**: it comes close to taking the place of the arm guard **because of the paleness caused by the confinement**.

(*PR* 2.64)

The name on the arrow is another addition related to the anagnorisis.[124] It constitutes a re-creation of a scene, not from the *Virāṭaparvan*, but from the *Bhīṣmaparvan* (*MBh.* 6). In *MBh.* 6, Bhīṣma recognizes Arjuna's arrows just by feeling them, whereas in *PR* he discerns Arjuna's arrow by looking at his signature, which needs no further deciphering. Bhīṣma has heard the message loud and clear.

kṛntanti mama gātrāṇi māghamāse gavām iva |
arjunasya ime **bāṇā** neme bāṇāḥ śikhaṇḍinaḥ | |

They **cut** my limbs just like someone cuts his cows from the herd during the month of Māgha: they must be **the arrows of Arjuna**, and not the arrows of Śikhaṇḍī.

(*MBh.* 6.114.60)

bāṇapuṅkhākṣarair vākyair jyājihvāparivartibhiḥ |
vikṛṣṭaṃ khalu pārthena na ca **śrotraṃ** prayacchati | |

By means of **words having their syllables in the feathers of his arrows** and being transmitted by the tongue of his bowstring, the Pārtha [sc. Arjuna] communicated with us, and this does not result in us **hearing** him?

(*PR* 3.17)

124 On the addition of the name on the arrow, see Steiner (2010): "In MBh 4.59 wird der Zweikampf zwischen Bṛhannalā und Bhīṣma geschildert, in dessen Verlauf beide gegenseitig ihre Standarte mit Pfeilen treffen. Im Pañcarātra wird ein auf Bhīṣmas Standarte geschossener Pfeil, auf dem Arjunas Name steht, für die Kauravas zum Hauptindiz für die Identifizierung Arjunas. Es wird dammit wohl auf MBh 6.114.55-60 (insbes. 60) angespielt, wo Bhīṣma für sich in Anspruch nimmt, die Pfeile Arjunas zu erkennen [In *MBh.* 4.59, the duel between Bṛhannalā and Bhīṣma is described, during which they both hit each other's banners with arrows. In *Pañcarātra*, an arrow shot at Bhīṣma's banner, with Arjuna's name on it, becomes the main indicator for the Kauravas for the identification of Arjuna. It is so alluded to in *MBh.* 6.114.55-60 (esp. 60), where Bhīṣma claims to recognize Arjuna's arrows]" (pp. 157-158).

However, the main emphasis of *PR* in terms of anagnorisis concerns Abhimanyu.[125] The epic showcases a gradual recognition of the Pāṇḍavas: prince Uttara learns about their true identities right before the second raid, but king Virāṭa is only let in on their secret three days thereafter. And the play turns it into an expeditious anagnorisis of the Pāṇḍavas: by featuring Abhimanyu in the ambush, on one hand, Uttara is not needed at the assembly hall until much later; and on the other, Arjuna gets to make himself known to someone closer to his heart. Father/son relations are, indeed, among (Ps.-)Bhāsa's favorite topics.[126] The change of Abhimanyu to the Kaurava side, the emphasis of his role, and the addition of his anagnorisis; they all come down to this.

That such father/son interactions bring out a man's true nature is an idea that Vyāsa had already developed, and he did so by focusing on none other than Arjuna. During the *Āśvamedhikaparvan* (*MBh.* 14), Arjuna, while securing the way for Yudhiṣṭhira's horse, comes across Babhruvāhana, his son born to Citrāṅgadā. Just as the epic Babhruvāhana is taunted by Arjuna, being paired up with women rather than with men, so too does the dramatic Abhimanyu interact with his father and uncles: he taunts them and gets taunted by them. The taunting is, in fact, what catalyzes the anagnorisis, here expressed in terms of making the son see who his father and uncles really are. Two sons, one encounter. Once again, the playwright is performing a merging.

Furthermore, anagnorisis is a very common procedure within Roman theater (Plautus, *Capt.* 872-874, *Cas.* 1012-1014, *Cist.* 664-665, *Curc.* 653-657, *Epid.* 635-636, *Men.* 1133, *Poen.* 1065-1075 and 1258, and *Rud.* 1160-1165; and Terence *An.* 904-956).[127] So, it could have been borrowed by Sanskrit theater ((Ps.-)Bhāsa *PR* 2 and *SV* 6; and Kālidāsa *Vikr.* 5 and *Śak.* 6).[128]

---

125 On the addition of Abhimanyu's anagnorisis, see Wulff Alonso (2020): "Third, the author has Arjuna's son, Abhimanyu, courageously fighting with the Kauravas, being captured by the Pāṇḍavas and carried to Virāṭa's court where he shows his dignity just before the corresponding discovery in terms of Aristotelian *anagnorisis* (See his *Poetics* 1452a)" (p. 239).

126 See Brückner (1999/2000, p. 502, n. 4).

127 See Vaccaro (1981/1983, pp. 88-89) and Ricottilli (2014, pp. 118-120).

128 See S. S. Dange (1994a). See also S. A. Dange (1994b), for the procedure of the "incognito heroine" in (Ps.-)Bhāsa *SV* 4, Kālidāsa *Śak.* 6, and Bhavabhūti

na tvayā **puruṣā**rthaś ca kaś cid astīha jīvatā |
yas tvaṃ **strī**vad yudhā prāptaṃ sāmnā māṃ pratyagṛhṇathāḥ | |

You live here but you have absolutely no ambition as **a man**! You are certainly like **a woman** in that you have received me only with conciliation when I came looking for a fight.

(*MBh.* 14.78.6)

na ruṣyanti mayā **kṣiptā** hasantaś ca **kṣipanti** mām |
diṣṭyā gograhaṇaṃ svantaṃ pitaro yena **darśitāḥ** | |

They, **taunted** by me, are not vexed; instead, they **taunt** me while laughing at me. Luckily, the cattle raid ends well, by **showing** me my father and uncles.

(*PR* 2.67)

[SA7] (Ps.-)Bhāsa changes the timing of Duryodhana's sacrifice. At the beginning of the *Gograhaṇaparvan*, Duryodhana is "in the middle of the assembly hall [*sabhāmadhye*]" (*MBh.* 4.24.8c), where he is visited by his spies; but, in the first act of *The Five Nights*, he arrives at a "forest [*vanaṃ*]" (*PR* 1.12b, *PR* 1.13a), where Brahmans are officiating at a sacrifice. Rather than a simple change of location, what is at play here is a change in timing: Duryodhana's sacrifice in the play seems to be an adaptation of his sacrifice during the *Ghoṣayātrāparvan* (*MBh.* 3.224-243) since both share some key elements: the officiating Brahmans (*MBh.* 3.241 ~ *PR* 1.2.2-18.5); the consecrated Duryodhana (*MBh.* 3.243 ~ *PR* 1.23.1); and the attending kings, marked by the significant absence of one of them (*MBh.* 3.242 ~ *PR* 1.27.2-13).

Furthermore, Duryodhana's sacrifice in *MBh.* 3 closes a minor book about a cattle raid against *gandharvas* (celestial musicians), which, in turn, has a lot in common with the cattle raids from *MBh.* 4: Dhṛtarāṣṭra/Duryodhana receives news about the Pāṇḍavas (*MBh.* 3.224 ~ *MBh.* 4.24), Karṇa urges Duryodhana (*MBh.* 3.226 ~ *MBh.* 4.25), the cattle raid is proposed by a complicit party (*MBh.* 3.227 ~ *MBh.* 4.29), Duryodhana reaches Dvaitavana/Matsya (*MBh.* 3.229 ~ *MBh.* 4.33), Citrasena/Arjuna fights back (*MBh.* 3.230 ~ *MBh.*

Uttar. 3.

4.41), and Duryodhana is defeated (*MBh.* 3.231 ~ *MBh.* 4.60). The thematic proximity of the cattle raids would account for the use of the sacrifice, and therefore, for the change in timing.

The epic sacrifice and the dramatic sacrifice, although correlated, are not mere images of each other. This is, precisely, the distinctive feature of any adaptation. A crucial change is that Duryodhana does not overreach for a royal consecration (*rājasūya*), and consequently, the Brahmans do not need to downsize it to a Vaiṣṇava sacrifice. The obstacle preventing a royal consecration, as per the source text, is the fact that both Yudhiṣṭhira and Dhṛtarāṣṭra are still alive. In the play, Yudhiṣṭhira's exile seems to suffice for counting him out of the running, and Dhṛtarāṣṭra is not even listed as one of the *dramatis personae*. Besides having his potential competitors out of the picture, the dramatic Duryodhana meets the criterion of being a good person, which is probably the reason why even his subordinates exhibit a friendly disposition towards him and the ceremony.

> tatra **yajño** nṛpaśreṣṭha prabhūtānnaḥ susaṃskṛtaḥ |
> pravartatāṃ yathānyāyaṃ sarvato hy anivāritaḥ | |
> eṣa te **vaiṣṇavo nāma yajñaḥ** satpuruṣocitaḥ |
> etena neṣṭavān kaś cid ṛte viṣṇuṃ purātanam | |
>
> O best of the kings, let **a sacrifice** according to the rules begin, with sufficient food, well prepared, unobstructed in every direction. This **sacrifice** of yours, **called Vaiṣṇava**, is appropriate for good men; no one besides Viṣṇu has sacrificed with it before.
>
> (*MBh.* 3.241.31-32)
>
> sarvair antaḥpuraiḥ sārdhaṃ prītyā prāpteṣu rājasu |
> **yajño** duryodhanasyaiṣa kururājasya vartate | |
>
> Once the kings joyfully arrive, along with all their queens, this **sacrifice** of the Kaurava king Duryodhana will proceed.
>
> (*PR* 1.2)

[SA8] Regarding the play's title, I suggest that the author changes the five villages from the *MBh.* into the five nights of the *PR*. In other words, although present in the form of a Vaiṣṇava sacrifice, the religious component would not have been the sole determinant for the title *The Five Nights*.[129] There might have been a literary component to it too. In *MBh*. 5, during Saṃjaya's embassy (*MBh*. 5.22-32), Yudhiṣṭhira sends Duryodhana the message that five villages, one for each of the five Pāṇḍava brothers, would end the quarrel once and for all.[130] The number five could be an adapted element coming from this recurring request.

> **bhrātṝṇāṃ** dehi **pañcānāṃ grāmān pañca** suyodhana |
>
> O Suyodhana, give **five villages to the five brothers**!
>
> (*MBh*. 5.31.20a-b)

> yadi **pañcarātreṇa pāṇḍavānāṃ** pravṛttir upanetavyā rājyasyārdhaṃ pradāsyati kila
>
> If someone brings him news **of the Pāṇḍavas within five nights**, he will accordingly give up half the kingdom.
>
> (*PR* 1.45.7)

[SA9] The author ignores Virāṭa's anger. According to Bharata,[131] violence and death on stage are to be avoided, specially in the acts: "**Anger**, favor, and grief, the pronouncing of a curse, withdrawal and marriage, the vision of a wonderful birth, all of them should not be made visible in an act [***krodha****prasādaśokāḥ śāpotsargo 'tha vidravodvāhau | adbhutasambhavadarśanam aṅke 'pratyakṣajāni syuḥ*]" (*Nāṭyaś*. 18.20), and "A battle, a kingdom's loss, **a death**, and a city's siege, should not be visible in an act, but contrived through interludes [*yuddhaṃ rājyabhraṃśo* ***maraṇaṃ*** *nagaroparodhanaṃ*

129 On the dramatic sacrifice as a *vaiṣṇavayajña* (Vaiṣṇava sacrifice) and the explanation of the title in relation to the religious movement of Pāñcarātra (Hindu tradition of Vaiṣṇava worship), see Steiner (2010, especially p. 163 ff.). Cf. Tieken's (1997) proposal about the dramatic sacrifice as a *rājasūya* (royal consecration) and the explanation of the title in relation to a *kṣatrasya dhṛti* (wielding of power): "This period of five days has evidently been grafted on the *kṣatrasya dhṛti*, a five-day sacrifice, which functions as a kind of interlude between the completed *rājasūya* and the next one, that is, in case a competitor shows up" (p. 23).

130 Yudhiṣṭhira's offer is later mentioned by Duryodhana (*MBh*. 5.54.29), Yudhiṣṭhira again (*MBh*. 5.70.14-16), Draupadī (*MBh*. 5.80.6-8), Vidura (*MBh*. 5.85.9), and Kṛṣṇa (*MBh*. 5.148.14-16). See Brodbeck (2020, p. 337).

131 I follow the Sanskrit text by the Göttingen Register of Electronic Texts in Indian Languages (2020). The translations are my own.

caiva | pratyakṣāṇi tu nāṅke praveśakaiḥ saṃvidheyāni]" (*Nāṭyaś.* 18.38).

In clear contrast with the narrative, which is full of gruesome bloodshed (e.g., *MBh.* 4.31.14, *MBh.* 4.56.6, *MBh.* 4.57.17-18, *MBh.* 4.60.4, *MBh.* 4.60.15), the play does not even allow Yudhiṣṭhira's nosebleed. However, the deleted scene is alluded to a couple of times, by referring to the anger that caused it. The most obvious allusion involves Yudhiṣṭhira proclaiming Arjuna's role in the Matysa victory, and consequently, bringing forth Virāṭa's wrath; the less evident one refers to Abhimanyu narrating Bhīma's role in his capture, but still being unable to vex Virāṭa with his attitude. The minimization of the epic Virāṭa's anger is such that the dramatic Virāṭa even admits finding a certain joy in other people's anger.

Given that avoiding violence on stage is a convention within Greek tragedy (Aeschylus *Supp.* 825 ff. and *Ag.* 1650 ff.; Sophocles *OT* 1146 ff.; and (Ps.-)Euripides *Andr.* 577 ff., *Hel.* 1628 ff., *IA* 309 ff., and *Rhes.* 684 ff.),[132] it could have been borrowed by Sanskrit theater ((Ps.-)Bhāsa *PR* 2).

> tataḥ **prakupito** rājā tam akṣeṇāhanad bhṛśam
> mukhe yudhiṣṭhiraṃ **kopān** naivam ity eva bhartsayan |
> balavat pratividdhasya nastaḥ śoṇitam āgamat
> tad aprāptaṃ mahīṃ pārthaḥ pāṇibhyāṃ pratyagṛhṇata ||
>
> Then, the **enraged** king hit Yudhiṣṭhira in the face with a die, threatening **out of anger** that it was not so. Having been hit hard, blood came out of his nose; but the Pārtha [sc. Yudhiṣṭhira] held it back with his hands, so that it did not reach the ground.
>
> (*MBh.* 4.63.44-45)

> bhagavan akāle svasthavākyaṃ **manyum** utpādayati
>
> O Bhagavān [sc. Yudhiṣṭhira], your untimely confident speech brings forth my **wrath**.
>
> (*PR* 2.20.1)

132 See Sommerstein (2010, Chapter 2).

na te kṣepeṇa **ruṣyāmi ruṣyatā** bhavatā rame |

I **am not annoyed** by your [sc. Abhimanyu's] haughtiness; I enjoy you **annoying** me.

(*PR* 2.58a-b)

Together with the ignoring of the on-stage anger, another innovation of *The Five Nights* is ignoring the outcome.[133] In *MBh.* 4, although there might be contrasting opinions about the exact number of days that it encompasses, everyone agrees on a deadline consisting of thirteen years. But in *PR*, a new, five-night deadline is fashioned, so that the conflict can have a speedy resolution. Therefore, when the epic Duryodhana learns about Arjuna's identity, he demands that the Pāṇḍavas go into exile for another twelve years, but when the dramatic Duryodhana is informed about it, he graciously admits his defeat, and is more than willing to give the kingdom back. A happy ending is strongly suggested, but sometimes the right thing is easier said than done.

anivṛtte tu nirvāse yadi bībhatsur āgataḥ |
punar dvādaśa varṣāṇi vane vatsyanti pāṇḍavāḥ ||

If Bībhatsu [sc. Arjuna] comes when the exile had not yet finished, the Pāṇḍavas will live in the forest **for another twelve years**!

(*MBh.* 4.42.5)

bāḍhaṃ dattaṃ mayā rājyaṃ pāṇḍavebhyo yathāpuram |
mṛte 'pi hi narāḥ sarve satye tiṣṭhanti tiṣṭhati ||

Of course, I am giving the Pāṇḍavas **the kingdom**, their suitable residence, for when truth lies dead, so too lie all men.

(*PR* 3.25)

133 On ignoring the outcome, see Wulff Alonso (2020): "It is remarkable to see how in this version, adapting the title of the famous Giraudoux play about Troy, the war of Kurukṣetra could not have taken place, and this requires new inventions, perhaps Śakuni's intrigues, to make it possible or a parallel world in which it never took place" (p. 239); and Hawley (2021): "The entire *Mahābhārata* has a false ending of its own: Yudhiṣṭhira goes to hell, only to discover that it is an illusion" (p. 92, n. 3).

Tokens of Recognition and Other Telling Details

Based on the analysis of the ambush motif as per *Il.* 10 and *Rhesus*, as well as according to *MBh.* 4 and *The Five Nights*, I have identified four instances of possible Greek influence in the adaptation techniques: [AM1][134] *twofold epic themes are merged in the plays, causing the occasional subtraction of other themes*, [AM2] *dramatic features are added with the purpose of emphasizing certain aspects of the characterization that are merely suggested in the source texts*, [AM3] *spaces, times, characters, and themes are changed in the plays, which otherwise would be dramatizations and not adaptations*, and [AM4] *death and violence on stage are ignored as per dramatic convention.*

[AM1] *Twofold epic themes are merged in the plays, causing the occasional subtraction of other themes.* Not only do Greek and Sanskrit epics share the parallel presentation of themes regarding the ambush, but also Greek and Sanskrit theater opt for merging them for the stage. In *Rhesus*, the Greek and Trojan camps are combined into an all-encompassing Trojan bivouac (GA1), and the interactions between Agamemnon and Menelaus, on the Greek side, and between Hector and Aeneas, on the Trojan one (GA2), are brought together against this new, merged background.

If the author of *The Five Nights* knew the Greek sources, the procedure could have influenced his parallel merging of themes. As a part of the major authorial decision of showcasing Duryodhana in a better light, the play fuses the epic Duryodhana with the epic Dhṛtarāṣṭra to produce a kinglier character (SA2). In this sense, the chief subtraction, i.e., that of Dhṛtarāṣṭra, mirrors that of Priam from the *Rhesus*; and the dominant merging, i.e., that of the two ambushes into one (SA1), recalls that exact same procedure in the *Rhesus* as well.

134 AM stands for "Ambush Motif". Hence, numbers AM1-AM4 refer to the proposed influences from *Rhesus*' adaptation of *Il.* 10 into *The Five Nights*' adaptation of *MBh.* 4.

Regarded as an instance of Greco-Indian *anukaraṇa*, the distinguishing trait here would be merging: a Greek text (*Rhesus*) about one raid (by Odysseus/Diomedes) adapted from a source (*Il.* 10) containing two separate ambushes (by Dolon and by Odysseus/ Diomedes), would have become an Indian text (*The Five Nights*) about one raid (by Duryodhana) adapted from a source (*MBh.* 4) containing two separate ambushes (by Suśarman and by Duryodhana). In this sense, the adapted elements would be Indian, but the adaptation techniques would come from the Greco-Roman world. In support of this claim, I adduce the same use by (Ps.-) Bhāsa of the two speeches in *The Embassy*.

[AM2] *Dramatic features are added with the purpose of emphasizing certain aspects of the characterization that are merely suggested in the source texts.* Additions and emphases are numerous and correlated in both plays. In *Rhesus*, Dolon's tricky bargaining (GA3) and Rhesus' braggartry (GA4) mirror each other in terms of characterization. Furthermore, the overall commotion (GA5) is presented by means of a pun through which the adaptation proclaims itself as such, and Hector's tardy anagnorisis of Odysseus as a foe rather than a friend (GA6) tells us more about the Trojan's lack of cunningness than about the Greek's mastery of it.

In *The Five Nights*, Droṇa's tricky request for a graduation fee (SA3) is correlated to Uttara's braggartry (SA4) too. There is also a proclamation of the adaptation as such, which now comes in the form of Bhīṣma's feud with Virāṭa (SA5). Lastly, there is room for several anagnorises (SA6): Uttara's recognition of Arjuna by means of a scar, Bhīṣma's recognition of Arjuna thanks to an arrow, and Abhimanyu's recognition of Arjuna because of the father/son encounter. The same event being presented from three different perspectives is a helpful resource when it comes to characterization. Out of all these parallel subjects, trickery and anagnorisis stand out.

On the subject of trickery, Dolon reveals himself as a great source for potential borrowings into (Ps.-)Bhāsa's tricky characters, such as Droṇa.[135] Ps.-Euripides' Dolon is well aware of the tricky way in which Homer's Dolon gets Hector to swear by his general offer about the best Greek horses, while also turning it into the specific offer of Achilles' horses. Being acquainted with the source text, Ps.-Euripides' Dolon proceeds to request his remuneration, just like any other fourth-century Greek mercenary would have normally done. (Ps.-)Bhāsa's Droṇa is also familiar with the way in which Vyāsa's Droṇa waited for Ekalavya to ask him what he wanted as his remuneration. However, he still opts for requesting his remuneration, against all social convention, before being asked to do so. In this, (Ps.-)Bhāsa's Droṇa seems so odd that even Duryodhana wonders about his behavior.

> οὔκουν πονεῖν μὲν χρή, πονοῦντα δ' ἄξιον
> **μισθὸν** φέρεσθαι. παντὶ γὰρ προσκείμενον
> **κέρδος** πρὸς ἔργῳ τὴν χάριν τίκτει διπλῆν.
>
> Well, it is necessary to work for it, and therefore, to give the worker a fair **wage**. **Remuneration** being attached to a job brings forth twice the pleasure.
>
> (*Rhes.* 161-163)
>
> DROṆAḤ
> **dakṣiṇe**ti
> bhavatu bhavatu
> vyapaśramayiṣye tāvad bhavantam
>
> DURYODHANAḤ
> **katham** ācāryo 'pi vyapaśramayiṣyate

135 If Dolon, as a human trickster, offers borrowable elements for Droṇa, similarly, Athena, as a divine trickster, does so for the Indra from *Karṇa's Task*: "Begone! Bear in mind that all that is yours **concerns me**, inasmuch as seeing that **my allies** prosper. You will also come to know about **my goodwill** [χώρει· μέλειν γὰρ πάντ' **ἐμοὶ δόκει** τὰ σά, / ὥστ' εὐτυχοῦντας **συμμάχους ἐμοὺς** ὁρᾶν. / γνώσῃ δὲ καὶ σὺ **τὴν ἐμὴν προθυμίαν**]" (*Rhes.* 665-667), and "Dear Karṇa, may **your renown** last like the sun, like the moon, like the Himālayas, and like the ocean [*bhoḥ karṇa sūrya iva candra iva himavān iva sāgara iva tiṣṭhatu* ***te yaśaḥ***]" (*KBh.* 16.8b). Both Athena's and Indra's statements could be interpreted as favorable (as Paris and Karṇa take them) or as unfavorable (as Athena and Indra intend them). Like that of Droṇa, Indra's request is odd enough to make Karṇa wonder about it: "O fortunate one, **should you not tell** me to have a long life? [*bhagavan* ***kiṃ na vaktavyaṃ*** *dīrghāyur bhaveti*]" (*KBh.* 16.9).

DROṆA
"**A graduation fee**", you say. So be it, so be it. I will make a request for you at once.

DURYODHANA
How will a preceptor make a request?

(*PR* 1.27.15 – 1.27.18)

Regarded as another instance of Greco-Indian *anukaraṇa*, the distinguishing trait here would be oddity: a Greek text (*Rhesus*) in which a tricky character (Dolon) normally requests a remuneration (the horses) when following a source (*Il.* 10), would have become an Indian text (*The Five Nights*) in which a tricky character (Droṇa) oddly requests a remuneration (the deal) when following a source (*MBh.* 1.123.10-39). Oddity in one culture, paired with a lack of it in the other, strongly suggests a borrowing.[136]

As for the anagnorisis, even though its achievement by means of a scar is certainly Homeric (e.g., *Od.* 19.466-475), its relation to a reinstatement could point to a borrowing from Roman theater. Plautus (254-184 BCE)[137] and Terence (185-159 BCE)[138] offer several examples: in *Capt.* 872-874, an account by a third party allows a freeman to recognize his "son [*filium*]", who had been living as a slave; in *Cas.* 1012-1014, the epilogue predicts the discovery of a female slave's noble birth, as the "daughter

136 See Wulff Alonso (2020): "I have also pointed out the need to recognize the importance of certain unusual cases, such as the odd, bizarre or fanciful components of a story. Thus, a rabbit in a narrative may well be commonplace, but not if it is pictured carrying a pocket watch, disappearing through a hole in the ground, talking, etc. Likewise, a man building a boat may well appear to be a commonplace trope; yet, a man building a boat because a god had warned him about an impending flood and instructed him on the finer points of boat building, is not. To find such similarities in two different stories is obviously meaningful as such details are, ostensibly, strange products of the human imagination which deepen the unlikelihood or sheer impossibility of independent creation. One very interesting variation of this case of the shared bizarre traits happens when it is so in one case, in one of the cultures, and not in the other" (p. 19).

137 I follow the Latin text by Nixon (Plautus, 1916, 1917, 1924, 1930, and 1952). The translations are my own.

138 I follow the Latin text by Sargeaunt (Terence, 1918). The translations are my own.

[*filia*]" of a freeman; in *Cist.* 664-665, a "baby rattle [*crepundia*]"[139] causes a mother to recognize her daughter, who had been living as a courtesan; in *Curc.* 653-657, a "ring [*anulum*]"[140] results in a soldier recognizing a supposed courtesan, with whom he was in love, as none other than his sister; in *Epid.* 635-636, a slave realizes that a young woman, who had been subject to slavery, is his master's "daughter [*filiam*]"; in *Men.* 1133, an abducted young man realizes that he is in the presence of his long-lost "brother [*frater*]", once he hears the other repeat the name of their mother; and in *An.* 904-956, an old man reminiscing brings about the recognition of a young woman as the "daughter [*filiam*]" of a freeman. Nonetheless, the most relevant examples come from Plautus' *The Little Carthaginian* and *The Rope.*

In *The Little Carthaginian*, a youth named Agorastocles is kidnapped and sold as a slave, only to be latter recognized as the nephew of a Carthaginian man who secures his wedding. Several of these details coincide with the plot of *The Five Nights*. Agorastocles and Abhimanyu are abducted youths: "is taken away [*surripitur*]" (*Poen.* 68) and "has walked right into his capture [*grahaṇaṃ gataḥ*]" (*PR* 2.34). They both endure a subordination: "sells him to a master [*vendit eum domino*]" (*Poen.* 75) and "made him descend [*avatāritaḥ*]" (*PR* 2.37). Their uncles take part in both recognitions: "my uncle [*mi patrue*]" (*Poen.* 1076) and "dear uncle [*bhos tāta*]" (*PR* 2.67.2). And they both end up married: "you must give her to me in marriage [*despondeas*]" (*Poen.* 1156) and "I take her as a wife [*pratigṛhyate*]" (*PR* 2.71).

However, the most telling commonality is that of a scar aiding the anagnorisis: bitten by a monkey, Agorastocles is left with a scar on his left hand, which is examined by Hanno, his older, long-lost relative, for his recognition; and, having his forearm slapped by the bowstring/confined by the bracelets, Arjuna is left with a scar on

139 This could have been borrowed by (Ps.-)Bhāsa for the "lute [*vīṇayā*]" (*SV* 6), and later, re-created by Kālidāsa as the "gem [*ratnam*]" (*Vikr.* 5).

140 This could have been re-created by Kālidāsa as the "ring [*aṅgulīyakaṃ*]" (*Śak.* 6).

his (presumably right)[141] forearm, which is interpreted by Uttara, his younger, soon-to-be relative, for his recognition.

Ag.	Ampsigura mater mihi fuit, Iahon pater.
Han.	Patrem atque matrem viverent vellem tibi.
Ag.	An mortui sunt?
Han.	Factum, quod aegre tuli. nam mihi sobrina Ampsigura tua mater fuit; pater tuos, is erat frater patruelis meus, et is me heredem fecit, quom suom obiit diem, quo me privatum aegre patior mortuo. sed si ita est, ut tu sis Iahonis filius, **signum esse oportet in manu laeva tibi,** **ludenti puero quod memordit simia**. ostende, inspiciam.
Ag.	Em ostendo.
Han.	Aperi. audi atque ades:
Agorastocles.	Ampsigura was my mother, and Iahon my father.
Hanno.	I wish your father and mother were alive!
Agorastocles.	Are they dead?

141 Since, in the *MBh.*, Arjuna is repeatedly said to be *savyasācin-* (a left-handed archer), it is not too far-fetched to assume that he would have slapped the interior of his right forearm with the bowstring.

Hanno.	Indeed, and I took it badly, because your mother Ampsigura was my cousin; and your father, he was my cousin on my father's side, and by the time of his death, he even made me his heir, so, ever since he died, deprived of him, I have been badly affected. But, if it is true that you are the son of Iahon, **there should be a sign on your left hand, where a monkey bit you, when you were playing as a kid**. Show it me, so that I can examine it!
Agorastocles.	There, I am showing it to you.
Hanno.	Open it up! Listen and witness!

(*Poen.* 1065-1075)

prakoṣṭhāntarasaṅgūḍhaṃ **gāṇḍīvajyāhataṃ kiṇam** |
yat tad dvādaśavarṣānte naiva yāti savarṇatām ||

The scar, which was inflicted by the string of Gāṇḍīva and remains hidden in the interior of his forearm, does not vanish, having the same appearance even at the end of the twelve years [sc. of exile].

(*PR* 2.63)

etan me pārihāryāṇāṃ vyāvartanakṛtaṃ kiṇam |
sannirodhavivarṇatvād godhāsthānam ihāgatam ||

This scar of mine was produced by me removing my bracelets: it comes close to taking the place of the arm guard because of the paleness caused by the confinement.

(*PR* 2.64)

Regarded as yet another instance of Greco-Indian *anukaraṇa*, the distinguishing trait here would be reversal: a Roman text (*The Little Carthaginian*), in which a younger character (Agorastocles) is recognized by an old relative (Hanno) because of a scar on his left side, would have become an Indian text (*The Five Nights*) in which an older character (Arjuna) is recognized by a younger soon-to-be relative (Uttara) because of a scar on his right side.

In *The Rope*, a woman named Palestra, after being kidnapped and sold as a courtesan, is later recognized as the daughter of a fisherman who, eventually, secures her wedding. In this case, the most compelling point of encounter are the names carved on weapons, which function as determinants for the anagnorisis: the woman Palestra is recognized by her father Daemones because she identifies, without seeing them, a little sword with the name of her father Daemones carved on it, as well as a little axe with the name of her mother Daedalis carved on it; and the man Arjuna is recognized by his grandfather Bhīṣma because he identifies himself, without being seen, through an arrow with the name Arjuna carved on it.

Daem.	dic, **in ensiculo** quid **nomen** est **paternum**?
Pal.	Daemones.
Daem.	Di immortales, ubi loci sunt spes meae?
Gr.	Immo edepol meae?
Trach.	Pergite, opsecro, continuo.
Gr.	Placide, aut i in malam crucem.
Daem.	Loquere **matris nomen hic quid in securicula siet**.
Pal.	Daedalis.
Daem.	Di me servatum cupiunt.
Gr.	At me perditum.
Daem.	Filiam meam esse hanc oportet, Gripe.
Daemones.	Tell me, what is **your father's name, which is on the little sword?**
Palestra.	Daemones.
Daemones.	O immortal gods, could my hopes be any higher?
Gripus.	By Pollux, never mind mine!

Trachalio.	Go on, I beg you, straightaway.
Gripus.	Do it leisurely, or else, I'll be hanged if...
Daemones.	Tell me **the name of your mother, which is on the little axe.**
Palestra.	Daedalis.
Daemones.	The gods want me to be saved!
Gripus.	And me to be lost!
Daemones.	O Gripus, this must be my daughter!

(*Rud.* 1160-1165)

bāṇapuṅkhākṣarair vākyair jyājihvāparivartibhiḥ |
vikṛṣṭaṃ khalu pārthena na ca śrotraṃ prayacchati ||

By means of **words having their syllables in the feathers of his arrows** and being transmitted by the tongue of his bowstring, the Pārtha [sc. Arjuna] communicated with us, and this does not result in us hearing him?

(*PR* 3.17)

Regarded as one more instance of Greco-Indian *anukaraṇa*, the distinguishing feature here would be merging: a Roman text (*The Rope*) in which a female character (Palestra) is recognized by an old relative (Daemones) because two names (Daemones and Daedalis) are spelled on two weapons (a little sword and a little axe), would have become an Indian text (*The Five Nights*) in which a male character (Arjuna) is recognized by an old relative (Bhīṣma) because a name (Arjuna) is spelled on a weapon (an arrow).

Before moving on to the next instance of possible Greek influence, I would like to adduce an additional argument to support the view of Abhimanyu's anagnorisis from a Greek/Aristotelian perspective. According to *Poet.* 1452a28-31, an anagnorisis encompasses three changes: from ignorance to knowledge, from enmity to friendship (or vice versa), and from prosperity to adversity (or vice versa). When those criteria are applied to the dramatic Abhimanyu, one sees that he goes from not knowing the identity of his father and uncles to being fully aware of it. Following such realization, he retrospectively understands why they were not taunted by him, and immediately he re-signifies their behavior as a friendly form of taunting. Moreover, any adverse effects that could have resulted from his capture are suddenly overshadowed by the prosperous family reunion. This is not the case in the *Virāṭaparvan*, where the Pāṇḍavas, even after being recognized, remain friends to their friends (the Matsyas) and foes to their foes (the Kauravas), and they just move on from one adverse situation (the exile) to the next (the war).

[AM3] *Spaces, times, characters, and themes are changed in the plays, which otherwise would be dramatizations and not adaptations.* As would be expected from any other text that critically engages with its canonical source, both adaptations incorporate various changes. In *Rhesus*, the general perspective is recast from the Greeks to the Trojans (GA7), whereas in *The Five Nights*, the remote sacrifice is remade as a proximate one (SA7). Additionally, while Ps.-Euripides maintains the nighttime from the Homeric ambush (GA8), (Ps.-)Bhāsa turns Vyāsa's five villages into the eponymous five nights (SA8).

If (Ps.-)Bhāsa was acquainted with (Ps.-)Euripides, the title itself could have been a Greco-Roman borrowing for *The Five Nights*. Assuming that the number five is an adapted element coming from the five-village request in the *MBh.*, the *Rhesus* would have provided a supplementary literary component. To put it another way, the *pañca-* part of the title would be Indian, but the *rātra-* part of it could be Greco-Roman. Thus, the spatial limit of five would have been re-created as a temporal limit of five, and the five "watches of the night" from the Greek play would have become the five "nights" in the Sanskrit play.

> – τίς ἐκηρύχθη πρώτην φυλακήν;
> – Μυγδόνος υἱόν φασι Κόροιβον.
> – τίς γὰρ ἐπ' αὐτῷ; – Κίλικας Παίων
> στρατὸς ἤγειρεν, Μυσοὶ δ' ἡμᾶς.
> – οὔκουν Λυκίους **πέμπτην φυλακὴν**
> βάντας ἐγείρειν
> καιρὸς κλήρου κατὰ μοῖραν;

– Who was announced for the first watch?
– They say that it was Coroebus, the son of Mygdon.
– Who, then, after him? – The Paeonian army woke the Cilicians; and the Mysians, us.
– Then is it not time, as per the drawing of the lots, to wake the Lycians, having gone to them, **for the fifth watch**?

(*Rhes.* 538-545)

yadi **pañcarātreṇa** pāṇḍavānāṃ pravṛttir upanetavyā rājyasyārdhaṃ pradāsyati kila

If someone brings him news of the Pāṇḍavas **within five nights**, he will accordingly give up half the kingdom.

(*PR* 1.45.7)

As an instance of Greco-Indian *anukaraṇa*, the hallmark here would be change: a Greek text (*Rhesus*) with a temporal deadline (five watches of the night) which has been adapted from the temporal deadline (three watches of the night) of the source (*Il.* 10) would have become an Indian text (*The Five Nights*) with a temporal deadline (five nights) which has been changed from the spatial deadline (five villages) of the source (*MBh.* 5).

[AM4] *Death and violence on stage are ignored as per dramatic convention.* In agreement with the Greek dramatic convention, *Rhesus* ignores the death of Dolon (GA9), as well as the total of deaths. Deaths on the Greek stage are highly unusual, and so are they on the Indian stage, as prescribed by *Nāṭyaś.* 18.38.[142] Similarly, *The Five Nights* opts to ignore the violence by Virāṭa (SA9) as well

142 The fact that Euripides and (Ps.-)Bhāsa are, respectively, the only Greek playwright and the only Sanskrit playwright who contravene this practice strongly suggests an influence. Furthermore, Hippolytus' death on stage in *Hippolytus* could have been borrowed for that of Duryodhana in *The Broken Thighs*: "O father, **my waiting is over**, for I am dead. Cover my face as fast as possible with veils [**κεκαρτέρηται τἄμ'**· ὄλωλα γάρ, πάτερ. / κρύψον δέ μου πρόσωπον ὡς τάχος πέπλοις]" (*Hipp.* 1457-1458), and "Ah, **my heart's desire is fulfilled**. My life is giving up on me… To fetch me, Time has sent a celestial vehicle, a chariot for heroes, yoked to a thousand geese. Here, here I come. (He goes to heaven) [*hanta* ***kṛtaṃ me hṛdayānujñātam*** | *parityajanti me prāṇāḥ… eṣa sahasrahaṃsaprayukto māṃ netuṃ vīravāhī vimānaḥ kālena preṣitaḥ* | *ayam ayam āgacchāmi* | *svargaṃ gataḥ*]" (*ŪBh.* 65.1-2… 9-11).

as the upcoming violence of the war. Here, the Greek convention could have been borrowed as an Indian rule.

Violence on the Greek stage is avoided at all costs by Aeschylus (524-455 BCE),[143] Sophocles (496-405 BCE),[144] and (Ps.-)Euripides: in *Ag.* 1650 ff., there are threats of a fight by "sword [ξίφος]"; in *OT* 1146 ff., of "torturing [αἰκίσῃ]" an old man; in *Andr.* 577 ff., of "staining with blood [καθαιμάξας]" the head of a king with a scepter; in *Hel.* 1628 ff., of "looking to die [κατθανεῖν ἐρᾷν]"; in *IA* 309 ff., also of "staining with blood [καθαιμάξω]" the head of an old man with a scepter; and in *Rhes.* 684 ff., of a "spear [λόγχην]" going through an enemy. This time, Aeschylus' *The Suppliants* seems to be the model.

The Suppliants present a lengthy confrontation between the Chorus and a Herald. There, one finds violent references to "the cutting off a head [ἀποκοπὰ κρατός]" (*Supp.* 841), the throwing of "punches [παλάμαις]" (*Supp.* 865), and "the dragging by the hair [ὁλκὴ... πλόκαμον (*Supp.* 884) and ἀποσπάσας κόμης (*Supp.* 909)]". But the precise borrowing would have come from a King who calls out the Herald for his arrogance, which in turn would have become the overconfidence and the haughtiness that Virāṭa criticizes, respectively, in Yudhiṣṭhira and Abhimanyu.

> οὗτος, τί ποιεῖς; ἐκ ποίου **φρονήματος**
> ἀνδρῶν Πελασγῶν τήνδ᾽ ἀτιμάζεις χθόνα;
> ἀλλ᾽ ἦ γυναικῶν ἐς πόλιν δοκεῖς μολεῖν;
> κάρβανος ὢν δ᾽ Ἕλλησιν ἐγχλίεις ἄγαν·
> καὶ πόλλ᾽ ἁμαρτὼν οὐδὲν ὤρθωσας φρενί.
>
> Hey there! What are you doing? Out of what kind of **arrogance** are you dishonoring this land of the Pelasgian men? Or do you think you have come to a city of women? Being a barbarian, you indulge yourself too much among the Greeks. Having erred a lot, you have done nothing right in your mind.
>
> (*Supp.* 911-915)

---

143 I follow the Greek text by Smyth (Aeschylus, 1922, 1926). The translations are my own.

144 I follow the Greek text by Storr (Sophocles, 1912, 1913). The translations are my own.

> bhagavan **akāle svasthavākyaṃ** manyum utpādayati
>
> O Bhagavān [sc. Yudhiṣṭhira], **your untimely confident speech** brings forth my wrath.
>
> (*PR* 2.20.1)
>
> na **te kṣepeṇa** ruṣyāmi ruṣyatā bhavatā rame |
>
> I am not annoyed by **your** [sc. Abhimanyu's] **haughtiness**; I enjoy you annoying me.
>
> (*PR* 2.58a-b)

As an instance of Greco-Indian *anukaraṇa*, the hallmark here would also be change: a Greek text (*The Suppliants*) where a monarch (the King) censures some explicit instances of violence (beheading, punching, and hair pulling) by one newcomer (the Herald), would have become an Indian text (*The Five Nights*) where a monarch (Virāṭa) censures some implicit instances of violence (being overly confident and being haughty) by two newcomers (Yudhiṣṭhira and Abhimanyu).

In a nutshell, from the ambush motif, I propose a Greek influence from *Il.* 10 and *Rhesus* into *MBh.* 4 and *The Five Nights*. I have pinpointed four adaptation techniques: theme subtraction-cum-merging (AM1), character addition-cum-emphasis (AM2), changing of spaces, times, characters, and themes (AM3), and ignoring-by-convention (AM4). In terms of the proposed Greco-Indian *anukaraṇa*, the influence would be marked by merging. Additionally, I put forward five Greco-Roman borrowings for the ambush motif: the remuneration, taken from *Rhesus* itself and characterized by oddity; the scarred limb, acquired from Plautus' *The Little Carthaginian* and defined by reversal; the signed weapon, gotten from Plautus' *The Rope* and distinguished by merging; the five night watches/five nights, also coming from *Rhesus* itself and differentiated by change; and a violent arrogance, to be found in Aeschylus' *The Suppliants* and marked by change as well. If the *MBh.* already relies on the Greek epic's version of the ambush, as seems to be the case,[145] then it would not come as much of a surprise that *PR* also profits from Greek sources, especially the *Rhesus*.

145 See Wulff Alonso (2020): "Book 10, the *Sauptika Parva*, for instance relies heavily on one Greco-Roman source. It recounts a nocturnal attack on sleeping enemies, mirroring Book 10 of *Iliad*" (2020, p. 243). Cf. Liapis' (2012, p. xxxii) view of an Indo-European shared background.

4. The Ogre

"Nobody Seeks to Kill Me!"

Book 9 of the *Odyssey* is divided into three episodes of unequal length: the Cicones, the Lotus-eaters, and the Cyclopes. Once he reveals his identity to the Phaeacians, Odysseus tells how, right after Troy, they encountered the Cicones, who managed to repel the ravaging Greeks and even to kill some of them; and on the tenth day thereafter, he dovetails the succinct tale of their get-together with the Lotus-eaters, whose alluring fruit nearly meant giving up on the homecoming. In both cases, the companions come out as imprudent, while Odysseus' prudence is what saves the day. However, the third episode is quite different, not only in terms of its lengthier narrative, but also concerning the hero's behavior.

The epic version of the episode goes like this: on the first day, Odysseus and his companions sail past the land of the Cyclopes, who are depicted as being unaware of such basic cultural practices as sowing or plowing, having assemblies or laws, or building ships. On the second day, the Greek warriors stay on the nearby island of the goats, where they eat and drink until nighttime. On the third day, Odysseus decides to take a small group of companions on an expedition to the neighboring land of the Cyclopes. Having sailed there, they find the cave of the mountainous Polyphemus, towards which only a still smaller group of twelve companions walk alongside the hero. Odysseus is carrying a special wine, which the priest Maron had given to him for sparing his life, as well as the lives of his wife and his son.

 https://doi.org/10.11647/OBP.0417.04

When they arrive, the Cyclops is out pasturing, and the twelve companions want to gather as much cheese and as many kids and lambs as they can carry, and then run back to the ship; but Odysseus recklessly chooses to wait for the Cyclops and ask him for a hospitable welcome. The Cyclops returns and closes the entrance to the cave with a boulder. When requested for hospitality, he openly disparages Zeus and the other gods, and proceeds to devour two of the companions. Odysseus is ingenious enough not to tell the Cyclops that they have a ship waiting for them – and not to kill him before the boulder has been removed from the entrance.

On the fourth day, the Cyclops devours two more men. By this point, Odysseus cleverly figures out a stratagem: with the help of his friends, he manages to carve a stake from the trunk of an olive that was laying around. By lot, four out of the eight remaining companions are chosen to aid the protagonist during the stabbing of the Cyclops. This new instance of selection presents the men as a group of four plus one. Once they are ready to implement the ruse, Odysseus gets the ball rolling by offering the Cyclops the special wine that he has been carrying, and by telling the ogre that his name is Nobody. An additional two men are eaten during the night.

As a gift of hospitality, the Cyclops offers Odysseus the gift of being the last one to be eaten, shortly before falling asleep with his neck exposed. Odysseus and his companions promptly stab the Cyclops in the eye. The other Cyclopes ask Polyphemus about his cries, to which he inadvertently replies with Odysseus' intended pun by saying that Nobody has harmed him. Odysseus laughs at the scene. Then, he fathoms the last step: he binds the rams in sets of three, and he secures a man below the middle one of each set. He himself rides below the strongest ram.

With the dawn of the fifth day, Polyphemus removes the boulder to take the rams for pasturing. He stands by the entrance while they exit the cave. But the smooth escape suffers from one last setback when the reckless Odysseus wants to make sure that Polyphemus is aware of what has happened to him. Furious, the Cyclops uproots the top of a mountain and throws it at the departing ship. Despite the best efforts of his companions to restrain him, Odysseus outdoes his previous foolishness by trumpeting his real name.

Thus, Polyphemus recognizes the fulfilment of an old prophecy, and prays to his father Poseidon to either prevent Odysseus from returning home or, at least, to do so tardily, alone, and ready to overcome still more challenges. Another mountaintop falls near the ship while they sail back to the island of the goats. Eating and drinking for the remainder of that day, much as they had done at the beginning of the episode, upon the arrival of the sixth day they sail away and continue their adventure.

Vis-à-vis Euripides' *Cyclops*, its multiple sources include the Homeric and Hesiodic Epics; the *Homeric Hymns*; the plays of Aeschylus, Sophocles, Aristophanes, and even Euripides himself;[146] and the works of other dramatists which have only been preserved in a fragmentary manner, such as Epicharmus, Aristias, Cratinus, Callias, and maybe even Thimotheus.[147] Nevertheless, the main source for the adaptation of the ogre motif is, without a doubt, *Od.* 9. In a nutshell, the plot of the play is as follows: throughout four episodes of varying length, the hero Odysseus alternately interacts with the chorus of Satyrs and with the Cyclops Polyphemus. The main events include Odysseus buying from the Satyrs, Odysseus plotting against Polyphemus, Odysseus being left high and dry by the Satyrs, and Odysseus revealing himself to Polyphemus.

In the prologue, the satyr Silenus explains that, while searching for the god Dionysus, who had been enslaved by pirates, he and his sons the Satyrs have ended up themselves as slaves at the house of Polyphemus, by the slopes of Mount Aetna. After a parodos[148] in which the audience learns that much of the day has already passed, the first episode introduces Odysseus. In their dialogue, Silenus and Odysseus go back and forth about civilization, government, agriculture, viticulture, and hospitality. Odysseus is, clearly, testing

146 E.g., *Cyc.* 222 ~ *Andromeda* fr. 125.

147 E.g., for Epicharmus, *Cyc.* 566-568 ~ *PGC* 72; for Aristias, *TrGF* 4; for Cratinus, *Cyc.* 358-359 ~ *PGC* 150; for Callias, *PGC* 6; and for Thimotheus, *PMGF* 780-783. See O'Sullivan & Collard (2013, p. 42), Shaw (2018, pp. 104-108), and Hunter & Laemmle (2020, pp. 4-8).

148 A parodos is the first choral part of a Greek play and it signals the entrance of the Chorus.

the waters. After learning that Polyphemus is out hunting, Silenus and Odysseus begin a commercial exchange involving, on one hand, meat, milk, and cheese, and on the other, not money but the wine previously supplied by the priest Maron. The subject of the Trojan war also comes up.

When Polyphemus returns to his cave, he finds his products on display, as well as a group of humans who make his mouth water. The drunken Silenus claims that Odysseus and his companions were trying to take everything by force, whereas Odysseus himself claims that it was all an agreed-upon transaction. With great comedic effect, Silenus swears by his sons the Satyrs that Odysseus and his companions were stealing the merchandise, while the Satyrs swear by their father Silenus that Odysseus and his companions were buying it. Following a new mention of the Trojan war, Polyphemus proclaims his ideology: he does not praise Zeus, but his belly; he does not follow any laws, but only the wishes of his heart; and he will only offer Odysseus, as hospitable gifts, a fire for cooking him, salt for seasoning him, and a bronze pot for completing the preparation of the meal.

After the first stasimon,[149] which gives time for some off-stage violence perpetrated by Polyphemus, the second episode begins with Odysseus narrating the culinary techniques displayed by the Cyclops. He does not only kill two of the companions, but he also carves, roasts, and boils as required. Immediately, Odysseus comes up with a plan. He must get Polyphemus drunk and away from the other Cyclopes, and then, he must use the olive stake from the cave to blind Polyphemus. If all goes well, Odysseus offers to rescue the Satyrs, and therefore, they offer to help him with the blinding. As intended, the drunken Polyphemus lies down just when the heat of the sun is at its peak. And just before falling asleep, he remembers to ask Odysseus about his name, to which Odysseus replies with the well-known "Nobody". Now it is time to put the alleged bravery of the Satyrs to the test.

149 A stasimon is any choral part of a Greek play other than the first one and the last one, and it serves to separate the episodes.

Following the second stasimon, the third episode quickly presents the unwillingness of the Satyrs to help Odysseus, who in turn, must appeal to his companions. The contribution of the Satyrs is limited to cheerleading. Lastly and after a third stasimon, which allows for the proportional off-stage violence orchestrated by Odysseus, the fourth episode showcases the blinded Polyphemus, who is relentlessly mocked by the Satyrs. As per the epic script, Odysseus finally reveals his identity, whereas Polyphemus, having remembered the prophecy of his blinding, proceeds to throw rocks at his witty adversary. In the exodos,[150] the Satyrs simply follow Odysseus, eager to go back to serving Dionysus.

In the dramatic version, the author profits from these twelve procedures: [GO1][151] he merges two stories into one, [GO2] he adds the father/son conflict, [GO3] he adds the Chance, [GO4] he emphasizes the tree, [GO5] he emphasizes the sex, [GO6] he emphasizes the mistaken identity, [GO7] he changes the place, [GO8] he changes the time, [GO9] he changes the authoritarian figure, [GO10] he changes the role of the priest, [GO11] he changes the lot into a choice, and [GO12] he maintains the hospitality.

[GO1] *Cyclops* brings together the stories about Odysseus and Polyphemus, on one side, and about Silenus and the Satyrs, on the other.[152] The addition of a chorus of Satyrs is a *sine qua non* for a satyr drama, but their integration with the narrative of the source

150 An exodos is the last choral part of a Greek play, and it signals the departure of the Chorus.

151 GO stands for "Greek Ogre". Hence, numbers GO1-GO12 refer to the adaptation of *Od.* 9 into *Cyclops*. Besides those that will allow me to argue for parallelisms with the Greco-Roman world, other adaptation techniques include changing Odysseus' and Polyphemus' genealogies, splitting the disregard for Zeus into the disregard for Zeus' plan and the derision of Zeus himself, adding the democratic perspective, changing the sheep pasturing into the hunting with dogs, emphasizing Polyphemus' eye, changing the timing of the ram trick and the boulder trick, adding the buying scene, emphasizing the Trojan war, adding the Cyclops' hedonism, adding the cooking, and changing the timing of the shipbuilding simile.

152 On merging two stories into one, see Shaw (2018): "As we have seen, Euripides actively acknowledges that the Cyclops is a reiteration of the constantly reiterated genre of satyr drama at the start of the play with Silenus' 'countless troubles' (v. 1), but these countless troubles also relate to Odysseus' legendary 'many pains' (πολλὰ ἄλγεα) at the start of Homer's *Odyssey* (1.4)" (p. 98).

text is quite innovative. The prologue of the *Cyclops* closely mirrors the proem of the *Odyssey*: the invocation to the Muse turns into that of Dionysus; the heroic Odysseus, into the antiheroic Silenus; and the many resources, wanderings, men, and sufferings, referring to the well-known, postwar homecoming, become the countless labors of a lifetime of servitude under the god of wine.

The overall reversal is further signaled by the abrupt switch, within the very first verse of the play, from the opening dactyl of the first foot, evidently recalling the Homeric hexameter, to the iambs of the last two feet of the trimeter, whose syncopated rhythm makes them stand in overt contrast with the preceding one. To put it another way, the metric of the first verse marks the transition between genres.

> ἄνδρα μοι ἔννεπε, μοῦσα, **πολύτροπον**, ὃς **μάλα πολλὰ**
> πλάγχθη, ἐπεὶ Τροίης ἱερὸν πτολίεθρον ἔπερσεν·
> **πολλῶν** δ' **ἀνθρώπων** ἴδεν ἄστεα καὶ νόον ἔγνω,
> **πολλὰ** δ' ὅ γ' ἐν πόντῳ πάθεν **ἄλγεα** ὃν κατὰ θυμόν,
> ἀρνύμενος ἥν τε ψυχὴν καὶ νόστον ἑταίρων.
>
> O Muse, tell me about the man **of many resources**, who wandered **very much** after he had ravaged the sacred citadel of Troy. He saw the cities **of many men** and came to know their minds, and he experienced **many sufferings** in his heart while being in the open ocean, striving to secure his own life and the return of his companions.
>
> (*Od.* 1.1-10)

> Ὦ Βρόμιε, διὰ σὲ **μυρίους** ἔχω **πόνους**
> νῦν χὤτ' ἐν ἥβῃ τοὐμὸν ηὐσθένει δέμας·
>
> O Bromius, thanks to you I tend towards **countless labors**, both now and back in my youth, when my physique was strong.
>
> (*Cyc.* 1-2)

But the interplay is not limited to the beginning of the dramatic composition. About halfway through and in a similar invocation to Zeus, the dramatic Odysseus rhetorically asks what he should say next. Clearly, the author is winking to his audience: this Odysseus knows the script from his epic counterpart, whose story is even explicitly criticized for being far-fetched, but acquaintance alone is no reason for him blindly following his predecessor. Thanks to the criticality that comes with every literary tradition, the playwright dares to question the canonical text, while still admiring it enough to adapt it.

> ὦ Ζεῦ, τί λέξω, δείν' ἰδὼν ἄντρων ἔσω
> κοὐ πιστά, **μύθοις** εἰκότ' οὐδ' ἔργοις βροτῶν;
>
> O Zeus, having seen, inside of the caves, things that were terrible and unbelievable, like those found **in stories** but not in deeds of mortal men, what will I say?
>
> (*Cyc.* 375-376)

[GO2] Euripides adds the father/son conflict. In the epic, there are two father/son relations at play: Poseidon/Polyphemus and Laertes/Odysseus. Unlike the hero, the ogre is the son of a god, and if humans like Achilles can hold a grudge (e.g., *Il.* 1.1), deities like Poseidon can do so too (e.g., *Od.* 1.20). When Odysseus finally reveals his identity, precisely by introducing himself as the son of Laertes, Polyphemus proclaims that he himself is the son of a worthier father, i.e., the god Poseidon. Shortly after, the Cyclops prays that, if possible, his father may cause Odysseus never to make it back home. In essence, the father from the first pair (Poseidon) would be responsible for the death of the son from the second pair (Odysseus).

In the play, the father/son relation is exploited in the form of the newly added characters: Silenus/Satyrs. *Sensu stricto*, Silenus is older than the Satyrs, but he is not their father. However, Euripides makes him so. The scene is quite comical: if the epic Polyphemus invokes Poseidon, the dramatic Silenus conjures not only Poseidon, Triton, Nereus, Calypso, and the Nereids, but also the waves and the fish. Silenus also profits from epithets combining superlatives and diminutives, and he falsely swears on the lives of his sons, only to be immediately called out on his lie by them, who in turn falsely swear on the life of their father.

> τοῦ γὰρ ἐγὼ **πάις** εἰμί, **πατὴρ** δ' ἐμὸς εὔχεται εἶναι.
>
> For I am his **son**, and he is proud to be my **father**.
>
> (*Od.* 9.519)

ΣΙΛΗΝΟΣ
μὰ τὸν Ποσειδῶ τὸν τεκόντα σ', ὦ Κύκλωψ,
μὰ τὸν μέγαν Τρίτωνα καὶ τὸν Νηρέα,
μὰ τὴν Καλυψὼ τάς τε Νηρέως κόρας,
μὰ θαἰερὰ κύματ' ἰχθύων τε πᾶν γένος,
ἀπώμοσ', ὦ κάλλιστον ὦ Κυκλώπιον,
ὦ δεσποτίσκε, μὴ τὰ σ' ἐξοδᾶν ἐγὼ
ξένοισι χρήματ'. ἦ κακῶς οὗτοι κακοὶ
οἱ παῖδες ἀπόλοινθ', οὓς μάλιστ' ἐγὼ φιλῶ.

ΧΟΡΟΣ
αὐτὸς ἔχ'. ἔγωγε τοῖς ξένοις τὰ χρήματα
περνάντα σ' εἶδον· εἰ δ' ἐγὼ ψευδῆ λέγω,
ἀπόλοιθ' ὁ πατήρ μου· τοὺς ξένους δὲ μὴ ἀδίκει.

SILENUS
O Cyclops, by Poseidon who begot you, by the great Triton and Nereus, by Calypso and the Nereids, by the sacred waves and the entire lineage of the fish, O pretty little Cyclops, O sweet little master, I swear that I was not going to sell your goods to the strangers; if not, may these bad **sons** of mine, whom I cherish more than anything, **perish** in a bad way!

CHORUS
Right back at you! I saw you selling his goods to the strangers; if I am telling lies, may my **father perish**! Do not do these strangers wrong.

(*Cyc.* 262-272)

[GO3] The playwright also adds the Chance. In the epic narrative, the outcome of the encounter depends on the gods, specifically on Athena. Even the term selected to refer to the ensuing glory (εὖχος) refers to the kind of glory that is conferred by the immortals. Conversely, in the adaptation, not only Zeus, but every god is degraded. And if there is no longer a difference between gods and humans, cosmos makes room for chaos, and all comes down to dumb luck. Unlike the older hierarchy, where gods outrank humans but are themselves outweighed by fate, this newer world order presupposes just an overarching, deified Chance (Τύχη) that renders deities useless.

πολλῇ δὲ ῥοίζῳ πρὸς ὄρος τρέπε πίονα μῆλα
Κύκλωψ· αὐτὰρ ἐγὼ λιπόμην κακὰ βυσσοδομεύων,
εἴ πως τισαίμην, δοίη δέ μοι εὖχος **Ἀθήνη**.

And with much whistling, the Cyclops turned his fat sheep towards the mountain, but I was left behind, deeply pondering an evil, in case **Athena** would grant me the glory, and I could somehow make him pay.

(*Od.* 9.315-317)

καὶ μὴ 'πὶ καλλίστοισι Τρωικοῖς πόνοις
αὐτόν τε ναύτας τ' ἀπολέσητ' Ὀδυσσέα
ὑπ' ἀνδρὸς ᾧ θεῶν οὐδὲν ἢ βροτῶν μέλει.
ἢ **τὴν τύχην** μὲν δαίμον' ἡγεῖσθαι χρεών,
τὰ δαιμόνων δὲ **τῆς τύχης** ἐλάσσονα.

And after his most beautiful Trojan endeavors, do not destroy Odysseus himself and his sailors at the hands of an individual to whom there is no care for gods or men. Otherwise, we will have to regard **Chance** as a deity and the deities as inferior to **Chance**.

(*Cyc.* 603-607)

[GO4] The author emphasizes the tree. There are two components to the dramatic depiction of the blinding. The first one concerns the planning process: Homer has Odysseus planning to get Polyphemus drunk before blinding him with the staff of green olivewood, but Euripides goes one step further, by having Odysseus plan to discourage Polyphemus from making any sort of contact with the Cyclopes before even attempting to get him drunk, let alone blinding him with the stake of olive. Clearly, the dramatic Odysseus is playing chess while the epic Odysseus is playing checkers.

Κύκλωπος γὰρ ἔκειτο μέγα **ῥόπαλον** παρὰ σηκῷ,
χλωρὸν ἐλαΐνεον...

Indeed, beside the pen lay the Cyclops' great **staff of green olivewood**...

(*Od.* 9.319-320)

κώμου μὲν αὐτὸν τοῦδ' ἀπαλλάξαι, λέγων
ὡς οὐ **Κύκλωψι** πῶμα χρὴ δοῦναι τόδε,
μόνον δ' ἔχοντα βίοτον ἡδέως ἄγειν.
ὅταν δ' ὑπνώσσῃ Βακχίου νικώμενος,
ἀκρεμὼν ἐλαίας ἔστιν ἐν δόμοισί τις,
ὃν φασγάνῳ τῷδ' ἐξαποξύνας ἄκρον
ἐς πῦρ καθήσω· κᾆθ' ὅταν κεκαυμένον
ἴδω νιν, ἄρας θερμὸν ἐς μέσην βαλῶ
Κύκλωπος ὄψιν ὄμμα τ' ἐκτήξω πυρί.

I intend to keep him away from that revel, by telling him that there is no need for him to give this drink **to the Cyclopes**, but to go through life pleasantly, keeping it to himself. Once he becomes drowsy, overcome by Bacchus, there is **a stake of olive** in his abode, whose tip, after sharpening it with this sword, I will put into the fire. When I see it kindling, having lifted it while still glowing, I will thrust it into the mid-forehead eye of the Cyclops and melt his eye with the fire.

(*Cyc.* 451-459)

[GO5] Euripides also emphasizes the sex by means of the "Ganymede : Zeus :: Silenus : Polyphemus" analogy. According to the *Iliad*, the Trojan Ganymede was the son of Tros, the eponymous king of Troy, as well as the brother of Ilus, from whom the city received the name of Ilium. Just as Aphrodite comes out from the Judgment of Paris as the most beautiful amongst female immortals, so too does Ganymede stand out as the most beautiful amongst male mortals. His beauty even earns him the job of wine steward to the king of the gods. Such conquest by Zeus reflected the Greek social norm of a sexual relationship between an adult man and a pubescent youth.

Out of this background, the author of the *Cyclops* constructs his analogy by assuming that "Ganymede is to Zeus what Silenus is to Polyphemus". In other words, the drunken Polyphemus sees in Silenus a potential passive-role sexual partner, thus allowing for the utilization of sex as one of the pillars of any satyr drama worth its ranking within the genre. Hence, the beauty of the most beautiful hero serves as a source of inspiration for a type of sexual encounter that would be more beautiful than one with a woman.

Ἶλός τ' Ἀσσάρακός τε καὶ ἀντίθεος **Γανυμήδης**,
ὃς δὴ **κάλλιστος** γένετο θνητῶν ἀνθρώπων·
τὸν καὶ ἀνηρείψαντο θεοὶ Διὶ οἰνοχοεύειν
κάλλεος εἵνεκα οἷο, ἵν' ἀθανάτοισι μετείη.

Ilus, Assaracus, and the godlike **Ganymede**, who was born as **the most beautiful** of mortal men: on account of his **beauty** the gods carried him off to pour out wine for Zeus, so that he could be among the immortals.

(*Il.* 20.232-235)

ἅλις· **Γανυμήδη τόνδ'** ἔχων ἀναπαύσομαι
κάλλιον ἢ τὰς Χάριτας. ἥδομαι δέ πως
τοῖς παιδικοῖσι μᾶλλον ἢ τοῖς θήλεσιν.

Enough! I will sleep **more beautifully** with **this Ganymede** than with the Graces. Anyway, I take more pleasure in youths than in women.

(*Cyc.* 582-584)

[GO6] Additionally, the playwright emphasizes the mistaken identity through a change in the timing of the name trick.[153] The epic highlights the relevance of the name trick by placing it in the middle of the sequence, after the boulder trick and before the ram trick. It also stresses the pun between the proper noun "Nobody" and the pronoun "nobody". The play on words is simple but effective: Polyphemus means that someone named Nobody is seeking to kill him, but his fellow Cyclopes interpret his statement as meaning that nothing is happening. Furthermore, Polyphemus tries to distinguish between a positive statement (Nobody is using trickery) and a negative one (Nobody is not using force), but such subtleties end up being conflated thanks to

153 On the emphasis on the mistaken identity, see O'Sullivan & Collard (2013): "Odysseus takes command of the situation early, speaking at times misleadingly (524, 526, 528) and preparing to use the trick of calling himself 'Nobody' (549), famous from Homer (cf. 672-5)" (p. 53), and "The blinded monster's reappearance and recognition of his own situation can be seen as a farce (663-709), in which the satyrs taunt their longtime tormentor with Odysseus' trick of Nobody (672-3). The satyrs' jokes with the name are certainly consistent with the Homeric hero's own mirth when he sees his trick take effect (*Od.* 9.413-14)" (p. 55). Cf. Hunter & Laemmle (2020, p. 16).

the presupposed negative of the name taken as a pronoun, and all that the Cyclopes hear is a double negative (nobody is using neither trickery nor force).

> ‘ὦ φίλοι, **Οὖτίς** με κτείνει δόλῳ **οὐδὲ βίηφιν**.’
> οἱ δ’ ἀπαμειβόμενοι ἔπεα πτερόεντ’ ἀγόρευον·
> ‘εἰ μὲν δὴ **μή τίς** σε **βιάζεται** οἶον ἐόντα,
> νοῦσον γ’ οὔ πως ἔστι Διὸς μεγάλου ἀλέασθαι,
> ἀλλὰ σύ γ’ εὔχεο πατρὶ Ποσειδάωνι ἄνακτι.’
>
> “O dear ones, **Nobody** seeks to kill me with trickery **and not by force**!” In answer, they pronounced these winged words: “If, indeed, **no one uses** their **force** against you who are alone, there is no way for you to avoid the sickness of the great Zeus, but still, pray to our father, the lord Poseidon.”
>
> (*Od.* 9.408-412)

Similarly, the drama profits from the comical implications of the confusion. But what was simple becomes complex: the assertion that Nobody destroyed Polyphemus can be taken as expressing that there was no wrong done to him; the claim that Nobody is blinding him, as stating that he is not blind; and even the question regarding the whereabouts of this Nobody, as deserving a nonsensical answer, for the word “there”, as part of an utterance such as “there is nobody”, does not denote an actual place. Where the Homeric Odysseus had a good laugh, the Euripidean Satyrs come close to rolling on the floor laughing.

> ΚΥΚΛΩΨ
> **Οὖτίς** μ’ **ἀπώλεσ’**.
>
> ΧΟΡΟΣ
> οὐκ ἄρ’ **οὐδείς** <σ’> **ἠδίκει**.
>
> ΚΥΚΛΩΨ
> **Οὖτίς** με **τυφλοῖ** βλέφαρον.
>
> ΧΟΡΟΣ
> **οὐκ** ἄρ’ εἶ **τυφλός**.
>
> ΚΥΚΛΩΨ
> †ὡς δὴ σύ†.

ΧΟΡΟΣ
καὶ πῶς σ’ οὔτις ἂν θείη τυφλόν;

ΚΥΚΛΩΨ
σκώπτεις. ὁ δ’ **Οὖτις** ποῦ ’στιν;

ΧΟΡΟΣ
οὐδαμοῦ, Κύκλωψ.

CYCLOPS
Nobody destroyed me.

CHORUS
Then, **nobody did wrong** to you.

CYCLOPS
Nobody blinds me right in my eye.

CHORUS
Then, you are **not blind**.

CYCLOPS
<Oh, that you were!>

CHORUS
And how could nobody make you blind?

CYCLOPS
You are mocking me. But where is this **Nobody**?

CHORUS
O Cyclops, he is **nowhere**.

(*Cyc*. 672-675)

The Euripidean Odysseus also has his fun. When he eventually reveals his name, he does so on the sly: he does not speak of Odysseus, but of his body; he does not act in defiance of Polyphemus, but out of self-preservation; and he is not close by, but at a safe distance. He is not acting the part of the well-trained warrior, but that of the well-read actor. In fact, it is not the Cyclops but Odysseus himself who alludes to the ancient prophecy as per the *Odyssey*.

ΟΔΥΣΣΕΥΣ
τηλοῦ σέθεν
φυλακαῖσι φρουρῶ σῶμ' Ὀδυσσέως τόδε.

ΚΥΚΛΩΨ
πῶς εἶπας; ὄνομα μεταβαλὼν καινὸν λέγεις.

ΟΔΥΣΣΕΥΣ
ὅπερ μ' ὁ φύσας ὠνόμαζ' Ὀδυσσέα,
δώσειν δ' ἔμελλες ἀνοσίου δαιτὸς δίκας·

ODYSSEUS
Far from you, I set a watch over this body of Odysseus.

CYCLOPS
What did you just say? Having changed your name, you boast of a new one.

ODYSSEUS
The very one my father gave me: Odysseus. And you were destined to pay the penalty for your impious banquet.

(*Cyc.* 689-693)

[GO7] In terms of spatial location, Euripides changes the action to a Mediterranean venue: the island of Sicily.[154] The Homeric

---

154 E.g., *Cyc.* 20, *Cyc.* 60, *Cyc.* 95, *Cyc.* 106, *Cyc.* 114, *Cyc.* 130, *Cyc.* 298, *Cyc.* 366, *Cyc.* 395, *Cyc.* 599, *Cyc.* 660, and *Cyc.* 703. On the change of location, see O'Sullivan & Collard (2013): "But those expecting a close emulation of Homer may have been surprised to learn of the location of Euripides' drama on Sicily, an innovation possibly attributable to the Sicilian poet Epicharmus (F 70-2 *PCG*); in *Odyssey* 9 the home of the Cyclopes is never made clear. Yet in Euripides' *Cyclops* the Sicilian location is made explicit fourteen times in a play of just of 700 lines (20, 60, 95 (twice), 106, 114 (twice), 130, 298, 366, 395, 599, 660, 703)" (p. 42); and Shaw (2018): "Not only has Euripides moved the action of the play from the geographically uncertain Homeric world to the island of Sicily, but he also mentions Sicily and Mt. Aetna a remarkable thirteen times over the course of the play" (p. 84), "He also appears to update the myth in a way that alludes to recent historical events, particularly the infamous Sicilian Expedition. From 415 to 413, the Athenians waged a battle to incorporate Sicily into their 'Empire'" (p. 83), and "Euripides may have even drawn on this myth because the audience would have been mindful of the poet's role in saving Athenian soldiers who were captured by barbarians and confined to a rocky prison. Polyphemus and the Cyclopes represent the Sicilian natives; Odysseus and his men are the arrogant and ill-prepared Athenians; Polyphemus' cave is the rocky quarry that imprisons the Greeks; and Euripides' poetry literally saves the day, with the prisoners escaping

geography is fictional, with its unlocated land of the Cyclopes, and its neighboring island of the goats. The Euripidean geography, in turn, is real: Malea is a cape in the southeast of the Peloponnese, which marked the sailing route towards Italy; and Aetna is a volcano in the east of Sicily. Although the characters and themes remain the subject of stories, there is an authorial intention of grounding spaces and times in historical facts. This agrees with the criticism of unbelievability that the play directs towards the epic.

> **Νῆσος** ἔπειτα λάχεια παρὲκ λιμένος τετάνυσται,
> **γαίης Κυκλώπων** οὔτε σχεδὸν οὔτ' ἀποτηλοῦ,
> ὑλήεσσ'· ἐν δ' **αἶγες** ἀπειρέσιαι γεγάασιν
> ἄγριαι...
>
> Now, a small, wooded **island** stretches outside the harbor, neither close to **the land of the Cyclopes** nor far from it, in which countless wild **goats** have been raised...
>
> (*Od.* 9.116-119)

> ἤδη δὲ **Μαλέας** πλησίον πεπλευκότας
> ἀπηλιώτης ἄνεμος ἐμπνεύσας δορὶ
> ἐξέβαλεν ἡμᾶς τήνδ' ἐς **Αἰτναίαν** πέτραν,
> ἵν' οἱ μονῶπες ποντίου παῖδες θεοῦ
> Κύκλωπες οἰκοῦσ' ἄντρ' ἔρημ' ἀνδροκτόνοι.
>
> Now, while we were sailing near **Malea**, an east wind blowing upon our mast made us go off course towards this rock of the **Aetna**, where the one-eyed sons of the sea god, the murderous Cyclopes, live in their solitary caves.
>
> (*Cyc.* 18-22)

[GO8] The author also changes the time, reducing several days of action to just one, and thus following the Greek theatrical convention. According to Aristotle,[155] "the latter [sc. tragedy] tries above all to be of under **one round trip of the sun**, or to exceed it by little; but epic is unlimited in time span and differs in this respect [ἡ μὲν ὅτι μάλιστα πειρᾶται ὑπὸ **μίαν περίοδον ἡλίου** εἶναι

---

through the poet's theatrical creation" (pp. 84-85). On the Sicilian Expedition, see Plutarch *Nic.* 29.2-5.

155 I follow the Greek text by Halliwell (Aristotle; Longinus; Demetrius, 1995). The translations are my own.

ἢ μικρὸν ἐξαλλάττειν, ἡ δὲ ἐποποιία ἀόριστος τῷ χρόνῳ καὶ τούτῳ διαφέρει]" (*Poet.* 1449b11-14).

The epic mentions the dawn of a new day on five separate occasions (*Od.* 152, *Od.* 170, *Od.* 307, *Od.* 437, and *Od.* 560), which means that the action stretches for at least six days. In addition, the Greek warriors are held captive inside of the cave for at least two nights: from days three to four, and four to five. In contrast, the play traces only the happenings of less than one round trip of the sun: a good part of the day has already passed, since the kids and lambs have been sleeping all day; but it is still daytime, because the daylight still allows for the trading of merchandise; and given the amount of sun-heat, the exact time of day must be the afternoon.

> Ἦμος δ' ἠριγένεια φάνη ῥοδοδάκτυλος **Ἠώς**,
>
> As soon as the early **Dawn** of rosy fingers showed herself...
>
> (*Od.* 9.152 = 170 = 307 = 437 = 560)

> ποθοῦσί σ' **ἀμερόκοι-**
> **τοι** βλαχαὶ σμικρῶν τεκέων.
>
> Among the little young ones, the bleating ones **who have slept all day** are longing for you.
>
> (*Cyc.* 58-59)

> ἐκφέρετε· **φῶς** γὰρ ἐμπολήμασιν πρέπει.
>
> Bring them, for **daylight** suits merchandise.
>
> (*Cyc.* 137)

> καὶ πρός γε **θάλπος ἡλίου** πίνειν καλόν.
>
> And, besides, it is nice to drink **in the heat of the sun**.
>
> (*Cyc.* 542)

[GO9] The playwright changes the authoritarian figure. There are two sides to this procedure. On one side, Dionysus' authority is positively highlighted, when the epic's wine drinking becomes the play's worshipping of the god of wine.[156] On a superficial level, the epic has vines and wine as antedating the arrival of the Greeks, whereas the drama stresses the fact that the inebriating liquor is a Greek invention. However, on a deeper level, there is the association of wine with Dionysus, and therefore, the reinterpretation of drinking as a form of worship. If wine/Dionysus is divine, then it/he must be worshipped. This idea receives further development. For instance, when the epic Odysseus offers the wine to Polyphemus, he introduces it as a special drink coming from his ship, but the dramatic Odysseus is no tagalong, so when he gets to this part of his script, he carefully makes sure to give it his personal touch: this drink is divine, precisely because of its association with Dionysus.

> Κύκλωψ, τῆ, πίε οἶνον, ἐπεὶ φάγες ἀνδρόμεα κρέα,
> ὄφρ' εἰδῇς **οἷόν τι ποτὸν τόδε** νηῦς ἐκεκεύθει
> ἡμετέρη...
>
> O Cyclops, here, drink the wine, after you have eaten human flesh, so that you know **this sort of drink** that our ship contained.
>
> (*Od.* 9.347-349)
>
> ...Ὦ τοῦ ποντίου θεοῦ Κύκλωψ,
> σκέψαι **τόδ' οἷον** Ἑλλὰς ἀμπέλων ἄπο
> **θεῖον** κομίζει **πῶμα, Διονύσου γάνος.**

156 On Dionysus' authority, see O'Sullivan & Collard (2013): "Interestingly, Homer emphasizes Odysseus' own thought processes in devising his revenge on the monster; it is a βουλή ('plan') that seems best to him (*Od.* 9.318, cf. 302). In Euripides' version the hero's escape plan is 'an idea sent from some god' (literally, 'something divine': τι θεῖον) that comes to him (*Cyc.* 411), and from here Dionysus is a more palpable presence in the play in the form of wine" (p. 51); Shaw (2018): "The name *Bacchios* is used twelve times, Bromios is mentioned six times, and *Dionysos* five, which averages out to about one mention of the god in every thirty lines" (p. 66), "His very first words in the first verse of the play are addressed to the god: 'Oh, Bromius!'" (p. 66), and "Then, at the end of the play, as the chorus of satyrs exit the stage, they sing one final couplet (708-9), exclaiming that they 'will be slaves to Bacchus for the rest of time'" (p. 68); and Hunter & Laemmle (2020): "The complete absence of wine from Cyclops-society, a striking difference from *Odyssey* 9, means that its introduction and destructive effect upon the Cyclops become, more sharply, another variation on the very familiar narrative and dramatic theme of the introduction of Dionysus' rites to a land or city which did not practice them before" (p. 17).

> O Cyclops, son of the sea god, look at **this sort of divine drink** that Greece procures out of the vines: **the crown jewel of Dionysus.**
>
> (*Cyc.* 413-415)

Furthermore, if human beings worship wine/Dionysus, then it/he favors them in return. Unlike the ingenious Odysseus from the epic, who comes up with a plan all on his own, the devoted Odysseus from the theater receives a divine idea. In this way, this self-proclaimed sommelier turns out to be the most enthusiastic of the devotees. From a structural point of view, the dramatist has re-created Zeus' plan as "Dionysus' plan": introducing an unwilling authoritarian to the liberating effects of wine. In a fifth-century context, relieving the world from overpopulation no longer makes sense as a divine plan, but preaching the gospel of Dionysus does. One might even recall that Euripides' *Bacchae* seem to have made it all the way to Parthia (Plutarch, *Crass.* 33.2).

On the other side of the procedure, Polyphemus' authority is negatively highlighted, when the adaptation introduces another treat suitable to this fifth-century context: the tyrannical perspective.[157] The dramatic Polyphemus is still an anthropophagus ogre, just like his epic counterpart, but as was the case with several other features of the adaptation, there is more to this than meets the eye. On one hand, the Euripidean Cyclopes might not yet be oenophiles, but by looking at their expertise vis-à-vis high-grade meat, one is tempted to view them as *bons vivants*. This is evinced in the first of the two following passages from *Cyclops*.

On the other hand, the re-created text encourages its audience to make a connection between the image of the mythical ogre, literally devouring the heroes of yore, and that of any historical tyrant, figuratively devouring the ordinary citizens – and alongside them,

157 On Polyphemus' authority, see O'Sullivan & Collard (2013): "Polyphemus' status as tyrannical ogre is central to his characterization in *Cyclops*, and he is often referred to negatively by the chorus as their 'master' (34, 90, 163, etc.) while they are his slaves (24, 78, 79, 442). The monster as slave-owning despot marks a key difference in his identity from his Homeric counterpart while still retaining much of the savagery of his epic incarnation. For the audience watching at the City Dionysia in democratic Athens, Polyphemus' tyrannical leanings would intensify his villainy" (pp. 49-50).

the democratic ideal. In other words, the adapted Polyphemus remains a man-eating monster, albeit one with a newly found refinement, but he also becomes a slave-owning despot. These two functions are distributed according to those surrounding him: Odysseus is his potential meal, but Silenus and his Satyrs are the actual slaves of this one-eyed "master", which is, precisely, the term used to refer to him in the second quoted passage from *Cyclops*.

> Ὣς ἐφάμην, τοῖσιν δὲ κατεκλάσθη φίλον ἦτορ
> μνησαμένοις ἔργων Λαιστρυγόνος Ἀντιφάταο
> Κύκλωπός τε βίης μεγαλήτορος, **ἀνδροφάγοιο**.
>
> I spoke thusly, and they were brokenhearted, having remembered the deeds of Antiphates the Laestrygonian, and the violence of the greathearted, **man-eating** Cyclops.
>
> (*Od.* 10.198-200)
>
> **γλυκύτατά** φασι **τὰ κρέα** τοὺς ξένους φορεῖν.
>
> They [sc. the Cyclopes] say that strangers bear **the tastiest flesh**.
>
> (*Cyc.* 126)
>
> τίνες ποτ' εἰσίν; οὐκ ἴσασι **δεσπότην**
> Πολύφημον οἷός ἐστιν ἄξενόν τε γῆν
> τήνδ' ἐμβεβῶτες καὶ Κυκλωπίαν γνάθον
> τὴν **ἀνδροβρῶτα** δυστυχῶς ἀφιγμένοι.
>
> Who can they possibly be? They must not know what our **master** Polyphemus is like, since they have set foot in this inhospitable land, and they have unfortunately arrived at the **man-eating** jaws of the Cyclops.
>
> (*Cyc.* 90-93)

[GO10] Euripides changes the role of the priest. Regarding Maron, the epic narrative is very thorough: he is the son of Euantes and the priest of Apollo. Presumably, when Odysseus met him, Maron would have been in the company of his wife and child. By "reverently embracing" the priest and his family, what would be meant is that they were let go unharmed, out of respect for the priestly condition of the father. Then comes the mention of the wine, which among several other epithets, is said to be of a divine nature. The story evolves backwards, to a time before the encounter, and it focuses on the house that would be located somewhere within the wooded grove. Other characters are mentioned as well: the slaves, the handmaidens, and a housekeeper. And there is even a picture of the prosperous lifestyle antedating the arrival of Odysseus: husband and wife secretly enjoying the divinely sweet liquor, without a care in the world.

As much as the clever Odysseus from the Homeric Epics wants to show off, in this case by boldly claiming some sort of clairvoyance when anticipating the encounter with the ogre, the truly resourceful spirit is that of the author, who announces some key elements that will eventually tilt the scales in favor of the hero: not only is the wine's alcohol content so high as to require some significant diluting, but also the wineskin is large enough to get Polyphemus drunk. Talk about being keen – Homer lets almost nothing slide.

Going back to Euripides, the authorial decision here is to ignore Maron's relation to Apollo, and to provide him with a similar link to Dionysus: if the drink coming from the epic Maron is twice characterized as being divine, the dramatic Maron himself is divine. He goes from priest of a god to son of a god. Moreover, given the overarching triumph of Dionysus in the satyr drama, there is no need to justify the high standing given to Maron.

> …ἀτὰρ αἴγεον ἀσκὸν ἔχον μέλανος οἴνοιο
> ἡδέος, ὅν μοι ἔδωκε Μάρων, **Εὐάνθεος υἱός,**
> **ἱρεὺς Ἀπόλλωνος**, ὃς Ἴσμαρον ἀμφιβεβήκει,
> οὕνεκά μιν **σὺν παιδὶ περισχόμεθ' ἠδὲ γυναικὶ**
> **ἁζόμενοι**· ᾤκει γὰρ **ἐν ἄλσεϊ δενδρήεντι**
> Φοίβου Ἀπόλλωνος. ὁ δέ μοι πόρεν ἀγλαὰ δῶρα·
> χρυσοῦ μέν μοι ἔδωκ' ἐυεργέος ἑπτὰ τάλαντα,
> δῶκε δέ μοι κρητῆρα πανάργυρον, αὐτὰρ ἔπειτα
> οἶνον ἐν ἀμφιφορεῦσι δυώδεκα πᾶσιν ἀφύσσας
> ἡδὺν ἀκηράσιον, **θεῖον ποτόν**· οὐδέ τις αὐτὸν
> ἠείδη **δμώων** οὐδ' **ἀμφιπόλων ἐνὶ οἴκῳ,**
> ἀλλ' αὐτὸς ἄλοχός τε φίλη **ταμίη** τε μί' οἴη.
> τὸν δ' ὅτε πίνοιεν μελιηδέα οἶνον ἐρυθρόν,
> ἓν δέπας ἐμπλήσας **ὕδατος ἀνὰ εἴκοσι μέτρα**
> χεῦ', ὀδμὴ δ' **ἡδεῖα** ἀπὸ κρητῆρος ὀδώδει
> **θεσπεσίη**· τότ' ἂν οὔ τοι ἀποσχέσθαι φίλον ἦεν.

> τοῦ φέρον ἐμπλήσας **ἀσκὸν μέγαν**, ἐν δὲ καὶ ᾖα
> κωρύκῳ· αὐτίκα γάρ μοι ὀίσατο θυμὸς ἀγήνωρ
> ἄνδρ' ἐπελεύσεσθαι μεγάλην ἐπιειμένον ἀλκήν,
> ἄγριον, οὔτε δίκας ἐὺ εἰδότα οὔτε θέμιστας.
>
> Moreover, I had a goat-hide wineskin of sweet, dark wine, given to me by Maron, **son of Euantes and priest of Apollo** – who, in turn, protected Ismarus. Because of that, we had **reverently embraced him, together with his wife and child** since he dwelled **in a wooded grove** of Phoebus Apollo. And he furnished me with some splendid gifts: he gave me seven talents of wrought gold, and he gave me an all-silver bowl, and having poured it into twelve whole jars, a sweet, unmixed wine, a truly **divine drink**. **In his house**, none of **the slaves** or **the handmaidens** knew about it, but only himself, his beloved wife, and a single **housekeeper**. And whenever they drank the honey-sweet, red wine, after filling one cup, he poured it **into twenty measures of water**, and a **divinely sweet** smell would come out of the bowl; then, it certainly was not easy to abstain from it. This is what I was carrying, after filling **a huge wineskin**, as well as some provisions in a leathern sack, for I anticipated, in my heroic spirit, going against a savage man, clad in great strength, and knowing neither justice nor laws.
>
> (*Od.* 9.196-215)
>
> καὶ μὴν Μάρων μοι πῶμ' ἔδωκε, **παῖς θεοῦ**.
>
> And surely, Maron, **the son of the god** [sc. Dionysus], gave me the drink.
>
> (*Cyc.* 141)

[GO11] The playwright changes the lot into a choice.[158] In book 9, during the final stages of planning the blinding, Odysseus leads his

158 On the change of the lot into a choice, see Hunter & Laemmle (2020): "In *Cyclops*, by contrast, the satyrs make much of the question as to which of them will handle the fiery torch together with Odysseus (vv. 483-6, 630-45); here there is no talk of the lot, it is just assumed that Odysseus will give the command. In the end, of course, no satyr comes anywhere near the 'serious action', but it is at least worth asking whether Euripides' employment of the motif implicitly recognises the improbability of Odysseus' Homeric narration that his comrades drew lots for this 'privilege' and that the lot produced just the result Odysseus would have chosen anyway" (pp. 10-11).

companions, not by appointing them to join him, but by ordering them to draw lots. Unlike previous instances, such as when he sailed from the island of the goats with a small but undetermined number of companions, or when he walked towards the cave of the Cyclops with a group of twelve companions, now Odysseus does not decide who will participate in this last phase of the adventure. When the stakes are higher, the hero leaves the decision-making up to chance. However, there is an exact correlation between the hero's wishes and the author's plans: the four allotted men would have been chosen anyway. When Odysseus himself takes the last spot, the group adds up to five, but it is still presented in terms of four plus one.

In *Cyclops*, Odysseus' lips are sealed, and the Satyrs call him out on it. The two contrasting passages offer examples of questions, as if the characters were wondering whether the protagonist has forgotten his lines. The recurring image of drawing them up suggests the direct order of a general, instead of the open-ended option of blind fate, which would follow a drawing of lots. The funniest thing here is the fact that the brave companions from the epic have been ironically supplanted by the cowardly Satyrs from the play. If the reference began with the Chorus calling out the protagonist for his apparent forgetfulness, it ends with him calling them out for their cowardice.

> αὐτὰρ τοὺς ἄλλους **κλήρῳ** πεπαλάσθαι ἄνωγον,
> ὅς τις τολμήσειεν ἐμοὶ σὺν μοχλὸν ἀείρας
> τρῖψαι ἐν ὀφθαλμῷ, ὅτε τὸν γλυκὺς ὕπνος ἱκάνοι.
> οἱ δ' **ἔλαχον** τοὺς ἄν κε καὶ ἤθελον αὐτὸς ἑλέσθαι,
> τέσσαρες, αὐτὰρ ἐγὼ πέμπτος μετὰ τοῖσιν ἐλέγμην.
>
> Then, I ordered the others to determine **by lot** which one would venture with me, after raising the stake, to work it into his [sc. the Cyclops'] eye, when sweet sleep had come upon him. Those four whom I would have wished to choose **were allotted**, and after them, I took the fifth place.
>
> (*Od.* 9.331-335)

> ἄγε, τίς πρῶτος, τίς δ' ἐπὶ πρώτῳ
> **ταχθεὶς** δαλοῦ κώπην ὀχμάσαι
> Κύκλωπος ἔσω βλεφάρων ὤσας
> λαμπρὰν ὄψιν διακναίσει;

> Come on, **having been drawn up**, who will be the first, and who the one after the first, to grip the haft of the firebrand, and after thrusting it between the eyelids of the Cyclops, who will gouge out his bright eye?
>
> (*Cyc.* 483-486)

> οὔκουν σὺ **τάξεις** οὕστινας πρώτους χρεὼν
> καυτὸν μοχλὸν λαβόντας ἐκκάειν τὸ φῶς
> Κύκλωπος, ὡς ἂν τῆς τύχης κοινώμεθα;

> Will you not **draw** us **up**, proclaiming those who, after grasping the stake, will be the first ones to burn out the eye of the Cyclops, so that we would partake of this fate?
>
> (*Cyc.* 632-634)

[GO12] Lastly, the author maintains the hospitality.[159] The epic presents the whole encounter with the ogre as a sort of counterexample of hospitality, and the gifts are no exception to such rule. Instead of being fed a proper meal, Odysseus is intended to serve himself as a meal for the man-eating monster. Therefore, the place of honor at the table suddenly turns into the specials section on the menu. But there is a double entendre here: for the character, eating "Nobody last" means ingesting Odysseus, while for the audience, eventually, it signifies being unable to finish his meal.

The dramatic rendition substitutes one gift for several gifts, all of which can be read ironically in relation to the poetics of hospitality: the fire is not for getting dry and warm, but for getting cooked; the salt, although "fatherly", is not a family heirloom coming from his father Poseidon, god of the sea, but merely the

159 On maintaining the gift of hospitality, see Shaw (2018): "The main theme that Euripides adopts from the Homeric original is the concept of *xenia*, the ancient notion of reciprocal hospitality..." (p. 75), and "Euripides adopts the theme of the guest-host relationship from Homer's story of Polyphemus and Odysseus, using the terms *xenos* (guest/host) and *xenia* (guest-host relationship) twenty-three times in the short play. In addition, Odysseus asks if the Sicilians are 'lovers of strangers' (*philoxenoi*, 125), Polyphemus is twice called 'guest-eater' (*xenodaitumos*, 610 and *xenodaita*, 658), and Sicily is dubbed 'unfriendly to guests' (*axenon*, 91). These examples amount to about one mention of guests, hosts, or the guest-host relationship every twenty-six lines, an average that confirms the thematic importance of *xenia* in the play" (p. 76).

right seasoning; and the cauldron is described through the same wording that would be used for any fancy clothing that could have been exchanged during a more hospitable welcome, thus turning the raggedy urchin into a snappy dresser.

> Οὖτιν ἐγὼ πύματον ἔδομαι μετὰ οἷς ἑτάροισιν,
> τοὺς δ' ἄλλους πρόσθεν· τὸ δέ τοι **ξεινήιον** ἔσται.
>
> I will eat Nobody last after his companions, and the others first: you will have this **gift of hospitality**.
>
> (*Od.* 9.369-370)
>
> **ξένια** δὲ λήψη τοιάδ', ὡς ἄμεμπτος ὦ,
> πῦρ καὶ πατρῷον ἅλα λέβητά θ', ὃς ζέσας
> σὴν σάρκα δυσφάρωτον ἀμφέξει καλῶς.
>
> So that I am not to blame, you will receive these **gifts of hospitality**: a fire, some fatherly salt, and a cauldron, which, having boiled, will duly clothe your ill-dressed body.
>
> (*Cyc.* 342-344)

"Hey! Middle One, Come Quick!"

Book 1 of the *Mahābhārata* consists of nineteen minor books, and it serves to frame the story as a form of storytelling in and of itself. Minor book 1 introduces the bard Ugraśravas and the seers of the Naimiṣa forest, who are the interlocutors of this dialogue-like narrative; and minor book 2 provides two lists of contents: one, in one hundred books, and the other, in eighteen books. Then come several stories about snakes: in minor book 3, a quest for some earrings leads to a conflict with the snakes, and then, to a sacrifice of the snakes; in minor book 4, a bride falls prey to a snakebite; and in minor book 5, a marriage is key to put an end to the snake sacrifice.

Minor book 6 offers a little perspective: Ugraśravas tells Śaunaka what Vaiśaṃpāyana told Janamejaya, that is, the *Mahābhārata*, going back to its very own author, known as Vyāsa. And minor book 7 packs in several stories: the origins of gods and humans; the tales of Śakuntalā, Yayāti, and Mahābhiṣa; the awesomeness of

Vyāsa's stepbrother Bhīṣma; the tale of Māṇḍavya; the births and marriages of Pāṇḍu and Dhṛtarāṣṭra, together with the ensuing births of the Pāṇḍavas and Kauravas; the tale of Vyuṣitāśva; and as a colophon, the story of Ekalavya. The main subject of minor book 8 is the fire at the house of lacquer: after burning it down and leaving behind six corpses, the five Pāṇḍava brothers and their mother Kuntī set out for their forest adventures, which include the killing of Hiḍimba (minor book 9) and the killing of Baka (minor book 10).

After the tales of Tapatī, Vasiṣṭha, and Aurva from minor book 11, Draupadī becomes the common wife of the five Pāṇḍava brothers in minor book 12: Arjuna wins her by being able to string a bow and hit a target, and Kuntī instructs her sons to share what food they have obtained during the day. Such an atypical wedding calls for Vyāsa himself to narrate the tale of the five Indras in minor book 13. Following this alliance with the Pañcālas, the steward Vidura mediates between the parties in minor book 14; and as a result, by minor book 15, the Kauravas are left with Hāstinapura, and the Pāṇḍavas with Indraprastha.

Minor book 16 opens with the tale of Sunda and Upasunda, intended to regulate the married life of the group, and ultimately responsible for Arjuna's exile, during which he begets Babhruvāhana. Then comes the securing of another major ally: the Vṛṣṇis. In minor book 17 Arjuna abducts Kṛṣṇa's sister Subhadrā; and in minor book 18 he begets Abhimanyu. In closing, and as a preview of what is yet to come, minor book 19 portrays the deeds of Arjuna and Kṛṣṇa during the fire at the Khāṇḍava tract, from which only a few, including the *śārṅgaka* birds, manage to escape.

In contrast with the preceding motifs, the Sanskrit narrative about the ogre comes from two sources: the story of Hiḍimba and the story of Baka. The ogre Hiḍimba (*MBh.* 1.139-144) lives in a tree close to the wood where the Pāṇḍavas are sleeping. Having identified a potential meal, the man-eater instructs his sister Hiḍimbā to kill the humans, and then to bring them over, so that they might cook them together. Four of the brothers and their mother are asleep, but Bhīma is awake. Hiḍimbā falls prey to love at first sight, and after changing her monstrous appearance for that of a beautiful woman, she confesses to him: his brother wants the whole family as his meal, but she prefers just him as a suitable husband.

Hiḍimba grows impatient and decides to finish the job all by himself. Self-confident enough, Bhīma rejects Hiḍimbā's offer to carry the whole family away. Hiḍimba is outraged by his sister's behavior, and he intends to kill her as well. Still confident in his abilities, Bhīma not only defends Hiḍimbā, but also attempts to defeat Hiḍimba without even waking up his family members. However, the havoc is stentorian. Kuntī wakes up first, and Hiḍimbā tells her what she had told Bhīma: she came for the meal but stayed for the eye candy. When the rest of the brothers wake up, Arjuna offers to help Bhīma, for as he says, ogres become mightier just before dawn. Bhīma quits horsing around, and he breaks Hiḍimba's body in half.

Then, Bhīma would have killed Hiḍimbā too if it was not for Yudhiṣṭhira. Persistently, Hiḍimbā asks Kuntī to let her marry Bhīma, but it is also Yudhiṣṭhira who ends up giving his blessing, which comes with some ground rules: they may love each other during the day, but Bhīma must return to his family at night. On the very same day of conception, she gives birth to Ghaṭotkaca, who is born already looking like a fully grown youth, and who vows to come and help the Pāṇḍavas when needed. The episode closes with Vyāsa leading them to the house of a Brahman priest at Ekacakrā, where the next adventure awaits them.

The ogre Baka[160] (*MBh.* 1.145-152) lives in a wood near the town where the Pāṇḍavas are staying. For some time, the brothers beg for alms, half of which feeds four of them plus their mother, and the other half of which barely suffices for the voracious Bhīma. One day, while the rest of the group is out begging, Kuntī notices the grief of the Brahman, and she exhorts Bhīma to help in whatever way possible. Mother and son find the Brahman at a crossroads: he is torn by the impossible choice of sacrificing either a member

160 As pointed by Hiltebeitel (2001, p. 138), Baka relates to the Crane disguise of Yama-Dharma.

of his family or himself, which in the long run, would also mean sacrificing those who depend on him to survive.

Shortly thereafter, all the family members, one after another, turn to martyrs: his wife steps up by claiming that, as per female duty and having already granted him progeny, her own life is the only thing left for her to sacrifice; his older daughter volunteers too, after asserting that, since daughters are meant to be given away anyway, he might as well get it over with; and in an extremely moving scene, his younger son innocently boasts that he can kill the ogre with a straw that he picks up from the floor.

At this point, Kuntī reveals herself, and the Brahman fills in the gaps of the story: there is an ogre named Baka, who in exchange for protecting the village from other enemies, demands free meals in the form of rice and buffalos, as well as the humans who, by turns that come after several years, must take them over to him. Kuntī saves the day by offering Bhīma to take the place of the Brahman, with the sole condition that the latter does not breathe a word about it to anyone. When the other Pāṇḍavas return, Yudhiṣṭhira misjudges Kuntī's actions as rash, only to be immediately corrected both by her knowledge on duty and by Bhīma's record against ogres, as recently proven with the death of Hiḍimba.

The next day, Bhīma arrives at the wood with the food for Baka, which he tauntingly begins to eat. After ignoring him for a while, Bhīma eventually responds to Baka, who has uprooted a tree and thrown it at him, and fights back. A tree battle unfolds. Then, in another instance of his trademark move, Bhīma breaks Baka in half. When other ogres come to see what is happening, Bhīma threatens to do the same to them if they do not stop bothering the townsfolk. Baka's corpse is left at the city gate. Another day later, the townsfolk visit the Brahman looking for an explanation, but the Brahman, in compliance with his promise, just credits another unnamed Brahman for such superhuman deeds. Thus, the Pāṇḍavas manage to keep on living there for a while.

Regarding *The Middle One*, its sources include the *Hiḍimbavadhaparvan*, "The Book about the Killing of Hiḍimba" (*MBh.* 1.139-144) and the *Bakavadhaparvan*, "The Book about the

Killing of Baka" (*MBh.* 1.145-152).[161] The plot of the play is as follows: After the standard invocation of the god Viṣṇu, the prologue has the stage manager introduce all the elements that will be key for the play: a father and a son, a Brahman and a rakshasa, a middle one. Then, the one and only act progresses from one encounter to the next: the Brahman Keśavadāsa and his family meet the rakshasa Ghaṭotkaca, Ghaṭotkaca meets the hero Bhīma, and Bhīma meets the female rakshasa Hiḍimbā.

During the first encounter, that of Keśavadāsa and his family with Ghaṭotkaca, the Brahman is walking, alongside with his wife and his three sons, when suddenly, a rakshasa starts chasing them. The mother and the sons fear his appearance, but the Brahman is put at ease by his words. Ghaṭotkaca presents himself as one who venerates Brahmans but is still willing to hunt them down, since his mother has instructed him to do so. Keśavadāsa proposes to ask the Pāṇḍavas for help because he knows them to be living close by. However, the eldest son provides him with three pieces of information that take him on an emotional rollercoaster: on that day, the Pāṇḍavas are away, attending a sacrifice; Bhīma was left behind, in charge of protecting the hermitage; but at that time, he has also departed, looking to get some exercise.

161 On the story of Baka as a secondary source for the adaptation, see Pavolini (1918/1920, pp. 1-2). See also Brückner (1999/2000): "The motives of the middle one and the substitution of a Kṣatriya for a Brahmin have structural parallels in the MBh-story of the killing of Baka (I.10.147, *Bakavadhaparvan*) as well as in the Śunaḥśepa-legend of the Aitareya-Brahmaṇa to which the text alludes almost literally (VII.15.7)" (p. 521); Salomon (2010): "Although Ghaṭotkaca does not figure in the story of the demon Baka, one may well surmise that this incident, given its proximity in the original epic, inspired the playwright's elaboration of the older Ghaṭotkaca legends. Thus the MV can be understood as an adaptation and expansion of the original Mahābhārata legends about Ghaṭotkaca, partly by way of a 'contaminatio'..." (pp. 7-8); and Sutherland Goldman (2017): "The theme of the unloved and unwanted middle child has antecedents in the Śunaḥśepa story, known in its earliest version in *Aitareya Brāhmaṇa* 7.15.14-18... The other most probable source of Bhāsa's play, as noted by Devadhar, is the story of the demon Baka in the *Mahābhārata*" (p. 239). Cf. on the story of Śunaḥśepa as a secondary source for the adaptation, *AitBr.* 7.15.7 and *AitBr.* 7.15.14-18, as well as retellings in *MBh.* 13.3.6, *R.* 1.60.61, and *BhP.* 9.7 (Sutherland Goldman, 2017, p. 239, n. 45).

At this point, the eldest son asks Ghaṭotkaca to let them go, to which the rakshasa agrees, on the condition that Keśavadāsa relinquishes one of his sons. One after another, the Brahman, the wife, the eldest son, the middle son, and the youngest son voluntarily offer to sacrifice themselves. Ghaṭotkaca rejects the Brahman and the wife, for his mother would not be satisfied either by an old man or by a woman. After that, each parent chooses their favorite: he wants to keep the eldest, and she prefers the youngest. The unwanted middle son asks, as his dying wish, to go to a nearby pond and quench his thirst. But Ghaṭotkaca realizes that he is taking too long, and it is getting a little late for his mother's breakfast, so he decides to call him. The rakshasa does not know how to address him, and Keśavadāsa is only willing to go so far in helping him, so the eldest son tells Ghaṭotkaca that he just goes by "Middle One".

Calling for one "Middle One" (sc. the middle son), Ghaṭotkaca accidentally summons another "Middle One" (sc. Bhīma), which prompts the second encounter, between Ghaṭotkaca and Bhīma. They look at each other and it is as if they were looking in a mirror. Ghaṭotkaca asks Bhīma if he is another "Middle One", to which Bhīma replies that he is the one and only "Middle One". By then, Keśavadāsa recognizes Bhīma, and he does so just in time, for when the middle son comes back from his self-procured libation, there is already someone who can help. At this point, the audience learns that the action is set in the Kuru jungle, between the villages of Yūpa and Udyāmaka, on the day of the initiation of Keśavadāsa's cousin.

Ghaṭotkaca and Bhīma start talking, and as soon as the rakshasa mentions Hiḍimbā to be his mother, the hero recognizes him as his son, but he still decides to play along a little longer. Bhīma volunteers to step in on behalf of the middle son, arguing that the life of a Brahman is worth more than that of a Kshatriya. Then, Bhīma starts taunting Ghaṭotkaca, especially by insulting his paternal heritage, and this leads to the rakshasa fighting the hero. Ghaṭotkaca throws trees and mountaintops at Bhīma, he wrestles him, and he even attempts to bind him; but nothing seems to work. When Ghaṭotkaca mentions, one more time, that he is following orders, Bhīma is reminded about Hiḍimbā, and he continues his path, towards the third and last encounter.

Hiḍimbā recognizes Bhīma just by looking at him, and she immediately scolds Ghaṭotkaca for his mistake. But Ghaṭotkaca wants proof of his wrongdoing: Hiḍimbā salutes Bhīma as her husband, and only then does Ghaṭotkaca finally recognize him. After the anagnorisis, father and son come together in an embrace. Figuratively out of the woods, Keśavadāsa is ready to get literally out of there as well, but Bhīma offers to take him to the hermitage where the Pāṇḍavas are staying, as an overdue token of hospitality. Keśavadāsa replies by claiming that him and his family having been given back their lives is more than enough. They go their separate ways, and the play ends as it began, with a prayer to Viṣṇu.

There are twelve procedures that the playwright displays in his adaptation: [SO1][162] he merges two stories into one, [SO2] he adds the father/son conflict, [SO3] he adds the chance, [SO4] he emphasizes the trees, [SO5] he ignores the sex, [SO6] he emphasizes the mistaken identity, [SO7] he changes the place, [SO8] he changes the time, [SO9] he changes the authoritarian figure, [SO10] he changes the role of the Brahman, [SO11] he changes the lot into a choice, and [SO12] he maintains the hospitality.

[SO1] (Ps.-)Bhāsa's merging of two stories into one would be an Indian example of *contaminatio*, i.e., incorporating material from another *Mahābhārata* episode into the primary episode which he is adapting.[163] The story of Hiḍimba functions as the primary

162 SO stands for "Sanskrit Ogre". Hence, numbers SO1-SO12 refer to the adaptation of *MBh.* 1 into *The Middle One.* Once again, the list is limited to those examples that will allow me to argue for Greco-Roman parallelisms. Other techniques include changing Ghaṭotkaca's attitude towards Brahmans, maintaining the willing mother, changing the older sister into the eldest brother, maintaining the younger brother, adding the water offering, changing the husband/brother dilemma into the mother/father dilemma, and emphasizing Hiḍimbā's absence.

163 On the Roman use of *contaminatio*, see Brown (2015, para. 1). On the Indian use of *contaminatio*, see Pavolini (1918/1920, p. 1) and Salomon (2010, p. 8). Cf. Tieken's (1997) proposal about a merging of two aspects of an *upanayana* (initiation): "The play is concerned with the *upanayana* ceremony on more than one level. On one level we have the Brahman family on its way to attend a relative's son's initiation. On another level we have the task set for Ghaṭotkaca by his mother, which is reminiscent of the test set by the *guru*

episode: from its beginning, the ogress Hiḍimbā meeting the Pāṇḍava family turns into the ogre Ghaṭotkaca meeting the family of Brahmans; and from its ending, the encounter with the order-giving Hiḍimba becomes the encounter with the order-giving Hiḍimbā. The story of Baka provides most of the incorporated material: mainly, the Pāṇḍava family from the story of Hiḍimba is substituted for the family of Brahmans of the story of Baka. But as I will show, other stories also contribute with additional material: for instance, the father/son conflict comes from the story of Babhruvāhana (*MBh.* 14.78-82).

From the story of Hiḍimba, there are several elements that have been maintained, albeit with slight modifications. First, an ogre/ogress entrusts an ogress/ogre to bring back some humans for them to eat. The epic has Hiḍimba ordering Hiḍimbā; the play, Hiḍimbā ordering Ghaṭotkaca. Second, the entrusted ogress/ogre comes upon a family. The epic narrative portrays the Pāṇḍavas and Kuntī; the adaptation, the Brahman and his family. Third, the entrusted ogress/ogre ponders whether to follow the order or to act freely. The *MBh.* depicts Hiḍimbā's reflection on *strīdharma* (wife duty), which leads her to choose her potential husband Bhīma over her brother Hiḍimba; the *MV*, Ghaṭotkaca's reflection on *kṣatradharma* (warrior duty), which leads him to choose sparing the life of a Brahman over following the order of a mother.

Fourth, the entrusted ogress/ogre fails to bring back the humans. Vyāsa makes Hiḍimbā act out of love, whereas (Ps.-)Bhāsa makes Ghaṭotkaca act out of respect. Fifth, a hero meets the entrusting ogre/ogress. The storyteller has Bhīma intentionally sticking around for Hiḍimba, while the playwright has Bhīma fortuitously stumbling onto Hiḍimbā. And sixth, the hero has a duel with the ogre. In the older version, Bhīma fights Hiḍimba to the death; in the newer one, he fights Ghaṭotkaca until the latter recognizes him as his own father.

(or his wife) for his pupil as part of the latter's initiation. After the successful completion of his task Ghaṭotkaca is reunited with his father and mother, which duplicates the return of the *snātaka* to his family. It may be asked if the sacrifice of the middle son of the brahmin should not be considered such a test as well" (p. 32).

Something similar could be said about the dialectics of tradition and innovation in terms of the story of Baka. First, the entrusted ogress/ogre comes upon a family. As a feature that is common to both the story of Hiḍimba and that of Baka, the family serves to establish the connection. In the epic, the family members are a Brahman, his wife, his older daughter, and his younger son; in the drama, they are a Brahman, his wife, and his three sons, i.e., the eldest, the middle one, and the youngest. Second, a single family member must be chosen for the entrusting ogre/ogress. In the epic narrative, the townsfolk sacrifice themselves by turns, and by the day on which the events take place, the Brahman's number is up; in the adaptation, the Brahman is directly asked to choose one of his sons as a victim.

Third, there is a discussion aimed at figuring out how to proceed. The *MBh.*'s arguments are that, with the death of the Brahman, his family will also die; that the lives of his two children are equally valuable; and that, if offered as a victim, his wife will probably be spared; the *MV*'s arguments, in turn, are that, with the death of the Brahman, his family will live; that the lives of his eldest and youngest sons are more valuable than that of his middle son; and that, if offered as a victim, his wife will definitely be spared. Fourth, the entrusting ogress/ogre does not receive the chosen family member. Vyāsa's choice is Bhīma, whom Kuntī offers as a substitute, and (Ps.-)Bhāsa's choice is Bhīma too, but in this case, he volunteers after appearing by chance.

Fifth, the potential victim requires an ablution. The storyteller presents the older daughter merely speaking about a water offering, whereas the playwright presents the middle son effectually going out for water. And sixth, the hero has a duel with the ogre. As was the case with the seemingly vulnerable family, the climactic duel is also a shared feature between the stories of Hiḍimba and Baka. In the Baka version, Bhīma fights Baka to the death; in the Ghaṭotkaca version, he fights Ghaṭotkaca until the latter recognizes him as his own father.

As an example of the postulated *contaminatio*, the following epic passages, respectively dealing with Ghaṭotkaca's birth from Hiḍimbā and with the Brahman's worries about Baka causing the death of his family, are merged into a dramatic passage combining the ogre's miraculous birth and the family's threat of death. The epic birth on the day of conception is reinterpreted as the dramatic birth of a fire-like ogre from an ogress like a kindling stick. The former is marvelous for its celerity, the latter, for its symbolism. In addition, both sets of families are presented in terms of a Brahman accompanied by his wife and children.

> bālo 'pi yauvanaṃ prāpto mānuṣeṣu viśāṃ pate |
> sarvāstreṣu paraṃ vīraḥ prakarṣam agamad balī | |
> **sadyo hi garbhaṃ rākṣasyo labhante prasavanti ca** |
> kāmarūpadharāś caiva bhavanti bahurūpiṇaḥ | |
>
> O lord of the people, although still a boy, he reached puberty among humans, and as a powerful hero, he attained great preeminence in every weapon. **Indeed, rakshasa women conceive and give birth on the very same day**, and their sons, assuming any shape at will, become multiform.
>
> (*MBh.* 1.143.31-32)

> na hi yogaṃ prapaśyāmi yena mucyeyam āpadaḥ |
> **putradāreṇa** vā **sārdhaṃ** prādraveyam anāmayam | |
>
> I certainly do not see any means by which I could get rid of my misfortune, unless, **together with my wife and children**, I could run away to a safe place.
>
> (*MBh.* 1.145.25)

> eṣa khalu pāṇḍavamadhyamasyātmajo **hiḍimbāraṇisambhūto** rākṣasāgnir akṛtavairaṃ brāhmaṇajanaṃ vitrāsayati
> bhoḥ kaṣṭaṃ kaṣṭaṃ khalu **patnīsutaparivṛtasya** brāhmaṇasya vṛttānto 'tra hi
>
> Now, this son of the middle Pāṇḍava [sc. Bhīma], the fire-like rakshasa **born from the kindling stick known as Hiḍimbā**, terrifies the estate of Brahmans, who have no feud with him. How sad is this incident of the Brahman **surrounded by his wife and children**!
>
> (*MV* 2.3-2.4)

[SO2] The playwright adds the father/son conflict.[164] As pointed out by Salomon (2010), this conflict is emphasized through an elaborate mirrored characterization, involving two literary techniques: repetition and key words. For instance, the same phrasing is used for/by both Bhīma and Ghaṭotkaca at *MV* 9b ~ *MV* 40.2, *MV* 24.6 ~ *MV* 40.17, *MV* 25.8 ~ *MV* 26.7, *MV* 26 ~ *MV* 27, *MV* 38.3 ~ *MV* 40.5, and *MV* 47.3 ~ *MV* 47.8; and the word *sadṛśa-* (like) is used at *MV* 24.12, *MV* 25d, *MV* 38.3, *MV* 39b, *MV* 41d, *MV* 42a, *MV* 42d, *MV* 43d, and *MV* 49.16. (Ps.-)Bhāsa takes Hiḍimbā's description of Bhīma, which has a certain lechery to it when coming from the hankering ogress, and he transfers it into Ghaṭotkaca's and Bhīma's descriptions of each other. There is clearly a doubling going on here.

The father Bhīma and his son Ghaṭotkaca are the ones interacting in the play, and consequently, they are also the ones voicing their thoughts about each other. Among the various similarities between the two dramatic portrayals, one stands out because of its presence in the epic version as well: the comparison with a lion. On one hand, the epic Hiḍimbā praises Bhīma's arms, shoulders, and eyes. On the other hand, the dramatic Bhīma extols Ghaṭotkaca's eyes, waist, arms, and shoulders, whereas the dramatic Ghaṭotkaca exalts Bhīma's arms, waist, and eyes. However, beyond any topical characterization, the recurrence of the lion image certainly supports the view that there are adaptation techniques in play. Lastly, the claim by the ogress that such a man is husband material

164 On the addition of the father/son conflict, see Salomon (2010): "From a modern point of view, the MV is, most obviously, an archetypal oedipal drama. On this point, Woolner and Sarup remark rather laconically in the introduction to their translation (p. 141) that "the motif of a father meeting and sometimes fighting his own son unawares is familiar." Still, for all its striking parallels with the Oedipus legend, the MV shows in at least two significant respects characteristically Indian features. First, as Woolner and Sarup (ibid.) note, "That a hero should find a son in such a monster seems original." The second and more important difference is the culmination in a recognition and reconciliation between father and son; this, in keeping with the conventions of the Sanskrit drama, which, with rare exceptions (notably the *Karṇabhāra*, also attributed to Bhāsa) ends happily" (p. 8); and Sutherland Goldman (2017): "Bhīma's entrance into the story now sets up an Oedipal struggle between father and son, while the nonpresent mother hovers on the outskirts of the narrative. As in the original Oedipal myth, the son is unaware that this person who confronts him is his father" (p. 241).

is substituted for a generic compliment that both hero and ogre pay each other.

ayaṃ śyāmo mahābāhuḥ **siṃha**skandho mahādyutiḥ |
kambugrīvaḥ puṣkarākṣo bhartā yukto bhaven mama | |

May this dark-skinned one be my lawful husband – the one with strong arms, **leonine** shoulders, great splendor, shell-like neck, and lotus eyes.

(*MBh.* 1.139.14)

aho darśanīyo 'yaṃ puruṣaḥ ayaṃ hi
siṃhāsyaḥ **siṃha**daṃṣṭro madhunibhanayanaḥ
snigdhagambhīrakaṇṭho
babhrubhrūḥ śyenanāso dviradapatihanur
dīrghaviśliṣṭakeśaḥ |
vyūḍhorā vajramadhyo gajavṛṣabhagatir
lambapīnāṃsabāhuḥ
suvyaktaṃ rākṣasījo vipulabalayuto lokavīrasya putraḥ | |

Ah, this man is certainly good-looking – the one with **leonine** face, **leonine** fangs, eyes like wine, deep voice coming from his throat, deep-brown eyebrows, aquiline nose, elephantine jaw, long loose hair, wide chest, adamantine waist, elephantine gait, long arms, and thick shoulders. Endowed with great strength, he is clearly the son of an earthly hero, born to him from a rakshasa.

(*MV* 25.8-26)

aho darśanīyo 'yaṃ puruṣaḥ ya eṣaḥ
siṃhākṛtiḥ kanakatālasamānabāhur
madhye tanur garuḍapakṣaviliptapakṣaḥ |
viṣṇur bhaved vikasitāmbujapatranetro
netre mamāharati bandhur ivāgato 'yam | |

Ah, this man is certainly good-looking – the one with **leonine** appearance, arms like palm trees, fine waist, and sides as painted as Garuḍa's wings. He could be Viṣṇu of eyes like open lotus leaves. He catches my eye like a recently arrived relative.

(*MV* 26.7-27)

Additionally, as is the case with *The Five Nights*, the anagnorisis of *The Middle One* draws materials from the story of Babhruvāhana (*MBh.* 14.78-82). This episode states that, during the horse sacrifice, the warrior Arjuna arrives at the kingdom of his son Babhruvāhana, who greets him with all due respect. However, Arjuna takes this as an insult, for it contravenes the duty of warriors, according to which a fight between the horse's guard and the kingdom's sovereign must ensue. Arjuna's accusations are aimed directly at Babhruvāhana's manliness. At this point, the naga Ulūpī intervenes, assuming a motherly role – Babhruvāhana's biological mother is, in fact, the princess Citrāṅgadā – and encouraging her putative son to seek the approval of Arjuna.

At first, Babhruvāhana fights from a chariot, and Arjuna does so from the ground. But once the son loses his horses, they proceed to an on-foot duel, during which Babhruvāhana severely wounds Arjuna: the latter drops dead and the former faints in a dead-like manner. Then, Citrāṅgadā laments her dead husband Arjuna, and blames it all on her co-wife Ulūpī, whom she asks to fix it, or else she will starve herself to death. Shortly thereafter, Babhruvāhana regains consciousness and, looking for an atonement that would fit such a contemptible deed as parricide, he too is determined to starve himself to death. And just as she had been responsible for Arjuna dying, Ulūpī must be credited for him coming back to life. She summons a miraculous jewel, which Babhruvāhana then places on Arjuna's chest. The revived hero has no memory of what has happened, and he is even baffled as to why there are so many long faces around him.

In retrospect, Ulūpī claims, it has all been for the best, since Arjuna dying means him being able to reach heaven, something that he would not have been allowed to do if he did not expiate the offence of killing his grandfather Bhīṣma while he was fighting someone else. Since Ulūpī had overheard the godly Vasus talking about cursing Arjuna to death, she had asked her own father to try his best to reduce the punishment. And the outcome was favorable, for a temporary death is certainly better than a lasting one.

Now, the adaptation reverses the sequence of events: instead of progressing from the revelation that Ulūpī is the mother to the encounter between Babhruvāhana and his father Arjuna, it first presents the father/son encounter, during which Bhīma comes to the full realization that Ghaṭotkaca is his son, while Ghaṭotkaca comes to the partial realization that Bhīma is a Kshatriya, and only then does it introduce the character of the mother Hiḍimbā, who, instead of introducing herself as such, openly addresses Bhīma as her husband, thus contributing to the completion of Ghaṭotkaca's anagnorisis. All three anagnorises reverberate backwards, as they should: Bhīma understands straightaway, by focusing on Ghaṭotkaca's pride; Ghaṭotkaca goes through two steps, by comprehending, first, Bhīma's general pride, and then, Bhīma's specific link to him.

> ulūpīṃ māṃ nibodha tvaṃ **mātaraṃ** pannagātmajām |
> kuruṣva vacanaṃ putra dharmas te bhavitā paraḥ | |
> yudhyasvainaṃ kuruśreṣṭhaṃ dhanaṃjayam ariṃdama |
> evam eṣa hi te prīto bhaviṣyati na saṃśayaḥ | |
>
> Know me to be Ulūpī, your [sc. Babhravāhana's] **mother** and the daughter of a naga. O son, follow my orders and your merit will be supreme. O enemy-tamer, fight with Dhanaṃjaya [sc. Arjuna], the best of the Kurus, for in this way, he will doubtless be pleased with you.
>
> (*MBh.* 14.78.11-12)

> **evaṃ** hiḍimbāyāḥ putro **'yam**
> sadṛśo hy asya **garvaḥ**
>
> **So, he** [sc. Ghaṭotkaca] is the son of Hiḍimbā. Then, his **pride** is fitting.
>
> (*MV* 38.2-38.3)

> **evaṃ** kṣatriyo **'yam**
> tena **garvaḥ**
>
> **So, he** [sc. Bhīma] is a Kshatriya. That is the reason for his **pride**.
>
> (*MV* 40.4-40.5)

> GHAṬOTKACAḤ
> *kaḥ pratyayaḥ*

HIḌIMBĀ
eṣa pratyayaḥ
jayatv ***āryaputraḥ***

GHAṬOTKACA
What is your proof?

HIḌIMBĀ
This is my proof: Glory to my **husband** [sc. Bhīma]!

(*MV* 48.23-48.25b)

[SO3] The author adds the chance.[165] Even though chance has little to do with the story of Hiḍimba, *The Middle One*'s plot advances from one lucky break into the next one. This could be owed to the fact that the story of Baka does factor in chance, when explaining why Bhīma is available for the match to begin with: his brothers went begging for alms, but someone had to keep Kuntī company. Likewise, the play stresses, by means of a threefold explanation, why Bhīma happens to be at the crime scene in the first place: the Pāṇḍavas are out, not begging for alms, but attending a sacrifice; Bhīma is in, not keeping his mother company, but holding the fort by protecting the hermitage; and in an unexpected twist, Bhīma is also momentarily out, trying to get some exercise. This last step is crucial for introducing the mistaken identity. But more on that later.

tataḥ kadā cid bhaikṣāya gatās te bharatarṣabhāḥ |
saṃgatyā bhīmasenas tu tatrāste pṛthayā saha ||

Then, one day, the bulls of the Bharatas [sc. the Pāṇḍavas] went begging for alms, but **by chance**, Bhīma remained there together with Pṛthā [sc. Kuntī].

(*MBh.* 1.145.8)

tasmād āśramād āgatena kenacid brāhmaṇena śatakumbhaṃ nāma **yajñam anubhavituṃ** maharṣer dhaumyasyāśramaṃ gatā iti

165 On the addition of chance, see also Salomon (2010): "The latter [sc. the Brahman] introduces himself as Keśavadāsa, explaining that he was on the way to his maternal uncle's home when he was attacked by the demon Ghaṭotkaca (32)" (p. 6).

A Brahman who came from that very hermitage told me that they had gone to the hermitage of the great seer Dhaumya **to help during the sacrifice** called "The one of the hundred vessels."

(*MV* 11.3)

tāta na tu sarva eva
āśramaparipālanārtham iha sthāpitaḥ kila madhyamaḥ

O father, but not all of them went. The middle one was stationed here **for the sake of protecting the hermitage**.

(*MV* 11.5-11.6)

sa cāpy asyāṃ velāyāṃ **vyāyāmaparicayārthaṃ** viprakṛṣṭadeśa iti śrūyate

And it is said that, at this moment, he too is at remote location **for the sake of getting some exercise**.

(*MV* 11.8)

[SO4] (Ps.-)Bhāsa emphasizes the trees.[166] Tree uprooting becomes something of a leitmotif in the story of Baka: after a quick mention of the shattering of trees and creepers in chapter 141, chapter 151 alone includes three such references. In the first one, Baka pulls up a tree and attacks Bhīma with it. The phrasing, specifically the repetition of rage as a catalyst, suggests that this first uprooting should be taken in tandem with that from chapter 141. In the second one, Baka lifts several trees and throws them at Bhīma, who returns the favor by doing the same. In this case, the wording reverberates into that of the adaptation, which highlights the idea of throwing.

In the third and last reference, one reads that both Baka and Bhīma can pulverize trees. Once again, the phrasing draws our attention back to the uprooting from chapter 141, particularly to the shattering. Furthermore, there are a couple of additional details in the epic passages from which the play profits. These trees

166 On the emphasis on the trees, see Sutherland Goldman (2017): "Ghaṭotkaca uproots huge trees to use as weapons, much in the manner of Baka in the *Mahābhārata* story, and finally he uproots the peak of a mountain" (p. 242).

are huge, and as a result, the mighty warriors must struggle to take them out/lift them up/pull them up.

> babhañjatur **mahāvṛkṣāṃl** latāś **cākarṣatus** tataḥ |
> mattāv iva **susaṃrabdhau** vāraṇau ṣaṣṭihāyanau | |
>
> Then, they **shattered huge trees** and tore off creepers, as if they were a couple of **greatly enraged**, sixty-year-old elephants in musth.
>
> (*MBh.* 1.141.23)
>
> tataḥ sa **bhūyaḥ saṃkruddho vṛkṣam ādāya** rākṣasaḥ |
> tāḍayiṣyaṃs tadā bhīmaṃ punar abhyadravad balī | |
>
> Then, **having taken out a tree**, the mighty rakshasa, still **more enraged** and trying to wound Bhīma, attacked him once more.
>
> (*MBh.* 1.151.12)
>
> tataḥ sa punar **udyamya vṛkṣān** bahuvidhān balī |
> **prāhiṇod** bhīmasenāya tasmai bhīmaś ca pāṇḍavaḥ | |
> tad **vṛkṣa**yuddham abhavan **mahīruha**vināśanam |
> ghorarūpaṃ mahārāja bakapāṇḍavayor **mahat** | |
>
> Then, once more **having lifted trees** of many kinds, the mighty one **threw** them at Bhīma, and the Pāṇḍava Bhīma at him. O great king, and a **huge** battle with **trees** arose between Baka and the Pāṇḍava, which was awful to look at and caused the destruction of those **trees**.
>
> (*MBh.* 1.151.15-16)
>
> tayor vegena mahatā pṛthivī samakampata |
> **pādapāṃś** ca **mahā**kāyāṃś **cūrṇayām āsatus** tadā | |
>
> The earth shook with their great impetuosity, and they **pulverized trees** of **huge** trunks.
>
> (*MBh.* 1.151.20)
>
> kathaṃ katham anṛtam ity āha kṣipasi me gurum
> bhavatv imaṃ **sthūlaṃ vṛkṣam utpāṭya praharāmi**
> katham anenāpi na śakyate hantuṃ kiṃnu khalu kariṣye
> bhavatu dṛṣṭam
> etad girikūṭam **utpāṭya praharāmi**

> How dare you say that it is not true? You insult my father! So be it. **Having pulled up** this **huge tree**, I **will throw** it at him. How is it that, even with this, it is not possible to kill him? What can I possibly do? That's it, I've got it! **Having pulled up** this mountaintop, I **will throw** it at him.
>
> (*MV* 43.3-43.6)

[SO5] The playwright ignores the sex.[167] Vyāsa's account of the sexual union between Bhīma and Hiḍimbā is quite detailed. Assuming an active role, Hiḍimbā not only seems to ask Kuntī for Bhīma's hand, but also carries Bhīma like a bride after laying hold of him. The copulating is presented almost like a Hierogamy, with special emphasis on the nature around them: from mountaintops to ocean floors, the close-up of their lovemaking resembles the journey through an *axis mundi.* With great narrative skill, the enjoyable landscape is smoothly transformed into an act of carnal enjoyment. After all, Hiḍimbā herself had chosen, over the ephemeral pleasure of eating Bhīma, the enduring one of marrying him (*MBh.* 1.139.16).

(Ps.-)Bhāsa remains silent on this subject. This notwithstanding, there is more than one double entendre. For example, the Brahman's wife from the epic says that, since the law is so clear in prohibiting the killing of a woman, even a poorly informed individual should spare her (*MBh.* 1.146.29-30); but the Ghaṭotkaca from the drama speaks of his mother not having any "desire" for a woman, nor for an old man. Perhaps the land and sea imagery from the source text has not become a literal surf and turf in the reworking, and perhaps the references to "eating", by means of sexual innuendo, are conveying the idea of "eating up".

167 On the ignoring of the sex, see Sutherland Goldman (2017): "Like other *rākṣasī* figures, such as Śūrpaṇakhā, Surasā, and Siṃhikā, Hiḍimbā too desires to "eat." Her voracious oral consumptive urges can also be seen as representative of her libidinal desires" (p. 235), and "The intersection of libidinal and gustatory desire creates a tension that Bhāsa employs in his drama to draw his character of Hiḍimbā. At the opening of the story the two traits that are most crucial in her construction are: (1) that she is a *rākṣasī*, which for the audience immediately associates her with negative libidinal and gustatory urges, and who, like the female vampire, is abject as she disrupts identity and order; and (2) that she is a mother, a fact also known from the epic story" (p. 236).

tatheti tat pratijñāya hiḍimbā rākṣasī tadā |
bhīmasenam upādāya ūrdhvam ācakrame tataḥ ||
śailaśṛṅgeṣu **ramyeṣu** devatāyataneṣu ca |
mṛgapakṣivighuṣṭeṣu **ramaṇīyeṣu** sarvadā ||
kṛtvā ca paramaṃ rūpaṃ sarvābharaṇabhūṣitā |
saṃjalpantī sumadhuraṃ **ramayām āsa** pāṇḍavam ||
tathaiva vanadurgeṣu puṣpitadrumasānuṣu |
sarahsu **ramaṇīyeṣu** padmotpalayuteṣu ca ||
nadīdvīpapradeśeṣu vaiḍūryasikatāsu ca |
sutīrthavanatoyāsu tathā girinadīṣu ca ||
sagarasya pradeśeṣu maṇihemaciteṣu ca |
pattaneṣu ca **ramyeṣu** mahāśālavaneṣu ca ||
devāraṇyeṣu puṇyeṣu tathā parvatasānuṣu |
guhyakānāṃ nivāseṣu tāpasāyataneṣu ca ||
sarvartuphalapuṣpeṣu mānaseṣu sarahsu ca |
bibhratī paramaṃ rūpaṃ **ramayām āsa** pāṇḍavam ||

After promising that she would proceed thusly and laying hold of Bhīma, the rakshasa Hiḍimbā strode upwards. On the **enjoyable** mountaintops and in the resting places of the gods, which are always **enjoyable** and resounding with deer and birds, having taken on a superb form, embellished with all sorts of ornaments, and speaking in a gentle manner, she **carnally enjoyed** the Pāṇḍava. Likewise, in thick forests, on mountains of flowering trees, by **enjoyable** ponds covered with lotuses and water lilies, on river islands of chrysoberyl-rich sands, by mountain streams of sacred woods and waters, on ocean floors scattered with gemstones and gold, in **enjoyable** towns, in woods of giant timber trees, in holy forests of the gods, on various mountaintops, in the dwelling places of the demigods, in the resting places of the ascetics, and by Lake Mānasa which bears fruits and flowers in every season, having taken on a superb form, she **carnally enjoyed** the Pāṇḍava.

(*MBh.* 1.143.19-26)

na khalu strījano **'bhimatas** tatrabhavatyā

Certainly not, my venerable mother does not **desire** a woman.

(*MV* 15.4)

ā vṛddhas tvam **apasara**

You are too old, **away with you**!

(*MV* 15.6)

[SO6] The author emphasizes the mistaken identity.[168] In *MBh.* 1, during his dialogue with his wife, the Brahman sometimes digresses, in a sort of inner monologue. For instance, when picturing a scenario where he gives up one of his children, he voices the *vox populi* about a son being more valuable than a daughter, but he does so only to immediately disagree with the view. For him, son and daughter are equal. In *MV*, the love of the father is split into the wants of the father and those of the mother. Although gender does not make a difference, age apparently does, for the eldest and youngest sons are chosen over the middle one. Within a family of five, the fact that each parent has their favorite results in the exclusion of two of the sons. In the end, all this is just a necessary step towards the scene of the mistaken identity, leading to the climactic anagnorisis.

Interactions of characters with their doppelgangers are not uncommon in the *Mahābhārata* as a whole, and certainly not in the ogre stories under discussion. The story of Hiḍimba evinces a sort of bilateral symmetry between the male Hiḍimba and the female Hiḍimbā. One can even argue that the story of Hiḍimba, highlighting the martial side of the coin, is in fact, a masquerade for the story of Hiḍimbā, emphasizing the amatory aspect, together with its genealogical repercussions. Instead of a tale about hate and death, when looked at from the right angle, it becomes one about love and life.

Not unlike this, the story of Baka does not fail to at least suggest a twofold nature. As anyone who has seen a crane roosting can attest, this namesake bird tucks one of its legs up into its body to keep it warm, thus giving the appearance of being one-legged. If Hiḍimba represents an entity that is doubled by means of the

168 On the emphasis on the mistaken identity, see Salomon (2010): "As a drama of mistaken identity, the MV actually turns on not one but two confusions: the confusion between the two "middle brothers" (the Brahman boy and Bhīmasena), and the misunderstanding between Bhīmasena and Ghaṭotkaca as to their real identities and relationship. Although these are essentially distinct incidents (the first being something of a dramatic decoy, or in traditional terms an *upakathā*), the poet cleverly intertwines them at the critical juncture of Bhīmasena's first appearance on stage (24/25)" (pp. 9-10).

sibling theme, Baka literally becomes a divided individual, once the hero subdues him with his strong grip and splits him in half.

A close reader like (Ps.-)Bhāsa would have undoubtedly noticed the many commonalities between these back-to-back stories about splitting identities (Hiḍimba/Hiḍimbā and Baka/the crane-like, half-and-half ogre), and here, he would have found inspiration for a nip and tuck *contaminatio* of his own, in which both ogre stories run neck and neck, thus managing to keep the audience's attention. If an adaptation is already *dviguṇa-*, "twofold", for bringing together the old and the new, a *contaminatio* is so on yet another level, by profiting from two sources. In a creative process that would have been anything but derivative, the author would have picked up the pieces of these broken ogres and sewn them back together in this "*bhāsa-saṃdha-* (joined by (Ps.-)Bhāsa)" re-creation.

In such reinterpretation, the two blood-related ogres/two bloody halves of the same ogre become two unrelated people, who happen to share the same spot within their respective family trees: having older and younger brothers, they are both middle sons. What better way to adapt the themes of multiplication and division than by presenting "two middle ones"? The ambiguity is key: Ghaṭotkaca needs a name to call back the young Brahman, but the father is not going to be responsible for providing him with the final nail in the coffin, so when ambiguously asked what his name is/what he is called, his older brother replies by referring to him as "the ascetic middle one" (i.e., the middle son). Little does he know that "the heroic middle one" (i.e., Bhīma) is just about to set him and his family free.

GHAṬOTKACAḤ
...atha kinnāmā tava putraḥ

VṚDDHAḤ
etad api na śakyaṃ śrotum

GHAṬOTKACAḤ
yuktaṃ bho brāhmaṇakumāra kinnāmā te bhrātā

PRATHAMAḤ
tapasvī **madhyamaḥ**

GHAṬOTKACAḤ
madhyameti sadṛśam asya
aham eva yāsyāmi
bho bho **madhyama madhyama** śighram āgaccha

GHAṬOTKACA
...But what is the name of your son?

OLD MAN
I cannot tell you this either.

GHAṬOTKACA
That makes sense. Hey! Young Brahman, what is the name of your brother?

FIRST SON
The ascetic **middle one**.

GHAṬOTKACA
"Middle one" – how fitting is that! I will go myself. Hey! **Middle One**. Hey! **Middle One**, come quick!

(*MV* 24.8-24.14)

Lastly, the fact that the two characters that trigger the scene of mistaken identity are brothers could be explained by considering its parallelisms within Greco-Roman theater: from Μέση (Middle Comedy), the works of Antiphanes', Anaxandrides', Alexis', Aristophon's, and Xenarchus' fragmentary *Twin Brothers*; from Νέα (New Comedy), Menander's and Euphron's fragmentary *Twin Brothers*; from *fabula togata* (comedy in Roman dress), Titinius' fragmentary *Female Twin*; from Atellan comedy, Pomponius' fragmentary *The Twin Brothers Maccus*, and Novius' fragmentary *Twin Brothers* and *The Two Dossennuses*; from Mime, Laberius' fragmentary *Little Twins*; and from *fabula palliata* (comedy in Greek dress), Plautus' *Bacch.* 568 ff. and *Men.* 273 ff.[169]

[SO7] (Ps.-)Bhāsa profits from changes of space and time for his adaptation. Regarding spatial locations, in the epic, the story of Hiḍimba takes place in an unnamed wood, and the story of Baka in a city called Ekacakrā. The transition from one ogre to the

169 See Panayotakis (2020, pp. 94-95).

other entails, as well, a change from nature to culture, and from the indistinctness of the former to the delimitation of the latter. The drama, once again, merges bits and pieces, and it does so in a creative manner: the key places are two villages in a jungle. Since Keśavadāsa – this newly christened "Servant (*dāsa-*) of Kṛṣṇa (*keśava-*)" – walks from his hometown to the house of his maternal uncle, his route through the ogre-infested jungle constitutes the ideal background for what the dramatist has in mind.

> tatra teṣu śayāneṣu hiḍimbo nāma rākṣasaḥ |
> avidūre **vanāt** tasmāc chālavṛkṣam upāśritaḥ | |
>
> While they were sleeping there, a rakshasa named Hiḍimba had taken refuge in a *śāla* tree not far from that **wood**.
>
> (*MBh.* 1.139.1)
>
> **ekacakrāṃ** gatās te tu kuntīputrā mahārathāḥ |
> ūṣur nāticiraṃ kālaṃ brāhmaṇasya niveśane | |
>
> Then, the combatant sons of Kuntī [sc. the Pāṇḍavas] went to **Ekacakrā**. For a short time, they lived in the house of a Brahman.
>
> (*MBh.* 1.145.2)
>
> ahaṃ khalu kururājena yudhiṣṭhireṇādhiṣṭhitapūrve **kurujāṅgale yūpagrāma**vāstavyo māṭharasagotraś ca kalpaśākhādhvaryuḥ keśavadāso nāma brāhmaṇaḥ
> tasya mamottarasyāṃ diśy udyāmakagrāmavāsī mātulaḥ kauśikasagotro yajñabandhur nāmāsti
>
> I am a resident of the **Yūpa village in the Kuru jungle**, which was previously governed by the Kuru-king Yudhiṣṭhira, a Brahman of the Māṭhara lineage, and a priest of the Kalpa school. My name is Keśavadāsa. I also have a maternal uncle who lives up north in the Udyāmaka village, a member of the Kauśika lineage named Yajñabandhu.
>
> (*MV* 31.12-13)

[SO8] As for the change in time, the playwright trims his sails to suit the theatrical convention. According to Bharata,[170] "The *vyāyoga* should be fashioned, by knowers of the rules, as one whose body is a well-known hero, employing few women, and **lasting one day** [*vyāyogas tu vidhijñaiḥ kāryaḥ prakhyātanāyakaśarīraḥ* | *alpastrījanayuktas tv* ***ekāhakṛtas*** *tathā caiva*]" (*Nāṭyaś*. 18.90).

The epic has the Pāṇḍava brothers and their mother Kuntī living for a short time in the wood during the story of Baka: the action begins at night (when the heroes are sleeping), the climax of its martial component comes just before dawn (when ogres become mightier), and the climax of its amatory component stretches throughout the day (when the couple is allowed to consummate the marriage), so that the action may end by the next night (when the fully grown youth has already been born). Nonetheless, their residency during the story of Baka is neither too short nor too long; instead, it goes on for an amount of time that is just right. This means that, at least, several days go by.

The adaptation has the best of both worlds. From the first story, it re-creates the one-day time lapse; from the other, the timely ritual involving one of its participants and lasting several days. Hence, the epic daughter's intended "marriage-like funeral [*vivāhasadṛśy antyeṣṭi*]" becomes the dramatic cousin's actual *upanayana* (initiation). If the author of *The Middle One* minimizes the sexual aspects that spread through his source, he also magnifies the religious ones. After all, adaptations are not only about filling in a plot and getting rid of some of its parts, but also about calling the shots and taking a stand.

> tathā tu teṣāṃ vasatāṃ tatra rājan mahātmanām |
> aticakrāma **sumahān kālo** 'tha bharatarṣabha ||
>
> O king, O bull of the Bharatas, while those eminent ones were living there in that manner, **a good amount of time** passed by.
>
> (*MBh*. 1.145.7)

170 I follow the Sanskrit text by the Göttingen Register of Electronic Texts in Indian Languages (2020). The translations are my own.

> tasya putr**opanayanā**nubhavanārthaṃ sakalatro ’smi prasthitaḥ
>
> For the sake of taking part in **the initiation** of his [sc. the maternal uncle’s] son, I set out together with my wife.
>
> (*MV* 31.14)

[SO9] The author changes the authoritarian figure by merging Hiḍimba ordering Hiḍimbā and Kuntī ordering Bhīma into Hiḍimbā ordering Ghaṭotkaca.[171] Hiḍimba ordering Hiḍimbā is a scene from the epic story of Hiḍimba. The epic Hiḍimba instructs his sister Hiḍimbā to go near the humans, find out who they are, kill them by herself, and bring them back for them to cook together. Similarly, the dramatic Hiḍimbā instructs her son Ghaṭotkaca to search for humans and then bring some of them back. The phrasing is very close, as seen in the following quotations.

> upapannaś cirasyādya bhakṣo mama manaḥpriyaḥ |
> snehasravān prasravati jihvā paryeti me mukham | |
> aṣṭau daṃṣṭrāḥ sutīkṣṇāgrāś cirasyāpātaduḥsahāḥ |
> deheṣu majjayiṣyāmi snigdheṣu piśiteṣu ca | |
> ākramya mānuṣaṃ kaṇṭham ācchidya dhamanīm api |
> uṣṇaṃ navaṃ prapāsyāmi phenilaṃ rudhiraṃ bahu | |
> **gaccha jānīhi** ke tv ete śerate vanam āśritāḥ |
> mānuṣo balavān gandho ghrāṇaṃ tarpayatīva me | |
> **hatva**itān mānuṣān sarvān **ānayasva** mamāntikam |
> asmadviṣayasuptebhyo naitebhyo bhayam asti te | |
> eṣāṃ māṃsāni saṃskṛtya mānuṣāṇāṃ yatheṣṭataḥ |
> bhakṣayiṣyāva sahitau kuru tūrṇaṃ vaco mama | |
>
> Today, at last, I [sc. Hiḍimba] have obtained my favorite food. Those flowing with fat make my mouth water and I keep licking my lips. Into their bodies and their fatty flesh, I will sink my eight, sharp-pointed teeth, which are unbearable when they bite after such a long time. Having approached their human throats and cut their arteries, I will drink their blood, which will be warm, fresh, bubbling, and abundant. **Go and find out** who those are who are lying down, having

171 On changing the authoritarian figure, see Sutherland Goldman (2017): “Note, too, that as in Bhāsa’s play, it is the mother’s [sc. Kuntī’s] command that must be obeyed and her judgment, although at first questioned by Yudhiṣṭhira, is never really doubted” (p. 240).

come to the wood. The strong aroma of humans seems to sate my scent. **Having killed** all those humans, **bring** them to me. Do not be afraid of those who are sleeping on our turf. Having cooked the flesh of those humans at leisure, we [sc. Hiḍimba and Hiḍimbā] will eat it together, so, quick, obey my orders.

(*MBh.* 1.139.5-10)

...putra mamopavāsanisargārtham asmin vanapradeśe kaścin mānuṣaḥ **parimṛgyānetavye**ti

...O son, **having searched for** a human in this wooded region, you [sc. Ghaṭotkaca] **must bring** him to me [sc. Hiḍimbā] for the sake of breaking my fast.

(*MV* 11.18)

Kuntī ordering Bhīma is a scene from the epic story of Baka.[172] The epic Kuntī commands her son Bhīma to fill in for the victim, so that he can appease the ogre's hunger. In this way, he can both pay their host back for his hospitality and pay it forward to the townsfolk, who have just about had it with this long-lasting tyrant. Correspondingly, the dramatic Hiḍimbā commands her son Ghaṭotkaca to fill the vacancy of the victim, so that he can appease her hunger. Once again, there are similarities in the phrasing, as can be appreciated in the next quotations.

mamaiva vacanād eṣa kariṣyati paraṃtapaḥ |
brāhmaṇārthe mahat kṛtyaṃ moṣkāya nagarasya ca ||

By my [sc. Kuntī's] **order**, the destroyer of his enemies [sc. Bhīma] will do a great deed for the sake of the Brahman and for the liberation of the town.

(*MBh.* 1.150.4)

asti me tatrabhavatī jananī
tayāham **ājñāptaḥ**...

I [sc. Ghaṭotkaca] have a venerable mother. **She** [sc. Hiḍimbā] **ordered** me to...

(*MV* 11.17-11.18)

172 Cf. Kuntī ordering the five Pāṇḍavas to share Draupadī as their common wife (*MBh.* 1.182.2).

[SO10] The most substantial changes in the adaptation come from (Ps.-)Bhāsas's handling of the family of Brahmans. For a start, he changes the unwilling father into a willing father. The epic Brahman lets emotion get the better of him. Before, he was afraid of the ogre; now, he is also angry at his wife. He wanted safety but could not secure it. And he talked a lot but achieved nothing. Now, he blames his wife for his own faults. He is condescending and disrespectful. And he can only see what affects him directly: when imagining the death of his family, he thinks not about their suffering, but about his loss; and when considering them living, he demonstrates not compassion, but guilt. Simply put, he does not want to die, hence the going in circles.

In contrast, the dramatic Brahman's words are as straightforward as his thoughts: instead of picturing his years ahead, he reflects upon those left behind; and instead of putting himself first, he thinks of his children. Where one character hesitates about whether he is going to be able to live with himself, the other is certain that he is going to be sacrificed and he dives into an altruistic death without giving it a second thought. As for the sacrifice itself, the imagery is clearly Vedic: it is phrased in terms of him offering (*hu*) to the fire (*agni-*), in agreement with the precepts (*vidhi-*).

> yatitaṃ vai mayā pūrvaṃ yathā tvaṃ vettha brāhmaṇi |
> yataḥ kṣemaṃ tato gantuṃ tvayā tu mama na śrutam ||
> iha jātā vivṛddhāsmi pitā ceha mameti ca |
> uktavaty asi durmedhe yācyamānā mayāsakṛt ||
> svargato hi pitā vṛddhas tathā mātā ciraṃ tava |
> bāndhavā bhūtapūrvāś ca tatra vāse tu kā ratiḥ ||
> so 'yaṃ te bandhukāmāyā aśṛṇvantyā vaco mama |
> bandhupraṇāśaḥ saṃprāpto bhṛśaṃ duḥkhakaro mama ||
> athavā madvināśo 'yaṃ **na** hi **śakṣyāmi** kaṃ cana |
> parityaktum ahaṃ bandhuṃ svayaṃ jīvan nṛśaṃsavat ||
>
> O my Brahman wife, as you know, I have previously tried to go where we would be safe, but you did not listen to me. O dim-witted one, when constantly asked by me, you kept saying that you were born and raised here, and so was your father. Now, your aged father is long gone, as is your mother, and all your relatives are deceased; then, what pleasure is there left in living here? While you were longing for your

family and not listening to my advice, I have undergone the destruction of my family, which causes great sorrow for me. Rather, this will be my own destruction, for I **will not be able** to abandon any of my own relatives and continue to live while filled with cruelty.

(*MBh.* 1.145.26-30)

kṛtakṛtyaṃ śarīraṃ me pariṇāmena jarjaram |
rākṣasāgnau sutāpekṣī **hoṣyāmi** vidhisaṃskṛtam | |

My body, decrepit from old age, has fulfilled its duty. Thinking of my children, I **will offer** it, purified by the precepts, to this fire-like rakshasa.

(*MV* 15)

[SO11] The playwright changes the lot into a choice. In the epic story of Hiḍimba, the Pāṇḍavas come across the ogre by chance; however, in the epic story of Baka, what is at stake is not if someone will face the ogre, but who it will be. The people of Ekacakrā have come to terms with eventually sacrificing themselves to Baka in exchange for both protection from fiercer adversaries and a meagre life waiting on death row. They die one by one, and their turn always comes. There is no escape and no hope for freedom. Contrarywise, by converting the one-by-one sacrifice into a single sacrifice, and by substituting the passive waiting for one's turn for an active pondering of strengths and weaknesses, the author of *MV* tinges both the notion of freedom and the character of the ogre.

ekaikaś caiva puruṣas tat prayacchati bhojanam |
sa **vāro** bahubhir varṣair bhavaty asutaro naraiḥ | |
tad**vimokṣāya** ye cāpi yatante puruṣāḥ kva cit |
saputradārāṃs tān hatvā tad rakṣo bhakṣayaty uta | |

One by one, people present him with food, and, after many years, every man's **turn** becomes unavoidable. And as per those people who at some point try to **free** themselves from him, having killed them, alongside their wives and children, the rakshasa eats them too.

(*MBh.* 1.148.7-8)

> patnyā cāritraśālinyā dviputro **mokṣam** icchasi |
> **balābalaṃ parijñāya** putram **ekaṃ** visarjaya | |
>
> You want your **freedom** as a father of two, together with your well-behaved wife. **Having pondered their strengths and weaknesses**, give up **one** of your sons.
>
> (*MV* 12)

[SO12] Lastly, the author maintains the hospitality. According to the epic, a Brahman's life is the most valuable treasure, and in turn, a Brahman's death is the greatest sin. Similarly, well-done hospitality can result in unimaginable benefits, and poorly done hospitality can be the cause of much distress. Even if the death of the head-of-the-household Brahman could arguably be regarded as comparable to that of the pretend-Brahman Bhīma, the latter is also a guest of the former. Here, the play offers one last example of time management: the theme is dealt with, not at the beginning, but at the end; and in consequence, it does not constitute an impediment, but a corollary. If taking a life is an inhospitable deed, giving it back is the ultimate gift.

> nāham etat kariṣyāmi jīvitārthī kathaṃ cana |
> brāhmaṇasy**ātitheś** caiva svārthe prāṇair viyojanam | |
>
> Clinging to my [sc. the Brahman's] own life, I would never prompt this: the loss of a life for my own benefit – much less that of a Brahman and **a guest** [sc. Bhīma]!
>
> (*MBh.* 1.149.4)

> kṛtam **ātithyam** anena jīvitapradānena
>
> By giving us [sc. the Brahman and his family] back our lives, you [sc. Bhīma] have fulfilled your **hospitality**.
>
> (*MV* 50.1)

(Plautine) Mistaken Identities

Following the analysis of the ogre motif in *Od.* 9 and *Cyclops*, as well as in *MBh.* 1 and *The Middle One*, I have identified three instances of possible Greek influence in the adaptation techniques: [OM1][173] *contaminatio of two epic stories into a single play*, [OM2] *dramatic themes which have no precedent in the source texts are added with the intention of providing an emphasis*, and [OM3] *spaces, times, characters, and themes are changed in the plays, which otherwise would be dramatizations and not adaptations.*

[OM1] *Contaminatio of two epic stories into a single play.* Regarding *Cyclops*, the characters of Silenus and the Satyrs, likely coming from the *Homeric Hymn to Dionysus* (GO1), are included by reason of their relevance within the new literary genre of the satyr drama, but they are also employed to focus the audience's attention on Dionysus' wine, instead of Odysseus' trickery. Thus, the epic's serious sneakiness is re-created as the play's humorous straightforwardness. Similarly, in *The Middle One*, the characters of the Brahman and his family, likely coming from the *Bakavadhaparvan* (SO1), shed a new light on a not-so-black-and-white Ghaṭotkaca.

[OM2] *Dramatic themes which have no precedent in the source texts are added with the intention of providing an emphasis.* The father/son conflicts surrounding the encounter of Odysseus and Polyphemus, on one side (GO2), and the encounter of Bhīma and Ghaṭotkaca, on the other (SO2) is one of two major additions. The other one is that of Chance (GO3) / chance (SO3), which is, indeed, a key component in Greco-Roman theater from Euripides onwards.[174] These parallelisms would make perfect sense by assuming a certain familiarity with Greco-Roman sources.

When considered as instances of Greco-Indian *anukaraṇa*, both procedures would be characterized by change: a Greek text (*Cyclops*) with heavenly fortuity (Chance) and a conflict between a father and a son (Silenus and the chorus of Satyrs) which has been adapted from a source (*Od.* 9) with a similar conflict (Poseidon and Odysseus), would have become an Indian text (*The Middle*

173 OM stands for "Ogre Motif". Hence, numbers OM1-OM3 refer to the proposed influences from *Cyclops*' adaptation of *Od.* 9 into *The Middle One*'s adaptation of *MBh.* 1.

174 For "chance" in Euripides (e.g., *Alc.* 785 and *Ion* 1512-1514) and "Chance" in Euripides (e.g., *IA* 1136), see Busch (1937).

One) with earthly fortuity (chance) and a conflict between a father and a son (Bhīma and Ghaṭotkaca) which has been adapted from a source (*MBh.* 14) with a similar conflict (Arjuna and Babhruvāhana). Moreover, the addition of the father/son conflict, coming from the story of Babhruvāhana, further supports the claim of *contaminatio*, which may very well have been close to the procedure that Euripides himself utilized for his *Cyclops*.[175]

In both cases, the addition of the conflict appears to be directly related to certain thematic emphases. On one hand, while the Greek hero blinds the ogre with the trunk of a tree (GO4), the Sanskrit hero ends up facing the ogre-like character in a tree battle (SO4). On the other hand, sex as a subject matter offers some interesting contrasts. In *Cyclops*, Polyphemus expresses his intention to "sleep" with Silenus (GO5). This explicit, homosexual desire aimed at the father figure would have been substituted, in *The Middle One*, for an implicit, heterosexual desire aimed at the son figure, when Hiḍimbā is said to prefer to "eat (up)" one of the Brahman's sons (SO5).

At the very core of the Sanskrit play lies the emphasis on the mistaken identity (SO6), as the title *The Middle One* suggests. Similarly, Odysseus' play on words when introducing himself as Nobody is probably among the best-known ruses in world literature (GO6). However, mistaken identity proper is a much more common procedure within Roman theater. Considering only non-fragmentary plays, Plautus (254-184 BCE)[176] stands out among Roman playwrights when it comes to mistaken identities involving siblings. For instance, in *Bacch.* 568 ff., when asked if he is, indeed, the lover of the courtesan called Bacchis, a young man answers with the revealing fact that there are, indeed, "two Bacchises [*duas... Bacchides*]", i.e., two courtesans that go by the same name,

175 On *contaminatio* in *Cyclops*, see Shaw (2018): "Euripides has rewritten a traditional myth in a humorous, self-conscious, and comedic manner, making Odysseus and his men the pirates of the Homeric Hymn as he combines two famous stories into a single satyr play" (p. 104).

176 I follow the Latin text by Nixon (Plautus, 1916, 1917, 1924, 1930, and 1952). The translations are my own.

and that are sisters. But the mistake is subject to a much more elaborated treatment in *The Two Menaechmuses*.

There are eleven examples of mistaken identity in *The Two Menaechmuses*.[177] The plot of the play is as follows: Menaechmus and Sosicles are the twin brothers that were born to a merchant. During a trip, Menaechmus got lost and ended up being adopted by another merchant and taken to a different city, where he now lives, unhappily married, and is having an affair with a courtesan. After many years of unfruitful searching, Sosicles, who was renamed as Menaechmus in honor of his presumably dead brother, finally arrives at the city where his long-lost brother resides. But now, they are not only twins, but also namesakes. A great portion of the play (*Men.* 273-1059) is dedicated to exploiting this authorially carved coincidence, until in the end, they recognize each other. As seen from this outline, the three key aspects from the Sanskrit play are present here as well: the brothers, the mistaken identity, and the anagnorisis.

The first four examples of mistaken identity involve the newly arrived "Menaechmus (Sosicles)" being taken for the well-known Menaechmus. One after the other, a cook (*Men.* 273-350), a courtesan (*Men.* 351-445), a parasite (*Men.* 446-523), and a maid (*Men.* 524-558) err in their assumptions and believe the newcomer to be their neighbor. The scene with the cook closely resembles the beginning of Bhīma's and Ghaṭotkaca's exchange during their encounter. One shared feature is that a brother, who is being mistaken for another brother, is addressed by a third party. In the Roman play, Cylindrus, mistaking Menaechmus (Sosicles) for Menaechmus, addresses him as such; in the Sanskrit play, Bhīma, believing the form of address "Middle One" to refer to him, comes to meet Ghaṭotkaca. Even their names, although etymologically unrelated, are phonetically similar: *me-naech-mo-* vs. *ma-dhya-ma-*.[178]

177 See Panayotakis (2020, p. 97).

178 On another phonetical similitude relating to the ogre motif and possibly owing to an Indian borrowing from the Greco-Roman world, see Wulff Alonso (2008a): "En términos puramente lingüísticos, no deja de ser interesante que los nombres de los hermanos sean el mismo, pero en femenino en los dos casos (Hidimba, Hidimbā, Caco, Caca) e incluso la similitud fonética entre este Caco-Caca y el nombre de otro *rakshasa* muerto

Another point of encounter is that the addresser asks a question about identity. In *The Two Menaechmuses,* Cylindrus rhetorically asks Menaechmus (Sosicles) about who he is; in *The Middle One,* Ghaṭotkaca genuinely asks how Bhīma can possible be a “Middle One” as well. A final commonality is the fact that both addressees respond in the negative. Menaechmus (Sosicles), as expected, denies any sort of acquaintance with Cylindrus; but Bhīma, instead of asserting his own identity, unexpectedly denies anyone else’s. As discussed, oddity is key when considering borrowings.

Cyl.	(...) **Menaechme**, salve.
Men. S.	Di te amabunt quisquis es.
Cyl.	**Quisquis** <sum? non tu scis, Menaechme, quis> **ego sim**?
Men. S.	**Non** hercle vero...
Cylindrus.	(...) O **Menaechmus**, hello.
Menaechmus (S).	May the gods be kind to you, whoever you are.
Cylindrus.	**Whoever** <I am? Do you not know, Menaechmus, who> **I am**?
Menaechmus (S).	By Hercules, I truly do **not**.

(*Men.* 278-280)

GHAṬOTKACAḤ
(...)
bho **madhyama** tvāṃ khalv ahaṃ śabdāpayāmi

---

por Bhima que aparece inmediatamente después de éste, Baca... [From a purely linguistic point of view, it is interesting that the names of the siblings are the same, but in the feminine in both cases (Hiḍimba, Hiḍimbā, Cacus, Caca), and so are the phonetic proximity of the Cacus-Caca and the name of the other *rākṣasa* killed by Bhīma, who appears immediately after this one, Baka...]” (p. 385).

BHĪMASENAḤ
atah khalv aham prāptaḥ

GHAṬOTKACAḤ
kiṃ bhavān api madhyamaḥ

BHĪMASENAḤ
na tāvad aparaḥ

GHAṬOTKACA
(...)
Hey! **“Middle One”**, now I am raising my voice for you!

BHĪMASENA
But that is why I came.

GHAṬOTKACA
How are you also “Middle One”?

BHĪMASENA
So far, **no** other is.

(*MV* 27.1-27.4)

The scene with the courtesan offers an *ad hoc* lineage which recalls the next portion of Bhīma’s and Ghaṭotkaca’s exchange during their encounter. In Plautus, when the interlocutor is listing biographical and historical details relating to the mistakenly identified brother, her style is simple: use of the second person, one mention of the name, reference to specific characters and spaces, all followed by a reply in the negative. In (Ps.-)Bhāsa, when the mistakenly identified brother is enumerating mythological and philosophical facts concerning himself, his style is complex: use of the first person, several mentions of the name, allusion to general characters and spaces, all crowned by a reply in the affirmative. Here, the key procedure would be reversal.

Erot.	Non ego **te** novi **Menaechmum**, Moscho prognatum patre, qui Syracusis perhibere natus esse in Sicilia, ubi rex Agathocles regnator fuit et iterum Phintia, tertium Liparo, qui in morte regnum Hieroni tradidit, nunc Hiero est?
Men. S.	**Haud falsa**, mulier, praedicas. (...)
Erotium.	Do I not know **you** to be **Menaechmus**, the son of your father Moschus, who was born – so they say – in Syracuse in Sicily, where king Agathocles ruled, and secondly Phintia, and thirdly Liparo, who, at his death, left the kingdom to Hiero, and now Hiero is king?
Menaechmus (S).	O woman, you utter **no falsehood**. (...)

(*Men.* 409-412)

BHĪMASENAḤ

madhyamo 'ham avadhyānām utsiktānāṃ ca **madhyamaḥ** |
madhyamo 'haṃ kṣiter bhadra bhrātṝṇām api **madhyamaḥ** ||

GHAṬOTKACAḤ

bhavitavyam

BHĪMASENAḤ

api ca
madhyamaḥ pañcabhūtānāṃ pārthivānāṃ ca **madhyamaḥ** |
bhave ca **madhyamo** loke sarvakāryeṣu **madhyamaḥ** ||

BHĪMASENA

I am the **"Middle One"** of the immortals, and the **"Middle One"** of the haughty ones. O good sir, **I** am the **"Middle One"** of the earth, and the **"Middle One"** even of my brothers.

GHAṬOTKACA
So be it.

BHĪMASENA
Moreover, I am the **"Middle One"** of the five elements, the **"Middle One"** of the kings, the **"Middle One"** in worldly existence, and the **"Middle One"** in all its affairs.

(*MV* 28-29)

When considered as instances of Greco-Indian *anukaraṇa*, the procedures at play in these last two pairs of passages would be characterized, respectively, by oddity and reversal: a Roman text (*The Two Menaechmuses*) where a character expectedly denies his acquaintance with someone else (Menaechmus (Sosicles) referring to Cylindrus) and listens to specific details about him (immediate family and place of birth), would have become an Indian text (*The Middle One*) where a character unexpectedly denies anyone else's identity (Bhīma referring to the second son) and speaks of general facts about himself (role within all of existence).

Continuing with the theme of mistaken identity in the Roman play, the fifth and sixth examples involve the well-known Menaechmus being mixed up with the newly arrived Menaechmus (Sosicles). This happens first to the wife (*Men.* 559-674) and then to the courtesan (*Men.* 675-700). With surgeon-like precision, the playwright juxtaposes, not only the two women making the same mistake, but also as the seventh example, the same woman wrongly identifying the two brothers (*Men.* 701-752), and as the next two examples, her father wrongly identifying the two brothers too (*Men.* 753-881 and *Men.* 882-965). The last two examples (*Men.* 966-1049 and *Men.* 1050-1059) relate to a slave taking, first, Menaechmus for Menaechmus (Sosicles), and then, the other way around.

The anagnorisis of the Roman twins is also worth discussing in tandem with that of the Indian middle brothers. A previous step for any kind of realization is the admission of having been wrong about something. This is a point that the Roman playwright explicitly makes: Menaechmus talks about being mistaken (*erro*). But just before wrapping things up, he also incorporates one last pun, concerning the notion of being set free (*libero*). Because of the saving (*servo*), which sounds a lot like a serving (*servo*), the master (*erus*) is now compelled to manumit his supposed slave. In turn, the Sanskrit playwright seems to be operating on a more implicit level: there is no mention of a mistake, but there is one allusion to the idea of being set free (*muc*). Furthermore, although no terms for masters or slaves are used, the selected verb (*anu-* + *gam*) at least suggests it, since it can mean both "follow" and "obey". It can even mean "imitate", thus winking at an eventual, overarching *anukaraṇa*, now marked by its obliqueness.

Mes.	Ergo edepol, si recte facias, **ere**, med emittas manu.
Men.	**Liberem** ego te?
Mes.	Verum, quandoquidem, **ere**, te **servavi**.
Men.	Quid est? adulescens, **erras**.
Mes.	Quid, **erro**?
Men.	Per Iovem adiuro patrem, med **erum** tuom non esse. (...)
Messenio.	O **master**, if by Pollux you did the right thing, you would then grant me my freedom.
Menaechmus.	Me **setting** you **free**?
Messenio.	Surely, seeing that I **saved** you, O **master**.
Menaechmus.	What was that? O young man, you **are mistaken**.
Messenio.	How **am I mistaken**?
Menaechmus.	I swear by Father Jupiter that I am not your **master**.

(*Men.* 1023-1026)

BHĪMASENAḤ
(...)
bhoḥ puruṣa **mucyatām**

GHAṬOTKACAḤ
na **mucyate**

BHĪMASENAḤ
bho brāhmaṇa gṛhyatāṃ tava putraḥ
vayam enam **anugamiṣyāmaḥ**

BHĪMASENA
(...)
Oh, **set** the man **free**!

GHAṬOTKACA
He is not **being set free**.

BHĪMASENA
Dear Brahman, take your son. We **will follow** him.

(*MV* 39.2-39.6)

When the recognition finally takes place, there is mention of the proofs that led to it. In this sense, both the Roman and the Sanskrit anagnorises would be following Aristotle's (*Poet.* 1452a28 ff.) subtype of ἡ διὰ τῶν σημείων (the one by signs). On the Roman side, the newly arrived Menaechmus (Sosicles) experiences a change from ignorance (believing Menaechmus to be a stranger) to knowledge (realizing that Menaechmus is his brother), which results in friendship (the rekindling of their brotherly bond) and great prosperity (Menaechmus has inherited a lot of wealth). On the Sanskrit side, Ghaṭotkaca experiences a change from ignorance (believing Bhīma to be an enemy) to knowledge (realizing that Bhīma is his father), which also results in friendship (the rekindling of their father/son bond) and great prosperity (no "Middle One" dies). It appears to be another case of change.

Men. S.	**Signa** adgnovi, contineri quin complectar non queo. mi germane gemine frater, salve. ego sum Sosicles.
Menaechmus. S.	I recognize **the proofs**: I cannot help but embrace you! Hello, my brother, my twin brother. I am Sosicles.

(*Men.* 1124-1125)

GHAṬOTKACAḤ
kaḥ **pratyayaḥ**

HIḌIMBĀ
eṣa **pratyayaḥ**
jayatv āryaputraḥ

GHAṬOTKACA
What is your **proof**?

HIḌIMBĀ
This is my **proof**: Glory to my husband!

(*MV* 48.23-48.25b)

When considered as instances of Greco-Indian *anukaraṇa*, the procedures at play in these last two pairs of passages would both be characterized by change: a Roman text (*The Two Menaechmuses*) where an actual slave (Messenio) obtains his freedom after the newcomer (Menaechmus (Sosicles)) takes part in an anagnorisis requiring proof, would have become an Indian text (*The Middle One*) where a soon-to-be-enslaved person (the second son) obtains his freedom after the newcomer (Bhīma) takes part in an anagnorisis requiring proof.

[OM3] *Spaces, times, characters, and themes are changed in the plays, which otherwise would be dramatizations and not adaptations.* Both adaptations change their location: from Homeric fiction to Sicilian quasi fact (GO7), and from a wilderness (in the story of Hiḍimba) and a town (in the story of Baka) to the wilderness between two towns (SO7). Nevertheless, time stands out as a more relevant intersection: not only do both dramas adhere to dramatic convention (*Poet.* 1449b11-14 ~ *Nāṭyaś.* 18.90) in compressing the action of several days into just one roundtrip of the sun (GO8 ~ SO8), but also both dramatists seem to have quite a few tricks up their sleeves when it comes to managing time. Since the audience of an adaptation is, presumably, familiar with the plot, this constitutes a major asset, as well as an adequate place for undertaking any examination of an author's creativity and criticality[179] within his respective tradition.[180]

Euripides changes the timing of the ram trick, the boulder trick, and the name trick. These well-known episodes go from the epic's boulder-name-ram sequence to the play's sequence of ram-boulder-name. If getting a laugh out of a canonical text such as the *Odyssey* is already a form of critique, scrambling its narrative points in the same direction. Now, (Ps.-)Bhāsa is no stranger to such subtleties, given that he also merges time as part of his seeming *contaminatio* of the stories of Hiḍimba and Baka.

In terms of characterization, the Greek author shapes the tyrant Polyphemus as a more up-to-date authoritarian figure (GO9), as does the Sanskrit author by fusing the authoritative rakshasa from the story of Hiḍimba and the authoritative mother from the story of Baka into the rakshasa-mother Hiḍimbā in the story of Ghaṭotkaca (SO9). The priest (GO10) / Brahman (SO10), as a religious figure sending off the hero with the provisions that he will need to face the ogre, is subject to changes in both adaptations. So too is the

179 For criticality in *Cyclops*, see Shaw (2018): "There are a few apparent intertexts, but on the whole the *Cyclops* goes beyond translating Homer for the stage. Instead, it functions more as a form of early literary criticism than of straightforward imitation" (p. 98); and Hunter & Laemmle (2020): "*Cyclops* offers a recasting of the Homeric story which amounts in fact to an interpretation, a 'critical reading' of it" (p. 17).

180 For tradition relating to *Cyclops*, see Hunter & Laemmle (2020): "Euripides' *Cyclops* both bears witness to, and was very likely formative for, an exegetical tradition which persistently wondered whether Odysseus was telling the truth and how things might 'really' have happened, if we had reports which did not emanate from the hero himself. Most of our evidence for that tradition comes from much later in antiquity and the Byzantine period – the Greek literature of the Roman empire, the scholia on Homer and the Homeric commentaries of Eustathius – but Euripides' satyr-drama is itself in part a commentary on the events of *Odyssey* 9, and one whose spirit finds some of its closest parallels in that later tradition" (p. 10).

drawing of lots (GO11 ~ SO11). And yet, many of the old themes remain, e.g., hospitality (GO12 ~ SO12).

To recapitulate, from the ogre motif, I propose a Greek influence from *Od.* 9 and *Cyclops* into *MBh.* 1 and *The Middle One*. Three adaptation techniques stand out: *contaminatio* (OM1), theme addition-cum-emphasis (OM2), and changing of spaces, times, characters, and themes (OM3). Considering the proposed Greco-Indian *anukaraṇa*, the influence would be marked by change. Additionally, I propound four Greco-Roman borrowings for the ogre motif: the response in the negative, characterized by oddity; the *ad hoc* lineage, defined by reversal; the end of the enslaving, distinguished by change; and the anagnorisis, differentiated by change as well. All four would come from *The Two Menaechmuses*.

Emily B. West's Ogres

Modern critics have highlighted the relevance of the aforementioned sets of texts, selected through the criterion of the ogre motif, when examining ancient methods and contexts of adaptation.[181] However, just a perusal of the previous footnote

181 For the Greco-Roman world, see O'Sullivan & Collard (2013): "Euripides' engagement with his Homeric model does not, however, simply entail a dramatization of the epic encounter between Odysseus and Polyphemus" (p. 41); Shaw (2018): "Euripides manipulates the Homeric plot to fit important themes of satyr drama, and to draw particular social, religious, and historical connections to Athens" (p. 65), "This created a performative fusion that helped make satyr drama a particularly self-reflective genre, where authors were not only engaging with the earlier literary sources of the myth being presented, but were also engaging with all other earlier satyr plays" (p. 69), and "Odysseus here [sc. *Cyc.* 375-376] states that the horrors which took place in the cave are the stuff of stories (*mûthois*), but the term *mûthos* also signifies 'myth', which creates a fascinating and overt reference to the mythological tale found in Homer's *Odyssey*" (pp. 101-102); and Hunter & Laemmle (2020): "'What might have *really* happened between Odysseus and the Cyclops?' is the question which *Cyclops* sets out to dramatise, and it can do this with a generous dose of irony because we are no longer at the mercy of Odysseus' own narration. Much of the fun of *Cyclops* is that all the characters, including even the Cyclops, know 'the Homeric script' and apparently allude to it with great freedom, but just as important for the spirit of the play is the (alternative) reality which it opposes to the Homeric Odysseus' narration" (p. 12), "Far from seeking to conceal the Homeric narrative which underlies his drama, Euripides revels

evinces that this has happened much more often in studies framed within the Greco-Roman world than in those dealing with India, and this is especially true for (Ps.-)Bhāsa.[182] But it is not all bad news. For instance, some work carried out in the field of Indo-European studies, like that by E. B. West (2005/2006), may also come in handy for an analysis presupposing cultural contact. There are deep, structural similarities between the Greek epic's ogre motif and the Sanskrit epic's ogre motif, and as a result, there is still more ground to cover for an adequate comparison of their two dramatic adaptations.

If my interpretation is correct, seven of E. B. West's (2005/2006) "thematic similarities" could have been direct borrowings from *Cyclops* into *The Middle One*, according to my numbering GO3 ~ SO3 (the addition of Chance/chance), GO4 ~ SO4 (the emphasis on the tree/trees), GO5 ~ SO5 (the emphasis on/ignoring of the sex), GO6 ~ SO6 (the emphasis on the mistaken identity), GO9 ~ SO9 (the change of the authoritarian figure), GO10 ~ SO10 (the change of the role of the priest/Brahman), and GO11 ~ SO11 (the change of the lot into a choice).

The hero leaving those close to him behind in *Od.* 9 and in *MBh.* 1 could be the trigger for incorporating Chance/chance as a factor in *Cyc.* and in *MV.*[183] In the Greek play, Odysseus faces the entire episode alone (GO3), because his companions have been

in the knowledge shared by characters and audience of that model" (p. 18), and "The dramatisation of an entire episode from the Homeric poems... is a particularly marked way of exposing the relationship between epic and drama and between Homer and the tragic poets" (p. 20). For India, see Salomon (2010): "As in the others [sc. the other *MBh.*-inspired plays], the author of the MV freely reworked the source material, expanding on various incidents and characters of the original" (p. 7).

182 On the relative lack of literary studies on (Ps.-)Bhāsa, see Brückner (1999/2000): "Detailed literary analyses and appreciations of the dramas are still wanting" (p. 503, n. 4); and Sutherland Goldman (2017): "...little attention has been given over to serious analysis of the plays themselves... the plays as literary and performative pieces seem largely to get bypassed" (p. 229). The latter is focusing, precisely, on *The Middle One.*

183 On the hero leaving those close to him behind in the Greek and Sanskrit epics, see E. B. West (2005/2006): "Odysseus leaves most of his men behind on the island of the wild goats (*Od.* 9.116-76) when he takes his handpicked band of men to explore the island of the Cyclopes. Though Bhīma takes no one else with him to his meeting with Baka, he leaves his mother and

substituted for the Satyrs. Along the same lines, in the Sanskrit play, Bhīma stands alone during the encounter (SO3), while his brothers and mother, at first, continue to sleep, and then, wake up to witness his prowess.

> καὶ μὴ 'πὶ καλλίστοισι Τρωικοῖς πόνοις
> **αὐτόν** τε ναύτας τ' ἀπολέσητ' **Ὀδυσσέα**
> ὑπ' ἀνδρὸς ᾧ θεῶν οὐδὲν ἢ βροτῶν μέλει.
> ἢ τὴν τύχην μὲν δαίμον' ἡγεῖσθαι χρεών,
> τὰ δαιμόνων δὲ τῆς τύχης ἐλάσσονα.
>
> And after his most beautiful Trojan endeavors, do not destroy **Odysseus himself** and his sailors at the hands of an individual to whom there is no care for gods or men. Otherwise, we will have to regard Chance as a deity and the deities as inferior to Chance.
>
> (*Cyc.* 603-607)
>
> tāta na tu sarva eva
> āśramaparipālanārtham iha sthāpitaḥ kila **madhyamaḥ**
>
> O father, but not all of them went. **The middle one** was stationed here for the sake of protecting the hermitage.
>
> (*MV* 11.5-11.6)

The trees, which were already relevant to the plots of *Od.* 9 and *MBh.* 1, would have been further exploited in *Cyc.* and *MV.*[184] In the Greek play, the prudent Odysseus goes over his entire plan before setting the wheels in motion (GO4). The stake of olive is crucial to his goal. In the Sanskrit play, Ghaṭotkaca follows in the footsteps of his epic begetter by easily uprooting a tree (SO4). In this case, the tree itself does not suffice, but it still contributes to the mirrored delineating of the father Bhīma and his son Ghaṭotkaca.

---

brothers behind at the house of their brahmin host. Both departures take place at dawn (*Od.* 9.170; *Mbh.* 1.151.1)..." (p. 131).

184 On the trees in the Greek and Sanskrit epics, see E. B. West (2005/2006): "In a foreshadowing of his eventual doom, Polyphemus enters the cave and throws down a load of wood, scaring the men with its tremendous crash (*Od.* 9.233- 5)... In the Baka narrative, the conflict's signature weapon is introduced as Bhīma continues to eat the food-offering, ignoring the *rākṣasa*'s yells and threats. Infuriated, Baka uproots a tree to use as a weapon (*Mbh.* 1.151.12)" (pp. 139-140).

κώμου μὲν αὐτὸν τοῦδ' ἀπαλλάξαι, λέγων
ὡς οὐ Κύκλωψι πῶμα χρὴ δοῦναι τόδε,
μόνον δ' ἔχοντα βίοτον ἡδέως ἄγειν.
ὅταν δ' ὑπνώσσῃ Βακχίου νικώμενος,
ἀκρεμὼν ἐλαίας ἔστιν ἐν δόμοισί τις,
ὃν φασγάνῳ τῷδ' ἐξαποξύνας ἄκρον
ἐς πῦρ καθήσω· κᾆθ' ὅταν κεκαυμένον
ἴδω νιν, ἄρας θερμὸν ἐς μέσην βαλῶ
Κύκλωπος ὄψιν ὄμμα τ' ἐκτήξω πυρί.

I intend to keep him away from that revel, by telling him that there is no need for him to give this drink to the Cyclopes, but to go through life pleasantly, keeping it to himself. Once he becomes drowsy, overcome by Bacchus, there is **a stake of olive** in his abode, whose tip, after sharpening it with this sword, I will put into the fire. When I see it kindling, having lifted it while still glowing, I will thrust it into the mid-forehead eye of the Cyclops and melt his eye with the fire.

(*Cyc.* 451-459)

kathaṃ katham anrtam ity āha kṣipasi me gurum
bhavatv imaṃ **sthūlaṃ vṛkṣam** utpāṭya praharāmi
katham anenāpi na śakyate hantuṃ kiṃnu khalu kariṣye
bhavatu dṛṣṭam
etad girikūṭam utpāṭya praharāmi

How dare you say that it is not true? You insult my father! So be it. Having pulled up this **huge tree**, I will throw it at him. How is it that, even with this, it is not possible to kill him? What can I possibly do? That's it, I've got it! Having pulled up this mountaintop, I will throw it at him.

(*MV* 43.3-43.6)

The detail of female ogres in both epics could be related to the treatment of sex in both plays.[185] *Cyclops* emphasizes Polyphemus' pleasure (GO5), and it creates a hierarchy thereof, placing youths

185 On female ogres in the Greek and Sanskrit epics, see E. B. West (2005/2006): "Both stories [sc. the *Cyclopeia* and the *Kirmīravadhaparvan*] are loosely paired with other encounters with man-eating giants, both of which open with interactions with less hostile female ogres (i.e. Odysseus' encounter with the Laistrygones at *Od.* 10.80-132, and the Pāṇḍavas' encounter with brother/sister Hiḍimba and Hiḍimbā at *Mbh.* 1.139-43)" (p. 129).

over women. *The Middle One,* in turn, ignores the subject, but it still leaves some telling details: Hiḍimbā's desire (SO5), which is both dietary and carnal, is directed neither at women nor at old men.

> ἅλις· Γανυμήδη τόνδ' ἔχων ἀναπαύσομαι
> κάλλιον ἢ τὰς Χάριτας. **ἥδομαι** δέ πως
> **τοῖς παιδικοῖσι** μᾶλλον ἢ **τοῖς θήλεσιν**.
>
> Enough! I will sleep more beautifully with this Ganymede than with the Graces. Anyway, I take more **pleasure in youths** than **in women**.
>
> (*Cyc.* 582-584)
>
> na khalu **strījano 'bhimatas** tatrabhavatyā
>
> Certainly not, my venerable mother does not **desire a woman**.
>
> (*MV* 15.4)
>
> ā **vṛddhas** tvam apasara
>
> You are too **old**, away with you!
>
> (*MV* 15.6)

The name trick from the *Odyssey* and the *Mahābhārata*, which also entails the provocation, the call for help, and the insufficient response, could have had an impact on the playfulness that surrounds the mistaken identities in the dramatic versions.[186] The

186 On the name trick in the Greek and Sanskrit epics, see E. B. West (2005/2006): "The trick of the name is the hallmark of the *Odyssey*'s story. At 9.355-6, the inebriated Cyclops asks for Odysseus' name, claiming he wants to give him a guest-gift. Odysseus recognizes that the overture is a trap, and gives his famous response (*Od.* 9.366-7)... But the most compelling argument for a lost name-trick in the story lies in a peculiar minor detail. Baka makes a final desperate rush for Bhīma "having trumpeted out his/ the name" (*nāma viśrāvya, Mbh.* 1.151.17) There is no explanation given for the utterance, it is not a battle convention in the epic, and Bhīma has taken great care to be anonymous" (pp. 142-144). On the provocation, see E. B. West (2005/2006): "After calling out to Baka, Bhīma sits down and eats the food he has brought until he is discovered by the ogre (*Mbh.* 1.151.3-5)... The *Odyssey*'s version lacks a deliberate attempt to inflame the monster here, postponing it until Odysseus' ill-advised decision to shout out his name to Polyphemus at 9.473-80 and 491-505, but at this point Odysseus confesses to a certain stubbornness which prevents him from taking his companions' advice to plunder the cave and leave (*Od.* 9.224-30). Though Polyphemus

Greek playwright has the Satyrs mock Polyphemus not for being blinded, but for being fooled by his blinder, who has the double name of “Nobody”/Odysseus (GO6). And the Sanskrit playwright presents the first son as causing a confused Ghaṭotkaca to end up going after the wrong prey, because there are two different people who answer to the name “Middle One” (SO6).

ΚΥΚΛΩΨ
Οὖτίς μ’ ἀπώλεσ’.

ΧΟΡΟΣ
οὐκ ἄρ’ **οὐδείς** <σ’> ἠδίκει.

ΚΥΚΛΩΨ
Οὖτίς με τυφλοῖ βλέφαρον.

ΧΟΡΟΣ
οὐκ ἄρ’ εἶ τυφλός.

ΚΥΚΛΩΨ
†ὡς δὴ σύ†.

ΧΟΡΟΣ
καὶ πῶς σ’ οὔτις ἂν θείη τυφλόν;

ΚΥΚΛΩΨ
σκώπτεις. ὁ δ’ **Οὖτις** ποῦ ’στιν;

ΧΟΡΟΣ
οὐδαμοῦ, Κύκλωψ.

CYCLOPS
Nobody destroyed me.

---

does not actually spot the men until he has lit his fire at 9.251, Odysseus and his companions are surprised in the act of eating the Cyclops’ carefully laid-up cheeses (*Od.* 9.231-3)” (pp. 136-137). On the call for help, see E. B. West (2005/2006): “The wounded Polyphemus calls out to the other Cyclopes (*Od.* 9.399-402)... Just as the Cyclops’ yells draw the other Cyclopes, Baka’s shouting of the name and his dying scream bring the other *rākṣasas*, in much the same way Page hypothesized that Polyphemus’ fellows would react to their leader’s cries (*Mbh.* 1.152.1)” (pp. 144-145). And on the insufficient response, see E. B. West (2005/2006): “In the *Odyssey*, the other Cyclopes are taken in by the trick of the name, and, failing to understand the urgency of Polyphemus’ situation, they abandon him (Od. 9.409-13)... In the *Mahābhārata*, Baka’s household members are easily cowed and pose no threat to Bhīma or the town (*Mbh.* 1.152.2-5)” (p. 145).

CHORUS
Then, **nobody** did wrong to you.

CYCLOPS
Nobody blinds me right in my eye.

CHORUS
Then, you are not blind.

CYCLOPS
<Oh, that you were!>

CHORUS
And how could nobody make you blind?

CYCLOPS
You are mocking me. But where is this **Nobody**?

CHORUS
O Cyclops, he is nowhere.

(*Cyc.* 672-675)

GHAṬOTKACAḤ
...atha kinnāmā tava putraḥ

VṚDDHAḤ
etad api na śakyaṃ śrotum

GHAṬOTKACAḤ
yuktaṃ bho brāhmaṇakumāra kinnāmā te bhrātā

PRATHAMAḤ
tapasvī **madhyamaḥ**

GHAṬOTKACAḤ
madhyameti sadṛśam asya
aham eva yāsyāmi
bho bho **madhyama madhyama** śighram āgaccha

GHAṬOTKACA
...But what is the name of your son?

OLD MAN
I cannot tell you this either.

GHAṬOTKACA
That makes sense. Hey! Young Brahman, what is the name of your brother?

FIRST SON
The ascetic **middle one**.

GHAṬOTKACA
"Middle one" – how fitting is that! I will go myself. Hey!
Middle One. Hey! **Middle One**, come quick!

(*MV* 24.8-24.14)

The ogre/ogress as a loner, a man-eater, and a giant in the two narratives could be responsible for their depiction as an authoritarian in the two adaptations.[187] Euripides' Polyphemus is a tyrant (GO9), who treats the Satyrs as a master would his slaves, and who regularly feasts on human flesh. Not unlike this, (Ps.-) Bhāsa's Hiḍimbā is a bossy mother (SO9), who demands for her meal to be promptly served.

τίνες ποτ' εἰσίν; οὐκ ἴσασι **δεσπότην**
Πολύφημον οἷός ἐστιν ἄξενόν τε γῆν
τήνδ' ἐμβεβῶτες καὶ Κυκλωπίαν γνάθον
τὴν **ἀνδροβρῶτα** δυστυχῶς ἀφιγμένοι.

187 On loner ogres in the Greek and Sanskrit epics, see E. B. West (2005/2006): "When we are introduced to the Cyclops at *Od.* 1.70-1, he is described as ἀντίθεον Πολύφημον, ὅου κράτος ἐστὶ μέγιστον / πᾶσιν Κυκλώπεσσι. 'Godlike Polyphemus, whose power is the greatest among all the Cyclopes.'... In contrast with the initial depiction of Polyphemus as a leader, on the onset of the *Cyclopeia* we are told that οὐδὲ μετ' ἄλλους / πωπλεῖτ' ἀλλ' ἀπάνευθεν ἐὼν ἀθεμίσται ᾔδη, 'nor with the others / did he consort, but stayed away, thinking lawlessly' (*Od.* 9.188)... Baka, too, is initially described a king, an *asurarāt... balī*, 'a strong Asura king,' (*Mbh.* 1.148.4), who is *iśo janapadasyāsya purasya ca mahābalaḥ*, 'extremely powerful, lording it over this countryside and town' (*Mbh.* 1.148.3). After the battle we learn that he possesses both a house and servants (*Mbh.* 1.152.1), but during the encounter itself he is nothing but a fearsome and uncivilized brute in the jungle (*Mbh.* 1.151.1)" (pp. 129-130). On man-eating ogres in the Greek and Sanskrit epics, see E. B. West (2005/2006): "At *Od.* 10.200, the Cyclops is remembered as an ἀνδροφάγος, 'man-eater,' and at 9.297 he lies down to sleep ἀνδρόνεα κρέ' ἔδων, 'having fed on human flesh.' At 9.347, while offering him the wine, Odysseus uses the same words to refer to the human flesh Polyphemus has eaten. Finally, at 9.374, he vomits up ψυμοί τ' ἀνδρόμεοι, 'chunks of human [meat].' Baka is repeatedly called a 'man-eater' (*puruṣādakaḥ*, at *Mbh.* 1.148.4; 1.150.26; 1.151.1; 1.152.6), whose preferred food is human flesh (*manuṣamāṃsa*)" (p. 131). And on giant ogres in the Greek and Sanskrit epics, see E. B. West (2005/2006): "Polyphemus' size, like most of his other qualities, is both amazing and terrifying (*Od.* 9.190-2)... In the same vein, the immense, lifeless body of Baka is a source of both wonder and horror to the liberated townspeople (*Mbh.* 1.152.8-9)" (p. 133).

Who can they possibly be? They must not know what our **master** Polyphemus is like, since they have set foot in this inhospitable land, and they have unfortunately arrived at the **man-eating** jaws of the Cyclops.

(*Cyc.* 90-93)

...putra mamopavāsanisargārtham asmin vanapradeśe kaścin **mānuṣaḥ** parimṛgy**ānetavye**ti

...O son, having searched for **a human** in this wooded region, you **must bring** him to me for the sake of breaking my fast.

(*MV* 11.18)

The priestly head of the family appearing both in the *Odyssey* and in the *Mahābhārata* could have determined the family trees in the theater versions.[188] The Greek playwright presents Maron as a son (GO10), thus recognizing his link to Apollo, while downplaying it for the sake of his Dionysus-favorable reworking. Taking a similar approach, the Sanskrit playwright showcases Keśavadāsa as a father (SO10), not without acknowledging the willingness of his relatives to come to his rescue, and yet causing the character himself to shine in a new light, thanks to that wisdom that only comes with old age.

καὶ μὴν Μάρων μοι πῶμ' ἔδωκε, **παῖς** θεοῦ.

And surely, Maron, **the son** of the god [sc. Dionysus], gave me the drink.

(*Cyc.* 141)

kṛtakṛtyaṃ śarīraṃ me pariṇāmena jarjaram |
rākṣasāgnau **sutā**pekṣī hoṣyāmi vidhisaṃskṛtam ||

188 For the priestly head of the family in the Greek and Sanskrit epics, see E. B. West (2005/2006): "Odysseus' meeting with Polyphemus is preceded by a brief aside describing the origin of the wine that figures so prominently in the episode. It was a gift from Maron, a priest of Apollo, in a carry-over from the preceding encounter with the Kikonians (*Od.* 9.196-200)... Where the *Odyssey* briefly mentions the existence of Maron's wife and son, the *Mahābhārata* contains 36 verses of the wife nobly offering to sacrifice herself to the monster (*Mbh.* 1.146.1-36), and a vignette of the lisping baby son telling his parents not to cry and offering to kill the ogre with a straw (*Mbh.* 1.147.20-22)" (pp. 134-135).

> My body, decrepit from old age, has fulfilled its duty. Thinking of my **children**, I will offer it, purified by the precepts, to this fire-like rakshasa.
>
> (*MV* 15)

Lastly, the precedent of drawing lots in the two narratives, together with its re-interpretation as a choice in the two adaptations, could be seen as a direct imitation.[189] Homer's Odysseus orders his companions to draw lots, but Euripides' just orders the Satyrs to line up. Which of them would be the ones that are going to help him is completely up to them (GO11). Likewise, Vyāsa's townsfolk die by turns, whereas (Ps.-)Bhāsa's Brahman must choose which of his sons to sacrifice (SO11).

> ἄγε, **τίς** πρῶτος, **τίς** δ' ἐπὶ πρώτῳ
> ταχθεὶς δαλοῦ κώπην ὀχμάσαι
> Κύκλωπος ἔσω βλεφάρων ὤσας
> λαμπρὰν ὄψιν διακναίσει;
>
> Come on, having been drawn up, **who** will be the first, and **who** the one after the first, to grip the haft of the firebrand, and after thrusting it between the eyelids of the Cyclops, who will gouge out his bright eye?
>
> (*Cyc.* 483-486)

> patnyā cāritraśālinyā dviputro mokṣam icchasi |
> balābalaṃ parijñāya putram **ekaṃ** visarjaya ||
>
> You want your freedom as a father of two, together with your well-behaved wife. Having pondered their strengths and weaknesses, give up **one** of your sons.
>
> (*MV* 12)

189 On the drawing of lots in the Greek and Sanskrit epics, see E. B. West (2005/2006): "In the *Mahābhārata*, the brahmin describes the system whereby the villagers pay tribute to Baka (*Mbh.* 1.148.6-8)... Later, the drawing of lots to determine who will wield the olive log is in the same vein as the turn taking described in the *Mahābhārata*; it is a cold-blooded determination of who must face down the ogre (*Od.* 9.331-3)" (p. 138).

5. Sanskrit Authors Adapting Greco-Roman Texts

Influences in the Adaptation Techniques

It is possible that the Greco-Roman world had an influence on the theater of India. The claim of a possible Greek influence on Sanskrit theater can be backed by the testimonies from ancient sources (Plutarch, *Mor.* 328d, *Alex.* 8.2-3, *Alex.* 72.1, *Crass.* 33.2; Philostratus, *V A* 2.32). It has also been acknowledged by modern specialists from the fields of Indology (Weber, 1852/1878, p. 207; Sinha & Choudhury, 2000, p. 32; Lindtner, 2002, p. 199; Bronkhorst, 2016, pp. 390-403), Classical Philology (Windisch, 1882; Reich, 1903; Tarn, 1938, pp. 381-382), Archaeology (Bernard, 1976, pp. 321-322), Theater Arts (Free, 1981, p. 84), and Comparative Literature (Walker, 2004). The possibility of a Roman influence on Sanskrit theater, on the other hand, has been acknowledged by at least one classicist (Rodríguez Adrados, 2012, p. 10).

Both Aeschylus (*The Myrmidons*, *The Nereids*, and *The Phrygians*, from *Il.* 16-24; *The Ghost-Raisers*, *Penelope*, and *The Bone-Gatherers*, from *Od.* 11-24) and Sophocles (*Nausicaa or the Washerwomen*, from *Od.* 6; *The Phaeacians*, from *Od.* 7-12; *The Foot-Washing*, from *Od.* 19) adapted the Homeric Epics (Sommerstein, 2015, pp. 461-462). Nonetheless, (Ps.-)Euripides (*Cyclops*, from *Od.* 9; *Phoenix*, from *Il.* 9; and *Rhesus*, from *Il.* 10) is the best source for studying Homer-*imitatio* (Lange, 2002, p. 22). Moreover, Homer and Euripides were

 https://doi.org/10.11647/OBP.0417.05

the best candidates for being exported into other cultural spaces (Tarn, 1938, pp. 382-384).

Likewise, (Ps.-)Bhāsa (*The Middle One*, from *MBh.* 1; *The Five Nights*, from *MBh.* 4; *The Embassy*, from *MBh.* 5; *Ghaṭotkaca as an Envoy*, from *MBh.* 7; *Karṇa's Task*, from *MBh.* 8; and *The Broken Thighs*, from *MBh.* 9), Kālidāsa (*The Recognition of Śakuntalā*, from *MBh.* 1.62-69; and *On Purūravas and Urvaśī*, from *Harivaṃśa* 10.26), Bhaṭṭa Nārāyaṇa (*The Binding Up of the Braided Hair*, from the entire *MBh.*), Vatsarāja (*On the Mountaineer and Arjuna*, from *MBh.* 3.13-42; and *The Burning of Tripura*, from *MBh.* 8.24), Kulaśekhara Varman (*On Tapatī and Saṃvāraṇa*, from *MBh.* 1.160-163; and *Subhadrā and Arjuna*, from *MBh.* 1.211-213), Rājaśekhara (*The Little Mahābhārata*, from the entire *MBh.*), Kṣemendra (*The Blossom-Cluster of the Rāmāyaṇa*, from *MBh.* 3.257-276), and Vijayapāla (*The Self-choice of Draupadī*, from *MBh.* 1.174-185) all adapted the *Mahābhārata*, and yet, (Ps.-)Bhāsa stands out as the best option for examining Vyāsa-*anukaraṇa* (Ghosh, 1963).

From the point of view of the treatises, there are various points of encounter between the Greek and Sanskrit theatrical traditions: both Aristotle and Bharata offer similar views on avoiding on-stage deaths (*Poet.* 1452b11-13 ~ *Nāṭyaś.* 18.38) and sticking to a one-day timeframe (*Poet.* 1449b11-14 ~ *Nāṭyaś.* 18.90). But most importantly, the Greek tragedies and the Sanskrit heroic-type plays (*nāṭaka*, *samavakāra*, *ḍima*, and *vyāyoga*) share an inclination to adapt traditional themes and characters, and to do so by reworking their epic precedents.[190]

From the perspective of the plays, the five-act division, the curtain, and the similarities in prologues, plots, and characters (Windisch, 1882), as well as in "choruses" (Sinha & Choudhury, 2000, p. 32) have all been adduced as arguments in favor of the influence hypothesis. So too have been the parallel practices, in both Greek and Sanskrit theater, of seeking their themes and characters in their respective epics (Wells, 1968, p. iii; Free, 1981, p. 84). And

190 See *Nāṭyaś.* 1.15: "Furnished with all the goals of the sciences, advancing all the arts, a fifth *Veda*, **accompanied by the epics** and called theater, I am fashioning [*sarvaśātrārthasampannaṃ sarvaśilpapravartakam* | *nāṭyākhyaṃ pañcamaṃ vedaṃ* ***setihāsaṃ*** *karomy aham*]".

more recently, there has even been an attempt (Walker, 2004, pp. 10-11) to link (Ps.-)Bhāsa to the beginning of such influence, since a *prakaraṇa*, such as his *Cārudatta in Poverty*, certainly recalls the Greek Comedy by Menander, whereas his *The Broken Thighs* – which some consider an *aṅka* – does the same with, for instance, the Greek Tragedy by Sophocles. Throughout this book, I have advanced some complementary arguments, not only to support the original claim, but also to spark a conversation about it.

For the embassy motif, both Euripides' *Phoenix* and (Ps.-)Bhāsa's *The Embassy* evince the same two techniques, and this proximity, when combined with the followed chronologies for the texts and the attested contacts of the cultures, suggests an influence from the Greek playwright to the Sanskrit one. Even though every shorter version of a story must make do with missing out some elements, the proposed character subtraction-cum-merging entails two correlated moves: subtracting characters and merging functions. Fragmentary as it is, *Phoenix* offers just enough evidence for allowing an appreciation of the fact that its author subtracts the character of the mother and merges her triggering function into the advances of the concubine. Similarly, *The Embassy* portrays a scenario in which the father is almost subtracted, and in which he and the son are merged. Two characters and two speeches become one of each: it is all reduced by means of a creative combination.

The theme addition-cum-emphasis is also a key component in any adaptation, since it presents authors with one of the best ways for showcasing their creativity and criticality. Euripides' main innovations vis-à-vis the embassy motif would be the accusation and the blinding, that is, the cause and the effect of the emphasized wrath of the father, who seeks a fitting punishment for a more severe crime. Likewise, (Ps.-)Bhāsa's chief contributions to this well-known story are the painting and the personified weapons, which both point to the emphasized mulishness of the son: the former, by bringing back the memory of the crime; the latter, by procuring an adequate pondering of the punishment.

Lastly, neither in Greece nor in India is the theatrical version a step-by-step summary of the epic plot. Canonical authors, such as Homer and Vyāsa, are worthy of the adaptors always going the extra mile. In *Phoenix*, the location changes from Troy, where the old ambassador currently is, to Thessaly, where he was born and raised; the time, from the present of the Trojan war to the past of the father/son conflict; the characters of the three messengers and their addressee, to those of the father, the concubine, and the son; and the themes of the pleading and the curse, to those of the accusation and the blinding. In fact, all of this – save the accusation and the blinding – is already present in the source text, but what was there a gemstone, i.e., one of the epic substories, is here, after much cutting and polishing, a piece of jewelry, i.e., an epic-inspired play.

If the Greek playwright is like a cameraman zooming in, his Indian counterpart is like someone who manages to see the elephant where the blind men cannot. *DV* works, not with one of the substories, but with the entire *MBh.* as its background: the location goes from the remoteness of the city to the immediateness of the camp; the time, from a moment when Bhīṣma is still not consecrated to one when the die is cast; the characters, from a plurality of advisors to just two contrasting views; and the themes of the sexual assault and the universal form, respectively, from the faraway experiences of the past tense and the divine realm, to the nearby ones of the ekphrastic painting and the tricky transformations.

In a sense, both Euripides' use of Homer and (Ps.-)Bhāsa's use of Vyāsa are ways of panning for gold. Out of the three parts of *Il.* 9, that is, assembly, council of chiefs, and embassy, the Greek author only focuses on the embassy. Out of the three ambassadors, that is, Odysseus, Phoenix, and Ajax, he concentrates on just Phoenix. And out of the three substories from his speech, that is, the story of Phoenix, the story of the Prayers, and the story of Meleager, he centers merely on the autobiographical portion. This laser focus makes sense within his literary tradition: Phoenix is already a father figure to Achilles, and therefore a worthy homage would not insist on that relationship, but exploit one close to it, such as that of Phoenix and his actual father, who, just like Achilles, ends up between a rock and a hard place because of a concubine.

Likewise, out of the four embassies, that is, the one of king Drupada's priest to the Kauravas, the one of king Dhṛtarāṣṭra's bard to the Pāṇḍavas, the one of Kṛṣṇa to the Kauravas, and the one of Duryodhana's cousin to the Pāṇḍavas, the Sanskrit author only focuses on that of Kṛṣṇa. He also moves past substories, like that of the victory of Indra, that of Dambhodbhava, and that of Ambā; other secondary narratives, like the deeds of Mātali and Gālava, and the colloquy of Vidurā and her son; didactic passages, like the instructions of the steward Vidura and of the sage Sanatsujāta; and even main events, like the yoking of the armies for battle, which gives name to *MBh.* 5. He is clearly taking a step back to see the bigger picture, and this also makes sense in the context of his canonical source: if the *Mahābhārata* is Vyāsa's entire thought, *The Embassy* is (Ps.-)Bhāsa's entire vision of this motif.

Even though there are messengers in Vedic literature (e.g., the dog messenger Saramā in *RV.* 10.108), there are two aspects that support a Greek influence here. On one hand, there is more in common between the Greek epic's version of the motif and the Sanskrit epic's version of the motif, both of which situate it in a war context and correlate it with substories. In fact, some critics (Lallemant, 1959; Duckworth, 1961) have pointed out the large-scale correspondences between the Sanskrit embassy and the Greco-Roman embassy. On the other hand, the fact that the embassy from the Homeric Epics is chosen for the Greek theater's version of the motif would have provided the perfect model for the *Mahābhārata* to be chosen for the Sanskrit theater's version as well. In other words, the elements would be Indian, but the techniques would be Greco-Roman.

For the ambush motif, both Ps.-Euripides' *Rhesus* and (Ps.-) Bhāsa's *The Five Nights* profit from the same four techniques. Such parallelism, together with the one discussed for the embassy motif, further supports the claim of a possible Greek influence upon India. To begin with, if dramas are more condensed, epics are more slow-paced. Through a series of narrative techniques, epics allow, not only for deferrals and suspense, but also for remembrances and gradual buildups. Nonetheless, of epic repetitions are among the better known of such procedures, in the adaptations, this is substituted: *Rhesus* and *The Five Nights* alike combine and eliminate. The best argument for the influence hypothesis here is that both playwrights merge two ambushes into one. Another technique is that of emphasized characterization. As parallel examples, one can cite Dolon's tricky bargaining and Droṇa's tricky request, Rhesus and Uttara as *milites gloriosi*, the references to "ambush [λόχος]" and "cattle raid [*gograha*(*ṇa*)-]" alluding the adaptations' respective sources, and Odysseus' anagnorisis by Hector mirroring those of Arjuna by Uttara, by Bhīṣma, and by Abhimanyu.

In terms of changes, Ps.-Euripides moves the action from the Greek camp to the Trojan camp, and (Ps.-)Bhāsa, from the Pāṇḍava side to the Kaurava side. The former showcases Rhesus in a better light, as does the latter with Duryodhana. This is done, respectively, by changing the perspective from the Greeks to the Trojans, and by changing the timing of the sacrifice. And if *Rhesus* opts for a minor adjustment when augmenting the night watches from three to five, *The Five Nights* effects a major variation when turning the five villages into the five nights, which may have also been the result of an influence coming from Ps.-Euripides. Finally, the author of *Rhesus* tiptoes around the subjects of death and violence, whether they relate to the Trojan spy Dolon or to the Trojan warriors accompanying Rhesus, just as the author of *The Five Nights* remains silent about Virāṭa occasioning Yudhiṣṭhira's nosebleed and about the outcome of the story. The correspondences between traditions in this instance even transcend the realm of literary practice, for theorists like Aristotle and Bharata see eye to eye on this as well.

For Aristotle (*Poet.* 1452b11-13) and the Greek theatrical tradition, both violence and death, by themselves, are a bit too much for the stage, but since they relate to suffering, and suffering, unlike those two, can and should be depicted in a play, there is still some wiggle room for them to be incorporated. For Bharata (*Nāṭyaś.* 18.20 and *Nāṭyaś.* 18.38) and the Sanskrit theatrical tradition too, violence and death are to be dispensed with, especially if they relate to the hero or if they are to be made part of the acts themselves, but for other characters, as well as for other moments, such as the interludes, the position varies. It is also worth remembering that only Euripides and (Ps.-)Bhāsa violate said conventions, and that

Alcestis and *Hippolytus*, on one hand, and *The Broken Thighs*, on the other, do present deaths on stage. It is possible that the Indian theorist and author could have profited from the Greek take on this, had they been aware of it.

Going back to the cameraman analogy, the Greek author is shooting from a different angle. One must remember that Greek theater, and especially tragedy for obvious reasons, favors the point of view of the defeated over that of the victor. And as for his Indian counterpart, he is gifting his audience with the director's cut that is *The Five Nights*, instead of the theatrical release that would have been the *Virāṭaparvan*. His public would have been familiar with the outcome of the year incognito, and therefore, would have expected the tension to grow during the unfruitful feats of diplomacy and into the two massacre-producing wars. Nevertheless, he rolls the credits just in time to eschew the death and violence that would have ensued.

Just as Ps.-Euripides is a close reader of Homer – and of Euripides, for that matter – so too is (Ps.-)Bhāsa when it comes to Vyāsa – and presumably to the Greco-Roman sources as well. Instead of moving back and forth from the Greeks to the Trojans, Ps.-Euripides centers on the latter and gives the story a tragic spin, something that Homer himself occasionally does, e.g., with the Trojan happenings in *Il.* 6. This procedure of giving a voice to the opposing side goes as far as turning Rhesus from silent participant to title character. The heroic victory of the Greeks is also the no-less heroic defeat of the Trojans, whose inadequate leadership may even shed some light on the politics of fourth-century Greece, and whose appealing presentation – after all, the play was transmitted as part of the Select Plays of Euripides – may have caught the attention of one or more first-or-second-century Indians.

In the same way, (Ps.-)Bhāsa could not be farther away from a careless butchering of Vyāsa. He knows the *Mahābhārata* like the palm of his hand, and this is particularly evident in his merging and splitting of several ambushes: Duryodhana's ambush against Citrasena in the *Ghoṣayātrāparvan*, Suśarman's ambush against Virāṭa in the *Virāṭaparvan*, Duryodhana's ambush against Uttara in the *Virāṭaparvan*. And if the influence hypothesis sustains itself, the list could also include Diomedes'/Odysseus' ambush against Dolon in *Od.* 10, Diomedes'/Odysseus' ambush against Rhesus in *Od.* 10, and Odysseus'/Diomedes' ambush against Rhesus in *Rhesus*. If the study of adaptations already presupposes a knowledge of various sources, for examining the proposed cross-cultural adaptations, the number of sources just keeps getting bigger.

Despite the various references to cattle raids in Vedic literature (e.g., *gáviṣṭi-* "quest for cows" in *RV.* 5.63.5, *RV.* 6.59.7, and *RV.* 8.24.5), and despite the undeniable presence of such cattle raids in several Indo-European traditions (e.g., in the Irish *Cattle raid of Cooley*), the points of encounter between the Greek and Sanskrit versions go way beyond an Indo-European connection. First, there is a certain consensus (Lincoln, 1976; Adams & Mallory, 1997) about the fact that, at the Indo-European stage, the cattle-raiding myth would have been part of the larger dragon-slaying myth, which has nothing to do with the studied plays. Second, while studying the various commonalities between different epic versions of the ambush motif, scholars have pointed out very specific Greco-Roman (Dué & Ebbott, 2010) and Greco-Indian (Wulff Alonso, 2008a) similarities, particularly in terms of devastating horses, nighttime deeds, and poetics of ambush. And third, just like with *Phoenix* and *The Embassy*, the Sanskrit author could have drawn his inspiration for adapting one of the *Mahābhārata* ambushes from his knowledge of *Rhesus* as a Greek adaptation of the Homeric ambush.

For the ogre motif, both Euripides' *Cyclops* and (Ps.-)Bhāsa's *The Middle One* resort to the same three techniques. This parallelism, together with those highlighted when examining both the embassy motif and the ambush motif, allows for more arguments in support of the claim of possible Greek influence. First and foremost, just as *Cyclops* appears to be the result of a *contaminatio* of elements coming from the *Homeric Hymn to Dionysus* into the main narrative of *Od.* 9, so too *The Middle One* seems to be the product of a *contaminatio* of elements originally precent in the *Bakavadhaparvan* into the main narrative of the *Hiḍimbavadhaparvan*.

If the author of *The Middle One* had just dramatized the epic story of Hiḍimba, the result would not have been even half as good. In contrast, by merging the story of Hiḍimba and the story of Baka he showcases the best of both worlds. The physical proximity of the stories, appearing back-to-back in the *Mahābhārata*, is certainly a compelling argument to support the *contaminatio*, but so is the thematic proximity, since they are both stories about man-eating rakshasas. If (Ps.-)Bhāsa had been acquainted with Roman theater, whose authors routinely blended together Greek plays, either because their plots resembled each other or because their author happened to be the same, then this could have motivated him to engage in a similar form of creative criticism.

Moreover, and still profiting from the analogy of filmmaking, the author of the *MBh.* presents the two stories of Hiḍimba and Baka separately and sequentially, that is, occurring one after the other, much like in an anthology film. But the author of the *MV*, being the close reader that he is, reinterprets and re-creates this as a single story, involving both Ghaṭotkaca and Hiḍimbā, which is constructed jointly and simultaneously, that is, with one of its plots being embedded within the other, not unlike what crossover films do. And on that note, does Euripides himself not write a sort of crossover of his own, when bringing together stories about Odysseus and Cyclopes, on one hand, and about Dionysus and Satyrs, on the other?

There are several commonalities related to emphases: the trees, the sex, the mistaken identities. There are numerous coinciding additions as well, among which two that stand out because of their thematic correspondences in both literary traditions: the father/son conflict and the Chance/chance. The father and the son, in *Cyclops*, are represented by Silenus and the chorus of Satyrs, who not only accommodate the needs of the new literary genre of satyr drama, but also highlight the absence, in the adaptation, of a *sine qua non* from the source, i.e., the wine. In a similar way, the father and son, in *The Middle One*, are typified by Bhīma and Ghaṭotkaca, who stress the absence, in the adaptation, of a must-have from the source, i.e., the mother.

The Chance, on which the Greek playwright proposes that any tragic outcome would be to blame, has its mirror image in the chance which the Sanskrit playwright credits for the happy ending.

Thus, it would be nothing but Chance if Odysseus, who had already managed to escape death during the decade-long Trojan war, were to meet his Waterloo during his brief encounter with Polyphemus. And it is also by chance that, even though the Pāṇḍavas have left for a sacrifice, Bhīma remains close by, and even though Bhīma himself has momentarily left for an exercising session, he can still hear his name being called. At this juncture, the main argument in favor of any sort of influence is the addition of chance by (Ps.-) Bhāsa, especially when considering the impact that Euripides' notion of Chance had on the Greco-Roman stage.

Regarding change, Euripides shifts the location from the vicinity of a fictitious island to the very real island of Sicily; and the timing, from the boulder-name-ram order to the one of ram-boulder-name. In much the same way, (Ps.-)Bhāsa modifies the location by combining the wilderness from the story of Hiḍimba and the town from the story of Baka; and the timing, by substituting the sequential encounters with Hiḍimba and Baka from the epic source for the almost simultaneous encounters with Ghaṭotkaca and Hiḍimbā in the dramatic adaptation. In both adaptations, the characters become more authoritarian (Polyphemus as a tyrant, and Hiḍimbā as a bossy mother), and more devoted (Maron as a son, and Keśavadāsa as a father). Also in both adaptations, one theme in particular catches the eye: what was drawn by lots in the epics is now chosen in the plays.

While rakshasas are only briefly alluded in Vedic literature (e.g., the demon-smiting Agni in *RV.* 10.87), ogres are some of the best-known characters in folklore (Thompson, 1955/1958). Still, one scholar (E. B. West, 2005/2006) has put forth some compelling arguments for a closer connection between the rakshasas of the *Mahābhārata* and the Cyclopes of the *Odyssey*. It is her view that such commonalities are due to a common, Indo-European origin. However, if the influence hypothesis were to be accepted as possible, her findings could also be interpreted from this alternative perspective. Even speaking conservatively, I claim with some degree of confidence that, for the epic versions of the ogre motif, Polyphemus, on one side, and Hiḍimba and Baka, on the other, have more in common with each other than they do with ogres coming from other traditions. This being the case, and if (Ps.-) Bhāsa had already shown an interest in Euripidean adaptations of Homer, what would have stopped him from imitating the Greek playwright when putting together this play as well?

Each one by itself, the Sanskrit adaptations of the embassy, the ambush, and the ogre seem to be nothing more than lucky coincidences, but the fact that a single author in India decided to rework the same three motifs that were associated with the name of a single Greek author, i.e., Euripides, is, at the very least, worth examining from the point of view of cultural contacts.

Folk, Indo-European, or Greco-Roman Literary Motifs?

The embassy, as a "folk motif", has very few occurrences. It can relate to a bride, "Royal bride conducted by embassy to husband's kingdom" (T133.2 in Thompson, 1955/1958); to a dog, "Dog's embassy to Zeus chased forth; dog seeks ambassador; why dogs sniff each other under leg" (A2232.8 in Thompson, 1955/1958) and "Zeus has embassy of dogs imprisoned for fouling his court" (Q433.3 in Thompson, 1955/1958); or to an imprisonment, "King imprisons another king's embassy" (R3 in Thompson, 1955/195).

Even though the link with a dog recalls the dog messenger Saramā in *RV*. 10.108, and even though the association with imprisonment resounds with the events from both Euripides' *Phoenix* and (Ps.-) Bhāsa's *The Embassy*, the war context and the applicable substories are nowhere to be found in the folklore, and neither is the sexual assault that brings together the Greek concubine, Phthia, and the Sanskrit wife, Draupadī. Still, the possibility of a folk origin of the embassy motif cannot be ruled out. Instead, what one can do is claim that the embassy being a folk motif is a possibility, but one with a very small probability.

Moving on, as an "Indo-European motif", the embassy does not receive a single mention either in Mallory & Adams (1997) or in M. L. West (2007). This absence can be very telling in its own way. Embassies are, without a doubt, a key element in the plots of the *Iliad*, the *Aeneid*, and the *Mahābhārata*, but not in those of *Beowulf* or *Nibelungenlied.* Once again, the embassy having an Indo-European origin is possible, but not highly probable. The embassy in the *Aeneid* is, much more likely, one of the many instances of Virgil's Homer-*imitatio*, and not the result of a centuries-long oral transmission. This opens the door to the possibility of a "Greco-Roman motif", for which one would also have to presuppose a contact with India.

There are at least two studies defending influences and borrowings between the Greco-Roman world and India within the epic versions of the embassy motif: Lallemant (1959) and Duckworth (1961), in reference to *MBh.* 5 and *Aeneid* (*Aen.*) 7.[191] According to Lallemant, the broader epic texts that frame such motifs not only present similarities, but also those common aspects are of such nature that chance alone would not satisfactorily account for them: "La lecture du *Mahābhārata*, le vaste et célèbre poème héroïque indien relatant le grand combat des Bhārata, nous a révélé des ressemblances avec l'*Énéide* qu'il nous a paru impossible d'attribuer au hazard [Reading the *Mahābhārata*, the vast and famous Indian heroic poem recounting the great battle of the Bhārata, revealed to us similarities with the *Aeneid*, which seemed to us impossible to attribute to chance]" (p. 262).

Therefore, she advances a "Sanskrit influence hypothesis": "L'hypothèse d'une imitation de l'épopée indoue par Virgile se présente alors [Then the hypothesis of an imitation of the Hindu epic by Virgil arises]" (p. 263). Apart from suggesting correspondences, such as the eighteen-day battle,[192] there are larger, structural parallelisms that could point towards direct borrowings. Given the chronology at the time of her publication,[193] she assumes an India-to-Rome direction. Even when disagreeing with these details of chronology and directionality, I appreciate her insight when phrasing the parallelisms in terms of an adaptation process.

---

191 I follow the Latin text by Fairclough (Virgil, 1918). The translations are my own.

192 See Lallemant (1959, p. 264).

193 For the *Aeneid*, the decade before 19 BCE. For the *Mahābhārata*, Hopkins' (1901) 400 BCE-400 CE. This dating of the *Mahābhārata* has, since then, been challenged by Adluri & Bagchee (2014). See Wulff Alonso (2018a, p. 92; 2018b, p. 459) for a 1-100 CE dating.

For the embassy motif, Lallemant (1959) offers the following comparative summary:

> L'*Udyoga parvan* (V) et le livre VII de l'*Énéide* montrent les armements: après une ambassade des Pāṇḍava aux Kaurava, des Troyens aux Latins, Dhṛtarāṣṭra – et Latinus – sont impuissants à maintenir la paix. Duryodhana refuse toute conciliation; de même Turnus, visité par Allecto, décide de se battre. Les Kauvara déclarent la guerre, et, du côté latin, s'ouvrent, poussées par Junon, les portes de la guerre. Les Pāṇḍava ripostent et à la fin du livre V du *Mahābhārata* , on assiste au défilé des deux armées. Seules les troupes latines défilent à la fin du livre VII de l'*Énéide*...
>
> The *Udyogaparvan* (V) and Book VII of the *Aeneid* show the armaments: after an embassy from the Pāṇḍavas to the Kauravas, from the Trojans to the Latins, Dhṛtarāṣṭra – and Latinus – are powerless to maintain the peace. Duryodhana refuses any conciliation; likewise, Turnus, visited by Allecto, decides to fight. The Kauvaras declare war, and, on the Latin side, the doors of war open, pushed by Juno. The Pāṇḍavas retaliate and at the end of Book V of the *Mahābhārata*, we witness the parade of the two armies. Only the Latin troops parade at the end of Book VII of the Aeneid...
>
> (Lallemant, 1959, p. 264)

Duckworth (1961), in turn, basically follows in Lallemant's footsteps. In addition to extending the list of examples and redirecting the comparison from the themes to the characters, he picks up where she left off, by providing some explanations of the supposed influences and borrowings: "either we must assume that these similarities result from a series of almost incredible coincidences, or we must accept the possibility that Vergil knew and utilized the Sanskrit epic as he used the Homeric poems, combining, modifying, and rearranging the material as it suited his purpose" (p. 124). Although still thinking them to be of the Rome-from-India type, in terms of the adaptation process, he points out that they parallel the procedures that Virgil follows for his Homer-*imitatio*.

For the embassy, Duckworth (1961) provides the following table:

Table 1 Parallels between the *Mahābhārata* and the *Aeneid* (after Duckworth, 1961, pp. 111-112).

The *Mahābhārata*	**The *Aeneid***
Book V	Book VII
Pāṇḍavas return from exile to receive kingdom promised to them by Kauravas.	Trojans come to Latium to receive land promised to them by Fate.
Pāṇḍavas desire peace (even willing to give up most of kingdom).	Trojans desire peace.
Embassies to Kauravas.	Embassy to Latinus.
Aged king Dhṛtarāṣṭra wants peace (supported by Bhīṣma, Droṇa, Vidura, and others).	Aged king Latinus wants peace, makes alliance with Trojans.
Duryodhana, urged by evil advisers, resolves on war.	Turnus, inspired by Allecto, resolves on war.
Dhṛtarāṣṭra helpless, but foresees disaster for Duryodhana.	Latinus helpless, but foresees disaster for Turnus.
Preparations for conflict.	Preparations for conflict.
Catalogue of warriors on each side.	Catalogue of Latin warriors.

In sum, given the embassy's scarcity in folklore and its apparent absence within the Indo-European framework, a Greco-Roman origin seems likely. And this, together with the reconsidered chronology of the Sanskrit sources, suggests that a Greco-Roman influence in India for the ambush motif stands, not only as a possible explanation, but also as a highly probable one. By accepting its higher probability, such influence could also be broadened to other Greco-Roman sources. For instance, Wulff Alonso (In Press),[194] when studying the embassy motif in *MBh.* 5, does not look solely into *Il.* 9. According to him, the sources for the *MBh.*'s embassy also include Euripides' *Phoenician Women* and

194 The author has kindly shared with me an unpublished version of his work *El cazador de historias: Un encuentro con el autor del Mahābhārata.*

Statius' *Thebaid* (Chapter 6). Moreover, *Il.* 9 would be mirrored by *MBh.* 9, but in aspects other than the embassy itself (Chapter 4). And as for the character of Kṛṣṇa in *MBh.* 5, influence might come from Euripides' *Bacchae* and Ovid's *Metamorphoses* (Chapter 6).

The ambush, as a "folk motif", also has few occurrences. It can relate to an animal, "Army saved from ambush by observation of bird's movements" (J53 in Thompson, 1955/1958), "Crocodile in ambush betrays self by talking" (K607.2.1 in Thompson, 1955/1958), "Bear killed from ambush as he leaves his cave" (K914.1 in Thompson, 1955/1958), and "Attacking animal is killed by another in ambush" (N335.6.1 in Thompson, 1955/1958); to an identity/appearance, "Enemy in ambush (or disguise) deceived into declaring himself" (K607 in Thompson, 1955/1958) and "Transformation to escape ambush" (D642.4 in Thompson, 1955/1958); and to a killing, "Murder from ambush" (K914 in Thompson, 1955/1958) and "Ambushed trickster killed by intended victim" (K1641 in Thompson, 1955/1958). Although there seems to be no relation, on this level, to night attacks, spying missions, or cattle raids, the reference to trickery does recall the Greek spy, Dolon. Just like with the embassy, one can, thus, claim that the ambush being a folk motif is possible, but also that its probability is low.

If the ambush's facet as a spying mission does, indeed, resound with folklore, its components of cattle raid and night attack are much more likely to correspond to an "Indo-European motif". The possibility of an Indo-European cattle raid, perhaps best represented by the *Cattle raid of Cooley*, has been studied by Weisweiler (1954, pp. 27-28), Venkantasubbiah (1965), Dillon (1975, p. 121), Lincoln (1975, 1976), Sergent (1995, pp. 285 ff.), Adams & Mallory (1997), and M. L. West (2007, pp. 451-452). And that of an Indo-European night battle, as depicted in *Il.* 10, *Ilias Parva* arg. 4, *MBh.* 10, *R.* 6.22.18-34, *Beowulf* 3, and *Brot af Sigurðarkviðu* 12, has been considered by M. L. West (2007, p. 475) and Dowden (2010, p. 118). Still, this does not rule out the possibility of a "Greco-Roman motif" that could have made it into India.

There are enough reasons to believe that the ambush of Nisus and Euryalus at *Aen.* 9.176-449 is an adaptation of the ambushes upon Dolon and Rhesus at *Il.* 10. In this case, Homeric influences and borrowings are defended by both ancient authors, such as Ovid (*Ib.* 625-630), Macrobius (*Sat.* 5.2.15), and Servius (*ad Aen.* 9.1), and modern scholars, like Duckworth (1967), Lennox (1977), Grandsen (1984, pp. 102-118), Hardie (1994, pp. 23-24), Horsfall (1995, pp. 170-178), Casali (2004), and Dué & Ebbott (2010, pp. 142-147). There are some who even propose Euripidean influences and borrowings; for example, Fenik (1960, pp. 54-96), König (1970, pp. 89-108), Pavlock (1985), and Fowler (2000).

The structural parallelism is obvious: Nestor's proposal (*Il.* 10.204-217) and Hector's proposal (*Il.* 10.303-312) are merged into Ascanius' proposal (*Aen.* 9.257-280).[195] In *Il.* 10, Nestor proposes a spying mission procuring glory (*Il.* 10.212) and a gift (*Il.* 10.213), while Hector proposes another spying mission, which would also result in a gift (*Il.* 10.304) and much glory (*Il.* 10.305). As a gift, Hector proposes the best horses (*Il.* 10.306-306). In *Aen.* 9, after Nisus proposes a spying mission that will bring him glory (*Aen.* 9.195), Ascanius presents a catalogue of gifts, including the horse of Turnus (*Aen.* 9.269-270). But there are also lots of small correspondences.

In the Greek epic, Diomedes gets ready by putting on a lion skin (*Il.* 10.177), as does Nisus in the Roman epic (*Aen.* 9.306).[196] Nisus' helmet (*Aen.* 9.307) also recalls those of Diomedes (*Il.* 10.257) and Odysseus (*Il.* 10.261). By a division of tasks, on one hand, Diomedes is to take care of the sleeping men, and Odysseus, of their horses (*Il.* 10.479-481); on the other hand, Euryalus is to watch their backs, while Nisus leads the way (*Aen.* 9.321-323). Following the bloodshed, the earth (*Il.* 10.484 ~ *Aen.* 9.334) is stained with blood (*Il.* 10.484 ~ *Aen.* 9.333). In a simile, just as a lion (*Il.* 10.485 ~ *Aen.*

195 On Nestor's proposal and Hector's proposal being merged into Ascanius' proposal, see Casali (2004, pp. 327-333). On Agamemnon's gifts (*Il.* 9. 122, *Il.* 9.128-131, *Il.* 9.139-140) being borrowed for Ascanius' gifts (*Aen.* 9.265 and *Aen.* 9.272-273), see Farrell (1997, p. 234), and Casali (2004, pp. 333-335). On the association with glory, see Dué & Ebbott (2010, p. 145).

196 On the parallelisms for the lion skin, see Dué & Ebbott (2010, p. 146); for the arming scene, see Dué & Ebbott (2010, pp. 145-146); for the division of tasks, see Dué & Ebbott (2010, p. 146); for the bloodshed, see Pavlock (1985, pp. 213-214); and for the lion simile, see Pavlock (1985, pp. 214-215), Dué & Ebbott (2010, p. 146), and Liapis (2012, p. xxxiii).

9.339) preys on sheep (*Il.* 10.486 ~ *Aen.* 9.339), so too, Diomedes and Nisus prey on the sleeping warriors. Lastly, Diomedes' prayer (*Il.* 10.284-294) is borrowed for Nisus' prayer (*Aen.* 9.404-409): two female deities, who had previously helped the fathers of the raiders, are now asked to help their sons.[197] And the decapitation of Dolon (*Il.* 10.455-457) is split into those of Nisus and Euryalus (*Aen.* 9.465-467).

Without a doubt, the most notorious aspects of this instance of Greco-Roman *imitatio* are the merging and the splitting: Virgil merges the themes from two Homeric books (the embassy from *Il.* 9 and the ambush from *Il.* 10),[198] but he also merges the two sides of the Homeric ambush (the ambush upon Dolon and the ambush upon Rhesus, both from *Il.* 10).[199] This is also followed by a subtraction-cum-merging, much like the one discussed in the Greek and Sanskrit adaptations of the ambush motif. Nisus and Euryalus receive features from Diomedes and Odysseus, such as the killing of the sleeping men, but they also inherit some of the aspects originally pertaining to Dolon, like the decapitation.[200] Furthermore, Virgil's adaptation eventually becomes a tradition (Liapis, 2012, p. xviii, n. 6 and p. xxxiii), for Ovid (*Met.* 13.243-252), Statius (*Theb.* 10.1-448), and Silius Italicus (*Pun.* 9.66-177) all dabble in night attacks following his lead. Now, as voluminous as this information is, it will never be enough to dispense with the possibility of an Indo-European origin. What I do is, conservatively speaking, support the idea of a similarly high probability of this being a "Greco-Roman motif".

The *Mahābhārata* has several ambushes. Considering only those discussed *supra*, the ones in the *Ghoṣayātrāparvan* and the *Virāṭaparvan* relate more to the cattle-raiding and the

197 On Diomedes' prayer being borrowed for Nisus' prayer, see Pavlock (1985, p. 218), Casali (2004, pp. 335-337), and Liapis (2012, p. xxxiii). On Dolon's decapitation being split into those of Nisus and Euryalus, see Dué & Ebbott (2010, p. 147).

198 On merging *Il.* 9 and *Il.* 10 into *Aen.* 9, see Farrell (1997, pp. 233-234).

199 On merging Dolon's ambush and Rhesus' ambush into Nisus' and Euryalus' ambush, see Casali (2004, p. 325).

200 On merging Diomedes' and Odysseus' characters and Dolon's character into Nisus' and Euryalus' characters, see Casali (2004, p. 26).

spying-mission facets, whereas that of the *Sauptikaparvan* clearly offers a better representation of the night-attack component.

The possibility of a Greek influence on India, vis-à-vis the night attack, has been explored by Wulff Alonso (2008a, 263-285; 2013, pp. 176-178; In Press, Chapter 4). In his opinion, the Greek ambush by Diomedes and Odysseus (*Il.* 10 and *Rhes.*) shares several elements with the Sanskrit ambush by Aśvatthāman, Kṛpa, and Kṛtavarman (*MBh.* 10): the location in the tenth book, the deity invocations and interventions, the animal attires and the special weapons, the role of sacrifice and the impossibility of averting the disaster, the lack of sentries and the sleeping victims, the nighttime and the beheadings, the setting at the end of the first of two wars, the back-and-forth between past and present, the destroying gods and the turn of events, the "horse" theme (from the Trojan *Horse* to the Kaurava *Aśva*-tthāman) and the unusual entering, among many others. Wulff Alonso (2018a, p. 87; 2020, pp. 129-130; In Press, Chapter 5) has also considered a Greco-Roman influence for the cattle raid. In this case, what catches the eye are the architectural similarities between the Trigartas' and Kauravas' ambush of Virāṭa's reign and the Itoni's ambush of Omphale's reign (Diodorus Siculus 4.31.7-8), as well as some smaller details, like the characterization of Arjuna in *MBh.* 4, which might have had some influence from Euripides' *Hippolytus*.

In a nutshell, considering the ambush's scantiness in folklore and its abundance in Indo-European traditions, the latter stands out as a far more likely explanation for its origin than the former. However, pondering the numerous views, both old and new, in support of a stronger link between the Greek and Roman ambushes, I propose, at least, the coexistence of both an Indo-European ambush motif and a Greco-Roman one. In this context, the Indian version of the motif could be a representative of either one of them. Furthermore, I argue that, if the origin of the embassy motif is Greco-Roman, as would very likely be the case, and if such a Greco-Roman motif would have had an influence in India, which appears as a highly probable explanation, then it is also possible that this second, Greco-Roman motif of the ambush could have made it into India as well. In other words, if there is a high probability that Indians adapted one Greco-Roman motif, then there is a possibility that they did it a second time.

Finally, the ogre appears as the best candidate for the "folk motif" explanation. Ogres constitute one of the seven major categories established by Thompson (1955/1958). To mention only the subtitles, his list includes "Cannibalistic ogres" (G10-G99), "Giant ogres" (G100-G199), "Other ogres" (G300-G399), "Falling into ogre's power" (G400-G499), "Ogre defeated" (G500-G599), and "Other ogre motifs" (G600-G699). For the most part, the Greek ogre Polyphemus has been approached as belonging to the realm of folklore. Such are the opinions of Glenn (1971), Page (1973, pp. 23-48), Mondi (1983), and even M. L. West (2007, pp. 297-298). Nonetheless, the option of an "Indo-European motif" is also possible, as has been suggested by E. B. West (2005/2006). And so is that of a "Greco-Roman motif", according to Jacobson (1989) and Sansone (1991).

Some classicists have defended the assumption that the ogre Cacus from *Aen.* 8.184-279 is an adaptation of the ogre Polyphemus from *Od.* 9. An argument in favor of such claim is that the myth of Cacus robbing cattle and being killed by Hercules is nowhere to be found in Greco-Roman literature prior to Virgil (Jacobson, 1989, p. 101), although he does present some similarities with the Hermes from the *Homeric Hymn* (Jacobson, 1989, p. 102). The first element shared with the Polyphemus from the *Odyssey* is the topographical description (*Od.* 9.182-192 ~ *Aen.* 8.193-197), centered in the cave (*Od.* 9.182 ~ *Aen.* 8.193) where the monstrous man (*Od.* 9.187 ~ *Aen.* 8.194) lives.[201] The next elements are the bloodshed (*Od.* 9.290 ~ *Aen.* 8.195-197) caused by the man-eater, and the boulder (*Od.* 9.240-243 ~ *Aen.* 8.225-227) used for closing the entrance. An additional point of encounter is that of the running water (*Od.* 9.484-485 ~ *Aen.* 8.240).

There are two notorious aspects in this instance of Greco-Roman *imitatio*. On one hand, Virgil splits a single Homeric ogre (the Polyphemus from *Od.* 9) into two of his own (the Polyphemus from

201 On the parallelisms for the topographical description, see Jacobson (1989, p. 101); for the bloodshed, see Jacobson (1989, p. 102); for the boulder, see Jacobson (1989, p. 101); and for the running water, see Sansone (1991, p. 171).

Aen. 3 and the Cacus from *Aen.* 8);[202] and on the other, he reverses the roles, by transferring the deceit from the hero Odysseus to the ogre Cacus, and the rock throwing from the ogre Polyphemus to the hero Hercules.[203] Similar reversals have also been suggested for the Sanskrit adaptations of the motifs considered for this study. Also, just like with the ambush motif, Virgil is to be credited with the establishment of a tradition, since, modelled upon his version, the story of Cacus is re-created in the works of Ovid (*Fast.* 1.543-578) and Propertius (4.9).

The Greek Polyphemus, the Roman Cacus, and the Indian Baka were first grouped together, on account of their commonalities, in the late nineteenth century. Lévêque (1880) says about Baka, "Il joue le rôle d'un ogre, comme le Cyclope de l'*Odysée*, et sa mort est une déliverance pour les habitants [He plays the role of an ogre, like the Cyclops of the *Odyssey*, and his death means the deliverance of the townsfolk]" (p. 441) and "Le personnage qui, dans la mythologie grecque, correspond réellement au rakchasa Vaka, c'est le Cyclops de l'*Odysée*, qui dévorait chaque jour des compagnons d'Ulysse [The character in Greek mythology who really corresponds to the rakshasa Baka is the Cyclops of the *Odyssey*, who devoured the companions of Odysseus day after day]" (p. 445, n. 2).

As Lallemant would do more than half a century later, Lévêque (1880) assumed that the Sanskrit epic's account of the story would have been the source, and therefore, that of the Roman epic would have been the adaptation. Disagreeing once again with the directionality, I appreciate the parallelisms that he established (p. 446): the tree throwing (*Aen.* 8.248-250 ~ *MBh.* 1.151.15-16), the grabbing (*Aen.* 8.259 ~ *MBh.* 1.151.22-23), the blood vomiting (*Aen.* 8.260-261 ~ *MBh.* 1.151.24), the peeping townsfolk (*Aen.* 8.264-267 ~ *MBh.* 1.152.8-10), and the newly established rite (*Aen.* 8.268-269 ~ *MBh.* 1.152.18).

If Polyphemus and Cacus have things in common (Jacobson, 1989; Sansone, 1991), and if Cacus and Baka also have things in

202 On splitting Polyphemus' character into Polyphemus' character and Cacus' character, see Jacobson (1989, p. 102).

203 On reversing the deceit from Odysseus to Cacus and the rock throwing from Polyphemus to Hercules, see Sansone (1991, p. 171).

common (Lévêque, 1880), then it does not come as that much of a surprise that Polyphemus and Baka do as well. E. B. West (2005/2006, pp. 129-148) lists up to seventeen parallelisms between the Greek Cyclopes and Laestrygonians, on one hand, and the Sanskrit rakshasas Hiḍimba, Baka, and Kirmīra, on the other.[204]

To recapitulate, the general notion of the ogre is, almost certainly, a folk motif. Nevertheless, the various arguments in favor of a subtype of this story specifically appearing in the Greek, Roman, and Indian traditions allow for a discussion of other possible explanations. As seen, the Greece-and-India connection, i.e., that of Polyphemus and Baka, has been interpreted from the point of view of an Indo-European origin, whereas the Greece-and-Rome connection, i.e., that of Polyphemus and Cacus, has been considered from the perspective of a Greco-Roman influence. Here, I have argued that the parallelisms found by E. B. West can also be accounted for by a hypothetical scenario of cultural contacts.

As with the ambush, the point of arrival of this ogre survey is that of the possibility of two separate versions of this motif: one would be a folk ogre, while the other might either be an Indo-European ogre or a Greco-Roman ogre. The most relevant one, for the purpose of this study, is obviously the latter. Fortunately, being unable to free this ogre from its Schrödinger's-cat-like status is not tantamount to being unable to hypothesize about it. After

204 "A. The Encounter Occurs During a Period of Dangerous Travel" (*Od.* 10.80-132 ~ *MBh.* 1.139-143), "B. The Ogre is Described as a Ruler of his Kind, but Later Revealed as Outcast and a Brute" (*Od.* 9.187-192 ~ *MBh.* 1.151.1-2), "C. Rest of Group Left Nearby" (*Od.* 9.116-176 ~ *MBh.* 1.150.1), "D. An Eater of Human Flesh" (*Od.* 9.347, *Od.* 9.374 ~ *MBh.* 1.148.4, *MBh.* 1.150.26, *MBh.* 1.151.1, *MBh.* 1.152.6), "E. The Ogre Lives Without Worries" (*Od.* 9.106-111 ~ *MBh.* 1.148.1-10), "F. The Ogre Compared to a Mountain" (*Od.* 9.190-192 ~ *MBh.* 1.152.8-9), "G. The Hero Helps a Priest" (*Od.* 9.196-200 ~ *MBh.* 1.145-149), "H. Priest's Food/Wine Taken to the Ogre" (*Od.* 9.212-215 ~ *MBh.* 1.151.1-2), "I. The Hero Eats the Ogre's Food" (*Od.* 9.231-233 ~ *MBh.* 1.151.3-5), "J. Victims/Attackers Drawn by Turn or Lot" (*Od.* 9.331-333~ *MBh.* 1.148.6-8), "K. The Tree as Weapon" (*Od.* 9.319-324 ~ *MBh.* 1.151.15-16), "L. Prominence of the Hero's Name" (*Od.* 9.502-505 ~ *MBh.* 1.151.17), "M. Other Ogres Congregate, but They Cause No Trouble" (*Od.* 9.399-413 ~ *MBh.* 1.152.1-5), "N. Rock Throwing" (*Od.* 9.481-486 ~ *MBh.* 3.12.51), "O. Encounter was Expected/Anticipated by the Ogre" (*Od.* 9.506-516 ~ *MBh.* 3.12.31), "P. The Accusation of Cheating" (*Od.* 9.511-516 ~ *MBh.* 3.12.30-31), and "Q. Sacrifice" (*Od.* 9.550-553 ~ *MBh.* 3.11.24).

all, an Indo-European motif that manifests itself in Greece, Rome, and India, is as much of a possibility as a Greco-Roman motif that travels to India. Moreover, if the embassy is, very likely, an example of the latter, so could be the ambush and the ogre. All three motifs being Greco-Roman influences on India is possible; the embassy being such, highly probable; the ambush and the ogre being such, at least probable.

If one accepts the possibility of a Greco-Roman influence on the Sanskrit ogre, the sources would not be limited to Homer's *Odyssey*. As with the embassy and the ambush, Wulff Alonso (2008a, pp. 385-388; 2008b, p. 89; 2020, p. 223, n. 76; In Press, Chapter 5) opines that other sources should be examined as well. These would include Herodotus' *Histories*, Euripides' *Alcestis*, and Virgil's *Aeneid*. As seen, there is still much work to be done in the comparison of the Greco-Roman world and India.

Before moving on to the next section, a few words on limitations are due. First, working with three-event probabilities means that, even if one of the three explanations – folk motif, Indo-European motif, Greco-Roman motif – corresponds to what has occurred, that does not mean that said explanation is the only one that does so. Second, working not with what has occurred but with what experts believe to have occurred – folk motifs, Indo-European motifs, and Greco-Roman motifs are nothing but agreed-upon hypotheses – means that there are no objective values whatsoever that one can input into such calculations. Third, even though these three are the most common explanations, there is, in theory, no limited number of explanations for the phenomenon of parallelisms (Stoneman, 2019, p. 419 ff.; Seaford, 2020, p. 8 ff.): a shared context of socio-economic change, shared story-patterns of the epic genre, Jungian archetypes, lucky coincidences – and the list could keep on growing.

Borrowings in the Adapted Elements

In (Ps.-)Bhāsa's *DV*, there are two possible instances of borrowing as a form of Greco-Indian *anukaraṇa*: the painting and the personified weapons. Paintings are never mentioned in Vedic literature, and their first mentions in Sanskrit literature are later than the Greco-Bactrian kingdom (Arora, 2011, p. 55). Likewise, the first attestations of personified weapons in Indian art, the so-called *āyudhapuruṣas*, are later than the Kushan Empire (Sivaramamurti, 1955, p. 134; Gail, 1980/1981, p. 181), and in Sanskrit literature, both epic (*R.* 7.99.7) and dramatic (*DV* 41.4-54.2 and *BC* 1.21-28), they are, at least, later than the contacts with the Greco-Roman world.

Taken as a borrowing, the painting in (Ps.-)Bhāsa's *The Embassy* would have responded to three authorial decisions. On a structural level, the Sanskrit playwright would have been carrying out a cross-cultural adaptation of Euripides' *Phoenix*, that is, of a Greek play that, like his own re-creation of the *Mahābhārata*, reinterpreted an epic version of the embassy motif, in this case, of the *Iliad*. On the level of details, the Sanskrit playwright would have been merging these materials with those from Terence's *The Eunuch*, that is, of a Roman play that, like his own rendition of the humiliation of Draupadī, included the ekphrasis of a painting. Lastly, and as an explanation for selecting those two supposed Greco-Roman sources, the Sanskrit playwright would have made a connection, focusing on the sexual assault: the Draupadī of the *Mahābhārata* is assaulted, just as the Phthia of the *Phoenix* alleges that she is; however, the assault of the Draupadī of the *Mahābhārata* is linked to a painting, like that of the Pamphila of *The Eunuch*.

As mentioned, there are also similarities in the phrasing: "this painting [*pictura haec*]" (*Eun.* 584) ~ "this painting [*ayaṃ citrapaṭaḥ*]" (*DV* 6.15), "a painted picture [*tabulam quandam pictam*]" (*Eun.* 584) ~ "this picture was carefully painted [*suvyaktam ālikhito 'yam citrapaṭaḥ*]" (*DV* 12.5), "And I, a puny man, would not do it? [*ego homuncio hoc non facerem?*]" (*Eun.* 591) ~ "Then, how am I the vile one of perverted mind? [*nīco 'ham eva viparītamatiḥ kathaṃ vā*]" (*DV* 11a).

Considered as a borrowing, the personified weapons in (Ps.-) Bhāsa's *DV* would have responded to similar authorial decisions. On a structural level, *The Embassy* is as much an adaptation of the *Mahābhārata*'s embassy motif as is the *Phoenix* of the *Iliad*'s embassy motif. On the level of details, there would have been a merging of these materials with those from *The Greek Anthology*, that is, with a selection of Greek lyric poems that, like this homage of the universal form of Kṛṣṇa, incorporated it-fiction with weapons.

Likewise, the choice of source here would respond to the Sanskrit playwright's association of ideas, presumably based on the *deus ex machina*: the Sudarśana of *The Embassy* brings the plot to an end, as the Chiron of the *Phoenix* probably did, but it does so by means of it-fiction, like the one found in poems of *The Greek Anthology* authored by Hegesippus the epigrammatist, Mnasalces of Sicyon, Nicias of Miletus, and Meleager of Gadara. There are a couple of commonalities in the phrasing as well: "I have been fastened [ἇμμαι]" (*Anth. Pal.* 6.124.1) ~ "I have sprung [*nirdhāvito 'smi*]" (*DV* 42b), and "I stay [μένω]" (*Anth. Pal.* 6.125.1) ~ "should I openly appear [*mayā pravijṛmbhitavyam*]" (*DV* 42d).

(Ps.-)Bhāsa's *PR* contributes with five more possible instances of borrowing as Greco-Indian *anukaraṇa*: the remuneration, the scarred limb, the signed weapon, the five nights, and the violent arrogance. The remuneration, even if it is not monetary, certainly recalls the Greek impact in India on subjects like commerce and coinage (Bopearachchi, 1991). The scarred limb and the signed weapons, as means for achieving anagnorises, are more relevant for the study of Sanskrit drama. In this sense, it is worth noticing that tokens of recognition, such as signet rings, are first documented in Indian culture only from the beginning of the Greco-Bactrian kingdom (Arora, 2011, p. 56).

As for the title of the Sanskrit play, one must consider that the religious tradition of *Pāñcarātra* (five nights), which worships Viṣṇu as the supreme god, dates from a time when Greeks and Indians had already established their contacts – sometime around the last centuries BCE (Rastelli, 2018, para. 1). And in regards to the violent arrogance, one must bear in mind that the dramatic convention of avoiding on-stage violence, as exemplified both by the treatises of Aristotle and Bharata and by the plays of (Ps.-)Euripides and (Ps.-) Bhāsa, has no precedents in India that are older than the contacts with the Greco-Roman world.

To begin with, the remuneration points to oddity as a feature of the proposed Greco-Indian *anukaraṇa*. Although remuneration is no strange subject to Vedic literature (e.g., *dakṣinā-* "gift" in the hymns of *dānastuti* (praise of gift giving), like in *RV.* 6.27.8), graduation fees are more a matter of the Sanskrit epics. In this context, even if the Droṇa of the *Virāṭaparvan* does not ask for his *gurudakṣinā* (graduation fee), the Droṇa of the story of Ekalavya (*MBh.* 1.123.10-39) certainly does. But unlike his epic predecessor, the dramatic Droṇa behaves in an odd manner when he does so. Like the Dolon of the *Rhesus*, who says to Hector that it is necessary "to give the worker a fair wage [πονοῦντα δ' ἄξιον / μισθὸν φέρεσθαι]" (*Rhes.* 161-162), the Droṇa of *The Five Nights* tells Duryodhana, "I will make a request [*vyapaśramayiṣye*]" (*PR* 1.27.17). That Greek asking, which makes sense within its fourth-century context of mercenary soldiers, would have become this Sanskrit telling, which conflicts with its epic context of preceptor/disciple relations. Even Duryodhana becomes confused by something so unbecoming of his preceptor.

Moving on to the tokens of recognition, i.e., the scarred limb and the signed weapon, the claimed borrowings seem to reveal, respectively, reversal and merging. The Agorastocles of Terence's *The Little Carthaginian*, who is recognized by his older relative by reason of a scar on his left hand, would have been partly re-created as the Arjuna of *The Five Nights*, who is recognized by his younger soon-to-be relative thanks to a scar, which is probably on his right forearm: "there should be a sign on your left hand, where a monkey bit you, when you were playing as a kid [*signum esse oportet in manu laeva tibi, / ludenti puero quod memordit simia*]" (*Poen.* 1074) ~ "The scar, which was inflicted by the string of Gāṇḍīva and remains hidden in the interior of his forearm [*prakoṣṭhāntarasaṅgūḍhaṃ gāṇḍīvajyāhataṃ kiṇam*]" (*PR* 2.63a-b).

Similarly, the Palestra of Plautus' *The Rope*, who is recognized by her old relative because her father's name is spelled on a little sword and her mother's name is spelled on a little axe, would have been reinterpreted, in part, as the Arjuna of *The Five Nights*, who is recognized by his old relative, when he sends an arrow with his own name carved on it. Two signed weapons would have become just one: "what is your father's name, which is on the little sword? [*in ensiculo quid nomen est paternum?*]" (*Rud.* 1160) and "the name of your mother, which is on the little axe [*matris nomen hic quid in securicula siet*]" (*Rud.* 1163) ~ "by means of words having their syllables in the feathers of his arrows [*bāṇapuṅkhākṣarair vākyair*]" (*PR* 3.17a).

Even while being aware of the great cultural relevance of this theme of "five nights" within Indian religious traditions, I hazard an alternative hypothesis, dealing instead with literary traditions that are both Sanskrit and Greco-Roman, and stating that, if (Ps.-)Bhāsa read and rewrote some of the plays attributed to Euripides, the *Mahābhārata*'s "five villages" theme could have been changed into the "five nights" theme of *The Five Nights*, by means of a borrowing involving the time aspect of the "five watches of the night" theme of Ps.-Euripides' *Rhesus*: "for the fifth watch [πέμπτην φυλακὴν]" (*Rhes.* 543) ~ "within five nights [*pañcarātreṇa*]" (*PR* 1.45.7).

Finally, there would have been another change in the matter of violent arrogance. The King of Aeschylus' *The Suppliants*, who censures the violence which the Herald has incurred, reminds one of the Virāṭa of *The Five Nights*: "Out of what kind of arrogance are you dishonoring this land of the Pelasgian men? [ἐκ ποίου φρονήματος / ἀνδρῶν Πελασγῶν τήνδ' ἀτιμάζεις χθόνα;]" (*Supp.* 911-912) ~ "your untimely confident speech brings forth my wrath [*akāle svasthavākyaṃ manyum utpādayati*]" (*PR* 2.20.1). Moreover, as discussed when looking into the possible influences, Aristotle (*Poet.* 1452b11-13) and Bharata (*Nāṭyaś.* 18.20) share similar views on the topic of on-stage violence. If the Greek theory of drama had any influence on the Sanskrit theory of drama, then the argument for this borrowing would make even more sense.

The list of possible borrowings comes to an end with four more examples, drawn from (Ps.-)Bhāsa's *MV*, and also pointing in the direction of a Greco-Indian *anukaraṇa*: the response in the negative, the *ad hoc* lineage, the end of the enslaving, and the anagnorisis. They all come from the same play by Plautus, whose name *me-naech-mo-* has already been linked to that of *ma-dhya-ma-*. Considering the response in the negative and the *ad hoc* lineage, one is, once again, faced with oddity and reversal. On one hand, the Menaechmus (Sosicles) of Plautus' *The Two Menaechmuses* logically responds in the negative when asked if he knows someone whom he does not: "By Hercules, I truly do not [*Non hercle vero*]"

(*Men.* 280). And the Bhīma of *The Middle One*, without it logically following, responds in the negative when asked if he is also named "Middle One": "So far, no other is [*na tāvad aparaḥ*]" (*MV* 27.4). The logical responses would have been that he is or that he is not. Instead, with this odd response, he avers that nobody else's name is the same as his.

On the other hand, the Menaechmus (Sosicles) of Plautus' *The Two Menaechmuses* faces a straightforward question, which reveals specific details about the identity of the other Menaechmus, whereas the Bhīma of *The Middle One* embarks on an elaborate self-praise, which serves to proclaim general information about his own identity as "Middle One": "Do I not know you to be Menaechmus [*Non ego te novi Menaechmum*]" (*Men.* 409) ~ "I am the "Middle One" [*madhyamo 'ham*]" (*MV* 28a and *MV* 28c). As seen, oddity and reversal appear to be recurring traits.

The last two examples, i.e., the end of the enslaving and the anagnorisis, relate to change. The Messenio of The *Two Menaechmuses* is a life-long slave, who obtains his freedom because of the events of the plot, while the middle brother of *The Middle One* has just been temporarily enslaved, pending the happy end: "Me setting you free? [*Liberem ego te?*]" (*Men.* 1024) ~ "He is not being set free [*na mucyate*]" (*MV* 39.3). As for the anagnorisis, I argue that both playwrights seem to be following Aristotle's (*Poet.* 1452a28 ff.) anagnorisis referred to as ἡ διὰ τῶν σημείων (the one by signs): "the proofs [*signa*]" (*Men.* 1124) ~ "your proof [*pratyayaḥ*]" (*MV* 48.24).

In brief, merging and changing, which are usual techniques for adapting within the same literary traditions, could also serve to characterize cross-cultural adaptations. Oddity and reversal might offer additional light on the matter. The borrowings would have come from various sources, including texts in Greek (*Phoenix*, *The Greek Anthology*, *Rhesus*, *The Suppliants*, and *Cyclops*) and in Latin (*The Eunuch*, *The Little Carthaginian*, *The Rope*, and *The Two Menaechmuses*), and texts pertaining to the genres of lyric (*The Greek Anthology*), and drama (*Phoenix*, *Rhesus*, *The Suppliants*, *Cyclops*, *The Eunuch*, *The Little Carthaginian*, *The Rope*, and *The Two Menaechmuses*). The predominance of theater is to be expected, but the same number of Greek plays (*Phoenix, Rhesus, The Suppliants,* and *Cyclops*) and Roman plays (*The Eunuch, The Little Carthaginian, The Rope,* and *The Two Menaechmuses*) begs for further explanation. I deal with this in the closing section.

A few words on the implications of the preceding findings are now due. First, similarities between the Greco-Roman world and India, even when numerous and precise, do not prove borrowings. The adaptation of Greek epic into Greek theater, on one hand, and of Sanskrit epic into Sanskrit Theater, on the other, is well accepted in the scholarly milieu. So too is the adaptation of Greek literature into Roman literature. But the adaptation of Greco-Roman texts into Sanskrit texts remains hypothetical. This situation is like that of Indo-European linguistics, but with the very relevant difference that there is no literary equivalent for the methods of historical linguistics.

Literatures just do not change in the same way that languages do. What this means is, on one hand, that promising tools should be employed, and their results evaluated;[205] and on the other, that an open mind must be kept, since Greco-Roman influence and Indo-European inheritance do not disprove each other, and since even less likely possibilities, such as coincidence or Indian influence, could hardly ever be eliminated altogether. That the borrowings are likely to have happened is as definitive a statement as can be made in this respect.

Second, just as similarities between the epic sources and the dramatic adaptations within each individual tradition do not necessarily imply that those exact passages were the ones adapted, so too is the case with line-by-line correspondences between different traditions. In narratives, themes recur. And the same is true for plays. Therefore, for every quotation from a Sanskrit play that recalls a specific passage of the Greco-Roman repertoire, there might be other sources of inspiration. Maybe Menander, or some other authors whose oeuvre has been preserved in a more

205 See Wulff Alonso (2020, pp. 15-16) on the applicability of the concept of "plagiarism", in the context of forensic linguistics, for the analysis of the hypothetical Greco-Roman borrowing in India.

fragmented way, or not at all. In literature, influence rarely comes from just one place, or arrives at just one place, for that matter.

The author of *The Embassy*, *The Five Nights*, and *The Middle One*, about whom one of the few certain things that can be said is that he must have admired the author of the *Mahābhārata*, could have been following in the latter's footsteps by making adaptive reuses. Wulff Alonso (In Press) envisions this when speaking of the presumed use of Greco-Roman sources by the author of the *Mahābhārata*: "Es un avezado cazador de historias que se mueve en terrenos que conocemos. Podemos ver cómo las utiliza como quien utiliza una cantera o viejos materiales de construcción y los adapta a un nuevo edificio que ha diseñado y construye [He is a seasoned hunter of stories, who walks on ground that is known to us. We can see how he uses them, like someone who uses a quarry, or some old construction materials, and adapts them into a new building, that he designed and constructs]" (Introduction).

Third and last, if (Ps.-)Bhāsa borrowed from the Greco-Roman world through procedures such as merging, changing, and reversal, he would have done so in accordance with the Sanskrit tradition, since Vyāsa himself, when presumably adapting Greco-Roman sources (Wulff Alonso, In Press), would have profited from "repartir [distributing]", "concentrar [concentrating]" (Chapter 4), and "invertir [reversing]" (Chapter 5). This would coincide with the view of reversal as a trademark of Greco-Indian *anukaraṇa*. Furthermore, if both Vyāsa and (Ps.-)Bhāsa borrowed from the Greco-Roman world, this would be an instance of traditional adaptation:

> Nuestro autor conoce sus obras, los textos griegos que utilizan, las técnicas con las que lo hacen y cómo continúan con el uso desprejuiciado de escritos anteriores que había caracterizado a la propia cultura griega y con los procedimientos adaptativos correspondientes.
>
> Our author [sc. Vyāsa] knows their [sc. Virgil's and Ovid's] works, the Greek texts that they use, the techniques with which they do so, and how they continue with the unprejudiced use of previous writings, which had characterized Greek culture itself, and with the corresponding adaptive procedures.
>
> (Wulff Alonso, In Press, Chapter 7)

Greco-Indian Historical Contexts?

By the late fourth century BCE, there are three main avenues of contact between the Hellenistic world and India: the Greeks in Bactria, the Seleucids in Syria, and the Ptolemies in Egypt (Wulff Alonso, 2008a, p. 44). By the third century BCE, the Greek imprint in Bactria is a well-accepted phenomenon (Holt, 1988, 1999, 2005, 2012), as is the cultural interaction between Greeks and non-Greeks in Central Asia (Coloru, 2009; Widermann, 2009; Mairs, 2014, 2020; Iliakis, 2015). During this time, there is also evidence for at least four theatrical performances during Alexander's expedition (Le Guen, 2014, p. 360), as well as record of a fragmentary Greek play preserved in the very ruins of Aï Khanoum (Stoneman, 2019, pp. 408-409).

These contacts seem to have developed into something more during the second century BCE. By then, the Kandahar Sophytos Inscription (Hollis, 2011, pp. 114-115) already bears witness to Greek influence: "As we have seen, however, throughout the epigraphic record we have evidence of Indians adopting Hellenistic culture in the Greek city-states of Bactria (Subhūti [sc. Sophytos])..." (Baums, 2017, p. 41). And, possibly, even to Greek borrowings, since the text from the inscription has been compared with various passages from the Homeric Epics (Wallace, 2016, p. 220, n. 51): line 1.2 ~ *Il.* 5.90, *Il.* 10.467, and *Il.* 17.53; and line 1.10 ~ *Od.* 1.3. Not to mention that Sophytos himself is portrayed as a kind of Odysseus. Up to this point, the contact is merely with Greece. However, a constantly expanding Rome is not far from entering the stage.

By the first century CE, one of the main avenues of contact with the Greco-Roman world was the Western Satraps in Bharukaccha/Barygaza (Wulff Alonso, 2011b, p. 25), as attested in both Greco-Roman (*Periplus Maris Erythraei* 14, 21, 27, 31, 32, 36, 40, 41, 42, 43, 44, 45, 47, 48, 50, 51, 52, 56, and 57) and Sanskrit sources (*MBh.* 2.28.50-53 and *MBh.* 2.47.7-8). But the most relevant context for eventual literary influences and borrowings would have been the Kushan Empire, whose link with the Roman Empire (Thorley, 1979) played a key role in Indo-Roman relations (Tomber, 2008).

In the middle of the territory occupied by the Kushans (Steward, 2016, p. 3), by the second or third century CE (Stoneman, 2019, p. 375), a depiction of a "Trojan Horse" in the style of Gandharan art is to be found (Karttunen, 2001, pp. 179-180). Near that time, (Ps.-) Bhāsa would have been the first Indian author to adapt this Greco-Roman theme (Homer, *Od.* 4.265 ff., *Od.* 8.492 ff., and *Od.* 11.523 ff.; Euripides, *Tro.* 511 ff. and *Hec.* 905 ff.; and Virgil, *Aen.* 2) into that of the "Trojan Elephant" in his *The Minister's Vows*. The philosopher Buddhaghosa (fifth century CE), in his *Path of Purification*; the poet Bāṇabhaṭṭa (seventh century CE), in his *Deeds of Harṣa*; and the writer Somadeva (eleventh century CE), in his *Ocean of the Streams of Stories*; they all would have eventually followed in (Ps.-)Bhāsa's footsteps, thus turning his adaptation into their tradition.

Besides some amazing discoveries, like that of an Indian figurine in Pompeii in 1938 (Weinstein, 2021), it is worth noticing the Greco-Roman practice of producing plastic representations related to plays, for instance, in the form of the terracottas from Roman Egypt depicting actors and theater masks (Sandri, 2012). It would be a good subject for future research to look at similar findings in India.

The relations between the Hellenistic and Roman worlds, on one hand, and India, on the other, are well established (Karttunen, 1989, 1997, 2001, 2015; Arora, 1996, 2011, 2018; Parker, 2008). Most of the reconstructed history of their contacts is based on numismatic and archaeological evidence (Turner, 1989; Bopearachchi, 1991, 2005), which has naturally strengthened the long-standing acceptance of commercial exchanges between the Greco-Roman world and India (Warmington, 1928; Sidebotham, 1986, 2011; Seland, 2010; Cobb, 2018). It is in this context that influences and borrowings from the Greco-Roman world to India are generally accepted in the exact sciences, such as astronomy and mathematics (Pingree, 1971, 1976, 1993; Falk, 2002; Plofker, 2011), as well as in the visual arts, such as architecture, painting, and sculpture (Acharya, 1927; Nehru, 1989; Boardman, 2015). On other subjects, such as medicine (Karttunen, 2021) or philosophy (Seaford, 2020), a lack of consensus is still the norm.

Although the extension of such cultural impact in India when it comes to literature is certainly a matter of speculation (Pisani, 1940), it is still interesting, for the sake of argument, to draw one's attention to a couple of well-attested, contemporaneous examples of "philhellenism". The first one comes from the Roman Republic, which during the third and second centuries BCE not only follows "the adoption of policy and behaviour actively represented as beneficial to, and respectful of, Greece and Greeks", but also is "characterized by the actively favourable reception of Greek language, literature, and philosophy within the Roman ruling class" (Derow, 2016, para. 1). The second example is provided by the Parthian kings, who during the second and first centuries BCE used the Greek script and language for their coins and, in some cases, went as far as taking the epithet of *philhellene*, i.e., "friend of the Greeks" (Aperghis, 2020).

Could there not have been in the India of the first and second centuries CE, whose interest in Greco-Roman arts and sciences has been sufficiently acknowledged, anything along the lines of what nineteenth-century classicists referred to as the "Scipionic Circle", i.e., "a group sharing the same cultural and even political outlook" (Erskine, 2016, para. 1), which would have included an appreciation for Greco-Roman literature? Could they have had access to those texts, in the form of either papyrus scrolls or parchment books, even in the Indian subcontinent? Could they have even read or understood them, let alone admired and adapted them?

That there was at least some degree of multilingualism bringing together the Greco-Roman world and India can be corroborated by the Kandahar Greek Edicts of Aśoka, which were written in both Greek and Prakrit (Schlumberger, 1964), and that this had an impact on literature can be assumed, considering that the *Yavanajātaka* was probably translated from the Greek to the Sanskrit during the second century CE. The Greek original would have come from Alexandria, and the Sanskrit translation would have been made under the rule of the Western Satraps (Pingree, in Sphujidhvaja, 1978). Moreover, that Greco-Roman literature was accessible throughout a chronologically and geographically vast extension in Eurasia around the turn of the millennium can be corroborated by the data. The Hellenistic world has book depositories since the foundation of the library of Alexandria, circa 300 BCE, a trend to which the Roman world also contributed, at least since the opening of Rome's first public library, around the 30s BCE (White, 2009).

At Alexandria (Casson, 2001, pp. 31-47), Ptolemy II (282-246 BCE) was responsible for the library's specialization in the Homeric Epics, while his successor Ptolemy III (246-222 BCE) went to great lengths to obtain the official versions of the plays of Euripides and the other Greek tragedians. The library had multiple texts in Greek and perhaps even some in Latin. And the work of this pioneering, groundbreaking institution was imitated thereafter to the point that by the first and second centuries CE and thanks to the Pax Romana that benefited most of the Indo-Mediterranean routes, libraries proliferated, at least in major centers. For instance, there is evidence that the works of Homer, Euripides, and many more were readily available in Asia Minor, in cities like Halicarnassus and probably several others.

At Rome (White, 2009, p. 271, n. 7), the sources reveal that bookshops made it relatively easy to purchase both Greek and Latin books, whether they were old or new. There, the works of Plautus, Terence, and several other authors could have begun a long journey that would have landed them virtually anywhere within the Roman Empire – or elsewhere. Literature traveled fast within the Greco-Roman world, and this can be corroborated by the fact that the first Roman adaptation of a play by Menander is dated less than fifty years after the death of the Greek author (Le Guen, 2014, p. 371). Likewise, literary techniques, such as those involved in adaptation, developed rapidly, as suggested by the overt contrast between the easily identifiable and understandable Greek influences and borrowings into the Roman tragedy from the Republic, on one side, and the more challenging ones coming from the Roman tragedy of the beginnings of the Empire, such as that of Seneca, on the other (Goldberg, 2014, p. 640).

Apart from the Greeks and the people of Greek tradition in India, there were also traders and travelers coming from the Greco-Roman world and settling in India. And more importantly, thanks to the new maritime routes, there were Indians in Alexandria, who could have served as cultural intermediaries for the hundreds of navigators who, year after year, completed the back-and-forth journeys (Wulff Alonso, 2008a, p. 50).

For the study of Greco-Roman *imitatio*, epic is the gold standard (Farrell, 1997): Virgil is probably the ancient author whose sources are best known from the point of view of a modern audience. Likewise, the still quite underrepresented study of Greco-Indian *anukaraṇa* has found its most valuable *comparanda* in the epics (Arora, 1981, 2011; Wulff Alonso, 2008a, 2008b, 2013, 2014, 2015a, 2018a, 2018b, 2019a, 2019b, 2020). And if the subjects of study coincide, so do the methods.

First, Homer's influences and borrowings in Virgil are "pervasive", that is, they are to be found almost in "every line" of the *Aeneid* (Farrell, 1997, p. 228), while Homer's influences and borrowings in Vyāsa would be of such "quantity" and "quality" that, by a "principle of improbability", causation would be more likely than mere correlation (Wulff Alonso, 2019a, p. 2; 2019b, pp. 226-227; 2020, pp. 18-19). Furthermore, there would be a "strong probability" of "many" of such epic themes having been adapted from Greece into India (Arora, 1981, pp. 178-179; 2011, p. 56). Second, Virgil's use of Homer is "analytical", thus evincing both his creative interpretation of the "sources involved" and his interpretative creation into an "allusive programme" (Farrell, 1997, p. 228), and Vyāsa's use of Homer would be "structural" or even "architectonic", implying the overall organization of the adapted plot "along the lines" of the source plot, and therefore, providing a "litmus test of the essential identity" (Wulff Alonso, 2019a, p. 3; 2020, pp. 20-21).

Third, the cross-cultural adaptation by Virgil is "thematically motivated", so that thematic proximity is usually responsible for the "modelling" of several elements into one, or the other way around (Farrell, 1997, p. 228), and the "working methodology" developed by Vyāsa would be characterized by recurring to "textual proximity" when merging or splitting literary "works" or "characters" (Wulff Alonso, 2019a, p. 3; 2019b, pp. 239-240; 2020, p. 21). Lastly, the *Aeneid*'s reworking of sources is "not limited" to the Homeric Epics, for even the works of Roman authors, like Lucretius (e.g., *Aen.* 9.224-228 ~ Lucr. 1.80-86), had an impact on Virgil (Ferrell, 1997, pp. 229-235), and neither would the *Mahābhārata*'s be, for it also would rely on Vedic sources (Minkowski, 1989, 1991, 2001; Feller, 2004).

If these four criteria, i.e., extensiveness, intentionality, proximity, and non-exclusiveness, suffice for characterizing Virgil's *imitatio* of Homer, why would they not when it comes to Vyāsa's supposed *anukaraṇa* of Homer – and perhaps even Virgil himself? The former is a fact, but the latter remains a hypothesis. Farrell (1997) even begins his exposition by stating, "The fact that Virgil's poetry exhibits many points of contact with the literature of the past is beyond dispute" (p. 222). But what gives this claim factual status? Virgil himself never announces that his intention was *Homerum imitari* (to imitate Homer), as Servius puts it in the prologue of his commentary. Instead, this is accomplished by a tradition of well-established "Homeric scholarship" (Hexter, 2010, p. 31), within whose ranks are various authors, both ancient (Macrobius, *Satur.* 5-6) and modern (Knauer, 1964; Barchiesi, 1984; Cairns, 1989; Berres, 1993; Dekel, 2005).

In India, neither does Vyāsa announce *yavanān romakāṃś cānukartum* (to imitate the Greeks and the Romans), nor are there any such explanations within the commentarial tradition. But more importantly, even if the methods were the same, the results were very different. And yet, as stated by Farrell (1997), "it is probably unwise to assume that the phenomena that we clearly observe at work in Virgil would be visible in others too" (p. 222). He is referring to Greco-Roman *imitatio*, but he might as well be talking about Greco-Indian *anukaraṇa*. Claiming that there could have been influences and borrowings from the Greco-Roman world into India will never be as "Eurocentric" as assuming that Greco-Roman *imitatio* is the only form of literary adaptation. If ancient Indians were at all impacted by the Greco-Roman world, it is obvious that they developed their own independent tradition thereafter.

Moving on to theater, the picture of Greco-Roman *imitatio* gets much blurrier. In Antiquity, Dio Chrysostom (*Or.* 52)[206] had the pleasure of contrasting firsthand Aeschylus' *Philoctetes*, Sophocles' *Philoctetes*, and Euripides' *Philoctetes*, and he did so with the availability of still more epic sources than are extant now. For instance, it is known from his critique that Homer's (*Od.* 13.429-438) Athena transforming Odysseus to avoid him being recognized by Philoctetes was changed by Aeschylus, but maintained by Euripides, who "having imitated [μιμησάμενος]" (13) the canonical author, is then "following [ἑπόμενος]" (6) him; and that, even when Euripides is not borrowing from specific passages of Homeric he still evinces a general influence, since he proceeds "in a Homeric manner [ὁμηρικῶς]" (14).

Similarly, Gelius (*NA* 2.23.11)[207] had the opportunity to compare Caecilius Statius' *The Necklace* with its Menandrian original, only to conclude that the Roman playwright had failed "to interpret [*enarrare*]" some of its best parts, and instead, he had "crammed in [*inculcavit*]" some bits and pieces from the Mime, while he "omitted [*omisit*]" others that the Greek author had devised. As seen, Dio Chrysostom's observations about Euripides' "maintaining" and Aeschylus' "changing", as well as Gelius' judgments on Caecilius Statius' "adding" and "subtracting" are, *mutatis mutandis*, analyses of their reinterpretations and re-creations, or in other words, on their adaptations.

Nowadays, the study of adaptation represents a greater challenge. Although "all the plays of Roman comedy are overt adaptations of originals of Greek 'New Comedy' (*nea*)" (Telò, 2019, p. 47), the scarcity of extant pairs of Greek source and Roman adaptation is notable. Considering the fragments, the examples are limited to Alexis' *Demetrios* (fr. 47.1-3) and Turpilius' *Demetrius* (fr. 5), Menander's *The Ladies Who Lunch* (fr. 337) and Plautus' *The Casket Comedy* (89-93), Alexis' *The Man from Carthage* (fr. 105) and Plautus' *The Little Carthaginian* (1318), Menander's *The Double Deceiver* (*POxy.* 4407 and fr. 4) and Plautus' *Bacchides* (494-562

206 I follow the Greek text by Crosby (Dio Chrysostom, 1946). The translations are my own.

207 I follow the Latin text by Rolfe (Gelius, 1927). The translations are my own.

and 816-817), and as mentioned, Menander's *The Necklace* and Caecilius Statius' *The Necklace* (Fontaine, 2014, pp. 409-414). The last one stands out, for not only can one compare the source and the adapted product, but also one can contrast those two with the commentary, in Gelius, about the process of adaptation. But this clarity is, indeed, a *rara avis*.

As said, blurriness is the norm, and it only gets worse when trying to extrapolate the findings from these sparse cases of Greco-Roman *imitatio* within the theater to the supposed Greco-Indian *anukaraṇa* within the theater. And yet, the context would have been favorable. Around the turn of the Millennium, India experienced both the transformation of Sanskrit into a code for literary expression (Pollock, 2006, p. 1), and the growth of manuscript culture (Pollock, 2006, p. 4). And the Greco-Roman world must have had an impact on this, since the Sanskrit word for "writing-reed [*kalama-*]" comes from the Greek word for "reed-pen [κάλαμος]", and the Sanskrit word for "ink [*melā-*]" comes from the Greek word for "ink [μέλαν]" as well (Jairazbhoy, 1963, p. 91; Mayrhofer, 1956, s.v. *kalámaḥ*[1], and 1963, s.v. *melā*).

Sailors, merchants, settlers, or even slaves could have made Greco-Roman literature available in the India of the first and second centuries CE (Jairazbhoy, 1963, p. 97). Some learned Indians could also have read Greek and Latin, and therefore, they could have written Sanskrit epics and dramas that incorporated at least some Greco-Roman influences and borrowings (Jairazbhoy, 1963, p. 97). The examples may not be as abundant in the theater as they are in the epics, but they are still there. And unless archaeologists gift us with some paradigm-shifting discoveries from the vicinities of modern-day Afghanistan in the up-coming years, it is up to the disciplines of Philology, Classics, and Indology to come together, in an interdisciplinary effort, to make sense of the various parallelisms between Greco-Roman and Sanskrit theaters, for instance, in other plays by (Ps.-)Bhāsa, in other Sanskrit playwrights, and even in other Sanskrit treatises on dramaturgy. *Audientes audiant*.

Proposed Influences

Table 2 Proposed influences in the adaptation techniques from the Greco-Roman texts to the Indian texts.

Greco-Roman texts	**Adaptation techniques**	**Indian texts**
Iliad 9 > *Phoenix*	1. character subtraction-cum-merging 2. theme addition-cum-emphasis	*MBh.* 5 > *The Embassy*
Iliad 10 > *Rhesus*	1. theme subtraction-cum-merging 2. character addition-cum-emphasis 3. changing of space and time 4. ignoring of death and violence	*MBh.* 4 > *The Five Nights*
Odyssey 9 > *Cyclops*	1. *contaminatio* 2. theme addition-cum-emphasis 3. changing of space and time	*MBh.* 1 > *The Middle One*

Proposed Borrowings

Table 3 Proposed borrowings in the adapted elements from the Greco-Roman texts to the Indian texts.

Greco-Roman texts	Adapted elements	Indian texts
The Eunuch *The Greek Anthology*	1. painting 2. personified weapons	*The Embassy*
Rhesus *The Little Carthaginian* *The Rope* *Rhesus* *The Suppliants*	1. remuneration 2. scarred limb 3. signed weapon 4. five nights 5. violent arrogance	*The Five Nights*
The Two Menaechmuses *The Two Menaechmuses* *The Two Menaechmuses* *The Two Menaechmuses*	1. response in the negative 2. *ad hoc* lineage 3. end of the enslaving 4. anagnorisis	*The Middle One*

Followed Chronologies

Table 4 Followed chronologies for the Greco-Roman world and India.

Greco-Roman world	Dates	India[208]
Homer (ca. 800-750) • *Iliad* (ca. 775) • *Odyssey* (ca. 775)	8th c. BCE	
Aeschylus (b. 524)	6th c. BCE	
Aeschylus (d. 455) • *The Suppliants* (ca. 463) Euripides (480-406) • *Phoenix* (ca. 425) • *Cyclops* (ca. 408)	5th c. BCE	
Ps.-Euripides • *Rhesus* (ca. 336) Aristotle (384-322) • *Poetics* (ca. 335)	4th c. BCE	Alexander's Indian Campaign (327-325)

208 The authors and texts included in the chronology are limited to those mentioned in this study. Even though, generally speaking, India's literary tradition antedates the Greco-Roman ones, in the case of epic and theater, especially in relation to the motifs of the embassy, the ambush, and the ogre, the situation is reversed.

Hegesippus the epigrammatist Mnasalces of Sicyon Nicias of Miletus Plautus (b. 254) • *The Little Carthaginian* (ca. 191) • *The Rope* (ca. 189)	3rd c. BCE	Pillars of Aśoka (first written sources) Greco-Bactrian kingdom (begins) Greek theater at Aï Khanoum (opened ca. 225)
Plautus (d. 184) • *The Two Menaechmuses* (ca. 186) Terence (185-159) • *The Eunuch* (ca. 161)	2nd c. BCE	Greco-Bactrian kingdom (ends) Indo-Greek kingdom (begins) Greek theater at Aï Khanoum (closed ca. 150)
Meleager of Gadara Virgil (70-19) • *Aeneid* (Posth. 17)	1st c. BCE	Indo-Greek kingdom (ends) Indian Embassies to Augustus (ca. 27)
Dio Chrysostom (b. in 40) Plutarch (b. in 46)	1st c. CE	Kushan Empire (begins) Vyāsa *Mahābhārata*
Dio Chrysostom's (d. in 115) Plutarch (d. in 119) Philostratus (b. in 170) Aelian (b. in 175)	2nd c. CE	Kushan Empire (continues) Bharata • *Nāṭyaśāstra* (Ps.-)Bhāsa • *The Embassy* • *The Five Nights* • *The Middle One*
Aelian (d. in 235) Philostratus (d. in 250)	3rd c. CE	Kushan Empire (ends)

References

Sources

Aelian. (1997). *Historical miscellany* (N. G. Wilson, Trans.). Cambridge, MA: Harvard University Press.

Aeschylus. (1922). *In two volumes, vol. 1* (H. W. Smyth, Ed. & Trans.). Cambridge, MA: Harvard University Press.

Aeschylus. (1926). *In two volumes, vol. 2* (H. W. Smyth, Ed. & Trans.). Cambridge, MA: Harvard University Press.

Aristotle; Longinus; Demetrius. (1995). *Poetics* (S. Halliwell, Trans.); *On the sublime* (W. H. Fyfe, Trans.); *On style* (D. C. Innes, Trans.). Cambridge, MA: Harvard University Press.

Bhasa-Projekt Universität Würzburg. (2007). *Multimediale Datenbank zum Sanskrit-Schauspiel: Texte, Manuskripte und Afführung klassischer indischer Dramen.* http://www.bhasa.indologie.uni-wuerzburg.de/

Catullus; Tibullus; Pervigilium Veneris. (1962). *Poems* (F. W. Cornish, Trans.); *Elegies* (J. P. Postgate, Trans.); *Pervigilium Veneris* (J. W. Mackail, Trans.). Cambridge, MA: Harvard University Press.

Dio Chrysostom. (1946). *In five volumes, vol. 4* (H. L. Crosby, Trans.). Cambridge, MA: Harvard University Press.

Euripides. (1994). *Volume I: Cyclops, Alcestis, Medea* (D. Kovacs, Ed. & Trans.). Cambridge, MA: Harvard University Press.

Euripides. (2003). *Volume VI: Bacchae, Iphigenia at Aulis, Rhesus* (D. Kovacs, Ed. & Trans.). Cambridge, MA: Harvard University Press.

Euripides. (2008). *Fragments: Oedipus-Chrysippus, other fragments* (C. Collard & M. Cropp, Eds. & Trans.). Cambridge, MA: Harvard University Press.

Gelius. (1927). *Attic nights: Volume I, books 1-5* (J. C. Rolfe, Ed.). Cambridge, MA: Harvard University Press.

Göttingen Register of Electronic Texts in Indian Languages. (2020). *Nāṭyaśāstra 1-16, 18-30, 33, 35-37*. http://gretil.sub.uni-goettingen.de/gretil/corpustei/transformations/html/sa_bharata-nATyazAstra-1-1618-303335-37.htm

Homer. (1995a). *Odyssey: Volume I, books 1-12* (2nd ed.) (A. T. Murray, Trans., & G. E. Dimock, Rev.). Cambridge, MA: Harvard University Press.

Homer. (1995b). *Odyssey: Volume II, books 13-24* (2nd ed.) (A. T. Murray, Trans., & G. E. Dimock, Rev.). Cambridge, MA: Harvard University Press.

Homer. (1999a). *Iliad: Volume I, books 1-12* (2nd ed.) (A. T. Murray, Trans., & W. F. Wyatt, Rev.). Cambridge, MA: Harvard University Press.

Homer. (1999b). *Iliad: Volume II, books 13-24* (2nd ed.) (A. T. Murray, Trans., & W. F. Wyatt, Rev.). Cambridge, MA: Harvard University Press.

Horace. (1942). *Satires, epistles, and ars poetica* (H. R. Fairclough, Trans.). Cambridge, MA: Harvard University Press.

Martial. (1920). *Epigrams, vol. 2* (W. C. A. Ker, Trans.). Cambridge, MA: Harvard University Press.

Philostratus. (1912). *Live of Apollonius of Tyana: In two volumes, vol. 1* (F. C. Conybeare, Trans.). Cambridge, MA: Harvard University Press.

Plautus. (1916). *In five volumes, vol. 1* (P. Nixon, Trans.). Cambridge, MA: Harvard University Press.

Plautus. (1917). *In five volumes, vol. 2* (P. Nixon, Trans.). Cambridge, MA: Harvard University Press.

Plautus. (1924). *In five volumes, vol. 3* (P. Nixon, Trans.). Cambridge, MA: Harvard University Press.

Plautus. (1930). *In five volumes, vol. 4* (P. Nixon, Trans.). Cambridge, MA: Harvard University Press.

Plautus. (1952). *In five volumes, vol. 5* (P. Nixon, Trans.). Cambridge, MA: Harvard University Press.

Plutarch. (1932). *Lives: In ten volumes, vol. 3* (B. Perrin, Trans.). Cambridge, MA: Harvard University Press.

Plutarch. (1962). *Moralia: In fifteen volumes, vol. 4* (F. C. Babbit, Trans.). Cambridge, MA: Harvard University Press.

Plutarch. (1967). *Lives: In ten volumes, vol. 7* (B. Perrin, Trans.). Cambridge, MA: Harvard University Press.

Sophocles. (1912). *In two volumes, vol. 1* (F. Storr, Ed. & Trans.). Cambridge, MA: Harvard University Press.

Sophocles. (1913). *In two volumes, vol. 2* (F. Storr, Ed. & Trans.). Cambridge, MA: Harvard University Press.

Sphujidhvaja. (1978). *The Yavanajātaka* (D. Pingree, Ed. & Trans.). Cambridge, MA: Harvard University Press.

Sukthankar, V. S., Belvalkar, S. K., Vaidya, P. L. et al. (Eds.). (1933/1971). *The Mahābhārata for the first time critically edited*. Pune: Bhandarkar Oriental Research Institute.

Terence. (1918). *In two volumes, vol. 1* (J. Sargeaunt, Trans.). Cambridge, MA: Harvard University Press.

The Greek Anthology. (1916). *In five volumes, vol. 1*. (W. R. Paton, Trans.). Cambridge, MA: Harvard University Press.

Virgil. (1918). *In two volumes, vol. 2* (H. R. Fairclough, Trans.). Cambridge, MA: Harvard University Press.

Bibliography

Acharya, P. K. (1927). *Indian architecture according to Mānasāra-Śilpaśāstra*. Oxford: Oxford University Press.

Adams, D. Q., & Mallory, J. P. (1997). Cow. In J. P. Mallory & D. Q. Adams (Eds.), *Encyclopedia of Indo-European culture* (pp. 134-139). London: Fitzroy Dearborn.

Adaptation (n.d.). In *Oxford English Dictionary* (online). https://www-oed-com.virtual.anu.edu.au/view/Entry/2115?redirectedFrom=adaptation #eid

Adluri, V., & Bagchee, J. (2014). *The nay science: A history of German Indology*. Oxford: Oxford University Press.

Adluri, V., & Bagchee, J. (2018). *Philology and criticism: A guide to Mahābhārata textual criticism*. London: Anthem Press.

Alexander, J. (2016). A systematic theory of tradition. *Journal of the Philosophy of History, 10*, 1-28.

Allen, J. (1946). A tabula iliaca from Gandhara. *The Journal of Hellenic Studies, 66*, 21-23.

Allen, N. J. (2020). *Arjuna-Odysseus: Shared heritage in Indian and Greek epic*. New York: Routledge.

Aperghis, G. G. (2020). The Greeks in the east in the Hellenistic period. In F. de Angelis (Ed.), *A companion to Greeks across the ancient world* (pp. 459-479). Oxford: Wiley-Blackwell. https://doi.org/10.1002/9781118341339.ch21

Arnott, P. (1972). Parody and ambiguity in Euripides' Cyclops. In R. Hanslik, A. Lesky, & H. Schwabl (Eds.), *Antidosis: Festschrift für Walther Krauss zum 70. Geburtstag* (pp. 21-30). Vienna: Böhlau.

Arora, U. P. (1981). *Motifs in Indian mythology: Their Greek and other parallels*. New Delhi: Munishram Manoharlal.

Arora, U. P. (1996). *Greeks on India: Skylax to Aristoteles*. Bareilly: Indian Society for Greek and Roman Studies.

Arora, U. P. (2011). India and the Hellenistic world. In K. Savvopoulos (Ed.), *Second Hellenistic studies workshop* (pp. 45-65). Alexandria: Alexandria Center for Hellenistic Studies.

Arora, U. P. (2018). *Greek sources on India: Alexander to Megasthenes*. New Delhi: Aryan Books International.

Baldick, C. (2001). *The concise Oxford dictionary of literary terms* (2nd ed.). Oxford: Oxford University Press.

Bansat-Boudon, L. (1992). *Poétique du théàtre indien: Lectures du Nāṭyaśāstra*. Paris: École française d'Extrême-Orient.

Barchiesi, A. (1984). *La traccia del modello: Effeti omerici nella narrazione virgiliana*. Pisa: Giardini.

Baums, S. (2017). Greek or Indian? The Questions of Menander and onomastic patterns in early Gandhāra. In H. P. Ray (Ed.), *Buddhism and Gandhara: An archaeology of museum collections* (pp. 33-46). New Delhi: Routledge. https://doi.org/10.4324/9781351252768

Bernard, P. (1976). Campagne de fouilles 1975 à Aï Khanoum (Afghanistan). *Comptes rendus de l'Académie des Inscriptions & Belles-Lettres, 120*(2), 287-322.

Berres, T. (1993). Vergil und Homer: Ein Beitrag zur Entmythologisierung des Verhältnisses. *Gymnasium, 100*, 342-369.

Bierl, A. (2012). Orality, fluid textualization and interweaving themes: Some remarks on the Doloneia, magical horses from night to light and death to life. In F. Montanari, A. Rengakos, & C. Tsagalis (Eds.), *Homeric contexts: Neoanalysis and the interpretation of oral poetry* (pp. 133-174). Berlin: De Gruyter. https://doi.org/10.1515/9783110272017.133

Bierl, A. (2015). New trends in Homeric scholarship (NTHS). In A. Bierl & J. Latacz (Eds.), *Homerś Iliad, the Bassel commentary: Prolegomena* (pp. 177-203). Berlin: De Gruyter. https://doi.org/10.1515/9781501501746-013

Boardman, J. (2015) *The Greeks in Asia*. London: Thames & Hudson.

Bopearachchi, O. (1991). *Monnaies gréco-bactriennes et indo-grecques: Catalogue raisonné*. Paris: Bibliothéque Nationale.

Bopearachchi, O. (2005). Contribution of Greeks to the art and culture of Bactria and India: New archaeological evidence. *The Indian Historical Review, 32*(1), 103-125.

Boyer, P. (1990). *Tradition as truth and communication: A cognitive description of traditional discourse*. Cambridge, UK: Cambridge University Press.

Bremond, C. (1980). Comment concevoir un index des motifs. *Le Bulletin du Groupe de Recherches en Sémio-linguistique, 16*, 15-29.

Brodbeck, S. P. (2006). Ekalavya and "Mahābhārata" 1.121-28. *International Journal of Hindu Studies, 10*(1), 1.34.

Brodbeck, S. (2020). The end of the Pāṇḍavas' year in disguise. *The Journal of Hindu Studies, 13*(3), 320-346. https://doi.org/10.1093/jhs/hiaa019

Bronkhorst, J. (2016). *How the brahmins won: From Alexander to the Guptas*. Brill. https://doi.org/10.1163/9789004315518

Brown, P. G. M. (2015). Contaminatio. In S. Goldberg & T. Whitmarsh (Eds.), *Oxford classical dictionary* (online). https://doi.org/10.1093/acrefore/9780199381135.013.1799

Brückner, H. (1999/2000). Manuscripts and performance traditions of the so-called 'Trivandrum plays' ascribed to Bhasa: A report on work in progress. *Bulletin d'Études Indiennes, 17/18*, 501-550.

Burgess, J. S. (2001). *The tradition of the trojan war in Homer and the epic cycle*. Baltimore, MD: Johns Hopkins University Press.

Burgess, J. S. (2017). The tale of Meleager in the Iliad. *Oral Tradition, 31*(1), 51-76.

Burkert, W. (1992). *The Orientalizing revolution: Near eastern influence on Greek culture in the early archaic age* (M. E. Pinder, Trans.). Cambridge, MA: Harvard University Press.

Burkert, W. (2004a). *Babylon, Memphis, Persepolis: Eastern contexts of Greek culture*. Cambridge, MA: Harvard University Press.

Burkert, W. (2004b). *Die Griechen und der Orient*. Munich: C. H. Beck.

Busch, G. (1937). *Untersuchungen zum Wesen der τύχη in den Tragödien des Euripides*. Heidelberg: Winter.

Cairns, F. (1989). *Virgil's Augustan epic*. Cambridge, UK: Cambridge University Press.

Casali, S. (2004). Nisus and Euryalus: Exploiting the contradictions in Virgil's "Doloneia". *Harvard Studies in Classical Philology, 102*, 319-354.

Casson, L. (2001). *Libraries in the ancient world*. New Haven, CT: Yale University Press.

Cobb, M. A. (2018). *Rome and the Indian Ocean trade from Augustus to the early third century CE*. Leiden: Brill. https://doi.org/10.1163/9789004376571

Coloru, O. (2009). *Da Alessandro a Menandro: Il regno greco di Bactriana.* Pisa: Fabrizio Serra.

Conte, G. B., & Most, G. W. (2015). Imitatio. In S. Goldberg & T. Whitmarsh (Eds.), *Oxford classical dictionary* (online). https://doi.org/10.1093/acrefore/9780199381135.013.3266

Corrigan, T. (2017). Defining adaptation. In T. Leitch (Ed.), *The Oxford handbook of adaptation studies* (pp. 23-55). Oxford: Oxford University Press. https://doi.org/10.1093/oxfordhb/9780199331000.013.1

Cuvardic García, D., & Cerdas Fallas, M. (2020). La “enunciación de objeto” en Catulo, Horacio y Marcial. *Káñina, 46*, 191-205.

Danek, G. (1988). *Studien zur Dolonie.* Vienna: Österreichischen Akademie der Wissenschaften.

Dange, S. A. (1994a). The order of the ‘Duryodhana’-plays of Bhāsa. In S. A. Dange & S. S. Dange (Eds.), *Critiques on Sanskrit dramas* (2nd ed., pp. 33-51). New Delhi: Aryan Books International.

Dange, S. A. (1994b). Three dramas and one motif. In S. A. Dange & S. S. Dange (Eds.), *Critiques on Sanskrit dramas* (2nd ed., pp. 77-87). New Delhi: Aryan Books International.

Dange, S. S. (1994a). Ghoṣavatī, Saṅgamanīya and the Aṅgulīyaka. In S. A. Dange & S. S. Dange (Eds.), *Critiques on Sanskrit dramas* (2nd ed., pp. 88-94). New Delhi: Aryan Books International.

Dange, S. S. (1994b). The citra-phalaka, a strategical device. In S. A. Dange & S. S. Dange (Eds.), *Critiques on Sanskrit dramas* (2nd ed., pp. 132-139). New Delhi: Aryan Books International.

Dekel, E. (2005). *Vergil’s Homer: The Aeneid and its Odyssean lens.* Doctoral dissertation, University of California at Berkeley.

Derow, P. S. (2016). Philhellenism. In S. Goldberg & T. Whitmarsh (Eds.), *Oxford classical dictionary* (online). https://doi.org/10.1093/acrefore/9780199381135.013.4970

Derrett, J. D. M. (1992). Homer in India: The birth of the Buddha. *Journal of the Royal Asiatic Society, 2*(1), 47-57.

Diamond, J. (1997). *Guns, germs, and steel: The fates of human society.* New York: W. W. Norton.

Dillon, M. (1975). *Celts and Aryans: Survivals of Indo-European speech and society.* Simla: Indian Institute of Advanced Study.

Dowden, K. (2010). Trojan night. In M. Christopoulos, E. D. Karakantza, & O. Levaniouk (Eds.), *Light and darkness in ancient Greek myth and religion* (pp. 110-120). Lanham, MD: Lexington Books.

Duckworth, G. E. (1961). Turnus and Duryodhana. *Transactions and Proceedings of the American Philological Association, 92*, 81-127.

Duckworth, G. E. (1967). The significance of Nisus and Euryalus for Aeneid IX-XII. *American Journal of Philology, 88*(2), 128-150.

Dué, C. (2012). Maneuvers in the dark of night: Iliad 10 in the twenty-first century. In F. Montanari, A. Rengakos, & C. Tsagalis (Eds.), *Homeric contexts: Neoanalysis and the interpretation of oral poetry* (pp. 175-184). Berlin: De Gruyter. https://doi.org/10.1515/9783110272017.175

Dué, C., & Ebbott, M. (2010). *Iliad 10 and the poetics of ambush: A multitext edition with essays and commentary*. Cambridge, MA: Harvard University Press.

Edmunds, L. (1997). Myth in Homer. In I. Morris & B. Powell (Eds.), *A new companion to Homer* (pp. 415-441). Leiden: Brill.

Eliot, T. S. (1919). Tradition and the individual talent, I. *The Egoist, 6*(4), 54-55.

Elliott, K. (2020). *Theorizing adaptation*. Oxford: Oxford University Press.

Erskine, A. (2016). Scipionic circle. In S. Goldberg & T. Whitmarsh (Eds.), *Oxford classical dictionary* (online). https://doi.org/10.1093/acrefore/9780199381135.013.5744

Esposito, A. A. (1999/2000). The two versions of *Dūtavakya* and their sources. *Bulletin d'Études Indiennes, 17/18*, 551-562.

Esposito, A. A. (2010). *Dūtavākya, die Worte des Boten: Ein Einakter aus den 'Trivandrum Dramen', kritische Edition, mit Anmerkungen und kommentierter Übersetzung*. Wiesbaden: Harrassowitz.

Falk, H. (2002). Frühe Zeitrechnung in Indien. In H. Falk (Ed.), *Vom Herrscher zur Dynastie: Zum Wesen kontinuierlicher Zeitrechnung in Antike und Gegenwart* (pp. 77-105). Bremen: Hempen.

Fantuzzi, M. (2020). *The Rhesus attributed to Euripides*. Cambridge, UK: Cambridge University Press.

Farrell, J. (1997). The Virgilian intertext. In C. Martindale (Ed.), *The Cambridge companion to Virgil* (pp. 222-238). Cambridge, UK: Cambridge University Press.

Feller, D. (2004). *The Sanskrit epics' representation of Vedic Myths*. Delhi: Motilal Banarsidass.

Fenik, B. (1960). *The influence of Euripides on Vergil's Aeneid*. Doctoral dissertation, Princeton University.

Fenik, B. (1964). *"Iliad X" and the "Rhesus": The myth*. Brussels: Berchem.

Finkelberg, M. (Ed.). (2011). *The Homer Encyclopedia*. Oxford: Wiley-Blackwell.

Fitzgerald, J. L. (2018). Mahābhārata. In K. A. Jacobsen, H. Basu, A. Malinar & V. Narayanan (Eds.), *Brill's encyclopedia of Hinduism Online*. Leiden:Brill. http://dx.doi.org/10.1163/2212-5019_BEH_COM_2020040

Fontaine, M. (2014). The reception of Greek comedy in Rome. In M. Revermann (Ed.), *The Cambridge companion to Greek comedy* (pp. 404-423). Cambridge, UK: Cambridge University Press. https://doi.org/10.1017/CCO9781139015356.027

Fowler, D. (2000). Epic in the middle of the wood: Mise en abyme in the Nisus and Euryalus episode. In A. Sharrock & H. Morales (Eds.), *Intertextuality: Greek and Roman textual relations* (pp. 89-113). Oxford: Oxford University Press.

Free, K. B. (1981). Greek drama and the Kutiyattam. *Theatre Journal, 33*(1), 80-89.

Freschi, E., & Maas, P. A. (Eds.). (2017). *Adaptative reuse: Aspects of creativity in south Asian cultural history*. Wiesbaden: Harrassowitz.

Fries, A. (2014). *Pseudo-Euripides, 'Rhesus': Edited with introduction and commentary*. Berlin: De Gruyter. https://doi.org/10.1515/9783110342253

Gail, A. J. (1980/1981). Āyudhapuruṣa: Die anthropomorphen Waffen Viṣṇus in Literatur und Kunst. *Indologica Taurinensia, 8/9*, 181-185.

Ganser, E. (2022). *Theater and its other: Abhinavagupta on dance and dramatic acting*. Leiden: Brill. https://doi.org/10.1163/9789004467057_003

Germany, R. (2016). *Mimetic contagion: Art and artifice in Terence's Eunuch*. Oxford: Oxford University Press.

Ghosh, J. (1963). *Epic sources of Sanskrit literature*. Kolkata: Sanskrit College Calcutta.

Glenn, J. (1971). The Polyphemus folktale and Homer's Kyklôpeia. *Transactions of the American Philological Association, 102*, 103-185.

Goldberg, S. M. (2014). Greek and Roman elements in Senecan tragedy. In G. Damschen & A. Heil (Eds.), *Brill's companion to Seneca: Philosopher and dramatist* (pp. 639-652). Leiden: Brill. https://doi.org/10.1163/9789004217089_050

Graf, F. (2011). Myth. In M. Finkelberg (Ed.), *The Homer Encyclopedia* (vol. 2, pp. 545-548). Oxford: Wiley-Blackwell.

Grafton, A., Most, G. W., & Settis, S. (2010). *The classical tradition*. Cambridge, MA: Harvard University Press.

Grandsen, K. W. (1984). *Virgil's Iliad: An essay on epic narrative*. Cambridge, UK: Cambridge University Press.

Greer, P. M. (2005). Ethical discourse in the Udyogaparvan. In T. S. Rukmani (Ed.), *The Mahābhārata: What is not here is nowhere else (yannehāsti na tadkvacit)* (pp. 211-224). New Delhi: Munishram Manoharlal.

Gutzwiller, K. (2017). Lyricism in Hellenistic epigram. *Trends in Classics, 9*(2), 317-338.

Hainsworth, J. B. (1993). *The Iliad, a commentary: Volume III, books 9-12*. Cambridge, UK: Cambridge University Press.

Hardie, P. (Ed.). (1994). *Virgil: Aeneid, book IX*. Cambridge University Press.

Hawley, N. S. (2021). The remembered self: Arjuna as Bṛhannalā in the Pañcarātra. In N. S. Hawley & S. S. Pillai (Eds.), *Many Mahābhāratas* (pp. 91-115). New York: State University of New York Press.

Hejib, A., & Young, K. K. (1980). Klība on the battlefield: Towards a reinterpretation of Arjuna's despondency. *Annals of the Bhandarkar Oriental Research Institute, 61*(1/4), 235-244.

Hexter, R. (2010). On first looking into Vergil's Homer. In J. Farrell & M. C. J. Putnam (Eds.), *A companion to Vergil's Aeneid and its tradition* (pp. 26-36). Oxford: Wiley-Blackwell.

Hiltebeitel, A. (2001). *Rethinking the Mahābhārata: A readerś guide to the education of the dharma king*. Chicago, IL: The University of Chicago Press.

Hollis, A. (2011). Greek letters from Hellenistic Bactria. In D. Obbink & R. Rutherford (Eds.), *Culture in pieces: Essays on ancient texts in honour of Peter Parsons* (pp. 104-118). Oxford: Oxford University Press.

Holt, F. (1988). *Alexander the great and Bactria: The formation of a Greek frontier in central Asia*. Leiden: Brill.

Holt, F. (1999). *Thundering Zeus: The making of Hellenistic Bactria*. Oakland, CA: University of California Press.

Holt, F. (2005). *Into the land of bones: Alexander the great in Afghanistan*. Oakland, CA: University of California Pres.

Holt, F. (2012). *Lost world of the golden king: In search of ancient Afghanistan*. Oakland, CA: University of California Press.

Horsfall, N. (1995). *A companion to the study of Virgil*. Leiden: Brill.

Hutcheon, L., & O'Flynn, S. (2012). *A theory of adaptation* (2nd ed.). New York: Routledge.

Hunter, R., & Laemmle, R. (Eds.). (2020). *Euripides: Cyclops*. Cambridge, UK: Cambridge University Press.

Iliakis, M. (2015). *The Bactrian mirage: Iranian and Greek interaction in western central Asia*. Edinburgh: Edinburgh University Press.

Jacobson, H. (1989). Cacus and the cyclops. *Mnemosyne, 42*(1/2), 101-102.

Jairazbhoy, R. A. (1963). *Foreign influence in ancient India*. New York: Asia Publishing House.

de Jong, I. F. J. (Ed.). (2012). *Space in ancient Greek literature: Studies in ancient Greek narrative, vol. 3*. Leiden: Brill.

de Jong, I. F. J., & Nünlist, R. (Eds.). (2007). *Time in ancient Greek literature: Studies in ancient Greek narrative, vol. 2*. Leiden: Brill.

Kakridis. J. T. (1949). *Homeric researches* (A. Placotari, Trans.). Lund: C. W. K. Gleerup. (Original work published 1944).

Karttunen, K. (1989). *India in early Greek literature*. Helsinki: Finnish Oriental Society.

Karttunen, K. (1997). *India and the Hellenistic world*. Helsinki: Finnish Oriental Society.

Karttunen, K. (2001). In India e oltre: Greci, Indiani, Indo-greci. In S. Settis (Ed.), *I Greci: Storia, cultura, arte, societá* (vol. 3, pp. 167-202). Turin: Einaudi.

Karttunen, K. (2015). *Yonas and yavanas in Indian literature*. Helsinki: Finnish Oriental Society.

Karttunen, K. (2021). Indian physicians in Greco-Roman literature? In T. L. Knudsen, J. Schmidt-Madsen, & S. Speyer (Eds.), *Body and cosmos: Studies in early Indian medical and astral sciences in honor of Kenneth G. Zysk* (pp. 363-368). Leiden: Brill. https://doi.org/10.1163/9789004438224_020

Keith, A. B. (1924). *The Sanskrit drama in its origin and development, theory & practice*. Oxford: Oxford University Press.

Kermode, F. (1975). *The classic: Literary images of permanence and change*. New York: The Viking Press; Faber and Faber.

Kirk, G. S. (1962). *The songs of Homer*. Cambridge, UK: Cambridge University Press.

Knapp, C. (1917). References to painting in Plautus and Terence. *Classical Philology, 12*(2), 143-157.

Knauer, G. N. (1964) *Die Aeneis und Homer: Studien zur poetischen Technik Vergils mit Listen der Homerzitate in der Aeneis*. Göttingen: Vandenhoeck & Ruprecht.

König, A. (1970). *Die Aeneis und die griechische Tragödie: Studien zur imitatio-Technik Vergils*. Doctoral dissertation, Princeton University.

Lallemant, J. (1959). Une source de l'Énéide: le Mahābhārata. *Latomus, 18*(2), 262-287.

Lange, K. (2002). *Euripides und Homer: Untersuchungen zur Homernachwirkung in Elektra, Iphigenie in Taurerland, Helena, Orestes und Kyklops*. Stuttgart: Steiner.

Le Guen, B. (2014). The diffusion of comedy from the age of Alexander to the beginning of the Roman empire. In M. Fontaine & A. C. Scafuro (Eds.), *The Oxford handbook of Greek and Roman comedy* (pp. 359-377). Oxford: Oxford University Press. https://doi.org/10.1093/oxfordhb/9780199743544.013.017

Lennox, P. G. (1977). Virgil's night-episode re-examined (Aeneid IX, 176-449). *Hermes, 105*(3), 331-342.

Lévêque, E. (1880). *Le mythes et les legends de l'Inde et la Perse dans Aristophane, Platón, Aristote, Virgile, Ovide, Tite Live, Dante, Bocacce, Arioste, Rabelais, Perrault, La Fontaine*. Paris: Eugène Belin.

Lévi, S. (1902). Sur quelques termes employés dans les inscriptions des Kṣatrapas. *Journal Asiatique, 19*(1), 95-125.

Lévi, S. (1963). *Le théâtre indien, tome 1er*. Paris: Honoré Champion. (Original work published 1890).

Lewis, C. T., & Short, C. (1879). *A Latin dictionary founded on Andrew's edition of Freund's Latin dictionary*. Oxford: Clarendon Press.

Lewis, G. A. (1980). *Day of shining red: An essay on understanding ritual*. Cambridge, UK: Cambridge University Press.

Liapis, V. (2012). *A commentary on the Rhesus attributed to Euripides*. Cambridge, UK: Cambridge University Press.

Liapis, V. (2017). Rhesus. In L. K. McClure (Ed.), *A companion to Euripides* (pp. 334-346). Oxford: Wiley-Blackwell. https://doi.org/10.1002/9781119257530.ch23

Lincoln, B. (1975). The myth of the "bovine's lament". *Journal of Indo-European Studies, 3*(4), 337-362.

Lincoln, B. (1976). The Indo-European cattle-riding myth. *History of Religions, 16*(1), 42-65.

Lindtner, C. (2002). Ludwig Asdorf: Kleine Schriften (2nd ed.), Ed. Albrecht Wezler; and Ernst Windisch: Kleine Schriften, Eds. Karin Steiner & Jorg Gengnagel. *Buddhist Studies Review, 19*(2), 197-200. https://doi.org/10.1558/bsrv.v19i2.14368

Mairs, R. (2014). *The Hellenistic far east: Archaeology, language, and identity in central Asia*. Oakland, CA: University of California Press.

Mairs, R. (Ed.). (2020). *The Greco-Bactrian and Indo-Greek worlds*. London: Routledge.

Mallory, J. P., & Adams, D. Q. (Eds.). (1997). *Encyclopedia of Indo-European culture*. London: Fitzroy Dearborn.

Matarrita Matarrita, E. (1989). Lo clásico: Una interpretación y una reflexión. *Káñina, 13*(1/2), 55-59.

Mayrhofer, M. (1956). *Kurzgefaßtes etymologisches Wörterbuch des Altindischen: A concise etymological Sanskrit dictionary, Band 1*. Heidelberg: Winter.

Mayrhofer, M. (1963). *Kurzgefaßtes etymologisches Wörterbuch des Altindischen: A concise etymological Sanskrit dictionary, Band 2*. Heidelberg: Winter.

Mayrhofer, M. (1976). *Kurzgefaßtes etymologisches Wörterbuch des Altindischen: A concise etymological Sanskrit dictionary, Band 3*. Heidelberg: Winter.

Menon, S. K. (2016). Ogres, ogresses and outcastes: The conflict of subaltern representation in the Mahabharata and Randam Oozham. *Indian Journal of Postcolonial Literature, 16*(2), 16-28.

Mills, S. (2015). Iphigenia in Tauris. In R. Lauriola & K. N. Demetriou (Eds.), *Brill's companion to the reception of Euripides* (pp. 259-291). Leiden: Brill. https://doi.org/10.1163/9789004299818_010

Minkowski, C. Z. (1989). Janamejaya's sattra and ritual structure. *Journal of the American Oriental Society, 109*(3), 401-420.

Minkowski, C. Z. (1991). Snakes, sattras and the Mahābhārata. In A. Sharma (Ed.), *Essays on the Mahābhārata* (pp. 384-400). Leiden: Brill.

Minkowski, C. Z. (2001). The interrupted sacrifice and the Sanskrit epics. *Journal of Indian Philosophy, 29*(1/2), 169-186.

Mondi, R. (1983). The Homeric cyclopes: Folklore, tradition, and theme. *Transactions of the American Philological Association, 113*, 17-38.

Morris, S. (1997). Homer and the near East. In I. Morris & B. Powell (Eds.), *A new companion to Homer* (pp. 599-623). Leiden: Brill.

Murnaghan, S. (2011). Tragedy and Homer. In M. Finkelberg (Ed.), *The Homer Encyclopedia* (vol. 3, pp. 884-885). Oxford: Wiley-Blackwell.

Nair, S. (2020). *Translating wisdom: Hindu-Muslim intellectual interactions in early modern south Asia*. Oakland, CA: University of California Press. https://doi.org/10.1525/luminos.87

Nehru, L. (1989). *Origins of the Gandhāran style: A study of contributory influences*. Oxford: Oxford University Press.

Orea Rojas, M. C. (2018). El motivo literario como elemento fundamental para la literatura comparada. *Actio Nova, 2*, 164-185. https://doi.org/10.15366/actionova2018.2

O'Sullivan, P., & Collard, C. (2013). *Euripides' Cyclops and major fragments of Greek satyric drama*. Liverpool: Liverpool University Press.

Pache, C. O. (Ed.). (2020). *The Cambridge guide to Homer*. Cambridge, UK: Cambridge University Press. https://doi.org/10.1017/9781139225649

Page, D. L. (1955). *The Homeric Odyssey*. Oxford: Clarendon Press.

Page, D. L. (1959). *History and the Homeric Iliad*. Oakland, CA: University of California Press.

Page, D. L. (1973). *Folktales in Homer's Odyssey*. Cambridge, MA: Harvard University Press.

Panayotakis, C. (2020). Plays of mistaken identity. In G. F. Franko & D. Dutsch (Eds.), *A companion to Plautus* (pp. 93-107). Oxford: Wiley-Blackwell. https://doi.org/10.1002/9781118958018.ch6

Papamichael, E. M. (1982). Phoenix and Clytia (or Phthia). *Dodone, 11*, 213-234.

Parker, G. (2008). *The making of Roman India*. Cambridge, UK: Cambridge University Press.

Patton, L. L. (Ed.). (1994). *Authority, anxiety, and canon: Essays in Vedic interpretation*. New York: State University of New York Press.

Pavlock, B. (1985). Epic and tragedy in Vergil's Nisus and Euryalos episode. *Transactions of the American Philological Association, 115*, pp. 207-224.

Pavolini, P. E. (1918/1920). I drammi Mahabharatiani di Bhasa: 1. Madhyamavyâyoga. *Giornale della Società Asiatica Italiana, 29*, 1-20.

Pingree, D. (1971). On the Greek origin of the Indian planetary model employing a double epicycle. *Journal for the History of Astronomy, 2*, 80-85.

Pingree, D. (1976). The recovery of early Greek astronomy from India. *Journal for the History of Astronomy, 7*(2), 109-123.

Pingree, D. (1993). Āryabhaṭa, the Paitāmahasiddhānta, and Greek astronomy. *Studies in History of Medicine and Science, 12*(1/2), 69-79.

Pisani, V. (1940). Riflessi Indiani del romanzo ellenistico-romano. *Annali della R. Scoula Normale Superiore di Pisa, 9*(3), 145-154.

Plofker, K. (2011). "Yavana" and "Indian": Transmission and foreign identity in the exact sciences. *Annals of Science, 68*(4), 467-476.

Pollock, S. (2006). *The language of the gods in the world of men: Sanskrit, culture, and power in premodern India*. Oakland, CA: University of California Press.

Powell, B. B. (2004). *Homer*. Malden, MA: Blackwell.

Powell, B. B. (2011). Near East and Homer. In M. Finkelberg (Ed.), *The Homer Encyclopedia* (vol. 2, pp. 559-562). Oxford: Wiley-Blackwell.

Pusalker, A. D. (1940). *Bhāsa: A study*. Lahore: Mehar Chand Lachhman Das.

Rastelli, M. (2018). Pāñcarātra. In K. A. Jacobsen, H. Basu, A. Malinar & V. Narayanan (Eds.), *Brill's encyclopedia of Hinduism Online*. Leiden: Brill. http://dx.doi.org/10.1163/2212-5019_BEH_COM_9000000055

Reich, H. (1903). *Der Mimus: Ein litterar-entwickelungsgeschichtlicher Versuch, Band 1*. Berlin: Weidmann.

Reinhardt, K. (1961). *Die Ilias und ihr Dichter*. Göttingen: Vandenhoeck & Ruprecht.

Ricottilli, L. (2014). Due aspetti della anagnorisis in Terenzio. *Dionysus ex machina, 5*, 114-127.

Rodríguez Adrados, F. (2012). Teatro griego antiguo y teatro indio: Su origen en danzas corales que miman algunos mitos. *Emérita, Revista de Lingüística y Filología Clásica, 30*(1), 1-12.

Salomon, R. (2010). Like father, like son: Poetic strategies in "The middle brother" (*Madhyama-vyāyoga*) attributed to Bhāsa. *Indo-Iranian Journal, 53*(1), 1-22. https://doi.org/10.1163/0019724 10X12686674794330

Sandri, S. (2012). Terracottas. In C. Riggs (Ed.), *The Oxford handbook of Roman Egypt* (pp. 630-647). Oxford: Oxford University Press. https://doi.org/10.1093/oxfordhb/9780199571451.013.0039

Sansone, D. (1991). Cacus and the cyclops: An addendum. *Mnemosyne, 44*(1/2), 171.

Saunders, V. (1919). Portrait painting as a dramatic device in Sanskrit plays. *Journal of the American Oriental Society, 39*, 299-302.

Schadewaldt, W. (1938). *Iliasstudien*. Leipzig: S. Hirzel.

Schein, S. L. (1970). Odysseus and Polyphemus in the Odyssey. *Greek, Roman and Byzantine Studies, 11*, 73-83.

Schlumberger, D. (1964). Une nouvelle inscription grecque d'Açoka. *Comptes Rendus de Séances de l'Académie des Inscriptions et Belle-Lettres, 108*(1), 126-140.

Scodel, R. (1982). The autobiography of Phoenix: Iliad 9.444-95. *The American Journal of Philology, 103*(2), 128-136.

Seaford, R. A. S. (1982). The Date of Euripides' Cyclops. *The Journal of Hellenic Studies, 102*, 161-172.

Seaford, R. A. S. (2020). *The origins of philosophy in ancient Greece and ancient India: A historical comparison*. Cambridge, UK: Cambridge University Press. https://doi.org/10.1017/9781108583701

Seland, E. H. (2010). *Ports and political power in the Periplus: Complex societies and maritime trade on the Indian Ocean in the first century AD*. Oxford: British Archaeological Reports.

Sergent, B. (1995). *Les Indo-Européens: Histoire, langue, mythes*. Paris: Payot & Rivages.

Shaw, C. A. (2014). *Satyric play: The evolution of Greek comedy and satyr drama*. Oxford: Oxford University Press.

Shaw, C. A. (2018). *Euripides, Cyclops: A satyr play*. London: Bloomsbury Academic.

Sidebotham, S. E. (1986). *Roman economic policy in the Erythra Thalassa: 30 B.C.–A.D. 217*. Leiden: Brill.

Sidebotham, S. E. (2011). *Berenike and the ancient maritime spice route*. Oakland, CA: University of California Press.

Sinha, B., & Choudhury, A. K. (2000). *Encyclopedia of Indian theater, vol. 1: Bhasa*. New Delhi: Raj Publications.

Sivaramamurti, C. (1955). The weapons of Vishnu. *Artibus Asiae, 18*(2), 128-136.

Sommerstein, A. H. (2010). *The tangled ways of Zeus and other studies in and around Greek tragedy*. Oxford: Oxford University Press.

Sommerstein, A. H. (2015). Tragedy and the epic cycle. In M. Fantuzzi & C. Tsagalis (Eds.), *The Greek epic cycle and its reception: A companion* (pp. 461-486). Cambridge, UK: Cambridge University Press. https://doi.org/10.1017/CBO9780511998409.027

Steiner, K. J. (2010). Ritual(e) im Drama: Spurensuche im Sanskrit Schauspiel Pañcarātra. In K. J. Steiner & H. Brückner (Eds.), *Indisches Theater: Text, Theorie, Praxis* (pp. 155-170). Wiesbaden: Harrassowitz.

Steward, P. (2016). The provenance of the Gandharan "Trojan Horse" relief in the British museum. *Arts Asiatiques, 71*, 3-12.

Stoneman, R. (2019). *The Greek experience of India: From Alexander to the Indo-Greeks*. Princeton, NJ: Princeton University Press.

Sullivan, B. M. (2016). An overview of Mahābhārata scholarship: A perspective on the state of the field. *Religion Compass, 10*(7), 165-175. https://doi.org/10.1111/rec3.12200

Sutherland Goldman, S. J. (2017). The monstrous feminine, rākṣasīs and other others: The archaic mother of Bhāsa's Madhyamavyāyoga. In G. Thompson & R. K. Payne (Eds.), *Meaning and Mantras: Essays in honor of Frits Staal* (pp. 247-274). Berkeley, CA: Institute of Buddhist Studies.

Swain, S. C. R. (1988). A note on Iliad 9.524-99: The story of Meleager. *The Classical Quarterly, 38*(2), 271-276.

Tarn, W. W. (1938). *The Greeks in Bactria and India*. Cambridge, UK: Cambridge University Press.

Telò, M. (2019). Roman comedy and the poetics of adaptation. In M. T. Dinter (Ed.), *The Cambridge companion to Roman comedy* (pp. 47-65). Cambridge, UK: Cambridge University Press. https://doi.org/10.1017/9780511740466.005

de Temmerman, K., & van Emde Boas, E. (Eds.). (2018). *Characterization in ancient Greek literature: Studies in ancient Greek narrative, vol. 4.* Leiden: Brill.

Thapar, R. (1984). *Śakuntalā: Texts, readings, histories*. New York: Columbia University Press.

Thieme, P. (1966). Das indischen Theater. In H. Kindermann (Ed.), *Fernöstliches Theater* (pp. 21-120). Stuttgart: Kröner.

Thompson, S. (1955/1958). *Motif-index of folk-literature: A classification of narrative elements in folktales, ballads, myths, fables, medieval romances, exempla, fabliaux, jest-books, and local legends* (rev. and enl. ed.). Bloomington, IN: Indiana University Press.

Thorley, J. (1979). The Roman empire and the Kushans. *Greece and Rome, 26*(2), 181-190.

Tieken, H. (1993). The so-called Trivandrum plays attributed to Bhāsa. *Wiener Zeitschrift für die Kunde Südasiens, 37*, 5-44.

Tieken, H. (1997). Three men in a row (Studies in the Trivandrum plays II). *Wiener Zeitschrift für die Kunde Südasiens, 41*, 17-52.

Tomber, R. (2008). *Indo-Roman trade: From pots to pepper*. London: Duckworth.

Tradition (n.d.). In *Oxford English Dictionary* (online). https://www-oed-com.virtual.anu.edu.au/view/Entry/204302?rskey=244lWO&result=1#eid

Turner, P. J. (1989). *Roman coins from India*. London: University College London Institute of Archaeology Publications.

Vaccaro, A. J. (1981/1983). Tratamiento de la personalidad en el teatro de Plauto. *Estudios Clásicos, 25*(86), 79-94.

Venkantasubbiah, A. (1965). On Indra's winning of cows and waters. *Zeitschrift der deutschen morgenländischen Gesellshaft, 115*(1), 120-133.

von Wilamowitz-Moellendorf, U. (1916). *Die Ilias und Homer*. Berlin: Weidmann.

Wallace, S. (2016). Greek culture in Afghanistan and India: Old evidence and new discoveries. *Greece & Rome, 63*(2), pp. 205-226.

Walker, S. F. (2004). The invention of theater: Recontextualizing the vexing question. *Comparative Literature, 56*(1), 1-22.

Warmington, E. H. (1928). *The commerce between the Roman empire and India.* Cambridge, UK: Cambridge University Press.

Weber, A. (1878). *The history of Indian literature* (J. Mann & T. Zachariae, Trans.). London: Kegan Paul, Trench, Trübner & Co. (Original work published 1852).

Weinstein, L. R. (2021). The Indian figurine from Pompeii as an emblem of east-west trade in the early Roman imperial era. In S. Autiero & M. A. Cobb (Eds.), *Globalization and transculturality from antiquity to the pre-modern world* (pp. 183-204). New York: Routledge. https://doi.org/10.4324/9781003096269

Weisweiler, J. (1954). Vorindogermanische Schichten der irischen Heldensage. *Zeitschrift für Celtische Philologie, 24*(1), 10-55.

Wells, H. W. (1968). *Sanskrit plays from epic sources.* Vadodara: University of Baroda Press.

West, E. B. (2005/2006). An Indic reflex of the Homeric Cyclopeia. *The Classical Journal, 101*(2), 125-160.

West, M. L. (1971). *Early Greek philosophy and the Orient.* Oxford: Clarendon Press.

West, M. L. (1997). *The east face of Helicon: West Asiatic elements in Greek poetry and myth.* Oxford: Clarendon Press.

West, M. L. (2007). *Indo-European poetry and myth.* Oxford: Oxford University Press.

West, D., & Woodman, T. (Eds.). (1979). *Creative imitation and Latin literature.* Cambridge, UK: Cambridge University Press.

White, P. (2009). Bookshops in the literary culture of Rome. In W. A. Johnson & H. N. Parker (Eds.), *Ancient literacies: The culture of reading in Greece and Rome* (pp. 268-287). Oxford: Oxford University Press.

Widermann, F. (2009). *Les successeurs d'Alexandre en Asie centrale et leur héritage culturel.* Paris: Riveneuve.

Windisch, E. (1882). *Der griechische Einfluss im indischen Drama.* Berlin: A. Asher.

Wulff Alonso, F. (2008a). *Grecia en la India: El repertorio griego del Mahabharata.* Madrid: Akal.

Wulff Alonso, F. (2008b). Heracles in the Mahābhārata. *Rivista degli Studi Orientali, 81*(1/4), 73-101.

Wulff Alonso, F. (2013). Greek sources in the Mahābhārata. In V. Adluri & J. Bagchee (Eds.), *Ways and reasons for thinking about the Mahābhārata as a whole* (pp. 155-183). Pune: Bhandarkar Oriental Research Institute.

Wulff Alonso, F. (2014). *The Mahābhārata and Greek mythology* (A. Morrow, Trans.). Delhi: Motilal Banarsidass.

Wulff Alonso, F. (2015). Cuando Hércules le espantaba las moscas a Buda: Negando el mundo greco-romano en la India. In L. Sancho Rocher (Ed.), *La antigüedad como argumento: Espejismos, mitos y silencios en el uso de la historia del mundo clásico por los modernos* (pp. 213-247). Zaragoza: Libros Pórtico.

Wulff Alonso, F. (2018a). The fourth book of the Mahābhārata and its Greek sources. In S. Brodbeck, A. Bowles, & A. Hiltebeitel (Eds.), *The churning of the epics and Purāṇas: Proceedings of the epics and Purāṇas section at the 15th world Sanskrit conference* (pp. 71-95). New Delhi: Dev Publishers.

Wulff Alonso, F. (2018b). Tres miradas que se cruzan en el mar: De Trajano a la China, pasando por la India. In A. F. Caballos Rufino (Ed.), *De Trajano a Adriano: Roma matura, Roma mutans* (pp. 459-481). Seville: Universidad de Sevilla.

Wulff Alonso, F. (2019a). Book 4 of the Mahābhārata and the Omphale-Heracles story: Methodological questions. In R. P. Goldman & J. Hegarty (Eds.), *Proceedings of the 17th world Sanskrit conference: Section 4 epics*. Vancouver, BC: University of British Columbia.

Wulff Alonso, F. (2019b). Book 4 of the Mahābhārata: Some methodological reflections on the use of Greco-Roman Sources. In A. K. Singh (Ed.), *Dialogue of civilizations: India and Greece* (pp. 225-249). New Delhi: Aryan Books International.

Wulff Alonso, F. (2020). *In search of Vyāsa: The use of Greco-Roman sources in book 4 of the Mahābhārata*. Malaga: University of Malaga.

Wulff Alonso, F. (In Press). *El cazador de historias: Un encuentro con el autor del Mahābhārata*. Madrid: Akal.

Zimmermann, B. (2014). Greek epic and tragedy. In H. Roisman (Ed.), *The encyclopedia of Greek tragedy* (vol. 2, pp. 595-601). Oxford: Wiley-Blackwell.

List of Tables

Table 1 Parallels between the *Mahābhārata* and the *Aeneid* (after Duckworth, 1961, pp. 111-112).

Table 2 Proposed influences in the adaptation techniques from the Greco-Roman texts to the Indian texts.

Table 3 Proposed borrowings in the adapted elements from the Greco-Roman texts to the Indian texts.

Table 4 Followed chronologies for the Greco-Roman world and India.

Index

addition-cum-emphasis 77, 130, 196, 209, 245
ad hoc lineage 189, 196, 232, 246
Aelian 13, 248
Aeschylus 4, 10–11, 81, 92, 116, 129–130, 135, 207, 232, 242, 247
The Suppliants 129–130, 232–234, 246–247
Aï Khanoum 236, 248
Alexander the Great 10–12, 236, 247
Alexandria 29, 238–239
anagnorisis 83, 90, 102, 110–112, 119, 121–122, 125–126, 162, 168–169, 175, 187, 191, 194, 196, 212, 232–233, 246
anger. *See* death on stage/violence on stage/anger on stage
architecture 16, 31, 237
argument of improbability 36, 240
argument of oddity 36–37
Aristotle 10–11, 90, 94, 147, 193, 208, 212, 230, 232–233, 247
Poetics 112, 247
astronomy 16, 22, 237
Yavanajātaka 16, 238

Bernard, P. 21–22, 25
Bharata 115, 179, 208, 212, 230, 232, 248
Nāṭyaśāstra 18, 115–116, 128, 179, 195, 208, 212, 232, 248
Bharukaccha/Barygaza 236
Bhavabhūti 54, 112
Bronkhorst, J. 25

cattle raid 81, 96, 99–100, 109, 113–114, 212, 214, 221, 224
Choudhury, A. K. 23
classicist 17, 20, 22, 25, 207, 225, 238
Classics 19, 24–25, 243
contaminatio 39, 160, 162, 164, 176, 185–186, 195–196, 214–215, 245

death. *See* death on stage/violence on stage/anger on stage
death on stage/violence on stage/anger on stage 94, 102, 115–118, 128, 213
deus/dea ex machina 48, 73, 75, 77, 82, 90, 230
Dio Chrysostom 7, 9, 13, 242, 248

end of the enslaving 196, 232–233, 246
Euripides 4, 7, 10–13, 15, 20, 23–24, 28, 33–35, 43–48, 73, 79, 81, 84, 86, 92–94, 116, 120, 127–129, 135, 137, 139, 141–142, 146, 148, 150–153, 155, 185–186, 195–196, 203, 205, 207, 209–217, 220–221, 224, 228–230, 232, 237, 239, 242, 247

folk motif 36, 217, 221, 225, 227–228
Free, K. B. 22

Gelius 242–243
Greco-Bactrian kingdom 229–230, 248
Greco-Indian *anukaraṇa* 24, 36, 67, 73, 77, 119, 121, 124, 126, 128,

130, 185, 191, 194, 196, 228, 230, 232, 235, 240–241, 243
change 128, 130, 185, 194, 196
merging 73, 77, 119, 126, 130
oddity 121, 191, 230, 232
reversal 67, 77, 124, 191, 232, 235
Greco-Roman *imitatio* 24, 36, 223, 225, 240–243
Greco-Roman motif 36, 218, 221, 223–225, 228
Greek Anthology, The 77, 229–230, 233, 246
Greek tragedy 22–23, 94, 116, 208

Hegesippus the epigrammatist 66, 74–75, 230, 248
Hellenistic lyric 66, 73–74
Homer 2–4, 7, 9–11, 14–16, 20, 24, 28, 33, 45–48, 68, 79, 81, 86, 91, 93, 95, 120–121, 127, 135, 137–138, 141, 143–144, 146, 148, 150, 152–153, 155, 185–186, 194–197, 205, 207, 209–211, 213–214, 217–219, 222–223, 225, 228, 236–237, 239–242, 247

Indo-European motif 36, 217, 221, 225, 228
Indologist 17, 20, 23
Indology 24, 207, 243

Kālidāsa 6, 49, 54, 65, 112, 122, 208
Kandahar Greek Edicts of Aśoka 238
Kandahar Sophytos Inscription 236

Lévi, S. 18–20, 25
Lindtner, C. 23

mathematics 16, 237
medicine 237
Meleager of Gadara 74, 230, 248
Menander 20, 177, 209, 234, 239, 242–243
miles gloriosus/milites gloriosi 87, 106, 212
Mnasalces of Sicyon 74, 230, 248

Nicias of Miletus 74, 230, 248

painting 16, 51–55, 67–71, 73, 77, 209–210, 228–229, 237, 246
personified weapons 52, 65, 67–68, 73, 209, 228–229, 246
philhellenism 238
philosophy 5, 16, 31, 237–238
Philostratus 13–14, 207, 248
Plautus 39, 54, 68, 87, 112, 121–122, 130, 177, 186, 189, 231–233, 239, 242, 248
The Little Carthaginian 122, 124, 130, 231, 233–234, 242, 246, 248
The Rope 122, 125–126, 130, 231, 233–234, 246, 248
The Two Menaechmuses 187–188, 191, 194, 196, 232–234, 246, 248
Plutarch 9–13, 42, 146, 150, 207, 248

Rājaśekhara 6, 54, 208
Reich, H. 18
remuneration 37, 86, 120–121, 130, 230, 246
response in the negative 188–189, 196, 232–233, 246
Roman lyric 66, 73
Roman theater 18, 24, 54, 68, 87, 112, 121, 177, 185–186, 215

Sanskrit literature 14, 228–229
scarred limb 110, 130, 230–231, 246
sculpture 16, 22, 237
signed weapon 130, 230–231, 246
Sinha, B. 23
Sophocles 4, 10–11, 81, 116, 129, 135, 207, 209, 242
subtraction-cum-merging 77, 130, 209, 223, 245
Śūdraka 54

Tarn, W. W. 20–22
Terence 39, 54, 68–69, 77, 112, 121, 229, 231, 239, 248
  The Eunuch 69–70, 73, 77, 229, 233–234, 246, 248
Trojan Horse 8, 224, 237

Vedic literature 211, 214, 216, 228, 230
violence. *See* death on stage/violence on stage/anger on stage
violent arrogance 130, 230, 232, 246

Walker, S. F. 23–24
Weber, A. 17, 18, 25
Windisch, E. 18, 23, 24
Wulff Alonso, F. 36, 220, 224, 228, 235

yavanikā 18

About the Team

Alessandra Tosi was the managing editor for this book.

Adèle Kreager was in charge of proofreading and indexing this manuscript.

Isaac Schoeber and Jeevanjot Kaur Nagpal designed the cover. The cover was produced by Jeevanjot Kaur Nagpal in InDesign using the Fontin font.

Cameron Craig typeset the book in InDesign and produced the paperback and hardback editions. The main text and heading font is Noto Serif.

Cameron also produced the PDF and HTML editions. The conversion was performed with open-source software and other tools freely available on our GitHub page at https://github.com/OpenBookPublishers.

Jeremy Bowman created the EPUB edition.

This book was peer-reviewed by two referees. Experts in their field, these readers give their time freely to help ensure the academic rigour of our books. We are grateful for their generous and invaluable contributions.

This book need not end here...

Share

All our books — including the one you have just read — are free to access online so that students, researchers and members of the public who can't afford a printed edition will have access to the same ideas. This title will be accessed online by hundreds of readers each month across the globe: why not share the link so that someone you know is one of them?

This book and additional content is available at:
https://doi.org/10.11647/OBP.0371

Donate

Open Book Publishers is an award-winning, scholar-led, not-for-profit press making knowledge freely available one book at a time. We don't charge authors to publish with us: instead, our work is supported by our library members and by donations from people who believe that research shouldn't be locked behind paywalls.

Why not join them in freeing knowledge by supporting us:
https://www.openbookpublishers.com/support-us

You may also be interested in:

Epidicus by Plautus
An Annotated Latin Text, with a Prose Translation
Catherine Tracy

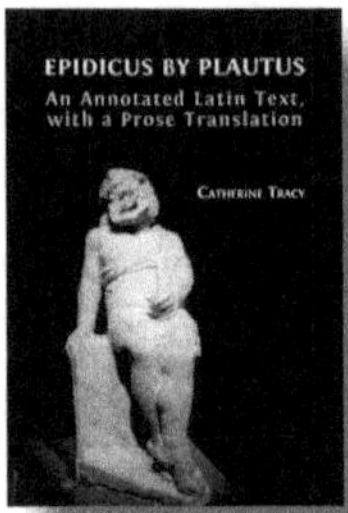

https://doi.org/10.11647/obp.0269

Ovid, Metamorphoses, 3.511-733
Latin Text with Introduction, Commentary, Glossary of Terms, Vocabulary Aid and Study Questions
Ingo Gildenhard and Andrew Zissos

https://doi.org/10.11647/obp.0073

Virgil, Aeneid, 4.1–299
Latin Text, Study Questions, Commentary and Interpretative Essays
Ingo Gildenhard

https://doi.org/10.11647/obp.0023

www.ingramcontent.com/pod-product-compliance
Lightning Source LLC
Chambersburg PA
CBHW051050230426
43666CB00012B/2631
* 9 7 8 1 8 0 5 1 1 3 6 1 4 *